An East Gate Book

China's
Establishment
Intellectuals

Edited by Carol Lee Hamrin
and Timothy Cheek

M. E. Sharpe, Inc.
ARMONK, NEW YORK/LONDON

To our mothers—

Rowena M. S. Lee

and

Alison M. Cheek

—with gratitude

East Gate Books are edited by Douglas Merwin
120 Buena Vista Drive, White Plains, New York 10603

Available in the United Kingdom and Europe from M. E. Sharpe, Publishers, 3 Henrietta Street, London WC2E 8 LU.

Library of Congress Cataloging in Publication Data

Main entry under title:

China's establishment intellectuals.
    "East gate books"—T.p. verso.
    Bibliography: p.
    Includes index.
    1. Communism and intellectuals—China—Addresses, essays, lectures. I. Hamrin, Carol Lee. II. Cheek, Timothy.
HX528.C48   1986   305.5'2'0951   85-22148
ISBN 0-87332-336-1
ISBN 0-87332-367-X (pbk.)

Printed in the United States of America

Contents

IV. ON THE FRINGE OF THE ESTABLISHMENT

Acknowledgments

This book is part of an ongoing intellectual project—to understand how a changing Chinese Marxism both reflects and shapes the lives of the intelligentsia in China. Our involvement with this issue began with individual research on Yang Xianzhen and Deng Tuo; our collaboration began with a panel for the annual meeting of the American Association for Chinese Studies in 1980, when we and Barry Naughton presented our views on three of the individuals in this volume. We are particularly grateful to John Israel and Merle Goldman, who offered their reflections on that panel and have since supported us in our continuing research efforts. Merle lent her enthusiasm and the institutional support of the New England China Seminar at Harvard for a workshop in May 1984 in which we explored the future prospects for the Chinese Leninism described in this book, as well as alternative intellectual stances, in post-Mao China. The product of that workshop, *China's Intellectuals and the State: The Search for a New Relationship*, now being edited with Merle, will provide a companion to this volume.

We want to thank each other, most of all, for the special friendship that has grown in the midst of both the sparkling intellectual interchange and the drudgery of editing and rewriting. Similarly, there has developed a strong support network among our contributing authors, who gave not only of their talents and patience, but also extra time and effort to share information and constructive criticism. We thank them for their generosity, which provided the basis for our introductory themes.

Roderick MacFarquhar has also lent his support, suggestions, and timely criticism to this project. We also thank Vera Schwarcz for her encouragement and contribution. Doug Merwin has been both amiable and flexible as editor; we thank him and Anita O'Brien at M. E. Sharpe for the opportunity to publish this work and for making the mechanics of it so painless. Thanks go to David Ownby and Hug Shapiro for casting a critical eye over the page proofs and particularly to David for assistance above and beyond the call of a chapter author. A special personal thanks goes to Bob Hamrin, for freeing up Carol's time for the final writing and editing, and to the Committee on Scholarly Communication with The People's Republic of China, for sending Tim to China in 1982-83.

In a more general sense, we are indebted to those who have guided our academic training and provided continued interest and support— for Carol, Maurice Meisner and Ed Friedman, and for Tim, Pierre Ryckmans, John Israel, and Philip Kuhn. Many other friends and colleagues have participated in the larger intellectual project of comprehending the personalities, institutions, and ideas shaping modern China. Their cooperative style has been an inspiration and a delight, not to mention being a good deal more efficient than isolated individualistic research. But in the end, the faults and errors are our own. We invite your criticism and suggestions as we continue to refine our understanding.

C.L.H. and T.C.

Foreword

John Israel

This volume depicts a stratum of Chinese intellectuals inextricably embedded in an authoritarian ruling elite. How did they get there? In the essays that follow, the force of social traditions comes through in rich detail, fleshing out earlier observations on the tenacity of attitudes, roles, and behavioral patterns among Chinese intellectuals in spite of a century's sweeping changes in the social system, their status in it, and the very definition of what it means to be an intellectual.[1]

The cooptation of intellectuals into bureaucratic alliances is by no means, however, a uniquely Chinese phenomenon. In America, where all have freedom to stick their necks out but few do, the concept of "establishment intellectuals" should be readily grasped. As alienated critics from C. Wright Mill to Noam Chomsky have reminded us, America has its own "establishment intellectuals" eager to hark to the clarion call of power. Among the more obvious examples are the brain trusters of the thirties, the Rand Corporation of the sixties, and the American Enterprise Institute of the eighties. Eloquent testimony to the spectrum of possibilities and constraints in establishment intellectual life could be offered by Eastern establishment editorialists who serve as cheerleaders for bureaucratic factions; by George Ball, who was favored by Lyndon Johnson as an in-house dissenter; and by Daniel Ellsberg's psychiatrist, whose address was placed on the plumbers' list because his patient had violated the sacred oath of silence. As any federal grant applicant knows, even when the government does not provide the answers, it can set the agenda. Given their own rich experience with establishment intellectuals, Americans have little reason to

[1]For a recent observation, see Merle Goldman, *China's Intellectuals: Advise and Dissent* (Cambridge: Harvard University Press, 1981), pp. 1–17.

assume that the terms are self-contradictory, that the only role for an intellectual is outside of—and in tension with—the political establishment.

Anti-establishment intellectuals in China have less to gain and more to lose than their American counterparts. Though an American Marxist may be denied the chairmanship of a political science department in the suburbs of the nation's capital, professional competence offers a certain degree of protection in a pluralistic society. In China, intellectuals become political critics at their own risk. Establishment intellectuals, on the other hand, enjoy protection and privileges available in China only through powerful bureaucratic allies. By playing assigned roles as supporters of the establishment and servants of the state, they gain patriotic self-esteem, outlets for their publications, power over their peers, and opportunities for scarce commodities such as housing and travel abroad.

Since all Chinese intellectuals are state employees, critics as well as supporters of the status quo must operate within a well-defined institutional framework and circulate their opinions only through authorized channels in which one's status and personal connections play a determining role. For expressing critical ideas, Wang Ruoshui lost his job as deputy editor of the *People's Daily,* but Democracy Wall activist Wei Jingsheng was sentenced to fifteen years in jail. The differential treatment derives not only from the content of the ideas and means of dissemination but also from the status of the two men. Newspaper editors express themselves with more impunity than zoo electricians. Wang may take satisfaction in the post-Mao reforms that have saved him from the fate of Deng Tuo; for Wei there is no such consolation. In contemporary China, if you are not some kind of establishment intellectual, you are not a legitimate intellectual at all.

In spite of historical precedents and tenacious patterns of behavior, contemporary establishment intellectuals did not evolve in linear fashion from China's imperial past. The transition from the independent critics of the May Fourth period to the bureaucratic-intellectual syncretism of the past quarter century occurred in stages and reflects the increasingly dependent status of intellectuals as centralized power became more pervasive:

1) 1917–1927: Weak, diffused authority in the hands of an ever-changing cast of rulers allowed intellectuals maximum independence. Supports for the role of culturally autonomous, independent critics, however, were inherently unstable: geographically, the foreign-con-

trolled treaty ports; institutionally, the universities, dependent upon government or missionary financing; psychologically, the notion of a cultural realm autonomous from politics. The last-mentioned was (and remains) highly vulnerable to the siren call of nationalism, championed since the 1920s by Leninist parties wary of the potential competition of independent intellectuals.

2) 1927–1937: One of these Leninist parties, the Nationalists, seized power and attempted to subject the intellectual and educational world to an orthodoxy based upon the ideas of Sun Yat-sen. The ruling party's liberal wing, however, insulated the academic realm from the full force of political coercion, and intellectuals continued to find some degree of shelter in universities and treaty ports.

3) 1938–1948: This decade witnessed the erosion of the social, economic, and political foundation for intellectual autonomy. Under wartime conditions, universities became dependent on the central government, inflation wiped out the financial security of salaried academics, and the rightward gravitation of power within the Nationalist party allowed fascist elements increasing scope for coercive practices. As the critics' role became ever more dangerous, many dissidents sought refuge in the Communist-administered areas or in Hong Kong.

4) 1949–1959: Having lost their independent power base, intellectuals were subjected to the strongest governmental controls in two millenia. They learned not to speak until spoken to. During the Hundred Flowers movement of 1957, official appeals for frank criticism briefly unleashed a flood of criticism. For their candor, the intellectuals were rewarded with brutal suppression.

5) 1960–1965: Mao's loss of authority in the wake of the Great Leap catastrophe and the resultant rifts in the leadership enabled a handful of bold Communist party intellectuals to revert to traditional roles as remonstrators within the bureaucracy.

6) 1966–1971: Availing themselves of the disintegration of Communist party control during the Cultural Revolution (1966–1969), a younger generation of aspiring intellectual and political leaders gave vent to long-suppressed frustrations and resentments. Aided by Mao, whose imprimatur had given sanction to rebellion, and an unrestrained security apparatus, they ruthlessly persecuted older intellectuals and officials and assumed their roles.

7) 1972–1976: Top leaders, including a chastened Mao, finally moved after Lin Biao's fall to dismantle the military-security dictatorship set in place at the height of the Cultural Revolution. Faced with

unrepentant extremists (headed by Mao's coterie—Kang Sheng and what is now called the "gang of four"), Cultural Revolution victims formed a convenient alliance under the aegis of Zhou Enlai and Deng Xiaoping. Intellectuals and Party officials began to reestablish the working arrangements of the early sixties.

8) 1976-present: After fifty years of one-party rule, most intellectuals now perceive that the only way to function is in cooperation with bureaucratic protectors. Both Party and intellectuals, however, play a dangerous game of cooptation. As in the early sixties, the Party recruits intellectuals, seeking to control them, broaden its own base, and restore weakened legitimacy. Intellectuals play a still riskier game by entering the Party, hoping to advance their own interests and to transform the establishment from within.

The post-Maoist drive toward constitutionalism and the rule of law can, at most, give limited security to intellectuals—as Pitman Potter reminds us in his treatment of Peng Zhen. Peng, whose entire career has been spent in pursuit of bureaucratic rationality as a prop to Party power, now champions due process as a means to the legitimacy and stability of the regime. Citizens' rights come as an afterthought and are merely instrumental. In rescinding the freedoms of political expression such as wall posters and labor strikes and outlawing the Democracy Wall, such legal reforms undermine whatever legitimacy might be claimed by anti-establishment critics while doing little to protect those within the establishment. As Potter notes, the reform that Peng advocates "does little to protect members of society from unjustified arrest" but "serves to protect members of the elite from attacks not sanctioned by official channels."

Readers of this volume will search in vain for heroes and villains. Yang Xianzhen, who brought the wrath of Mao upon his head for daring to suggest that "two unites into one," emerges in Carol Hamrin's treatment as "the voice of Leninist orthodoxy"—scarcely the kind of figure with whom Western intellectuals can readily identify. Yang, to be sure, deserves our sympathy for his suffering during the Cultural Revolution, but when we read Hamrin's account, we discover that Yang has since joined in the recent persecution of Wang Ruoshui, the *People's Daily* editor whose liberated views were excoriated during the campaign against "spiritual pollution" in 1983. Wang too, however, emerges as something less than a heroic figure for, we are told, as early as 1964 he had depicted Yang as an "agent of the bourgeoisie donning the cloak of Marxism,'' linked him with Trotsky and Bukharin, etc. By helping to destroy a current "object of struggle," Wang, of course, was simply playing by the rules expounded so well in the Maoist injunction, "Beat to death the drowning dog!" Among those who seized the opportunity to push Yang under was his erstwhile patron, Peng Zhen—but Potter has already alerted us not to expect too much from Peng.

One conclusion that we can draw from these dreary internecine vendettas is the familiar one that the revolution devours its children. What establishment intellectual, to echo Lu Xun's madman, has not eaten human flesh? But a more striking message for students of recent Chinese history highlights both the ambiguity of the Maoist legacy and the contradictory nature of the Dengist coalition. As Hamrin observes, the same populist tendencies that brought Wang Ruoshui to Mao's side in assaulting the evils of the bureaucratic establishment in the early 1960s reemerged in more liberal garb during the Deng period in his call for outside controls on the Party. Deng's invocation of the need to uphold Party hegemony was aimed less against the outside dissidents of the Democracy Wall than against the relatively democratic-minded elements within Deng's coalition, including Wang Ruoshui. In leaping aboard the juggernaut that crushed advocates of relaxation, Yang Xianzhen managed to settle an old score while remaining true to his Leninst convictions. The endless rounds of mutual pummeling, whether with Leninist hammer or Maoist cudgel, demonstrate, as Hamrin so accurately puts it, "the poverty of thought forms with which Chinese theorists have to work."

Although classified, along with Yang Xianzhen, as a Party intellectual, Deng Tuo was a breed apart. Yang and others like him were foremost bureaucratic administrators, Deng a man of ideas. Timothy Cheek's essay shows that a Leninist loyalist could be a cultivated exemplar of the amateur scholar in the Chinese humanistic tradition but also that even such an intelligent and civilized person could still function on occasion as a Party hack. The same man who sacrificed his life for the right to question the omniscience of Chairman Mao was himself a paternalistic authoritarian, a zealous guardian of state secrets and advocate of a "need to know" criterion for the dissemination of knowledge, who declared that "the highest standard in our society's rule of life is to subordinate the rights of the individual to the rights of the group." He assailed the Chairman not because he believed that all men are created equal and are endowed by their creator with certain inalienable rights—but rather because, intellectual aristocrat that he was, he did not suffer fools gladly.

Wu Han is another example of a talented intellectual, firmly rooted in China's humanistic traditions, undone by his own cleverness. While Deng Tuo pursued journalistic activities in the Communist border areas, Wu was launching his career as a historian at Southwest Associated University (Xinan Lianda) in Kunming. The hallmark of his political writings was the use of historical analogy to criticize the increasingly oppressive Nationalist party just as he was later accused of using the same weapon against Mao Zedong.

Like Deng Tuo, Wu Han demonstrates that not all martyrs to Maoist madness are totally sympathetic characters. Wu's political pilgrimage shows the interaction of psychological, economic, social, political, and ideological forces in the making of an establishment intellectual. At Kunming during the 1940s he was the poor but brilliant scholar who had to struggle to prove his worth. An uncommonly talented man, Wu Han had a burning need for recognition. His personal agenda reflected the psychology of an underappreciated *wunderkind*. His economic security sabotaged by inflation at the same time that Nationalist officials were getting rich, he found devastating analogies in Nationalist China to corruption and injustice during the Ming dynasty. When his friend and comrade-in-arms Wen Yiduo was murdered by Chiang K'ai-shek's assassins, Wu's hatred of the ruling dictatorship was confirmed.

In the People's Republic, Wu found the recognition, security, and political fulfillment that had escaped him in the old order. As vice mayor of Beijing, he became a pillar of the establishment, and he used his power to help whip fellow intellectuals into line. Soon after his long-unfulfilled ambition of Party membership was realized, he threw himself into the anti-Rightist campaign, the pitiless assault on dissenters who had dared raise their voices during the Hundred Flowers liberalization. He was particularly zealous in attacking Luo Longji, a one-time colleague at Lianda and a fellow critic of the Nationalists, who had also become an official in the People's Republic, though never a Communist. Luo's political credo, unlike Wu's, was solidly based upon Anglo-American concepts of democracy, due process, and pluralism. Liberals like Luo were easily disposed of in 1957; their persecutors like Wu had less than a decade to wait before they, too, became victims. Wu, but not Luo, has enjoyed—if that is the word—posthumous rehabilitation and honor, the difference between a Party reformer who tried to work from within and a non-Party collaborationist who tried to organize intellectuals as an outside force.

What is obviously needed to break through the impasse in thought and political participation is intellectual imagination fortified by political courage, but the pattern of official policy since the late 1970s has done little to foster these qualities. The regime—or, rather, different sectors of the regime—has given contradictory signals, first encouraging intellectuals to "seek truth from facts," then warning them to seek no political truths beyond the parameters of Party supremacy. As Vera Schwarcz observes, "A certain amount of refutation of wrong ideas has been sanctioned in the realm of the intellectuals' own expertise," but "it is quite a different matter . . . for the intellectuals to take their critical point of view into the realm of politics."

Here we encounter the familiar distinction between the intellectual *qua* scholarly specialist and the intellectual *qua* wide-ranging sociopolitical critic. In China, as in the West, most intellectuals are, presumably, content to confine themselves to their areas of expertise and to leave politics to politicians. For the laboratory scientist, technician, or engineer, such a role is both natural and comfortable. For those in the social sciences, humanities, and arts, however, it is not always so easy to draw the line between the narrowly professional and the broadly political. Even though the slogan "politics takes command" has been consigned to the dustbin of history, few areas of Chinese life are untouched by the Communist Party and by whatever its current version of Marxist-Leninist ideology may be. For many intellectuals, it is difficult to make a significant statement—even within their spheres of expertise—without transgressing the political realm.

Nonetheless, if the Party is gambling on pacifying intellectuals by granting merely professional autonomy, it enjoys favorable odds, at least among those persecuted during the Cultural Revolution. For senior scientists and technical experts and even some social and humanistic scientists, professional autonomy is not to be scorned. There is an overwhelming feeling of satisfaction in simply being allowed to do one's own thing in one's own field. How many would imperil this long-denied privilege to join a crusade of critical intellectuals in pursuit of broader freedom—a high-risk enterprise in which few have more than marginal interests?

The kind of deal intellectuals end up striking with the political establishment may eventually resemble the "contract" that has been sealed in Taiwan. There the regime demands unquestioned conformity on fundamental issues: the legitimacy of the political order, the illegitimacy of Taiwanese independence, the utter depravity of mainland communism. Around these unchallengeable precepts is a vaguely defined no-man's land into which critics venture at their own risk. Hence the periodic shutdowns of opposition publications and intimidation and punishment of dissenters. The ultimate bases for the Taiwan contract, however, are political cooptation and economic prosperity. The former means a gradual broadening of the democratic sector to offer peaceful avenues for change and career outlets for non-ruling-party politicians. The latter means the channeling of energies toward material goals that at once enrich the individual and promote national pride. On the mainland side of the Taiwan Strait, Party leaders have alluded to such a formula by suggesting, in their deterministic Marxist way, that political relaxation will follow economic development.

Any polity that seeks to drown political discontent in a tide of economic progress directs our attention to sociopolitical phenomena that transcend the cultural universe of the People's Republic and Taiwan. To find politicians able to build careers upon blatant appeals to self-interest, we need not look beyond our own shores. Youth in China, "the Chinese 'me generation' "—as Tim Cheek has dubbed it—find more than nominal counterparts in Reagan's America. In both cases, youth have come to political consciousness in the wake of profoundly disillusioning experiences that left indelible marks even if the events themselves are dimly perceived. Their earliest childhood memories are of the Cultural Revolution or Vietnam—"noble crusades" that ended in disaster, with their initiators (Mao/LBJ) in historical limbo and their subsequent perpetrators ("gang of four"/Nixon) in disgrace. Fumbling efforts by transitional figures (Hua Guofeng/Ford and Carter) failed, and in their wake a new leadership of profit-oriented "realists" (Deng/Reagan) has emerged.

The birthright of the me generations, Chinese and American, is a pervasive lack of interest in altruistic crusades. The most eloquent spokesmen for noble values (Mao/Kennedy) are dead and the organizations that sought to encapsulate these values (Communists/Democrats) are ideologically bankrupt. Into the vacuum emerges a new leadership whose moral precepts are limited to conventional simplicities—the most powerful of which is pride in the nation's heritage and destiny— and whose immediate appeal is based upon a promised fulfillment of self-interest. Ambitious youths seeking an outlet for talents respond with alacrity, delighted to cloak naked careerism in the vestments of patriotic purpose.

Deng Xiaoping, like Ronald Reagan, is adamant about broadening the sphere of economic freedom while remaining ambivalent about (if not hostile toward) other types of individual freedom. Both administrations are under pressure from ideological purists (moral majoritarianists/anti-spiritual-polluters) to see that freedoms go no further than the profit margin. Unable to address themselves to the spiritual needs of young intellectuals, they seek to keep them quiet with material rewards.

What stretches our (already thin) analogy to the breaking point becomes clear in the present volume. In authoritarian China's society of scarcity, the risks of intellectual autonomy are greater and the rewards fewer than in democratic America's land of abundance. Habitual obedience is the rule even when, as David Ownby observes, China's leaders speak in an outdated vocabulary, irrelevant to the needs of youth.

If the current generation of young Chinese requires anything to strengthen its skepticism about the limits of reform, it need only examine the case of Bai Hua, analyzed by Richard Kraus, in which a movie, viewed in closed showings by the elite, was declared too dangerous for the masses because it raised unwelcome questions about the moral legitimacy of the regime. Bai wound up "slapping his own face" in a public confession—and everyone breathed a sigh of relief because he did not suffer worse. In Bai, Kraus shows an artist with profoundly anti-establishment instincts working within the bureaucracy like a good establishment intellectual. The Bai affair shows how lack of autonomous vocations and strong professional associations denies shelter for the tender shoots of intellectual freedom. Little wonder that incipient liberals become political operators, prepared to deny in deed—and sometimes in word—fundamental tenets that Western liberals take for granted.

Beyond abstract patriotism and concrete self-interest, what is left? The politics of mass mobilization stands discredited. Within the Party, the politics of rectification may be nearing a dead end. Ideological indoctrination falls upon deaf ears. Little wonder that establishment authorities seeking to reach the educated young turn to the time-honored device of touting moral exemplars—including establishment intellectuals who can be presented as paragons of virtues sought in the next generation.

While living figures like Wei Jingsheng and Bai Hua must suffer the consequences for rash opinions expressed during halcyon intervals of liberalization, victims of the Cultural Revolution like Wu Han and Deng Tuo, having paid in blood the final installment of their Party dues, can be posthumously shaped to contemporary specifications. What is notable is the effort to establish them not as free spirits who paid the price for outspoken candor but as the loyal Party faithful sacrificed in the line of duty. Similarly, Wu's friend Wen Yiduo, an independent-minded fellow traveler murdered by Nationalist party thugs, is treated—like Lu Xun—as one who died a Communist in all but name. From the officially authorized post-Cultural Revolution perspective, the moral to be drawn from the tragedies of Wu Han and Deng Tuo is not that official restraints on free speech were too severe but that they were too lax. Rather than appearing as martyrs to the cause of civil liberties, Wu and Deng are presented as victims of uncontrolled criticism of the ruling elite. Official hagiographies supply the pantheon of saints with establishment intellectuals shorn of any doubts or ambiguities that might have qualified their allegiance to the Party during their lifetimes.

Deng Tuo, suggests Cheek, might be held up to future establishment intellectuals as "a model of culturally rich but politically orthodox intellectual and professional life." If that is true, the question arises as to how much impact this thoroughly cultivated, empirically grounded, critically minded Communist intellectual can have on China in the 1980s. David Ownby has shown that Chinese youths have taken the political vocabulary force fed to them by the Party and used it to explore *their* experiences, which differ so much from those that shaped their establishment elders. Indeed, as Ownby concludes, "The question is whether the revolutionary leaders can communicate with their revolutionary successors." The generation now in its forties and fifties will move into power before the end of the century. Products of the narrowly specialized Soviet-style curriculum that replaced liberal education during the 1950s, these middle-aged experts may share Deng Tuo's orthodoxy but they lack his breadth. The generation in its thirties, molded by the Cultural Revolution, is tough, skeptical, and experienced in the ways of the world but may fall short on grounds of both political orthodoxy and cultural sophistication. Few of the generation in its twenties, survivors of the current rigorously Darwinian process of educational advancement, are likely to duplicate Deng's virtuosity. Perhaps Deng Tuo is both the first and last of a breed—a "Mozartian commissar."

A more readily emulated model for future establishment intellectuals is Sun Yefang, the Soviet-trained economist who wrote like a technocrat but responded to dogma with flexibility and to persecution with integrity. Barry Naughton highlights two characteristics of the Sun model: the official Party recognition of a realm of individual conscience within the Party walls, granting some protection to dissenters, and the acceptance by these dissenters of restrictive rules of discourse, keeping much of the debate behind closed doors. Here we have the notion of freedom of expression *within* the establishment, a notion that may work well enough for economic planning but scarcely furthers the cause of vitality in the creative arts, *vide* Bai Hua.

Even as we find in this volume cause for optimism in the intelligence, integrity, and, sometimes, courage of China's establishment intellectuals, we are also led to wonder whether a moral-intellectual-political priesthood is capable of leading the Chinese people into the full realization of their latent potential. What China's establishment refrains from doing may be just as important as what it does. Viewing the kaleidoscopic landscape of post-Mao China, we cannot help but ask whether the ruling elite's most promising tendencies are not those that are shifting the balance from Party to state and from state to society, returning to the Chinese people some of the awesome powers of the Leninist machine. To what extent the rule of the marketplace will be extended from the economic sphere into the realm of ideas remains, however, an unanswered question.

China's
Establishment
Intellectuals

Introduction

Collaboration and Conflict in the Search for a New Order

Timothy Cheek and Carol Lee Hamrin

This book explores the motives and means for collaboration, as well as the sources of tension and conflict, between leading intellectuals and the top Chinese Communist Party leadership.* It grew out of individual studies, begun in the early 1970s, aimed at understanding those whom Mao rejected and attacked in the Cultural Revolution—what they stood for, what alternatives there were to Maoism in China. This introduction discusses the common themes that we, the editors, perceive as emerging from the lives and thought of these intellectuals.

Our subjects were members of the *establishment*, serving and operating within the governing institutions of the People's Republic. They collaborated in a system by which the Leninist Party exercised its claim to uncontested power and authority. As a subgroup within the ruling elite, they had a deep interest in perpetuating the system. These men, with the exception of Peng Zhen, a Party leader who has been included in this volume because he was the protector or "patron" of several of them, were also *intellectuals* in the sense of specialists with advanced training involved in the practice of the arts, economics, journalism, history, and philosophy.

Our subjects were not at the apex of power on the Politburo or

*We would like to thank the chapter authors and other scholars who read and commented on various drafts of this introduction, particularly Timothy Brook, David Chu, Joshua Fogel, Merle Goldman, Philip Kuhn, Roderick MacFarquhar, Frederick Teiwes, and Edwin Winckler.

Secretariat, and only one (Yang Xianzhen) sat on the Central Committee, but they played a key mediating role in coordinating a symbiotic exchange of services—an implicit social contract—between rulers and the larger intellectual elite. In this exchange, the intellectuals provided expertise and buttressed the moral legitimacy of the governing group by explaining and popularizing its policies. The leadership in turn gave the intellectuals the opportunity to serve the country and engage in their professional pursuits, while enjoying a relatively affluent and culturally rich lifestyle.

The scholar-officials who mediated this exchange traveled in the most influential of China's metropolitan cultural and political circles. They were at the same time both high-level intellectuals (*gaoji zhishifenzi*) and high-level officials (*gaoji ganbu*). This category corresponds with Edward Shils' discussion in the *International Encyclopedia of the Social Sciences* of intellectuals "who share the high and general intellectual culture," are primarily engaged in intellectual activities that define the "ultimate" or the ideal—issues inseparable from political authority—and have "affirmed, accepted and served the ruling authorities."[1] While this type of intellectual might be found in any culture, there is a particularly powerful tradition in China, as Shils notes, whereby scholar-officials (*shi*) have gained tremendous political power and social stature by serving at the higher levels of state administration and as personal counselors or agents of the sovereign. In our view, this is a special stratum of intellectuals that exists only in a system in which political control of culture is widely perceived as legitimate.

As part of a larger political generation, China's leading intellectuals shared formative experiences and resultant outlooks with other leftist intellectuals, some self-educated like Mao Zedong, who became China's top leaders. This founding generation was shaped by the antitraditionalism and anti-imperialism of the May Fourth movement in the 1920s and then was radicalized by the growing oppression of leftists after the Communist-Nationalist split of 1927.[2] With the forma-

[1]Edward Shils, "Intellectuals," in *International Encyclopedia of the Social Sciences*, vol. 7, ed. David Sills (New York: Macmillan, 1968), pp. 413–14.

[2]We follow the general definition of political generation—based on the formative political experiences of individuals between age seventeen and twenty-five—used by Michael Yahuda, "Political Generations in China," *The China Quarterly* 80 (1979):796–805, and by Li Zehou and Vera Schwarcz, "Six Generations of Modern Chinese Intellectuals," *Chinese Studies in History* 17, 2 (Winter 1983–84):42–56. The political generation of these men falls into Yahuda's "Older Intellectuals" and "Older Cadres" and crosses Li and Schwarcz's third "Generation of the 1920s" and fourth "Anti-Japanese War Generation."

tion of the People's Republic, some of these educated Party activists became top administrators; others, like the subjects of this study, either took on the dual role of scholar-officials serving as personal advisers and cultural administrators or, as noted scholars, put their academic skills in the service of the Party's policies. In the 1940s and 1950s, these establishment types helped found the basic institutions of the new order. They served as the back-room boys editing Mao's first *Selected Works,* writing Central Party School texts, formulating economic policy, and rewriting China's history along Marxist lines.

After the disastrous economic results of the Great Leap Forward (1958–1960) brought home the need for improved Party leadership, there was genuine soul searching throughout the ruling elite. The troubled scholar-officials addressed their recommendations for reform of the Chinese polity not only to their patrons within the elite but to a brooding Chairman Mao Zedong.[3] This book looks at five such intellectuals who made significant policy suggestions between 1959 and 1964 based on their efforts to adjust Chinese Communist theory and practice to suit better the new tasks of economic development and to appeal to new urban constituencies. Their intellectual enterprises at that time set the norm with which current experiments must now come to grips.

This effort to "modernize" Chinese Marxism on the part of the establishment after the Great Leap was aborted by Mao's own search for a new order, which led to the anti-establishment Cultural Revolution. Mao and his radical followers have been the subject of numerous studies; in this volume we have tried to discover why and how some key members of the Chinese Party establishment came to quite different conclusions, which eventually brought down upon them the wrath of Chairman Mao. The author of each chapter has sought to understand what these intellectual enterprises meant, searching backward in time to the personal histories of these men and the genesis of their ideas, reaching out into the social and political context surrounding their activities in the 1960s, and looking at their recent rehabilitations and the current rethinking of Communist ideology and the Party's role in the 1980s. It appears to us that the founding generation of establish-

---

[3]Frederick Teiwes introduced a similar analysis concerning the efforts of Party leaders, such as Liu Shaoqi, Peng Zhen, and Deng Xiaoping, to gain Mao's approval for their policy packages in the early 1960s. See *Politics and Purges in China* (White Plains, N.Y.: M.E. Sharpe, 1979), pp. 493–600. The brooding Mao is analyzed in Teiwes's *Leadership, Legitimacy, and Conflict in China* (Armonk, N.Y.: M.E. Sharpe, 1984).

ment politicians and intellectuals were competing among themselves and with younger radicals for the loyalty of still younger generations. An emerging technocracy, predominately urban in orientation, was in turn being followed by a new generation of literate youth born in the 1950s who were to become the skeptical "lost generation" of the Cultural Revolution, described in the last chapter of our volume. As radicalism has been discredited in recent decades and the frail and aging survivors of the 1950s establishment have returned, the question has become, what does the establishment have to offer China's future?

In bringing together the political-intellectual biographies of a group of men with like experiences, we have begun to mine a new treasure trove of data released in recent years, and we are encouraged by the prospects for further studies that combine biography with generational studies and link intellectual history with political studies of institutions and social groups. Our data not only have shed light on central policy and politics—the main concern of this volume—but also have pointed to fruitful lines of research outside that realm. The details of these lives have revealed other worlds of social interaction that touched on national politics but also had their own dynamics. While in these arenas, actors had to take central political concerns into account, conversely, at times they allowed their "local" concerns to affect the formation or implementation of central policy in ways that had little to do with the intent of the Party center. Thus, we have been able to analyze the relationship between micropolitical behavior and macropolitical concerns among highly placed metropolitan officials. Sociological analysis now seems possible regarding matters of material wealth, social prestige, and political influence at different stages of their political careers.

We have also begun to see the personalities and personal concerns of these men, albeit through a glass darkly. And it is here in the last analysis that we may search for the deepest roots of their behavior— their beliefs and their operating styles, whether compliant or combative, slippery or straightforward. Several of these intellectuals consciously looked to traditional models of the scholar-officials of dynastic China, and influences from the May Fourth period and from education abroad have become apparent. The chapters that follow reveal a rich variety of combinations of the inherited culture of the Chinese elite literatus and self-chosen Leninist commitments.

Shared Outlook

From this collection of lives, there has emerged evidence of a significant overlap in political views. After the Leap, the subjects of this book were attempting to improve on Lenin's concept of Party organization, which operated according to the rules of democratic centralism, collective leadership, and minority rights and provided the elite status for intellectuals from which they could exercise a traditional style of benevolent paternalism. Mao and his direct followers, however, began creating a much more populist version of Leninism based on Mao's personal charisma operating in a patrimonial manner among its adherents.[4] The establishment intellectuals, in our view, at heart remained loyal to institutional *Leninism* even in their efforts to make Leninist norms suit China better. Mao, even though he clearly intended to "purify" the Leninist party, ended up destroying it in the name of a new ideological variant, *Maoism*. The unraveling of the bond between China's more moderate, bureaucratic Leninists and the increasingly radical, charismatic leader (Mao) very likely began in the spring and summer of 1959 when central Party meetings debated how to respond to the obvious economic failures of the first year of the Great Leap Forward.[5]

In our view, the ideals of *liberalism* played only an indirect, minor role in this contest between world views. Although the establishment intellectuals wanted to preserve a degree of intellectual and professional autonomy from politics and also were willing to allow some degree of intellectual and social pluralism, these attitudes were mediated by their primary loyalty to Party domination.[6] Their interest in inheriting some of the ideals of traditional *Chinese humanism* was similarly limited. In fact, the establishment's advocacy of moral and disciplinary restraints, common to both Chinese tradition and Leninism, provided them a means of strengthening Party power and avoiding adoption of truly democratic institutional restraints on Party power. Thus, while

[4]Teiwes, *Leadership*, ch. 3, discusses the "normative rules" of Party life, which the subjects of this book increasingly emphasized, and the "prudential rules" of Party life, which Mao's group increasingly stressed after 1959.

[5]This is demonstrated by Roderick MacFarquhar, *The Origins of The Cultural Revolution 2: The Great Leap Forward 1958–1960* (New York: Columbia University Press, 1983), chs. 7–10. This split between the bureaucracy and the leader parallels a tension inherent in Marxism-Leninism between a rational managerial approach to political action, which emphasizes technico-economic progress, and a messianic individual approach, which sees history as a moral drama. Benjamin Schwartz has identified this *problematik* in "China and the West in the 'Thought of Mao Tse-tung,'" in *China in Crisis, book 1, vol. 1, China's Heritage and the Communist Political System*, ed. Ping-ti Ho and Tang Tsou (Chicago: University of Chicago Press, 1968), pp. 368 ff.

[6]Thus we have chosen not to use Merle Goldman's description of these men as "liberal intellectuals," though we agree with much of her circumscribed definition of the term. See *China's Intellectuals: Advise and Dissent* (Cambridge: Harvard University Press, 1981), p. 2.

Leninist inner-Party norms may be a faint echo of Western constitutionalism, which works against one-man dictatorship, they serve basically illiberal ends with respect to the rest of Chinese society.[7] In this regard, we believe that Peng Zhen's views on the utilitarian role of law in a Leninist state accurately reflect the attitudes of the majority of China's scholar-officials. Truly dissident thinkers and writers who demanded constitutional and legal restraints on Party power had been removed from the stage by the time of the Great Leap, often by the subjects of this volume. The distinctive combination of Chinese and Leninist features that has characterized the attitudes of China's establishment intellectuals is discussed in greater detail below.

In the realm of *theory* or ideology, for Mao as well as his colleagues, acceptance of Marxism meshed with ancient Chinese attitudes about orthodoxy: the need for one absolutist moral ideology and the need to assert publicly its infallibility. But the Chinese Leninist approach came to rely on a relatively orthodox version of Marxism-Leninism in comparison with Mao's voluntarism. The organization men in the establishment tended increasingly to reflect the more moderate strains both in Neo-Confucian political culture and in Marxism-Leninism that stressed the need for doctrine to be applied cautiously within the limits of objective conditions and to be tested against practical results.[8] This was to be carried out by an elite cadre of morally cultivated and technically trained intellectuals. They had, as well, an abiding faith in the historical materialism of Engels and those parts of the Leninist-Stalinist canon that confirmed his historical materialist belief; this served as an inoculation against Maoist voluntarism. They also viewed doctrine primarily as an educational tool to forge unity of purpose, especially within the Party, while allowing diversity of interests and perspectives in the larger society. The Maoists, in contrast, increasingly stressed the more radical strains in both traditional and Marxist heritages—utopian faith in correct thought and unity of will as a means of overcoming practical limitations. Intolerant dogmatism and anti-intellectualism developed in the effort to forge mental and social uni-

---

[7]See Benjamin Schwartz, "A Personal View of Some Thoughts of Mao Tse-tung," *Ideology and Politics in Contemporary China*, ed. Chalmers Johnson (Seattle: University of Washington Press, 1973), p. 364.

[8]Thomas Metzger discusses certain moderate and radical strains in Neo-Confucian thought. See *Escape from Predicament: Neo-Confucianism and China's Evolving Political Culture* (New York: Columbia University Press, 1977), p. 3, on the role of political culture, and p. 12 and ch. 5 on specific traits.

formity among all sectors of society.[9]

There was also an important difference in degree of openness to other traditions of thought. China's Leninists maintained an interest in proto-socialist ideas to be found in China's past and socialist experiments in other cultures, even though their cosmopolitanism fell short of embracing all Western thought. In contrast, the closed, purist approach of Mao's later thinking was one of its most notable characteristics. In this regard, Mao's thinking appeared to retain more of China's traditional "totalistic" view that cultures are indivisible wholes, to be adopted or rejected *in toto*. The Party establishment thinkers were moving toward a more syncretic, incrementalist approach that would allow discrete borrowing.

In the realm of *political organization,* most of the Chinese leadership shared the traditional statist belief that political institutions should dominate culture and society. Like most intellectuals shaped by the May Fourth experience, they viewed themselves as an historic, select group with a mission to transform China's culture and its political, social, and economic structures. Thus, they easily accepted the Leninist concept of the Party as vanguard and viewed its domination of all aspects of Chinese society as a good and necessary thing. The rules of political life were the norms of rectification laid down in Yan'an in the 1940s. Collective leadership was assumed, but it was modified by the appreciation of the need in Chinese society for a charismatic leader to personify the Party organization.[10]

The tension between these two modes of leadership became increasingly problematic, however, as the historical mission of the Party shifted from taking power to administering modernization programs. Problems arose with disagreement over the January 1956 "little leap" and the 1957 Hundred Flowers campaign, and serious division into incompatible leadership styles came in response to the problems emerging from the Great Leap Forward. Central bureaucrats were horrified by the excesses perpetrated by uneducated, low-level officials and allowed by misinformed leaders, whereas Mao became increasingly concerned that the practices of traditional-style bureaucratism at higher levels were to blame.

Thereafter, the Chinese Leninists increasingly placed a premium on Party discipline and social order. Yet they were painfully conscious of

---

[9]Ibid., pp. 115 ff. and 188 ff. On Mao's ideas see Maurice Meisner, *Marxism, Maoism and Utopianism* (Madison: University of Wisconsin Press, 1982).

[10]Teiwes, *Leadership*, ch. 3.

human imperfection, technical limitations, and the probability of error in the process of social transformation. Thus they allowed differences of opinion within the Party in the name of scientific experimentation and were slow to attack deviance *within* the Party for fear of making irreparable errors. This freedom of inner Party debate was posited on the basis of strict adherence to Central Committee resolutions after the fact, regardless of personal rank or opinion. Mao in the meantime began experimenting with new forms of education and organization that would revive wartime norms of official flexibility and mass initiative. To assert his views, he set himself above the rules. This split between bureaucratic and charismatic tendencies in Leninism obviously reflected the roles of the actors involved: establishment intellectuals and their patrons on the Central Committee were team members; Mao was the charismatic leader.

In *social policy*, for Chinese Leninists, there was little tolerance for criticism from the larger society, despite the role for institutionalized pluralism within the Party. Subgroup interests were to be taken into account by realistic investigation, strict discipline, strong moral training, and rational decision-making by the Party acting on behalf of the people—not by non-Party organizations. Therefore, leeway given to unorthodox ideas or behavior was tactical, not permanent. The gradual achievement of harmonious unity of interests among individuals, social groups, and the state was assumed as historically inevitable. Unlike the theories positing alienation between a society's state and its people, which emerged in Eastern Europe in the 1950s and again in China since 1980, as well as in the critique of the "bourgeois class" in the Party found in Maoist writings, Chinese Leninism did not admit the possibility that the state could, other than by temporary error or individual malevolence, become alienated from the interests of the people.[11] There was little patience for mass-based activism, whether populist or democratic, since independent political or social institutions were considered neither necessary nor legitimate.

In the realm of *professional activity,* the Chinese Leninist approach relied on specialists and technocrats. Compared with Mao's populist bent, it was an elitist approach in line with Lenin's high hopes for the "Party member." State-society relations were viewed paternalistically,

---

[11]For this alternative to the establishment approach, see D. A. Kelly, "The Emergence of Humanism: Wang Ruoshi and the Critique of Socialist Alienation," in *Chinese Intellectuals and the State: Search for a New Relationship*, ed. Merle Goldman, with Timothy Cheek and Carol Hamrin (forthcoming).

with the Party cadre and the technical specialist alike claiming considerable privileges and perquisites in return for carrying out their services for the people. The general population was assumed to be the passive recipient of their ministrations, although the individual citizen was explicitly encouraged to become one of them—a Party member or professional specialist. Class background mattered less than diligent study. Professional standards were strongly emphasized as a close second to Party loyalty. The dominant concern of establishment leaders and intellectuals was to strengthen Party legitimacy and authority, which had been weakened by the Leap, and on this they found themselves in growing conflict with Mao's determination to upset the status quo.

In the realm of *private life* this establishment approach acknowledged the legitimacy of personal interests and family concerns, so long as they did not interfere with the broad social policies of the Party. Considerable latitude was granted for private habits and opinions. This was not, however, due to any liberal concept of individual rights, but stemmed from a somewhat deterministic social philosophy, which posited that ownership and control over the means of production (the economic base) automatically gave the Party power in determining the future of China's political institutions, culture, and thought (the superstructure). Thus, unorthodox ideas, so long as they were kept private, were not viewed as grave threats to this ultimate control and could easily be tolerated. Mao increasingly diverged from this view as his desire to eradicate "bourgeois" thought and lifestyles grew along with his concern over the "retrogression" of Chinese society from socialism to capitalism.

The Chinese Leninist approach did acknowledge the importance of individual thinking, particularly the role of "thought reform" (*sixiang gaizao*) as an indispensable companion of economic development in the achievement of socialism. The establishment view was that thought reform was a rational transformation based on an appreciation of scientific history, not a cataclysmic emotional experience.

Common Experience

The shared views that emerged among these establishment intellectuals in response to the failures of the Leap likely stemmed in part from the similar earlier experiences and career patterns of these men. As indicated in table 1, they were not directly exposed to democratic societies

Table 1

Shared Career Patterns

	Yang Xianzhen	Deng Tuo	Wu Han	Sun Yefang	Bai Hua
Higher education	Europe/ USSR	China	China	USSR	China
Joined CCP	1926	1930	1957	1925	1945
Long March	No	No	No	No	N.A.
War Years (1937–1945)	JCJ*	JCJ	Kun- ming	Central China†	N.A.
Early Leap**	Pro	Pro	Pro	Pro	N.A.
Late Leap	Critical	Critical	Critical	Critical	Critical
Purge	1964/66	1966	1966	1964/66	1957
By 1976	Alive	Dead	Dead	Alive	Alive
Rehabilitation	11/80	9/79	9/79	1978	1974
Role by 1980	Adviser	Post- humous model	Post- humous model	Adviser	Writer

Notes: *Jin Cha Ji Border Region (Hebei-Shanxi-Chahar).
**The dividing line between the early and late Leap was fall 1959.
†Sun was in Yan'an in 1943–44.

as were Western-educated intellectuals, many of whom were more liberal-minded as a consequence. They also did not participate in the Long March or share, for the most part, in the Yan'an experience during the war, as did the military leaders and intellectuals in Mao's personal coterie.

These five intellectuals, with Bai Hua clearly a junior member, had by the eve of the Great Leap in 1957 become part of a distinct social stratum within the established order. Reflecting their common interests, they all had reservations about the speed-up of collectivization in 1955–56, and they were cool toward the public criticism program in the 1957 Hundred Flowers, but they openly supported the anti-Rightist drive in the summer of 1957. They publicly supported the Leap in early 1958 as it was originally conceived—as an economic production drive. But they were all soon critical of the irrational economic excesses and utopian political style of the Leap and voiced reservations about early signs of this through internal mechanisms within their particular professional spheres. They went public with some versions of these criticisms after 1961 when the Central Committee allowed it. They were all purged in the anti-intellectual campaigns of 1964–1968. Two died under duress during the Cultural Revolution. After the landmark Third Plenum of the 11th Central Committee in December 1978 at which Deng Xiaoping consolidated his control of the Party leadership, the reputations of these men were restored. Those dead were posthumously honored and their works republished with praise. Those still alive were formally exonerated and given responsible jobs. Since then we have seen establishment intellectuals and their Leninist views again operating in all arenas.

Structures and Mechanisms of Participation

Although we have noted common threads in the lives of the intellectuals in this volume, the salient details of each man's life, thought, and work, documented in the chapters that follow, suggest the rich variety within this stratum of the elite. The structure of the book highlights the spectrum of political participation relevant to establishment intellectuals, ranging from a senior Party patron who acted at the very center of power, to Party intellectuals working in close cooperation with such patrons, to establishment scholars more distant from high-level politics as they served national institutions, to the fringe of the establishment where creative writers and youth debate the issues of the day with much less knowledge and influence. This structure, indicating a gradation of political involvement, underscores our view that to speak of the Party in conflict with intellectuals is to suggest a dichotomy of interests that is misleading.[12]

Thus in figure 1 we see Peng Zhen at the center of power, the Politburo, as the member responsible for cultural matters in the 1960s. Although Peng was not the direct patron of all of the intellectuals discussed in this volume, his "Beijing stable" included Deng Tuo and Wu Han, and he had long-standing ties with Yang Xianzhen, whose direct patron, Liu Shaoqi, had once been Peng's.

Our examples of Party intellectuals active in central Party organs are Central Committee member Yang Xianzhen, director of the Central Party School, and Deng Tuo, editor of *People's Daily* and member of the Beijing Party Committee. In the next ring out from the center of power are Sun Yefang, who directed the Institute of Economic Re-

---

[12]An example of this fairly common assumption of a dichotomy of interests between intellectuals and the state is Peter R. Moody's *Opposition and Dissent in Contemporary China* (Stanford: Hoover Institution Press, 1977), esp. pp. 167–84.

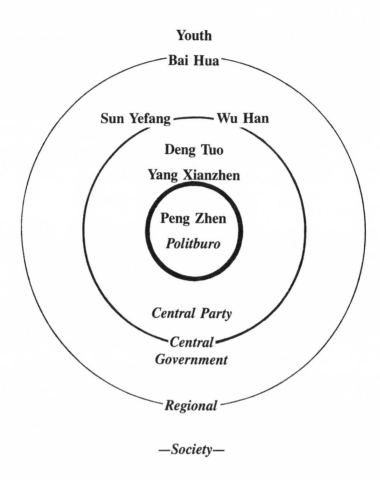

Figure 1

Relationship to Central Power

search in the Academy of Social Sciences and advised the State Council, and Beijing Vice-Mayor Wu Han, a nationally famous historian who taught at Beijing University and was active in government-sponsored political and professional associations. On the fringe of the establishment is the creative writer Bai Hua, a cultural worker in the military who was located in the provincial city of Wuhan. And in the outer circle are the youth, still only potential members of the ruling elite.

Once we envisioned the map of these men's social worlds, we noticed that we had very little data for something one might assume would be natural: horizontal alliances, or interest groups.[13] The career histories of the intellectuals studied in this volume confirm Merle Goldman's model of vertical patron-client relations as the dominant pattern of communication linking top Party leaders and intellectuals.[14] We stress, however, that there is no clear gap between the Party and intellectuals. Rather, there are interlocking sets of patron-client relationships, with a mix of political and intellectual roles and interests at each level. The strength and perennial nature of these vertical personal ties also undercuts the view that patron-client alliances are activated primarily in times of crisis and that they serve purely utilitarian, power purposes on the part of the Party and moral-policy purposes on the part of the intellectuals. Instead, we discovered a pattern of close, career-long collaboration, involving mutual influence between superiors and subordinates and complex motivations including moral, policy, and material considerations in the case of each individual. The seeming activation of such ties in times of crisis appeared to be the result primarily of changes in tactics and the exacerbation of disagreements to the point of public name-calling rather than a genuine change in the nature of political relationships.

As our research illuminated the mode of political discourse, the complexity of political strategy became apparent. The rounds of unpublicized investigations, report meetings, and writing in internal channels have now been partially disclosed and provide a richer context in which to assess the public allegorical essays, media debates, and academic symposiums. For example, the key to Sun Yefang's character emerged precisely in his balancing of careful public conduct with a strong, principled internal stance. Here, the impact of Leninist disciplinary regulations on intellectual behavior was clear.

Throughout our investigations, the weakness of horizontal professional or interest group ties stood out. Even Deng Tuo and Wu Han,

---

[13]Andrew Walder has found a pattern of networks and patron-client relationships in Chinese factories that is similar to that which we have found at the elite level. He finds group politics an inadequate model for explaining labor relations in China. See Walder, *Communist Neo-Traditionalism: Work and Authority in Chinese Industry* (Berkeley: University of California Press, forthcoming), ch. 1. David S. G. Goodman notes the difficulty, as well as the benefits for comparative study, of applying group theories of politics to China. David Goodman, ed., *Groups and Politics in the People's Republic of China* (Armonk, N.Y.: M.E. Sharpe, 1984), pp. 5–7.

[14]Goldman, *China's Intellectuals*, pp. 2–3.

who worked in the same municipal government and wrote in the same magazine column, had few personal contacts and no informal associations through which to express their common concerns. The view, typified in Peng Zhen's writings, that informal or professional groups exist purely to serve Party needs rather than autonomous interests has prevailed in the People's Republic. Leninist norms of behavior have strongly reshaped traditional modes of intellectual behavior; analogies between traditional opinion groups or schools and contemporary formal or informal organizations are particularly weak.

Understanding this makes the outpouring of criticism of the excesses of the Leap and exploration of traditional Chinese culture in 1961 all the more noteworthy. First, this rethinking was approved by the central Party as a leadership project. *Hai Rui Dismissed from Office* and *Notes from a Three-Family Village* were not anti-Party dissent that slipped out during leadership squabbles, such as the 1978–79 Democracy Wall materials; they were conscious efforts to defend and strengthen the status quo. Second, the unity of the response among establishment intellectuals despite the lack of any organization for interest group politics reflects the depth of their shock from the Great Leap as well as the underlying unity of their assumptions—both traditional and Leninist—regarding the best political order for China and their role in it.

Our findings on the strength of traditional patron-client networks also addressed the strategies involved in power relationships. As we began to understand how high-level debates were shaped by the research, controversies, and policy recommendations one level below the Central Committee leadership, it became clear that these advisers were casting their criticisms and recommendations in terms designed to appeal to Mao. As Frederick Teiwes has argued for central leaders in 1961–1964, at this lower level, too, there was no simple, "two-line struggle"; rather, establishment intellectuals tried, ultimately, to convince Mao, the final arbiter, of the wisdom of their approach.[15] The evolution of Mao's thinking in turn was shaped by the competing alternatives being placed before him, and to which he was often reacting.

In this competition for legitimacy, the question of what is orthodoxy became central. Exploring beneath the surface of the commonly shared language of Marxism-Leninism-Mao Zedong Thought, our exegesis of what these symbols of orthodoxy meant to each actor helped to isolate

[15]Teiwes, *Leadership*, ch. 1.

different rules of logic and appeals to different types of legitimacy in defending a position. For example, many of our subjects consistently cited pre-1949 works of Mao in order to compete with emerging views that Mao eventually chose to endorse; they fought off more voluntaristic interpretations of dialectics based on early works of Lenin by citing the later Lenin. And yet this competition was far from static. Mao was not the only inconsistent actor in the play. Even the fundamentalist Yang Xianzhen, whose Bible was Lenin's *Materialism and Empirio-Criticism,* responded to the publication in the late 1950s of the works of the "early" Marx and Lenin, and later to the rampant ultra-leftism during the high tide of the Leap, by rethinking his views.

Even though our conclusions at times appear to depict "two-line struggles," since most of our subjects shared many views with their patrons, Liu Shaoqi and Peng Zhen, in fact there was a minimum of the collusion between or even within these personal networks that is assumed by a two-line analysis. For example, Sun Yefang and Yang Xianzhen both had Soviet connections, ties to Liu Shaoqi, and common views on economic policy; both headed prestigious and influential policy think tanks. Yet there was no evidence that they ever spoke to each other. Only at low levels and quite sporadically did their staffers come in contact at meetings or on investigation teams.

The attacks on the rest of the Party hierarchy in the Cultural Revolution emerged as a series of "one-line struggles" by Mao against the individual personal networks of other leaders. The lack of coordination of the defense against the radical attacks contributed to the ironic and tragic outcome, whereby the majority of the Party elite opposed radicalism but, constrained in part by adherence to Leninist precepts, were unable or unwilling to unite against it.

The Modernization of Chinese Marxism

The efforts by establishment intellectuals in the early 1960s to "retool" Chinese Communism are profoundly significant in the history of modern China. Their ideas and activities reflect a reinterpretation of Marxism-Leninism intended to adapt Yan'an communism to a new constituency—urban intellectuals and professionals—and a new historical task—economic modernization. The process in Yan'an of reshaping Chinese Marxism to suit a peasant nationalist revolution has been termed, both by the Chinese and by outside observers, a sinification. Thus, the effort underway in the early 1960s might be called a second sinification. Leaders today speak of developing a "Chinese-style" socialism. Of course, such terms tend to ignore even earlier versions of Chinese Marxism, such as Li Dazhao's in the 1920s, but more important to us than numbering sinifications is to note that the rethinking after the Leap was in essence an effort to modernize official ideology, to make it more suitable to legal-rational means of organization, in Weberian terms. We use the term retooling to avoid the pejorative term revisionism, applied by the Maoists to suggest an abandonment of basic principle, and also to distinguish this earlier, aborted effort in the 1960s from more fundamental changes underway in ideology today. In our view, China's establishment intellectuals were interested in "fixing" Leninism only enough to preserve the heart of its precepts. This approach is in tension with approaches to ideology that fundamentally alter the definition of the Party's role, whether from a radical Maoist or a radical reformist perspective.

We have found the analysis of non-Chinese Leninist parties by Kenneth Jowitt helpful in our effort to assess both the original success of Yan'an communism in helping the Chinese leadership unite to found a nation in a wartorn, undeveloped country and the later dissolution of this ideology into conflicting charismatic and bureaucratic tendencies under the pressures of development. Jowitt accepts Max Weber's analytical distinction between status (or traditional) society and class (or modern) society. He posits that when traditional societies have faced threatened or actual domination by a powerful, modern society, resulting in political, cultural, and economic "national dependency," Leninism has often been more successful than alternative sets of ideas for organizing the efforts of traditional societies to throw off intruders and to begin to modernize. The key to the "Leninist response" is the "enmeshment of class and status" in the "charismatic impersonal Party"—a peculiar organization that combines attributes of charismatic rule, which can speak to and mobilize traditional elements (particularly the peasantry), and attributes of modern rule based on norms of achievement, which can promote the modernization of industry and rationalization of the bureaucracy. The key legitimizing principle of the Leninist response is not the views of a single leader, but the "correct line" determined by a collective leadership, which, theoretically, transcends individual failings, including mortality.[16]

[16]Kenneth Jowitt, *The Leninist Response to National Dependency*, Research Series No. 37 (Berkeley: Institute of International Studies, 1978), pp. 34–62.

Applying Jowitt's model to China, it would seem that the mix of charismatic and rational-bureaucratic modes of operation in the first sinification of Marxism hammered out in Yan'an in the 1940s did indeed suit the needs of the Party's constituency then—a status society of peasants and kinship groups in rural China. However, in the face of massive, chronic problems inhibiting Chinese economic development, the assumptions and attendant methods of this ideology fell short. Perceiving the reappearance of traditional elite bureaucratism and social class differentiation, the charismatic leader, Mao, pushed for a revival of the mass movement approach of Yan'an in 1958 and 1966. Perceiving in turn the re-creation of traditional emperor worship and what they thought to be dysfunctional populism, Party leaders and establishment intellectuals deeply involved in administration naturally turned to the more rational-bureaucratic side of the Yan'an amalgam. Both approaches aimed to modernize China; both failed inasmuch as their premodern roots emerged to block their aspirations. In response to the crisis of the Great Leap Forward, "one divided into two."

This volume, by exploring the ideas of those who chose bureaucratic Leninism, complements the many available studies of the charismatic populism that evolved into the Maoism of the Cultural Revolution.[17] Individual chapters show how establishment intellectuals plumbed both Chinese and foreign, primarily Soviet and East European, thought for ideas with which to retool Leninism. In particular, our research is teaching us that intellectual and political developments in the larger socialist world have been much more influential on Chinese developments than the current literature would suggest. On one level, we have discovered how much Yang Xianzhen and Sun Yefang were involved in a larger, international dialogue. At another level, it has become clear that de-Stalinization prompted even the most orthodox of Marxist Chinese thinkers like Yang to look for a model better rooted in the Chinese past.

The research in this volume can contribute to another set of studies in comparative communism, that on the "class role" of intellectuals. The life histories of these scholar-officials clearly parallel those of intellectuals in Eastern Europe as analyzed by George Konrád and Ivan

---

[17]John Bryan Starr, *Continuing the Revolution: The Political Thought of Mao* (Princeton: Princeton University Press, 1979); Stuart Schram, "To Utopia and Back: A Cycle in the History of the Chinese Communist Party," *The China Quarterly* 87 (1981):407–39; Meisner, *Marxism, Maoism and Utopianism.*

Szelényi in *Intellectuals on the Road to Class Power*.[18] The Chinese Communist Party gave intellectuals the first sustained opportunity to participate in national politics since the demise of the Confucian bureaucracy in 1911. We have tried in this book to emphasize that these intellectuals were a privileged stratum well-entrenched in the established order. In the 1960s, they were not attacking Party rule but defending their interests in the name of Leninism against competitors who supported Mao's assault on the technocracy. From Konrád and Szelényi's perspective this would suggest that "in China, conflicts we normally regard as being conflicts between the Party and intellectuals are conflicts amongst intellectuals."[19]

The effort to complete the "modernization" of Chinese Marxism in China continues today. The evolution of Chinese Communist theory will reflect the appreciation for realistic economic practices and modern scientific and administrative criteria typical of the technocratic establishment intellectuals. Although some of the founding generation, such as Peng Zhen and Yang Xianzhen, are on the scene, both new generations of establishment intellectuals and a new mood color the continuation of this enterprise. This new mood stems from the searing experience of the Cultural Revolution. Its twin lessons—the depth of human corruptibility and the consequent need for institutional change, but also the pain of social chaos—have been burned in the consciousness of all, but have somewhat contradictory implications for change. The first lesson has led to a much deeper and broader exploration for political and cultural alternatives in both traditional and nonsocialist Western social theory than at any time since the May Fourth period. The second lesson, however, has brought greater terror of the unknown. Virulent antidogmatism and a deep desire for a psychological "center," for ideological certainty in the midst of change, now reside uneasily in the hearts of China's establishment intellectuals. Thus, it is still quite possible that the reforms being offered today eventually will lean more toward authoritarian checks on intellectual and political excess than toward liberal democratic institutions that require greater tolerance of competition.

[18]George Konrád and Ivan Szelényi, *Intellectuals on the Road to Class Power* (New York: Harcourt, Brace, Jovanovich, 1979). We are particularly interested in their idea, based on Eastern European experience, that intellectuals in nations that lack a proletariat used Marxism as a means to obtain state power.

[19]This is the interpretation of Susanne Weigelin-Schwiedzrik, Ruhr-Universitat, Bochum, personal communication.

I. The Party Center

PENG ZHEN

Evolving Views on Party Organization and Law

Pitman B. Potter

Laws are the finalization of the Party's principles and policies; they are fixed general lines and specific policies of the Party put in a legal form.

Peng Zhen, speech to the Central Party School,
September 1, 1979

Our Party leads the people in enacting the Constitution and the laws and leads the people in obeying the Constitution and the laws.

Peng Zhen, discussing the PRC Draft Constitution,
May 20, 1982

The rehabilitation of Peng Zhen in 1979 after twelve years of disgrace and his subsequent rise to become one of the dozen top Party leaders and chairman of the National People's Congress Standing Committee represent one of the most significant turnabouts in the political history of the People's Republic of China. After his rehabilitation, Peng was given responsibility for resuscitating the Chinese legal system. Just as the current legalization program constitutes a reemergence of the legal system of the 1950s and early 1960s, Peng Zhen's stewardship over the system represents the resumption of his role during the earlier period. He has become the single Chinese official whose responsibilities and

I would like to thank James R. Townsend, Elizabeth Perry, Roderick MacFarquhar, and Barrett McCormick, all of whom made helpful comments on an earlier draft.

experience enable him to enforce directly and virtually independently his views on the role of law in China.

An examination of Peng's career reveals a great deal of consistency in his views toward the role of law as an expression of Party policy manifested through command rules enacted by the state apparatus. These rules serve not only to identify the thrust of Party policy, but also to provide an organizational framework for the enforcement of policy. Peng's concept of the function of law in China is generally in accord with the views expressed by Liu Shaoqi, Deng Xiaoping, and other Leninist-oriented officials. Nonetheless, Peng was more involved in legal affairs than any other top Party leader prior to the Cultural Revolution and thus expressed views and opinions on topics that other leaders, due to their different areas of responsibility, did not address directly. Thus, in their content and scope, Peng Zhen's views as they developed over the decades represent the fullest expression of the Party's idea of law in China.

Given the emphasis in China on the role of law as embodying the Party's policy commands, the balancing of rights and interests that requires elaborate legal reasoning in some systems of jurisprudence is carried out in the PRC according to Party principles. Thus Peng's stewardship over the legalization program brings to play his Party experience and organizational skills without requiring formal legal training, which he lacks.

In the absence of a system characterized by "legal determinism," Chinese judicial officials have wide discretion in interpreting and applying the laws that exist on the books according to the "principles" embodied in certain regulations or the "spirit" of various legal work conferences.[1] Under these conditions, the views of top political legal officials such as Peng Zhen have a significant impact on defining the spirit according to which laws are interpreted and applied.

[1]See, for example, "Peng Zhen fuweiyuanzhang zuo ren da changweihui gongzuo baogao he guanyu jige fulu caoan de shuoming" [Vice Chairman Peng Zhen Makes a Report on the Work of the Standing Committee and Gives an Explanation of Several Draft Laws], *Zhongguo fazhi bao* [China Legal System News], September 5, 1980. Also "Quanguo zhengfa gongzuo huiyi zaijing juxing" [National Political-Legal Work Meeting Convenes in Beijing], *Zhongguo fazhi bao*, July 30, 1982. For broad treatment of the absence of "legal determinism" in the Chinese legal system, see William C. Jones, "An Approach to Chinese Law," *Review of Socialist Law* 4 (1978):3–25; Frank Munzel, *The Reform of Chinese Economic Law* (Heidelberg: Verlagsgesellschaft, Recht und Wirtschaft, 1979). Also see Hungdah Chiu, "Socialist Legalism: Reform and Continuity in Post-Mao People's Republic of China," *Occasional Papers/Reprint Series in Contemporary Asian Studies* 1 (1982):1–32.

Biographical Sketch

Peng Zhen was born of poor peasant stock in 1902 in Quwu county, Shaanxi.[2] His education was limited to primary and middle school. Peng joined the Chinese Communist Party in 1923 and during the late 1920s and early 1930s was active in labor organization work, first in Taiyuan and then in Tianjin. Peng was an important force in the upsurge of student nationalism known as the December 9th movement of 1935. It was during this period that Peng began to develop personal ties that would continue throughout his career. He was arrested three times during this period and was released for the last time in 1935. In 1936, Peng began what was to become a long-standing relationship with Liu Shaoqi when Liu took over the Party's North China Bureau in Tianjin. When the Sino-Japanese War erupted in 1937, Peng briefly went to Yan'an and then to Shanxi, where he became chairman of the Government Council of the Jin Cha Ji (Shanxi, Chahar, Hebei) Border Region. During this period, Peng had organizational ties with border region commander Nie Rongzhen and *Jin Cha Ji Daily* editor Deng Tuo. Peng returned to Yan'an in 1941 to become vice-president of the Central Party School, where he played a major role in carrying out the 1942 Party rectification campaign.

After being appointed director of the Party Organization Department in 1943, Peng became head of the Central Party School in 1944. He worked together with Chen Yun to draft regulations for handling Nationalist cadres who had surrendered to the Communists. Peng was elevated to the Politburo in 1945. After the Japanese surrender, he moved to Manchuria where he was secretary of the Northeast Bureau and political commissar of the army commanded by Lin Biao. Peng was removed from these posts in 1946, allegedly for his sluggish response to Mao's military directives but more probably due to personal and policy conflicts with Lin Biao. Peng's antagonistic relationship with Lin continued in subsequent years and was an important factor in

---

[2]Most authorities agree that Peng came from a poor peasant family. During the Cultural Revolution, however, Red Guard criticisms of Peng claimed that his was a rich peasant background. See, for example, "Counterrevolutionary Revisionist Peng Zhen's Towering Crimes of Opposition of the Party, Socialism and the Thought of Mao Tse-tung," *SCMM* 639, p. 30. For the majority view, see Donald Klein and Anne Clark, *Biographical Dictionary of Chinese Communism 1921-1965* (Cambridge: Harvard University Press, 1970), p. 713. Also see "Peng Zhen: From Disgrace to Rehabilitation," *Issues and Studies* (September 1979):93. The brief biographical sketch included here is based primarily on these two sources.

the attacks on Peng during the Cultural Revolution. From 1947 to 1949, Peng's energies again were directed toward the administration of Jin Cha Ji. Here, Peng renewed his ties with Liu Shaoqi and Deng Tuo.

After the Communist victory, Peng was made secretary of the Beijing Party Committee and held concurrent posts in the Chinese People's Political Consultative Conference and in the Central People's Government Council. His power base in Beijing continued right up to 1966; indeed, Mao was to comment that under Peng's leadership the municipality of Beijing was controlled so tightly that not even a needle or a drop of water could penetrate.[3] Peng was also appointed vice-chairman of the government's Political-Legal Affairs Commission, beginning his long career in this arena. In 1953, he was appointed a member of the election-law drafting committee under Deng Xiaoping, and in 1954 he served as head of the Central Political-Legal Cadre School. During the middle and late 1950s, Peng made several trips abroad, including a major visit to the Soviet Union and Eastern Europe in 1957.

In the early 1960s, Peng was given responsibility for Party cultural policy. In the politically combative atmosphere following the Great Leap Forward, indirect criticism of Mao became prominent in the literary forums under Peng's control. His sponsorship of Deng Tuo and Wu Han was to play an important role in Peng's downfall. In 1965 he headed the Five-Man Cultural Revolution Group charged by Mao to direct the criticism of Wu Han and his play, *Hai Rui Dismissed from Office*. Peng's attempt to confine criticism of Wu to academic rather than political issues led to the final break with Mao. On June 3, 1966, it was announced that Peng had been dismissed from his posts. On December 4, 1966, he was "arrested" by Red Guards and on the 12th was paraded through the streets of Beijing to a violent struggle session.[4] Peng was later transferred to his native province of Shaanxi, where he labored in obscurity for twelve years. Aside from heralding a new level of violence in the Cultural Revolution, the persecution of Peng Zhen was particularly ironic because it represented the imposition of extralegal punishment on the Politburo member most closely associated with the Chinese legal system.

[3]Roderick MacFarquhar, *The Origins of the Cultural Revolution, I: Contradictions among the People* (London: Columbia University Press, 1974), p. 204, citing *Zhengfa hongqi* [Political-Legal Red Flag] (October 17, 1967):5.

[4]For a description of Peng's arrest and subsequent struggle session, see *The China Quarterly* 29 (January-March 1967):188.

After the decision of the landmark Third Plenum of the Eleventh Central Committee to rehabilitate Peng, he immediately returned to Beijing in December 1978.[5] He reappeared publicly for the first time on January 27, 1979 at a tea party celebrating the Spring Festival.[6] On February 23, at a session of the National People's Congress (NPC) Standing Committee, Peng was appointed chairman of its Committee for Legislative Affairs,[7] and in July he was once again elected a vice-chairman of the Standing Committee. In September he also regained his former position on the Politburo.[8] On June 10, 1981, Peng resigned his post on the Legislative Affairs Committee to take up responsibilities as vice-chairman of the Committee for Revising the Constitution.[9] After its promulgation in December 1982, Peng became first secretary of the Party's Central Political-Legal Committee. He became chairman of the Sixth NPC Standing Committee in June 1983.[10]

The Formative Period: The Jin Cha Ji Border Region

Having concentrated his efforts on Party organization during the 1920s and early 1930s, Peng Zhen's first experience in law-making came while he was secretary of the Jin Cha Ji Border Region. Under his direction, specific regulations were enacted governing punishment of traitors, control of corruption, mediation of disputes, elections, the organization of various administrative and judicial bodies, and economic activity.[11] These specialized laws were formulated according to

[5]James D. Seymour, *The Fifth Modernization, China's Human Rights Movement, 1978–1979* (Stanfordville, N.Y.: Human Rights Publishing Corporation, 1980), pp. 193–94.

[6]*Selections from World Broadcasts* (Far East), February 1, 1979, p. BII/23.

[7]Ibid., February 27, 1979, p. BII/2.

[8]Wolfgang Bartke, *Who's Who in the People's Republic of China* (Armonk, N.Y.: M. E. Sharpe, 1981), pp. 287–89.

[9]*Xinhua yuebao* [New China Monthly] 6 (1981):80. Although Peng was nominally subordinate to Ye Jianying on the committee, Ye's state of semiretirement gave Peng de facto leadership.

[10]*Zhongguo fazhi bao*, June 7, 1983.

[11]For texts of these and other regulations, see Han Yanlong and Chang Zhaoru, *Zhongguo xin minzhuzhuyi geming shiqi genju di fazhi wenxian xuanbian* [Collection of Legal Documents from the Base Areas During China's New Democratic Revolution], 3 vols. (Beijing, 1981). See also Jin Cha Ji Bianqu Xingzheng Weiyuanhui, *Xianxing faling huiji* [Collection of Current Laws], 2 vols., 1945. For general discussion of laws and regulations in Jin Chi Ji and other border areas, see Lan Quanpu, *Jiefangqu fagui gaiyao* [Outline of Laws and Regulations in the Liberated Areas] (Beijing: Qunzhong, 1982).

the "Current Administrative Program Concerning the Jin Cha Ji Border Region," issued in 1940 by the North China Bureau.[12]

Peng's program served first of all as a broad statement of Party policy regarding such issues as the establishment of organizations for resisting Japan, economic and tax policies, property rights, education, and measures for the punishment of "traitors." More importantly, the program also detailed the organizational steps to be taken in the realization of these policies. Article 5 set forth the manner by which Party dominance of popular and administrative organizations was to be achieved. All popular and government bodies were to reserve one-third of their membership for the Chinese Communist Party, leaving two-thirds to be made up of "other parties resisting Japan together with independent persons." For such tasks as disaster relief, cooperation among nationalities, mutual aid among the peasants, and the improvement of health and hygiene, Article 11 established a variety of specialized bodies in which the Party was to enjoy a minimum of one-third guaranteed membership. Aside from these organizational means of ensuring the Party's dominance over popular and governmental organizations, Article 17 called for the active repression of enemies, traitors, anti-Communists, and diehards—thus providing a basis for the elimination of potential opponents to Party rule.

In contrast to the organizational framework established for the enforcement of Party dominance, there existed no such framework for the protection of personal and property rights promised for "all those who resist Japan" (Article 7). Subsequently, in 1943 and 1944, regulations were enacted pertaining to the governments's power of inspection, search, arrest, and detention.[13] These regulations, however, were designed primarily to restrict the independent authority of individual officials rather than impose limits on the power of government over the citizenry generally. For, while the arrest of citizens was subject to approval by higher-level organs, such approval could be obtained after the arrest had been carried out.[14]

[12]Original text appears in Jin Cha Ji Bianqu Xingzhen Weiyuanhui, *Xianxing faling huiji*, vol. 1, pp. 1–5. The "Program" was reprinted in Peng Zhen, *Guanyu Jin Cha Ji bianqu dang de gongzuo he juti zhengce baogao* [Report on Party Work and Specific Policies in the Jin Cha Ji Border Region] (Beijing, 1981), pp. 210–14. After comparing it to the original for accuracy, I used the reprint for reference.

[13]For a discussion of these procedural regulations, see Lan Quanpu, *Jiefangqu fagui gaiyao*, pp. 127–37. Also Han and Chang, *Zhongguo xin minzhuzhuyi geming*, vol. 3, pp. 91–97, 392–93.

[14]See sec. 2, arts. 3–8, "Decision of the Jin Cha Ji Border Region Concerning Arrest, Search, Investigation, and Handling of Crimes and Serious Criminals," in Han and Chang, *Zhongguo xin minzhuzhuyi geming*, vol. 3, pp. 92–93.

Peng's concern, as indicated in the program and in subsequent regulations, focused on the dangers posed for centralized control by individual offices and officials exercising unfettered authority. This use of organizational regulations carefully to control the power of government officials was to emerge consistently throughout Peng Zhen's career. During this period, Peng also developed the practice of presenting a careful analysis of specific local conditions before introducing policy proposals, revealing a characteristically strong faith in the value of rational objective analysis in the preparation of policy.[15] These policies—on the economy, land, labor, finance, and banking—were to be carried out under the direction of local Party committees.[16]

Peng's primary concern was revealed in a speech addressing the "Question of Building Political Power," a theme which Peng described as the "fundamental issue of all revolutions" and to which he would return repeatedly.[17] Peng emphasized the need to replace the old system with a system of village representative congresses.[18] These popular organizations would in turn serve as the pool from which officials in administrative organs would be drawn.[19] Peng explained that the reason for this system of indirect representation was the need to prevent "the stealthy deprivation of the people's real democratic rights under extreme democracy." Distinguishing between the concepts of political power (*zheng quan*) and the power of rule (*zhi quan*), Peng argued that the political power of the people did not include the powers of direct election and recall of officials.[20]

The logic of Peng's approach was threefold. As representatives of the still-formidable landlord power structure, the village heads would probably have been able to garner enough votes to pose a significant threat to Communist-supported candidates in any elections for single leadership posts. Thus, the system of elected councils was intended to

[15]Peng Zhen, *Guanyu Jin Cha Ji*, pp. 5–19, gives his analysis of conditions in the border area. While the original version of this report was unavailable, the veracity of the reprint is suggested by the accuracy of the reprint of the "Current Administrative Program for the Jin Cha Ji Border Region," contained in the same volume.

[16]For discussion of the role of Party committees in carrying out land policy, see Ibid., pp. 87–101.

[17]Ibid., p. 20.

[18]Ibid., pp. 24–25. For text of the "Regulations for Country, District, and Village Organizations in the Jin Cha Ji Border Region," see Han and Chang, *Zhongguo xin minzhuzhuyi geming*, vol. 2, pp. 272–81.

[19]Peng Zhen, *Guanyu Jin Cha Ji*, pp. 27–31. Also see Han and Chang, *Zhongguo xin minzhuzhuyi geming*, vol. 2, pp. 272–81.

[20]Peng Zhen, *Guanyu Jin Cha Ji*, pp. 27–28.

diminish the power of the village heads by forcing them into a situation of collective leadership in which they could be outnumbered by Communist candidates. Secondly, by setting up popular organizations as a precursor to the establishment of administrative bodies, Peng sought to reduce the number of possible candidates, thus facilitating the Party's control over the selection process. Finally, the Party could use its one-third membership in popular organizations as a voting bloc to gain more than its guaranteed one-third membership in governmental organizations.

While imposing organizational filters on the exercise of popular democracy, Peng also sought to loosen the prerequisites for candidacy to administrative office. By opposing the requirement that candidates for the posts of district or county head have more than two years of administrative experience, Peng extended the selection process to inexperienced but politically favorable individuals.[21] He disallowed procedural provisions that would have ensured that the traditional rural officials, those with long experience in power, retained their posts.

Peng's discussions of specific policies ended on a note that revealed much about his analysis of the development of Chinese society. While noting that traitors and opposing groups still needed to be suppressed, Peng asserted that the old system of oppression—embodied in the police and security units of the old regime—had been destroyed.[22] Arguing that with the overthrow of the Nationalist dictatorship, the feudal system of political power was also overthrown, Peng indicated his view that the transitional stages in Chinese society were determined by changes in control over political institutions rather than by more fundamental socio-economic transformation. Given the mixed economy in this period, his approach does not fully accord with orthodox Marxism, which would view transformation of the superstructure as presupposing transformation of the economic base. Peng's approach took for granted, and indeed diminished, the importance of continuing to change class relations. This approach to analyzing China's transition to socialism was to form the basis for many of Peng's later views on the role of law in the People's Republic.

Peng's views on intra-Party affairs also became evident in this early period. He stressed the realistic formulation of policy; the strengthening of leadership and supervision over cadres; and the practical

---

[21]Ibid., p. 29.
[22]Ibid., pp. 51–54.

reeducation of Party members. Peng emphasized the need for discipline in the formulation and fulfillment of Party policies. Noting that the Party often was accused of "being able to talk but unable to act," Peng advocated realism in the formulation of policy and rigor in the fulfillment of policy.[23] Observing that many Party cadres were new and inexperienced, Peng stressed the need for leadership to ensure the timely and complete fulfillment of various tasks. He also cautioned that while the education of cadres should give proper weight to the theoretical study of basic issues of the Chinese revolution, the more important aspect of cadre education was the requirement that "Party cadres steel themselves in actual activity."[24] Peng's statements made in his report to the Politburo in 1941 on cadre policy served notice of higher approval of his approach to the rectification campaign to begin five months later.[25]

That Peng's views accorded generally with those of Liu Shaoqi is not altogether surprising given the close career relationship between Liu and Peng.[26] Nonetheless, a difference in style and tone is apparent. Liu's strong emphasis on self-cultivation reflected an abstract sense of "communist morality" that led to stringent standards for cadre behavior.[27] Peng viewed rigorous cadre training as the most crucial factor in ensuring the Party's practical effectiveness, allowing him a more restrained response to the shortcomings of local cadres.

Nation-Building in the Early 1950s

After the establishment of the People's Republic, Peng's experience in Jin Cha Ji was to prove useful in government legal work.[28] Although

[23]Ibid., p. 166.

[24]Ibid., pp. 180, 194-95.

[25]For a discussion of the 1942 rectification campaign, see Mark Selden, *The Yenan Way in Revolutionary China* (Cambridge: Harvard University Press, 1971), pp. 188 *et seq.* Also see Boyd Compton, *Mao's China: Party Reform Documents, 1942-44* (Seattle: University of Washington Press, 1966), pp. xxxiv-xxxix.

[26]See generally Klein and Clark, *Biographical Dictionary,* p. 713 *et seq.*

[27]For Liu's views on cadre training, see e.g. Liu Shaoqi, *Three Essays on Party-Building* (Beijing: Foreign Languages Press, 1980), pp. 3-11.

[28]That Peng may also have been influenced by Kuomintang law is indicated by Red Guard charges that Peng and Liu Shaoqi "openly advocated that law has the nature of continuity" and that "the old laws of the Kuomintang may be continued." See James Seymour, *China: The Politics of Revolutionary Reintegration* (New York: Crowell, 1970), p. 92.

Peng was subordinate to Dong Biwu on the Political-Legal Committee, Dong's relative inactivity made Peng the most influential member.[29] In this capacity, Peng became an important force in the new regime's consolidation of power.

In February 1951 Peng delivered to the Government Administrative Council a "Report on Questions Concerning the Suppression of Counterrevolutionary Activity and Regulations for the Punishment of Counterrevolutionaries."[30] In it he underscored the role of the regulations in providing standards for judicial personnel in the current "Constitution"—the Common Program of 1947—to prevent leftist (overly harsh) and rightist (overly lenient) errors in the suppression of counterrevolutionaries.[31]

Later, in May 1951, Peng presented a "Report on Political-Legal Work and the Present Tasks,"[32] in which he addressed the problems brought on by a lack of legal personnel. He cautioned against mass participation unfettered by legal procedure and stressed the need to establish political/legal committees "responsible for directing and linking up the work of organs concerning civil affairs, public security, judicial affairs, bureaux of investigations, law courts, and supervision as well as for the disposal of mutual relations between organization and work" (p. 9). These committees would serve to control further mass participation in the campaign against counterrevolutionaries.

Characteristically for Peng, law served first as a statement of policy and then as an organizational framework for the enforcement of policy. As a statement of the regime's policy of repression of "those who collude with imperialism," "inciters," "tempters," "officials receiving bribes," "traitors," and "those using arms to cause disruption of the masses," the regulations provided a "legal weapon" against opponents of the regime by stipulating the varying sanctions to be employed

---

[29]Klein and Clark, *Biographical Dictionary,* p. 715.

[30]Peng Zhen, "Guanyu zhenya fangeming huodong he zhengzhi fangeming tiaoli wenti de baogao," *Zhongyang zhengshi gongbao* 25 (1951):4–6.

[31]Art. 7 of the Common Program of the Chinese People's Political Consultative Conference addresses directly the respective roles of harshness and leniency in handling counterrevolutionaries. See Chen Hefu, *Zhongguo xianfa leibian* [Compilation of Chinese Constitutions] (Beijing: Zhongguo Shehui Kexue Chubanshe, 1980).

[32]Peng Zhen, "Report on Political and Legal Work," *Current Background* 91 (July 10, 1951):1–9.

against such elements.[33] The regulations also provided for an organizational framework that, while allowing anyone to denounce counterrevolutionaries to the people's government, restricted the power of individuals and groups to apply sanctions. This power was limited to military courts, which in turn were limited to the period of military rule.[34]

Peng similarly employed law during the later campaigns against corruption to strengthen Party power as well as Party discipline. In his "Explanations of the PRC Draft Regulations for the Punishment of Corruption" (1952), he noted that the struggle against corruption and theft was one between two work styles.[35] Law was to promote central control over local cadres, impose Party-directed rules on non-Party officials, and control mass movements. Peng wanted to routinize the results of the campaign by emphasizing institutional processes and dampening mass participation. Such routinization involved the establishment of a framework of judicial and commercial management organizations to detect and punish corruption.[36] As was the case with the campaign against counterrevolutionaries, the regulations gave such bodies great flexibility and discretion in carrying out their tasks.[37] Central control over the movement was also exercised through the system of Party committees rather than through restrictive procedural regulations.[38]

---

[33]See arts. 3, 4, and 5 of PRC Regulations for the Punishment of Counterrevolutionaries in *Zhongyang renmin zhengfu guanyu gongbu shixing Zhonghua renmin gongheguo zhengzhi fangeming tiaolie de mingling* [Orders of the Central People's Government Concerning Promulgation and Implementation of the PRC Law for Punishment of Counterrevolutionaries] (Beijing, 1951), p. 2.

[34]Art. 20 in ibid., p. 6.

[35]"Guanyu Zhonghua renmin gongheguo zhengzhi tanwu tiaoli caoan de shuoming" [Explanation of Draft Regulations for Punishment of Corruption in the PRC], in *Renmin shouce* [People's Handbook], 1952, pp. 52–55. Also see "Zhonghua renmin gongheguo zhengzhi tanwu tiaoli" [PRC Draft Regulations for Punishment of Corruption], *Renmin shouce*, 1952, pp. 50–51.

[36]See art. 10 of "Zhonghua renmin gongheguo zhengzhi tanwu tiaoli," p. 51.

[37]While the regulations established a hierarchy of sanctions for crimes of varying degrees of seriousness measured by value of loss, there is little in the way of standards for computation or for determining other types of seriousness. See ibid., pp. 51–52.

[38]Peng Zhen, "Zhengzhi tanwu tiaoli caoan," p. 52.

Consolidating Organizational Power in Beijing

Peng's emphasis on the role of organization in consolidating the achievements of revolutionary mass mobilization was also evident in his administration of Beijing municipality. Peng's speech to the First Beijing Representative Congress in 1954 served as a summary of the city's development during the first five years after liberation. He cautioned that the elimination of the poisons of the old society required a long-term struggle, and he bemoaned the lack of systematic handling of these problems. In addressing the need for ideological reform, Peng criticized the sloppiness borne of lack of organization and discipline. He went on to admonish all government workers and people to develop the practice of following law and legal methods. This concern was applied also to economic, educational, and cultural questions.[39]

Later, the Hundred Flowers movement and the anti-Rightist campaign of 1957 presented a particular challenge to Peng's views because he was Party chief in Beijing, the center of the disturbances. Western observers have suggested that Peng Zhen's behavior during this period indicated his resistance to criticism of the Party and his hostility toward non-Party elements in China.[40] Liu Shaoqi's criticism of Peng's "sectarianism" has often been cited as evidence of this.[41] Yet Peng has repeatedly evinced the view that cooperation with non-Party members was a necessary and beneficial component in the regime's development program.[42] During the Cultural Revolution, Peng was criticized stridently for advocating tolerance toward capitalists.[43] Thus, at the

[39]Peng Zhen, "Beijing shi wu nian lai zhengfu gongzuo qingkuang he jinhou gongzuo renwu" [Government Work in Beijing During the First Fifteen Years and Work Tasks for the Future], *Xinhua yuebao* 9 (1954):28–30.

[40]MacFarquhar, *Origins of the Cultural Revolution, I*, p. 203 *et seq.*

[41]Liu was quoted by Red Guards as saying at a forum of democrats, "Peng Zhen is quite a capable man. His mistakes are only his serious sectarian feelings." *SCMM* 651 (April 22, 1969):39.

[42]In the section on the political life of the state in Liu Shaoqi's Political Report to the Eighth National Party Congress, Peng criticized "some members of our Party who hold that everything should absolutely be of one color, who are unwilling to see non-Party people work in state organs, who do not consult with them when circumstances require, and do not respect the authority that goes with their posts." Peng is widely credited as the author of this section of Liu's report. See MacFarquhar, *Origins of the Cultural Revolution, I*, p. 100, citing *A Compilation of Dossiers* (suppl. to *Gong nong bing* [Worker, Peasant, Soldier]) (September 1967), trans. in *SCMM* 527:5.

[43]See "Counterrevolutionary Revisionist P'eng Chen's Towering Crimes of Opposing the Party, Socialism, and the Thought of Mao Tse-tung," *SCMM* 639:5. Also *A Compilation of Dossiers*, pp. 38, 39.

April 20, 1957 Beijing propaganda conference belatedly called by Peng to signal his support for the Hundred Flowers slogan, when he asked for cooperation between Party and non-Party elements, his comments can only partially be ascribed to political expediency.

Peng's reluctance to support the rectification campaign may be explained better by reference to his insistence on subjecting social movements to organizational control. In signaling his acquiescence to the campaign, Peng stressed the role of Party committees at all levels, indicating that the criticism campaign should be confined to existing organizations.[44] He also stressed the need for centralized control and the importance of preventing the outbreak of unbridled criticism.[45] Thus, his concern about the conduct of "blooming and contending" focused on the mechanics of soliciting criticism of the Party rather than on the principle of whether criticism was due.[46] The Party should set the parameters for criticism, in his view, and ultimately define the relationship between itself and society. Only when the organizational controls over non-Party critics threatened to break down did Peng urge the leadership to crack down.

Whether or not Peng was amenable to accepting from outsiders criticisms of Party work style, he was certainly aware of shortcomings in the Party's leadership at the basic level. He was frequently critical of the heavy-handed attitude of local Party cadres and of the chronic problems of incompetency and inefficiency, which were the target of much of the criticism during the Hundred Flowers movement.[47] Peng's awareness of these problems may well have made him cautious of allowing unfettered criticism of Party rule. Peng's 1957 visit to Eastern Europe, then in the throes of post-Stalin unrest, had undoubtedly impressed on him the potential for underlying popular resentment of Party rule. Peng's report on his visit revealed his concern for the

[44]"Peng Zhen zai Beijing shi xuanchuan gongzuo huiyi shang zuo baogao" [Peng Zhen's Report to the Beijing Municipal Propaganda Work Conference], *Renmin ribao* [People's Daily], April 22, 1957, p. 1.

[45]"Peng Zhen tongzhi tan jianchi hefeng xiyu de fangfa" [Comrade Peng Zhen Discusses Adhering to the Methods of Mild Wind and Gentle Rain], *Renmin ribao*, May 10, 1957, p. 1.

[46]Peng did not dismiss the usefulness of accepting criticism, but rather criticized "wholly incorrect policies and methods of resolution" regarding the handling of contradictions—i.e., regarding the management of the campaign. "Peng Zhen zai Beijing."

[47]Peng's previous criticisms of Party work styles were made at meetings such as the First Beijing Municipal Representative Conference (*Xinhua yuebao* 9, 1954) and in Peng's 1951 Report on Political and Legal Work (*Current Background* 91 [July 10, 1951], p. 6 et seq.).

potential for social upheaval resulting from such resentment.[48] Such concern seemed to be justified in light of the broad critiques of Party rule that did emerge during the movement.

Peng's response to critiques of the Party's ruling position, revealed in his speech to the second Beijing Representative Congress in August 1957, was a scathing rejection that set the tone for the anti-Rightist campaign. Carefully distinguishing between criticisms of Party work style and attacks on the rule of the Party, Peng made it clear that the latter were unacceptable, amounting to an appeal for the restoration of capitalist overlords.[49] His response to the criticisms of the Hundred Flowers movement seems to have derived primarily from the content rather than the sources of the criticism. It was the content that revealed the "rightist" character of the source rather than vice versa. Thus, his reaction to the criticisms of Hundred Flowers is traceable not to Peng's "sectarianism" but rather to his fundamental commitment to Party power.

Advent of the Cultural Revolution

Although Peng continued to be identified as the Politburo member responsible for the legal system, after the Great Leap Forward he gave few speeches dealing directly with legal issues. His attentions were occupied primarily with his new responsibilities for culture and education, an arena in which central-level political tension was growing. After the purge of Peng Dehuai in 1959, policy decisions increasingly involved serious political in-fighting. Peng Zhen's predisposition in favor of organizational solutions to political problems was evident in three major developments leading up to the Cultural Revolution— investigative reports on the Leap, the Socialist Education campaign, and the campaign against Wu Han.

Economic Policy

The events surrounding the Chang Guan Lou incident revealed Peng's commitment to rational, collective decision-making based on "objec-

---

[48]Peng's report was carried in *Renmin ribao*, April 1, 1957.

[49]"Peng Zhen tongzhi zai Beijing shi renmin dai hui shang chanshu fan youpai douzheng de weida yiyi" [Comrade Peng Zhen Explains the Great Significance of the Struggle Against Rightists to the Beijing Representative Congress], *Xinhua yuebao* 17 (1957):144–46. Also see *SCMP* 1588 (August 12, 1957):2–3.

tive truth."[50] Presumably with the knowledge of Liu Shaoqi and perhaps Deng Xiaoping as well, Peng directed Deng Tuo to supervise an investigation of mistakes in central economic policy that had caused the recent economic disaster. In November 1961 several meetings were held at the Chang Guan Lou (Broad View Tower) in the Beijing Zoo during which central policy documents were analyzed. Finally, a lengthy report was generated and delivered to Peng.[51] Peng apparently intended to use the report and its accompanying materials at an enlarged meeting of the Central Committee in an attempt to repudiate Mao's economic policies, particularly the communes.[52] However, Mao's self-criticism at the 7,000 Cadre Conference in January 1962 rendered the attack superfluous and the Chang Guan Lou report was never formally presented. Whether its contents had been circulated, helping to prompt Mao's "apology," is not known.

That Peng was later accused of breaking discipline in bringing about the "secretive" Chang Guan Lou sessions suggests that his views on Party discipline may not have been absolute. Peng appears to have organized an overall critique of the Leap in the guise of a review of its local impact on Beijing. In any case, in authorizing the collection of materials revealing errors in central policies, Peng revealed his assumption that, when presented with such evidence, the Party leadership would act rationally and withdraw its support for Mao's policies.

Party Reform

Peng's involvement in the Socialist Education campaign of 1963-65, intended to improve the quality of local Party officials, provided further evidence that his views on organization, both in Party reform and

---

[50]Red Guard criticisms of the Chang Guan Lou Incident include "Events Surrounding the Chang Guan Lou Counterrevolutionary Incident," *Dongfang hong*, April 20, 1967, in *SCMP* 5, 187 (June 15, 1967):23-37; "Thoroughly Disclosing the Inside Story of Chang Guan Lou Counterrevolutionary Incident, *Diyi zhanxian*, May 18, 1967, in *SCMP* 4001 (August 15, 1967); and "Big Exposure of a Conspiracy to Usurp the Party and State Leadership," *Guangming ribao*, August 9, 1967, in *SCMP* 4014 (September 15, 1967). Also see Kenneth Lieberthal, *A Research Guide to Central Party and Government Meetings in China: 1949-1975* (White Plains, N.Y.: International Arts and Sciences Press, 1976), pp. 176-77.

[51]Lieberthal, *Research Guide,* p. 177, credits Xiao Jia with writing the report. *Guangming ribao*, August 9, 1967, p. 3, claims the report was made to Zheng Tianxiang. Zheng is now president of China's Supreme People's Court.

[52]Lieberthal, *Research Guide,* p. 177. For further details, see Timothy Cheek's chapter on Deng Tuo in this volume.

in controlling mass campaigns, contrasted with those of Mao Zedong. Mao's "first ten points" on the campaign emphasized the importance of poor and lower-middle peasant organizations as the main force for mobilizing popular participation.[53] Peng, in his "later ten points," put local officials in charge, supported by higher-level Party work teams as staff.[54] While both documents admonished against interference in local administration, Peng allowed work teams to replace "bad" officials in some instances.[55] Peng's view of the work teams, however, was in turn more restrained than that expressed in Liu Shaoqi's "revised later ten points," which urged that work teams take charge of local Party reform.[56] Indeed, Peng's willingness to protect local officials from work team interference was strengthened by personal interest evident in his decision to replace Zhang Banshi as head of the work team sent to Beijing University when Zhang continued to press criticism against Peng's associate Lu Ping, head of the school's Party Committee.[57]

Additionally, Peng's later ten points established concrete regulations for officials' participation in labor in place of earlier vague generalizations.[58] Peng thereby made lower-level officials accountable, but he also set standards for evaluating their behavior. This issue also revealed his concern with practicality, for while Mao explained these labor activities as a way of building symbolic ties with the masses, Peng viewed the process as an important method by which officials could gain a more complete understanding of local conditions.

The issue of the treatment of landlords in these documents also reflected divergent views on the development of Chinese society. Mao's "points" emphasized the need for ongoing class struggle and advocated reliance on poor and lower-middle peasants in establishing

---

[53]The first ten points are included as appendix B in Richard Baum and Frederick C. Teiwes, *Ssu-Ch'ing: The Socialist Education Movement of 1962-1966* (Berkeley: University of California Press, 1968), p. 62.

[54]The later ten points are included as appendix C in ibid., p. 76. Peng Zhen is widely credited as the author of the later ten points. See Richard Solomon, *Mao's Revolution and the Chinese Political Culture* (Berkeley: University of California Press, 1971), p. 435; Byung-joon Ahn, *Chinese Politics and the Cultural Revolution: Dynamics of Policy Process* (Seattle: University of Washington Press, 1976), p. 62.

[55]See art. 7, First Ten Points, and art. 2, para. 4, Later Ten Points, Baum and Teiwes, *Ssu-Ch'ing,* p. 76.

[56]Ibid., pp. 29 *et seq.*

[57]See Ahn, *Chinese Politics and the Cultural Revolution,* p. 115.

[58]See art. 9, First Ten Points, and art. 7, Later Ten Points, Baum and Teiwes, *Ssu-Ch'ing,* pp. 88-90.

proletarian dictatorship over hostile elements, thus authorizing a broad attack on a rather poorly defined enemy.[59] Peng's, by contrast, tended to downplay the threat posed by "bad" elements, admonished against broadening the scope of attack, and set out clearcut procedures for their suppression.[60]

Clearly, in Peng's view, since the Party had already seized and consolidated political power, the impact of the preexisting bad classes was diminished. He therefore emphasized behavior rather than class origin in determining political qualities of individuals.[61] The "later ten points" noted explicitly that the sons and daughters of landlords and rich peasants could break from their class backgrounds and criticized the practice of applying parents' class labels to their children.[62] This approach was rejected in Liu's "revised later ten points," which stated flatly that "Children of landlords and rich peasants should be barred without exception from taking positions of local basic-level teaching cadres," implying grave doubts as to whether the children of bad classes could adopt a correct class standpoint.[63]

Cultural Policy

Peng's use of organizational solutions to political issues was perhaps most evident in his handling of the campaign against Wu Han. Peng's position of responsibility for the Party's cultural policy had coincided with an increase in criticism of "bureaucratic" work styles on the part of Party officials, after the excesses of the Leap. Mao approved this effort, but it resulted in what could be read as indirect critiques of Mao himself—one of which was Wu Han's play, *Hai Rui Dismissed from Office*.[64] Peng, who had already clashed with Jiang Qing over the

[59]See arts. 3 and 5, First Ten Points, ibid., pp. 60–64.

[60]See arts. 3 and 9, Later Ten Points, ibid., pp. 84–85, 91–93.

[61]In his January 31, 1965 speech to the second session of the Fourth National Committee of the All-China Youth Federation and the simultaneously held Eighteenth National Students Representative Conference, Peng pointed out that the "Party, in dealing with young people with different family origins and experience, attached importance to their behavior." *SCMP* 3395 (February 11, 1965). Also see Stanley Rosen, *Red Guard Factionalism and the Cultural Revolution in Guangzhou (Canton)* (Boulder, Colo.: Westview Press, 1982), p. 85.

[62]See art. 10, Later Ten Points, Baum and Teiwes, *Ssu-Ch'ing*, pp. 93–94.

[63]See art. 10, Revised Later Ten Points, ibid., p. 117. For discussion of Liu Shaoqi's authorship of the revised later ten points, see Lowell Dittmer, *Liu Shaoch'i and the Chinese Cultural Revolution* (Berkeley: University of California Press, 1974), p. 50.

[64]For the context and details of this criticism, see the introduction to this volume and the chapters on Wu Han and Deng Tuo.

reform of Beijing opera, resisted attempts by Mao's supporters to influence cultural policy.[65] Having tried and failed to prevent the formation of the special Cultural Revolution Group and the publication of Yao Wenyuan's critique of *Hai Rui*, Peng was charged with directing the criticism of Wu Han.[66] Peng's 1966 "February Outline" report sought to restrict the campaign to the academic issue of Wu's historiography and established a smaller working group, which excluded Kang Sheng, Mao's representative on the original group.[67]

By such organizational tactics, Peng sought to manipulate the criticism of Wu Han so as to avoid the broader issue of whether there existed in the Beijing Party Committee an organized group resistant to Mao's leadership. This, together with Peng's manipulation of Beijing University, confirmed his penchant for using his organizational strengths to further his political interests.[68] In this respect, Peng's political tactics may be contrasted with the style of Liu Shaoqi. Liu not only espoused in his writings the principle that cadres should accept criticism and not engage in factional intrigue, but he practiced it to the point where he seemed to accept his own political demise without much of a fight.[69] Peng, on the other hand, was not above engaging in factional conflict when his political power and position were threatened. But his efforts to restrict discussion to academic issues also revealed his view that a broad range of views should be allowed, so long as Party control and Marxist-Leninist categories of thought were upheld.

Conceptual Framework

Two of Peng's slogans that were particularly criticized during the Cultural Revolution—"Everyone Equal Before the Law" and "Every-

[65]Peng Zhen, "Zai jing ju xiandai xi guanmo yanchu dahui shang de jianghua" [Speech at the Conference on Model Performances of Contemporary Plays by the Beijing Opera], *Hongqi* 14 (1964):18–24. See analysis of dispute in Ahn, *Chinese Politics and the Cultural Revolution*, pp. 171–72.

[66]Ahn, *Chinese Politics and the Cultural Revolution*, p. 196.

[67]For text of the February Outline, see Union Research Institute, *Main Documents of the Great Proletarian Cultural Revolution* (Hong Kong, 1968), pp. 3–12. For criticisms of the February Outline, see *Hongqi* 9 (1967):25–28.

[68]For a general discussion of Peng's ties with the "Beida" administration, see "P'eng Chen, Peking, and Peking University," in *China News Analysis* 615 (June 10, 1966).

[69]Liu Shaoqi, "On Inner-Party Struggle," in Liu Shaoqi, *Three Essays on Party-Building*. Also see Liu Shaoqi, "Training of a Communist Party Member," in Compton, *Mao's China*, p. 136 *et seq.*; Dittmer, *Liu Shao-ch'i*, pp. 116–18.

one Equal Before the Truth''—sum up his basic views.[70] The first reflects his understanding of the relationship of state to society, which is a function of Peng's ideas on the evolution of Chinese society. During the immediate postliberation period, Chinese society still contained hostile elements such as landlords, rich peasants, and KMT elements who were not considered "citizens" and were not entitled to legal equality. Peng took the view that, with the elimination of these class enemies, the remainder of society should enjoy the evenhanded application of law. Peng clearly did not accept the notion that, once the Party-directed campaigns against class enemies were concluded, such elements could continue to pose a threat to the rule of the proletariat.

The second slogan reflects Peng's views on decision making and organizational discipline, which are functions of his belief in the power of objective rationality.[71] Peng's faith in "objective laws" (*keguan guilu*)—not to be confused with his attitudes toward law (*falu*)—that could be discerned by rational analysis and be implemented in practical terms was evident not only in his pronouncements but in his style of work.[72] With the failure of the Great Leap Forward and the subsequent debates over economic policy, Peng and others stressed the importance of respecting objective truth even more than before. Questions as to whether Mao's voluntarist economic policies had any rational foundation surfaced in a number of ways and found expression in the Beijing Party Committee's journal, *Frontline*, under Deng Tuo's leadership. For example, one article took the guise of discussing whether truth had a class character, or whether one could distinguish between objective laws and various class-based theories about those objective laws.[73] By questioning Mao's view that everything has a class nature, Peng's group participated in a larger effort to shape a theoretical alternative to

[70]See art. 85 of the 1954 Constitution in Chen Hefu, *Zhongguo xianfa leibian*, p. 232. Peng was credited with asserting in 1954 that equality before the law should extend to all the people. *Zhengfa hongqi*, October 17, 1967, p. 8. Also see *Cuijiu zhanbao* [Militant Journal for Smashing the Old], May 25, 1967, p. 3.

[71]See "Counterrevolutionary Revisionist P'eng Chen's Towering Crimes," p. 2. Also Y. C. Chang, *Factional and Coalition Politics in China: The Cultural Revolution and Its Aftermath*, (New York: Praeger, 1976), p. 14; P'eng Shu-tse, *The Chinese Communist Party in Power* (New York: Monad Press, 1980), p. 279.

[72]See, for example, Peng Zhen, *Guanyu Jin Cha Ji*, pp. 166–67.

[73]"Zai tan zhenli you meiyou jiejixing" [A Further Discussion on Whether or Not Truth Has Class Nature], *Qianxian* 17 (1965):47–49. For discussion of *Qianxian* and its significance, see Timothy Cheek, "Deng Tuo: Culture, Leninism, and Alternative Marxism in the Chinese Communist Party," *The China Quarterly* (September 1981):484.

Mao's thought.[74] They also implicitly rebuked Mao for his refusal to heed the advice of his colleagues on economic policy since, in the view of Peng and others, objective truth was arrived at through the involved process of mutual consultation and rational discussion.[75]

During the Cultural Revolution, Peng was accused of using the notion of equality before the law to halt class struggle and using the concept of objective truth as a weapon against Mao.[76] While these charges are clearly distorted and exaggerated, they contained grains of truth. In any event, Peng Zhen's twelve years in the wilderness gave him ample opportunity to reflect on the validity of his political viewpoints.

Return to Power

Resurrection and Endorsement of Peng's Thought

In March 1979—two weeks after Peng's appointment to the NPC's Legal Affairs Commission—*Beijing Daily* reprinted an article by Peng written for the 1958 inaugural issue of *Frontline* and subjected to vitriolic abuse as a "big poisonous weed" in 1966.[77] The original article had emphasized the need for officials to be objective in their analysis of right and wrong, good and bad, and to assess their own work in the light of current historical conditions. Peng at the time seemed indirectly to be arguing against Mao's subjective vision in 1958 concerning the capabilities of the peasantry. Criticizing those who have "too high an opinion of themselves," Peng contended that standing in the forefront of revolution meant acting in accordance with the capabilities and needs of objective reality.[78]

These antivoluntarist views naturally had been the target of Cultural Revolution radicals who accused Peng of vilifying Mao by admonish-

---

[74]For discussion of Mao's contention that all understanding has a class character, see Stuart Schram, *The Political Thought of Mao Tse-tung* (New York: Praeger, 1969) pp. 180–85, 190–94.

[75]"Peng Zhen zai Beijing." Also see Peng Zhen, *Guanyu Jin Cha Ji*, pp. 180–84.

[76]See *Cuijiu zhanbao*, May 25, 1967, p. 3, and "Counterrevolutionary Revisionist P'eng Chen's Towering Crimes," p. 2.

[77]*Beijing ribao*, March 8, 1979, p. 1; "Counterrevolutionary Revisionist P'eng Chen's Towering Crimes," pp. 7–8.

[78]"Zhanzai geming he jianshe de zui qianxian" [Standing at the Forefront of the Revolution and Construction], *Beijing ribao*, March 8, 1979, p. 1.

ing people "not to stay in the air like kites or balloons."[79] Such criticisms were not far from the mark, although Peng had not limited his critique to the chairman. Peng's rejection of "the doctrine of the mean" and his criticism of those who "swim in the middle of the stream" had been aimed at officials who went along with Mao's policies when they should have stood up for their beliefs and resisted.

Beijing Daily in its preface to the reprint of the article asserted that "practice has already proved that the ideas and policies published in the article were correct and that it was a good article particularly for popularizing the Party's fine work style of seeking truth from facts." Noting that the article had continuing practical significance, the *Beijing Daily* commentary directed cadres and officials to study it in the context of promoting the Marxist style of study promoted at the Third Plenum.[80]

Peng's views were further resurrected in 1979 with an article in *People's Daily* on the question, "Shouldn't Everyone Be Equal Before the Truth?"[81] The publication in 1981 of Peng's comprehensive "Report on Party Work and Concrete Policies in the Jin Cha Ji Border Region,"[82] by then four decades old, accompanied his reemergence as a major force in national politics.

Renewed Influences

Peng promptly set about promoting his views on the role of law in China through his positions on the Legislative Affairs Committee and, later, on the Committee for Revising the Constitution. The establishment of the *Legal Studies Journal* in 1980 gave him a medium through which to communicate his views to legal professionals.[83] As Peng

[79]"Counterrevolutionary Revisionist P'eng Chen's Towering Crimes," p. 7.

[80]*Beijing ribao*, March 8, 1979, p. 1.

[81]Xing Fengsi, "Zhenli mianqian bu yingdang renren pingdeng ma?" [Shouldn't Everyone Be Equal Before the Truth?], *Renmin ribao*, June 13, 1979. Also see *Selections from World Broadcasts* (Far East), June 19, 1979, pp. BII1-BII3.

[82]Peng Zhen, *Guanyu Jin Cha Ji*.

[83]The relationship between Peng and *Faxue zazhi* is indicated by a number of factors. The journal's name is written in Peng's calligraphy; Peng's photograph is featured prominently in many issues while the photographs of other political-legal officials are not so featured; and *Faxue zazhi's* contribution to the volume *Lun falu mianqian renren pingdeng* [On Everyone Is Equal Before the Law] (Beijing: Falu Chubanshe, 1981) is the only one that names Peng Zhen as a contributor to the concept of equality before the law.

began to carry out his new duties, his earlier views reemerged in full. In his explanation of the policy basis for various substantive laws, Peng emphasized that such legislation was designed to serve the regime's policies of economic modernization.[84] He reiterated his adamant, long-time support of the Eighth Party Congress Resolution of 1956, which declared that Chinese society had progressed beyond the stage of class struggle to that of developing the productive forces. Under Peng Zhen's direction, the current legalization program has embodied policy pronouncements in the form of substantive laws.

The Criminal Law Code, enacted in 1979, reflected Peng's view that the pursuit of economic development above all required social stability to "ensure the smooth advance to socialist modernization."[85] By protecting personal as well as state property, the code reinforced the regime's turn away from the policies of excusive state ownership that had plagued economic development in the past. At the third session of the Fifth National People's Congress Standing Committee in September 1980, Peng emphasized the need to draft a law for economic contracts.[86] Enacted in December 1981, the Economic Contract Law was intended to regulate the tension between the imperatives of central planning and resurgent local market forces.[87]

Peng next supervised the drafting of the 1982 Constitution, which enshrined such policies as economic modernization, support for intellectuals, and family planning.[88] In keeping with his previously ex-

[84]See "Peng Zhen tongzhi xiang canjia quanguo gong, jian, fa youguan huiyi de tongzhi zuo zhongyao jianghua" [Comrade Peng Zhen Gives an Important Speech to Comrades Participating in Meetings Related to National Public Security, Procuracy, and Courts] *Xinhua yuebao* 7 (1979):281.

[85]Peng Zhen, "Guanyu qige falu caoan de shuoming" [Explanation of the Seven Draft Laws], *Jiaqiang shehui zhuyi fazhi* [Strengthen the Socialist Legal System] (Chengdu, 1979), p. 14.

[86]*Zhongguo fazhi bao,* September 5, 1980. Also see Peng Zhen, "Report on the Work of the Standing Committee of the National People's Congress of the PRC," *Main Documents of the Third Session of the Fifth NPC* (Beijing: Foreign Languages Press, 1980), p. 98.

[87]See Liang Huixing, "Lun wo guo hetong falu zhidu de jihua yuanze yu hetong ziyou yuanze" [On the Principles of Planning and Contract Freedom in Our Country's Contract Law System], *Faxue yanjiu* 4 (1982). Also see Gu Ming, "Jingji hetong fa shi baozhang guojia jihua zhixing de youli de gongji" [The Economic Contract Law Is a Powerful Tool for Ensuring Fulfillment of the State Plan] *Faxue zazhi* 3 (1982).

[88]See preamble and arts. 6, 7, and 25 of the Constitution of the PRC, in *Beijing Review* 25, 52 (December 27, 1982):10–15.

pressed views against overly detailed and restrictive regulations, he has cautioned, ''We must avoid subjective, one-sided attempts to formulate a multiplicity of all-embracing laws and must not allow our laws to become too complicated and elaborate for our cadres and people to learn and apply.''[89] Thus, the constitution and many of the laws are subject to broad interpretation. While the scope of such interpretation may be limited by official explanations of the intent and meaning of various laws, the imprecise nature of the laws themselves raises the possibility of divergence in interpretation and application. The problem was underscored when in 1981 the Congress issued a resolution explaining detailed procedures for interpreting ambiguous laws and regulations.[90] Clearly, it is the Party that ultimately determines the true meaning of specific statutes and regulations, giving it maximum flexibility in strengthening and exercising control over society.

Similarly, the various organizational laws regarding local people's governments address the Party's concern with bureaucratic foot dragging in the enforcement of policy.[91] Peng has repeatedly urged paying ''close attention to extending appropriately the powers of the local authorities under unified central leadership.''[92] Nonetheless, the vagueness of the dividing line between permissible initiative and punishable disregard for central policy may curb the initiative of local officials and render powerless Peng's organizational reforms.

The organization laws of the people's courts and people' procurates also reflect Peng's approach to judicial behavior and law enforcement.[93] Overlapping jurisdiction among the basic (county), intermediate (district), and higher (province) courts allows the higher levels to rule directly on cases arising at lower levels.[94] This effectively restrains judicial independence. Similarly, lower-level procuracy offices, which supervise arrests and prosecutions, are subject to direct supervision by higher levels. Party dominance—through the committees at each level

---

[89]Peng Zhen, *Speech to First Session of 6th NPC June 21, 1983* (Beijing: Foreign Languages Press, 1981), p. 140.

[90]*Selections from World Broadcasts*, FE/67 48/BII/3/13, June 1981, p. 3.

[91]Peng Zhen, ''Guanyu qige falu,'' pp. 12–13.

[92]Peng Zhen, Speech to First Session of 6th NPC, p. 140.

[93]The text of these statutes appears in Yu Man-king, *Criminal Law Code and Three Other Codes of the PRC* (Hong Kong: Great Earth Book Co., 1980).

[94]See arts. 25 and 28 of the Court Organization Law in ibid.

of the court system—is further strengthened by the provision that violations of Party discipline are not within judicial jurisdictions. Moreover, while the courts and procuracies are empowered to act independently of other administrative organs, there is no parallel restriction on interference by Party organs.[95]

The ever troublesome dilemma of maintaining central control over the localities without stifling local initiative clearly remains a problem. This issue was also the source of concern during the 1950s. At that time, however, the issue involved the need for centralization, increased control over mass activities, and state building. At present, the need is to loosen state control and to allow for controlled decentralization through an organizational framework established by legislation. This is evident, for example, with respect to the role of standing committees in the people's congresses at local levels. These committees are to enjoy a greater degree of autonomy while still being subject to supervision by the National Standing Committee.[96] Similarly, Peng Zhen's organizational approach to controlled decentralization is evident in the provisions in the Economic Contract Law for a hierarchy of offices to supervise the contract formation process.[97]

To supplement the role of legislation in providing the basis for controlled decentralization, Peng has, predictably, emphasized the role of the Party in providing overall supervision. This is evident in his persistent espousal of the importance of following the "four basic principles"—the most basic of which is the leadership of the Chinese Communist Party.[98] Thus in his speech to the first session of the Chinese Legal Studies Society, Peng stressed that "the work of the Legal Studies Society is to uphold the four basic principles."[99] Among

[95]See Peng Zhen, "Guanyu qige falu," pp. 19–20.

[96]See Peng Zhen, "Report on the Work of the Standing Committee of the NPC," pp. 102–103.

[97]See ch. 6, Economic Contract Law of the PRC, *Zhonghua renmin gongheguo jingji hetong fa tiaowen shiyi* [Explanation of Articles in the Economic Contract Law of the PRC] (Beijing: Falu Chubanshe, 1982), pp. 120–25; art. 111, Constitution of the PRC, in *Beijing Review* 25, 52 (December 27, 1982):27.

[98]The principles are: (1) Uphold the Socialist Road; (2) Uphold Proletarian Dictatorship; (3) Uphold the Leadership of the Party; and (4) Uphold Marxism, Leninism, Mao Zedong Thought. See Deng Liqun, "Meiyou gongchandang lingdao jiu meiyou shehuizhuyi xiandaihua jianshe" [Without the Leadership of the Communist Party There Can Be No Socialist Modernization Contruction], *Sixiang jiben yuanze tongsu jiangzuo* [Popular Lectures On the Four Basic Principles] (Beijing, 1981), pp. 9–15.

[99]Peng Zhen, "Fazhan shehuizhuyi minzhu, jianquan shehuizhuyi fazhi" [Develop Socialist Democracy, Perfect the Socialist Legal System], *Faxue zazhi* 5 (1982):5–6.

the tasks he enumerated at the July 1982 National Conference on Political-Legal Work was that of strengthening the leadership of basic-level Party organizations in the campaign against economic crimes.[100]

Despite his promotion of overall Party supervision, however, Peng has cautioned that Party officials should not get involved in individual cases, so as to avoid arbitrary intervention. He told an audience at the Central Party School that "leadership by the Party Committee does not mean it must examine and approve concrete cases. . . . If the Party Committee has a hand in every case, it will surely become too busy with trifles to bother about important matters." While seemingly contradictory to the concept of Party leadership, Peng's comment in fact indicates merely that such leadership should take on a new form of indirect supervision. For Peng also stated that instead of involving itself in concrete cases, the Party Committee "must lead, supervise, and support the independent public security organs and the functioning of procuratorial and law enforcement organs. . . . It must support the correct things they have done. It must criticize and rectify the mistakes they have made."[101]

Peng evinces a genuine concern that direct supervision of cases by Party officials will lead to abuse of power to the detriment of the legalization program and the Party's prestige and authority generally. In his discussion of equality before the law, Peng stated specifically that the principle was directed against the seeking of special privileges.[102] In his discussion of "Seven Draft Laws," Peng noted that the pursuit of special privileges would undermine the legal system. Moreover, continued reference to the ongoing presence of "leftist remnants" reveals concern that such remnants in particular yet will seek to manipulate the judicial system for their own political benefit.[103]

Nonetheless, Peng has declined to enact an all-embracing prohibition on direct Party involvement, as indicated by the absence in the final draft of the constitution of any prohibition on Party interference in the handling of cases.[104] In fact, Peng has stressed that the Party

[100]See "Quanguo zhengfa gongzuo huiyi zai Beijing juxing" [National Political Legal Work Meeting Convenes in Beijing], *Zhongguo fazhi bao* (July 30, 1982).

[101]Peng Zhen, "Guanyu shehuizhuyi fazhi de jige wenti" [On Several Questions in the Socialist Legal System], *Hongqi* 11, p. 7.

[102]See Chen Changhang, " 'Falu pingdeng' de lixiang, xianshi, lishi" [The Ideals, Reality, and History of 'Everyone Is Equal Before the Law'], *Lun falu mianqian renren pingdeng* [On Everyone Is Equal Before the Law] (Beijing, 1981).

[103]See Peng Zhen, "Guanyu qige falu," pp. 22–24.

[104]See art. 126, Constitution of the PRC, in *Beijing Review* 25, 52 (December 27, 1982):28.

Secretariat must give final approval for congressional enactment of the constitution, criminal law, and all other legislation.[105] Thus, the threefold process of Party approval of legislation, interpretation of statutes, and appointment and supervision of Party personnel is intended to ensure Party control over the legalization program without incurring the costs that direct supervision of cases might bring.

New Thinking

Peng's emphasis on the need to codify law can be explained by several factors aside from his long-held assumption that social and political control can be achieved best through formalized law in the form of command rules. Peng's old view that China has progressed beyond the need for class struggle, combined with distaste for the Cultural Revolution, has led to his greater acceptance of the need for some protection of citizens' rights.[106] This view is partially a concession to the need to build legitimacy for the regime in the eyes of the populace. For, even if not involved directly in national-level political conflict, members of society at large were nonetheless affected by the Cultural Revolution and its aftermath, such that a profound distrust of the Party has become evident. Providing ordinary members of society with a measure of legal protection against arbitrary political attack may serve to alleviate such distrust.

A more fundamental factor, however, is protection of members of the elite, including intellectuals and low-level officials, from political attack. Marshalling their support is crucial to the regime's modernization program. Peng's new concern in this area clearly stems from a commitment to ensuring that the brutalities of the Cultural Revolution are not repeated. Aside from his personal suffering at the hands of Red Guards in December 1966, Peng is no doubt responding to the suffering of his friends and associates. Through his attendance at one memorial service after another in 1979 and 1980, Peng was constantly reminded of the political and personal demise of colleagues such as Liu Ren, Deng Tuo, An Ziwen, and Liu Shaoqi. In step with the posthumous honoring of these colleagues, Peng reiterated the theme that

[105]See Peng's discussion of the role of the Party Secretariat in "Shiyi renmin zhijie canjia guojia guanli de yizhong zhongyao xingshi" [An Important Form by which a Billion People Directly Participate in Management of the Country], *Xinhua yuebao* 5 (1982):33.

[106]See "Peng Zhen tongshi xiang canjia quanguo," p. 28.

codes of law are a necessary step in preventing a reemergence of the radical excesses of the Cultural Revolution.[107] He also emphasized the provision in the "Organic Law of Local People's Congresses and Local People's Governments" that prohibits the arrest of deputies to these bodies without the approval of their standing committees.[108] The constitution was also revised to include similar provisions in addition to prohibitions against holding deputies to the National Congress legally liable for their speeches or votes at its meetings.[109]

Many of Peng's current views on law are in broad conformity with views held by Liu Shaoqi, Peng's pre-Cultural Revolution mentor.[110] One can see differences, however, in their concepts of the role of the Procuracy. Liu thought the Procuracy should carry out general supervision over government as well as over legal organizations, pursuing a broad range of governmental misconduct and corruption as well as the prosecution of law-breakers.[111] Peng, agreeing with Chen Yun, has expressed the more limited view that the Procuracy is to supervise only the enforcement of the Criminal Law,[112] leaving Party and governmental discipline to the Party Discipline Inspection Commission. Peng's more restrained view expresses his concern that legal institutions not be used again to carry out factional attacks on establishment officials as they were during the Cultural Revolution—a concern Liu might have shared had he survived.

Additionally, another new facet in Peng's thinking regarding the role of legal procedure has emerged. Whereas during the 1950s he was concerned primarily with the enactment of substantive regulations to strengthen state and Party control over economic and social activity, after his rehabilitation he began to stress the need for formal codes of legal procedure. The regulations of the 1950s either contained procedural provisions or were supplemented by administrative guidelines circulated internally,[113] but there were no formal codes of procedure

[107]See Peng Zhen, "Guanyu shehui zhuyi fazhi," p. 4.

[108]Peng Zhen, "Guanyu qige falu," pp. 17–18.

[109]See arts. 74 and 75, Constitution of the PRC, in *Beijing Review* 25, 52 (December 27, 1982):21.

[110]"Selected Edition On Liu Shao-ch'i's Counterrevolutionary Revisionist Crimes," *SCMM* 653 (May 5, 1969):33–36.

[111]Ibid., pp. 37–39.

[112]Peng Zhen, "Guanyu qige falu," p. 20.

[113]See William C. Jones, "An Approach to Chinese Law," *Review of Socialist Law* 4 (1978):3–25. Informants in Hong Kong indicate that such guidelines are still the basis for most judicial activity.

enforced by specialized institutions.[114] Peng's recent emphasis on the need for formal codes of legal procedure is indicated by his description of the Criminal Procedure Law as the primary guarantee of the "legal rights" of citizens.[115]

The importance of legal procedure in preserving political stability is emphasized by the purposeful dispersal of authority among the people's courts, the Procuracy, and the Public Security Bureau. Since the latter still retains virtually unfettered power to hold individuals under administrative detention, this dispersal of authority is less effective in protecting members of society from unjustified arrest than in protecting members of the elite from attacks not sanctioned through official Procuracy channels. The Procuracy thus serves primarily to ensure that the Ministry of Public Security—still filled with "leftists"—is not again so easily manipulated in the course of political conflict.

Conclusion

Peng Zhen's career in the Chinese political elite spans a period of some forty years. During this time, he has espoused a consistent view that law should be an instrument of Party policy, enforced through centrally controlled organizations. His views on the relationship between state and society have stemmed from a reliance on institutional rather than class analysis of China's progress toward socialism. Believing that arbitrary abuses of power can be curtailed through organizational control, Peng has sought to use procedural provisions to dilute the independent authority of individual officials.

Peng's greatest effect on the performance of the Chinese legal system will stem from his long-standing commitment to the principle of Party dominance. In this regard, Peng's organizational ties to the state bureaucracy do not dilute his role as a proponent of Party leadership, but rather exemplify the emerging pattern of indirect Party control. Peng Zhen's ranking position on the Politburo indicates that his role is one of translating the broad programmatic decisions of the Party center into the state institutional and legislative framework. In an important speech to a meeting of Beijing journalist circles, Peng conceded that the form of Party leadership must undergo change as China makes the

[114]The Procuracy was a step in this direction, but it fell into disuse after 1957. See Jerome A. Cohen, *Criminal Process in the People's Republic of China, 1949–1963* (Cambridge: Harvard University Press, 1968), pp. 10–18.

[115]Peng Zhen, "Guanyu qige falu," pp. 17–18.

transition from the stage of revolution to that of construction. Nonetheless, he indicated, the basic aim remains the same: "Party policies become state policies through the state structure. We must fix into legal form policies that are proved correct by practice."[116] That Peng may try to use his state positions to interpret Party policies selectively to suit his own political agenda, or even to maneuver his way onto the Politburo's Standing Committee, does not dilute his commitment to the principle of Party control.

Peng's views on the importance of Party dominance contribute to his utilitarian approach to the role of non-Party intellectuals. Asserting that unless legal studies are tied to the needs of reality they become merely the "hobby of individuals," he has combined a limited reliance on the role of trained legal scholars in providing necessary investigation and research with a prohibition against deviating from the ideological precept of Party power.[117] Thus, in directing the formulation of the new constitution, Peng authorized extensive research into foreign constitutions while ensuring that the document contained a provision for combating "capitalist, feudal, and other decadent ideas."[118] That such strict Party dominance over the legislative process has caused dissatisfaction within the Chinese legal community was indicated in part by the contention of one legal scholar, later retracted under pressure, that equality before the law must extend to law making.[119]

With respect to legal personnel, Peng has conceded the need for technical training but has shied away from granting political authority to professionals—as indicated by the appointment of his associate Zheng Tianxiang (a Party official and nonlawyer) to the presidency of the Supreme People's Court. Peng recognizes that their education and expertise render professionals less willing to accept Party norms at face value. For, while conceding the need to raise the cultural, scientific, and technical levels of the politically more reliable workers and

[116]"Jiaqiang fazhi xuanchuan shi xinwenjie de zhongyao zhize" [Strengthening Popularization of the Legal System Is an Important Responsibility of Journalistic Circles], *Zhongguo fazhi bao* (May 14, 1984):3.

[117]Peng Zhen, "Fazhan shehuizhuyi minzhu jianquan shehuizhuyi fazhi," *Zhongguo fazhi bao* (October 1, 1982):1.

[118]"Shiyi renmin zhijie canjia guojia guanli de yizhong zhongyao xingshi" *Xinhua yuebao* 5 (May 1982); art. 24, *The Constitution of the PRC* (Beijing, 1983), p. 24.

[119]Pan Nianzhi and Qi Naikuan, "Guanyu falu minqian renren pingdeng de wenti" [Several Questions Regarding Everyone Is Equal Before the Law] *Shehui kexue* (Shanghai) 1 (1980), reprinted in *Lun falu mianqian renren pingdeng* [On Everyone Is Equal Before the Law] (Beijing, 1981).

peasants, Peng has urged that "state cadres and intellectuals in particular should study dialectical materialism and historical materialism so that all our people will base their thinking on the scientific world outlook and, of their own accord, take the socialist road."[120]

As its main architect for nearly thirty years, Peng Zhen has left an imprint on the performance of the legal system that will be evident in the years ahead. Legislation in China can be expected to expand both in scope and detail while continuing to reinforce indirectly the Party's dominance. Legal institutions may well become less subject to arbitrary abuse in the course of political conflict but will continue to take Party policies as their basis for action. Legal personnel will receive increasingly specialized education and training but political authority within the legal system will remain in the hands of Party officials. Thus, imbued with Peng Zhen's views on the relationship between Party dominance and law, China's legal system will combine greater specialization with undiluted, albeit more subtle, Party control.

[120]Peng Zhen, "Speech to First Session of 6th NPC," pp. 145–46.

II. Party Intellectuals

YANG XIANZHEN

Upholding Orthodox Leninist Theory

Carol Lee Hamrin

Why is it that we have always made mistakes in carrying out our work over the past twenty years and more? Why is it that we have suffered so many twists and turns? Our violation of the Marxist principle regarding the basic question of philosophy [that theory should reflect reality] and our defiance of the elementary knowledge of materialism are the epistemic roots of the mistakes and twists and turns. . . . Many previous years' facts show that in order to adhere to materialism, we must oppose "preconceived ideas and prejudices" and oppose all brands of subjective idealism and voluntarism.

Yang Xianzhen, *Guangming Daily*, March 2, 1981

With these harsh words, Yang Xianzhen summed up the recent history of Chinese Marxist theory and policy, based on his experiences during the decade of controversy from 1955 to 1965 and the decade of persecution that followed.[1] Yang had suffered severely after 1958, as his theoretical views and his policies in running the Party school system were called into question. His close personal and professional ties with Peng Dehuai, Liu Shaoqi, and Peng Zhen brought him scathing denunciation as a counterrevolutionary, as well as torture and imprisonment. Dozens of his closest associates were killed or committed suicide. In early 1979, at the age of eighty-three, Yang reappeared in public along with Liu's widow and Peng Zhen, nearly twenty years after he had

[1]The views expressed below are those of the author, not of any U.S. government organization. I am grateful for the help of Timothy Cheek and H. Lyman Miller in finding recent Chinese-language material by and about Yang Xianzhen, and for the support of Professor Maurice Meisner and the Fulbright program for my earlier research, which can be found in "Alternatives Within Chinese Marxism 1955-1965: Yang Hsien-chen's Theory of Dialectics," Ph.D. dissertation, University of Wisconsin, 1975. Steve S. K. Chin helped me find key material on Yang in 1972-73 in Hong Kong.

ceased regular public activity.[2] Shortly thereafter, he became the chief adviser to the Central Party School, helping to rebuild the institution that had been his only home. In 1982, Yang was elected to the Party's Central Advisory Commission.

Post-Mao writings have detailed the attacks against Yang beginning in 1959 and argued that they were personally directed by Mao's close associate, secret police chief Kang Sheng, in a successful bid to gain control of the Party school system. Less detailed accounts of Yang's case written by the school's "revolutionary" writing group in the early 1970s tend to confirm this.[3] The open theoretical debates and the private feuding at the school in turn were part of a larger rivalry for control over theoretical and cultural affairs. In a mirror image of that earlier period, the theoretical discussions of 1978–79 were components of an effort by Deng Xiaoping to regain control of key Party organs from Kang Sheng's successors. Yang was particularly useful to the Dengists in undermining radical Maoist dogma since he more than any other theoretician had developed a comprehensive explication of a more orthodox Chinese Marxism-Leninism. Yang, in turn, has used this mandate to launch a personal crusade against voluntaristic tendencies in doctrine and policy still infecting even the Dengist wing of the Party.

Despite Yang's useful rehabilitation, many of the theoretical, political, and policy issues involved in his case have not been resolved—or even addressed in some instances—well into the 1980s. Some of the ambiguities in the treatment of Yang's case may have been due to Mao's well-known personal interventions against him. But there is more to the story than residual respect for Mao. Beneath the surface of some articles that seemed to give Yang only grudging respect were the buds of a theoretical debate that burst open only in 1981 but had roots in a long history of differences of view among key theoreticians jostling within the broad reform coalition patched together by Deng Xiaoping. A number of writers now closely tied to Deng and Hu Yaobang had

---

[2]Yang was born in Hubei province on July 24, 1896, according to *Zhongguo zhexue nianjian 1983* [Chinese Philosophy Yearbook 1983], p. 358, which gives a brief biography. Yang's family background and the details of his personal life are unknown.

[3]See Fan Ruoyu, "The Origin of the Polemic Against 'Two Combining Into One,'" *Hongqi* [Red Flag], October 2, 1979, pp. 64–69, in *Joint Publications Research Service Translations from Red Flag* (hereafter JPRS-RF) 74680 (November 30, 1979):109–18. See *Three Major Struggles on China's Philosophical Front (1949–64)* (Beijing: Foreign Languages Press, 1973) for a collection of articles by the Revolutionary Mass Criticism Writing Group of the Party School.

once argued the Maoist position against Yang. The most prominent of these erstwhile Maoists is Wang Ruoshui, until late 1983 the deputy editor-in-chief of *People's Daily*. Wang was a principal critic of Yang from 1960 through 1965, along with his mentor Ai Siqi, the renowned Party theorist and close friend of Mao who died in 1966, reputation intact. No doubt Wang and others have found it embarrassing to be linked implicitly in Yang's exposés with the likes of Kang, Chen Boda, and "ultra-leftist" Guan Feng.

A careful review of the debates over dialectics in the 1960s and in the 1980s involving Yang Xianzhen reveals persisting differences among China's top theorists on fundamental questions of epistemology that have important implications for policy. In disputing whether "human consciousness" or "material conditions" should weigh most heavily in determining policy, these theorists continue to rehash disputes that have appeared at some time throughout the socialist world—what demarcates idealism from materialism, how to operate on the middle ground between determinism and voluntarism, and whether politics or economics should be "in command." These rather ethereal doctrinal disputes reflect systemic problems and thus did not die with Mao, but have found new life in post-Mao efforts to steer a new course for China. Moreover, there is a clear, if intricate, interrelationship among theoretical differences, policy disputes, and power struggles throughout. Earlier interpretations of incidents involving Yang Xianzhen, based primarily on the content of academic articles, without the inside story now available on personal rivalries, were by necessity superficial.[4] But to place sole weight on later revelations that focus on the competition for power and obscure the theoretical and policy differences would also be incomplete. The fact is, personal ties and factional appointments were often based on shared views.

Thus, the persistence of fundamental differences of view since at least the 1950s among the founding generation of Chinese Marxist-Leninists calls for a closer look at their early, formational experiences and a reexamination of the seemingly intractable intellectual problems that keep resurfacing in contemporary China. Yang Xianzhen's life provides a window into these matters. His is the voice of Leninist orthodoxy from the united front periods of both Soviet and Chinese Communist history—the voice of gradualism and caution associated

[4]Earlier studies of Yang include Hamrin, "Alternatives Within Chinese Marxism"; Donald J. Munro, "The Yang Hsien-chen Affair," *The China Quarterly* 22 (April-June 1965):75–82; and Merle Goldman, *China's Intellectuals* (Cambridge: Harvard University Press, 1981), pp. 95–101.

with Bukharin and Liu Shaoqi. Yang was one of those Chinese Marxists who learned early on through a series of painful experiences to oppose adventurism from any quarter.

The Formative Years

Yang Xianzhen belongs to a political generation of Chinese Communists whose early intellectual life was shaped by pre-Stalin Soviet thinking. Following famine and peasant uprisings in 1920, Soviet officials were in full retreat from the forced wartime collectivization. In the prevailing atmosphere of self-criticism and reassessment within the regime, lively debates over theory and policy were accompanied by a relaxation of cultural and social life. In particular, debate abounded on how to apply dialectics to all fields, a subject not broached again until after Stalin's death. Bukharin was the prime architect of the New Economic Policy (NEP) and its theoretical underpinnings, which projected a gradual and voluntary transition from capitalist to collectivist practices. His ideas dominated Comintern training activities worldwide, which he and his protégés directed.[5]

Liu Shaoqi was among the first eight students sent from China in early 1921 to train in Moscow, but he left dissatisfied with the quality of the fledgling school and impatient for the active life. The next, larger group of Chinese students stayed longer, while others were trained in China under Comintern oversight. Liu and these other leaders became responsible then for organizing labor and student activities in the coastal cities. Joining the Party in 1926, Yang was assigned along with other newly trained recruits to work with them.[6]

[5]Alfred G. Meyer, introduction to Nikolai Bukharin, *Historical Materialism* (Ann Arbor: University of Michigan Press, 1969), pp. 1A-7A, discusses Bukharin's involvement with the Comintern and the NEP. Jane L. Price, *Cadres, Commanders, and Commissars: The Training of the Chinese Communist Leadership, 1920-45* (Boulder, Colo.: Westview Press, 1976), ch. 3, discusses the Party schools in Moscow and in China dominated by Bukharin's approach.

[6]Information in Price, *Cadres, Commanders, and Commissars*, pp. 31-33, 48-49, and in Donald W. Klein and Anne B. Clark, *Biographical Dictionary of Chinese Communism, 1921-1965* (Cambridge: Harvard University Press, 1971), pp. 973-75, suggests that Yang was educated in Moscow in the early 1920s, following graduate training in China and Germany, but this has not been confirmed by official Chinese sources. *Zhongguo zhexue nianjian 1983* states only that Yang graduated from the Wuchang College of Commerce in 1920 and joined the Party in 1926. Yang's own reminiscences start there. Yang is known to have translated a number of

Imprisonment

Many of these organizers sat out the 1930s in jail after the Nationalist-Communist united front broke down in 1927. Liu was said to have complained bitterly about reckless, "leftist" policies from headquarters that made it easier for the Nationalists to deplete his ranks.[7] Yang's seven-year experience in a Beijing prison has recently been detailed in a history of the "sixty-one traitors" case, which was used during the Cultural Revolution to justify rescinding Party membership for Liu Shaoqi, Bo Yibo, An Ziwen, Liu Lantao, and Yang along with dozens of others who had worked in the Communist underground in North China.[8] In the fall of 1936, on the eve of the Japanese drive south, Liu obtained permission, apparently from General Secretary Zhang Wentian, to negotiate the release of those in prison in exchange for their public renunciation of Communism. An investigation of the case in 1945 approved this stratagem and declared the records of the former prisoners clear. Mao even commended the prison's Party Committee, headed by Bo Yibo and including Yang, for having turned the prison into a "school" where they translated and studied Marxist-Leninist texts and taught the other prisoners. In 1968, this judgment was reversed and Liu and the others were judged traitors for having sold out to the Nationalists, allegedly against Party orders. It was implied that they had been spies in the service of the Nationalists ever since.

Soviet texts, but at least some were translated from English, not Russian, so that his knowledge of the Russian language also must remain in question. See Yang Xianzhen and Guan Shan, "Ru Caolanzi jianyou qianhou" [Before and After Entering Caolanzi Prison], *Geming shi ziliao* [Revolutionary History Materials] 1 (Beijing, October 1980):17–18.

[7]This was apparently a source of tension between Liu and Chen Yun, who oversaw his work. James Pinckney Harrison, *The Long March to Power: A History of the Chinese Communist Party, 1921–72* (New York: Praeger, 1972), pp. 235 and 245.

[8]The best information on this case, which confirms less detailed information available earlier from Red Guard sources, comes from Tai Huaiji, *Tiandi you zhengqi:Caolanzi jianyu douzheng yu "liushi yi ren an"* [Heaven and Earth Have Upright Spirit: The Struggle in Caolanzi Prison and the "61-Man Case"] (Beijing: Beijing Dichu Geming Shi, Beijing Chubanshe, December 1982). Timothy Cheek has translated the list of names, with biographical information, of the sixty-one involved. Yang, in Bai Ye, "Fang Yang Xianzhen" [An Interview with Yang Xianzhen], *Xinwen zhanxian* [News Front] 12 (1980):2–7, says that he was imprisoned twice for "almost seven years" between 1926 and 1936.

Work in the "Base Areas"

Liu assigned the released cadres to help in the formation of the new Jin Cha Ji Border Region in 1937, working out of Taiyuan in southern Shanxi. Led by Bo and Yang, they organized peasant and student associations, under orders from Liu to follow "genuine" united front policies that respected concrete, local interests and to avoid "empty talk" and leftist practices. For several years, Yang was in the Taihang Mountains, near the 8th Route Army headquarters. His recent reminiscences from the anti-Japanese war period speak of close working relationships with Bo Yibo, Yang Shangkun, and Deng Xiaoping and a warm friendship with Peng Dehuai and his wife forged admidst narrow escapes from Japanese encirclement.[9]

In 1940, Yang began his career in cadre training. In addition to administering the work of the North China Bureau's Secretariat and later its investigation/research office, as well as writing many editorials for the local Party daily, Yang was charged with building up the bureau's Party school. At first, Yang has recalled, as part of a small teaching staff with little material, he frantically reviewed (Moscow's current version of) Lenin's works and the Soviet Party history text, both just published in Chinese in Yan'an, and listened to reports from local Party secretaries to create teaching material that would help connect theory with reality. He also remembered with disdain his conflicts with incoming "arrogant, individualistic" cultural cadres who looked down on popular literature and whose "ostentatious" writing was sloppy with regard to facts. These themes in Yang's remembrances were not just fashionably created for the post-Mao "line" of "seeking truth from facts," although they served it well. Nor did they reflect a purely personal bias against academics. Yang throughout his career gave highest priority to teaching Party officials how to

---

[9]See Tai Huaiji, *Tiandi you zhengqi*; Harrison, *Long March to Power,* pp. 297–302; and Tetsuya Kataoka, *Resistance and Revolution in China: The Communists and the Second United Front* (Berkeley: University of California Press, 1974), pp. 87, 90, 125, 137, 177, and 271, for information on Bo Yibo's "dare to die" groups and the Party's Northern Bureau. Yang's personal experiences as the secretary general of the bureau are found in Bai Ye's interview and in Yang Xianzhen, "Cong Taihang wenhuaren zuotanhui dao Zhao Shuli di 'Xian Erhei jiehun' chuban" [From the Taihang Cultural Work Conference to the Publication of Zhao Shuli's "The Marriage of Xiao Erhei"], *Xianwenxue shiliao* [New Literature Historical Materials] 3 (1982):28–35. Timothy Cheek has summarized in English the many names, dates, and events in this lengthy article.

translate theoretical knowledge into a realistic, down-to-earth work style. This was evident not only in articles he wrote in the 1940s, but also in his lectures and public addresses through the 1950s.

Yang's experience during these formative years—a relatively cosmopolitan education followed by harrowing times in prison and in the primitive countryside during wartime—was different from that of other theorists who later became his competitors. As Yang set out for Jin Cha Ji, Mao was gathering around himself in Yan'an an inner circle of theoreticians steeped in Stalinist ideology and experienced in propaganda work. Ai Siqi was well-acquainted with the wide scope of Marxist-Leninist classics as well as much of the rest of European philosophy from his years of study in Japan, but he was especially taken with the writings of Stalin's in-house philosopher, Mark Mitin, who became something of a personal model.[10] Ai and Chen Boda, Mao's Yan'an secretary, had collaborated during the 1930s in Shanghai, popularizing Marxism-Leninism (as interpreted by Stalin) among a whole generation of Party converts. Kang Sheng meanwhile spent much of the decade in Moscow, probably being trained in secret police work at the height of Stalin's purges. Toward the end of the decade, Chen Boda received theoretical training at Sun Yat-sen University, which along with other Party schools by then was dominated by Mitin's men. There is some evidence that Mao was already impressed by Ai's efforts to popularize Marxism in China, even before Ai's arrival in Yan'an in 1936. Others have documented the pervasive influence of the views of Ai, Chen, and through them Mitin and Stalin on Mao's *On Contradiction* and *On Practice*, which he first compiled as lectures to be given in Yan'an.[11]

The evidence indicates that Yang already had some differences with Chen and Ai over theory, economics, and teaching methods by the late 1940s and early 1950s, when all three were directly involved with the Party school.[12] It thus seems likely that from early on there was a

[10]Ai Siqi's background and views have been researched by Joshua A. Fogel; I am grateful for his discussions with me about Ai, through personal correspondence. See his chapter on Ai in *Chinese Intellectuals and the State: Search for a New Relationship*, ed. Merle Goldman, with Timothy Cheek and Carol Lee Hamrin (forthcoming).

[11]See Raymond F. Wylie, *The Emergence of Maoism: Mao Tse-tung, Ch'en Po-ta, and the Search for Chinese Theory: 1935-1945* (Stanford: Stanford University Press, 1980).

[12]From 1948 to 1955, Liu Shaoqi was president and Chen and Yang were vice-presidents of the school. One Red Guard source, Liaison Station Attached to the August 18 Red Rebel Regiment of Nank'ai University, "Pledging to Fight a Bloody Battle with Liu-Teng-T'ao to the End," April 1967, in *Survey of China Mainland Maga-*

spectrum of interpretations within Chinese Marxism, stemming from different life experiences during these years of upheaval. At least two important variants were in the making, one at headquarters in "liberated" Yan'an and one in the base areas behind Japanese lines in North China. In the later careers of these men can be seen something of how the radical, populist "Maoism" of the Cultural Revolution drew on the more voluntarist strains found in Lenin and Stalin, which in turn are rooted in an idealist Hegelian view of dialectics, while a more moderate, bureaucratic Leninism drew sustenance from the determinist strains found in Lenin and Bukharin, which are consonant with Engels' mechanistic approach to dialectics.

Founding an Institution

In January 1945, Yang Xianzhen arrived in Yan'an, newly assigned to the Central Party School, which was to be his home base through its several incarnations for the next twenty years. The school had grown from 300 students in 1937 to 5,000 in 1944, with several branches.[13] From 1948 until 1955, under the general guidance of school president Liu Shaoqi, Yang as vice-president was responsible both for creating a

---

zines (hereafter SCMM) 651 (April 22, 1969), claimed that in 1952–53, Liu backed Yang in a dispute with Chen over a management issue. It is likely that Ai Siqi was in charge of theory classes at the school; Yang, in " Weiwulun de mingyun" [The Destiny of Materialism], *Shehui kexue zhanxian* [Social Science Front] 1 (1982), has claimed that his dispute with Ai over theoretical matters began in a teaching situation in 1950.

[13]Harrison, *Long March to Power*, p. 321. According to Harrison, the predecessor of the Central Party School (CPS) was the Marxist-Communist School, founded in March 1933 under Dong Biwu's headship. The CPS was next directed by Li Weihan from 1937 to 1939 and Deng Fa from 1940 to 1943. The school became an important center of the Yan'an rectification campaign, during which it was reorganized several times and run by a high-level committee including Mao and Kang Sheng; Peng Zhen administered the school and formally took over in 1943. The school's history is unclear between 1945, when Peng left Yan'an, and July 1948, when it was reconstituted in Hebei as the Marxist-Leninist Institute under Liu's leadership. Its official name from 1955 until the Cultural Revolution was the Higher Party School; in its new incarnation, it is known once again as the Central Party School. I have referred to it as the Party school to avoid confusion. According to an unnamed former official who had attended the school, there were 1,200 students in 1952, 2,500 in 1953, and 3,000 from 1954 to 1956; the numbers are smaller than in Yan'an due to the post-1949 formation of hundreds of lower-level Party schools attached to ministries and provinces. See "Zhonggong Ma Lie xueyuan" [The CCP's Marxist-Leninist Institute], *Xingdao ribao* [Star Island Daily] (Hong Kong), August 20 and 30, 1964.

formal teaching and research program and for building new facilities near the Summer Palace. Upon completion of the complex, he became the new president. Yang has recalled Liu's directive in 1948 on procedures for regularizing cadre education after years of war. Liu urged teachers and students to overcome the fear of being labeled "dogmatic" (probably stemming from the criticism of Soviet-trained Chinese "bolsheviks" during the Yan'an rectification campaign) and boldly to integrate "foreign [e.g., Soviet] things" through the assiduous study of theory.[14]

In the early 1950s, the differences among variants of Chinese Marxism such as those sketched above were not serious, as Chinese revolutionaries together experimented with adapting the Stalinist model to the founding of new China's governing institutions. In early 1953, the draft first five-year plan was circulated and a study movement initiated to "learn from the Soviet Union." The plan was discussed widely, by Party school researchers as well as others. A flood of Soviet reference materials was translated for use in all of China's research and educational institutions, and Soviet advisers helped shape management styles. Yang Xianzhen led a Party school work delegation to Moscow in October 1954 and early the next year published letters from his Soviet counterparts praising the work of the school. Yang's program was approved by the Central Committee in February 1956 and then widely publicized.[15]

Yang's Growing Reputation

In the competition between Yang Xianzhen and Ai Siqi behind the scenes at the school, Ai at first would have had the advantage of greater prestige as the most notable Chinese expert on "dialectical materialism" and the editor of the Party's journal, *Study*. In 1955, however, Yang's new post as head of the school enhanced his prestige. He, as well as Ai, was active in the formation of the Academy of Science's Institute of Philosophy, and this gave him greater entree to public forums. Yang participated in campaigns critiquing "idealist" alternatives to Marxist materialism, such as those alleged to have been offered by Hu Shi and Hu Feng. He developed a set of lectures called

[14]Yang Xianzhen, "One Who Inspired and Guided the Building of the Party School—In Memory of Comrade Liu Shaoqi" (hereafter "On Liu"), *Hongqi* 7 (April 1, 1980):21–25, in JPRS-RF, pp. 35–43.

[15]*Zhongguo zhexue nianjian 1983*, and ibid.

"What Is Materialism?" which was distributed in late 1955 to all institutions of higher education as a text for political study. In 1956, he was elected first alternate candidate to the Central Committee at the Eighth Party Congress, becoming a full member at its second session in 1958.[16]

Shifting Trends in Party Education

The ink was barely dry from the Central Committee chop affirming the Party school's sixteen-character policy ("study theory, unite with reality, raise understanding, and reinforce Party spirit") when controversy arose. According to Yang, "a few students in the theoretical training class" (then under Ai Siqi) suggested that Mao's writings be treated as classics along with those of Marx, Engels, Lenin, and Stalin. At a Party delegates meeting held at the school in the summer of 1956 it was decided (probably first at higher levels) that they should be so considered.[17]

Following the Eighth Party Congress in September, Liu Shaoqi ordered yet another revision of the curriculum to reflect the new emphasis on economic development by devoting 70 percent of the time to the "urgent" study of philosophy and political economics, leaving 30 percent for Party history and policies. In May 1957, Liu also asked the school to organize a staff project researching how to make the planned socialist economy more diverse and flexible. Yang and his associates responded to these new demands with a seven-year plan for expanding the staff, organizing new education-research sections in addition to the seven then existing, and introducing an academic rank system so as to "normalize" the school and make the work of theory education more professional. According to Yang, Kang Sheng killed these plans. Newly appointed in 1956 as the Politburo's supervisor of the school, Kang was intent on remaking his reputation after six years of obscurity and

[16]Yang Xianzhen, *Gongchanzhuyi shijieguan yu zhuguan weixinzhuyi shijieguan de douzheng* [The Struggle Between the Communist World View and the Subjective Idealist World View] (Beijing: San Lian Shudian, 1955); and "Shenmo shi weiwuzhuyi?" [What Is Materialism?], serialized in the Hong Kong journal *Zhanwang* [Outlook] 207–229 (September 16, 1970-August 16, 1971). The contents of these two collections overlap considerably. Yang was a member of the standing committees of the Second and Third National People's Congresses. See *Zhongguo zhexue nianjian 1983*.

[17]Yang, "On Liu." Liaison Station had claimed that at this meeting, Liu and Yang had played down the study of Mao's works. Yang's vague account leaves open the possibility that Mao's "classics" were still given low priority in the curriculum.

partially feigned physical and mental illness. He already had placed his wife, Cao Yi'ou, in the school administration as his eyes and ears, and she had been raising questions about Yang's management.[18]

Kang used the Party rectification campaign of 1957 to press for another approach. He called for cessation of all activity except rectification, tied to the study of Mao's February 1957 speech. From April through October, a school staff work group was sent down to the Hebei countryside. Yang and his associates thought these activities should be integrated with rather than replace the regular program. They appealed to Liu Shaoqi, who backed them. In May, Liu addressed the subject in a speech at the school, saying that far from studying too much, there still had been too little study. Kang was later to use this as "evidence" of Liu's opposition to the use of the Thought of Mao Zedong as guiding policy in the school. Kang also claimed that the long-term plans were a mere copy of the Soviet experience and were incompatible with the spirit of the Yan'an rectification. He proposed instead that the existing research sections be condensed into one "Thought of Mao Zedong Education-Research Section." Stalemate ensued; both plans were dropped.[19]

Disputes Over Economic Policy

In discussions at the Party school between 1952 and 1955 regarding the first five-year plan, Yang and Ai Siqi came to different conclusions. In late June 1955, following a national rural work conference that hotly debated the proper speed of collectivization in the countryside, Yang summed up his views in a draft article, which he presented in a lecture at the school.[20] Coming down on the side of gradualism, he argued that

[18]Ibid., and Yang Xianzhen, "A Sinister Conspirator Who Butchered and Persecuted the Loyal and Innocent—Exposing Kang Sheng's Features of a Counterrevolutionary Doubledealer" (hereafter "On Kang") *Hongqi* 1 (1981):34–37, in JPRS-RF 77587 (March 13, 1981):53–59. A number of recent articles on Kang Sheng, not directly linked to Yang, give details about his career and the role of his wife that tend to confirm Yang's account.

[19]Yang, "On Kang."

[20]Yang has explained the background to this dispute in an author's note upon publication of his article, "Guanyu Zhonghua renmin gongheguo zai guodu shiqi de jichu yu shangceng jianzhu de wenti" [On the Problem of Base and Superstructure in the PRC During the Transitional Period], in a collection of early works by Yang and several colleagues, *Wei jianchi bianzheng weiwuzhuyi er zhandou* [Struggle to Uphold Dialectical Materialism] (Hubei Renmin Chubanshe, 1980). Accurate excerpts of this article were released in the polemics against Yang in 1964, along with the article by Ai Siqi cited in note 22.

the policies of the Second Plenum (of the Seventh Party Congress) in 1949, which called for "peaceful coexistence" between capitalist and socialist elements in the economy, should persist long into the future. He argued for an "integrated" (mixed) economic base in opposition to those like Ai who had been calling for a "solitary" (fully collectivized) economic base. The disputes at the school reflected higher-level debate, evident since the summer of 1953 when comments by Mao at a national financial-economic conference were indirectly critical of the "united front" attitudes of Liu and other white-areas cadres.[21] Nevertheless, as late as March 1955, Mao had reaffirmed the line of 1952 calling for a lengthy, fifteen-year transition to socialism; he set forth the goal of catching up with the developed world by the year 2000. Thus, Yang was not "out of line" in June, but arguing against a change in line.

In July, however, Mao startled almost everyone by calling for a speedup in rural cooperativization, essentially negating the carefully wrought first five-year plan that had just been announced at the National People's Congress. Ai Siqi, under the safety of this umbrella, wrote an article criticizing Yang's views.[22] Chen Boda was likely involved in this dispute, at least indirectly. At the national level, he was the primary backer of the speedup, and in 1955 he was appointed as deputy director of the Party's rural work department. Yang prudently decided to withdraw his article from publication; Ai followed suit, settling the issue "out of court." Thus, stalemate ensued on yet another front at the school. In the 1980s, when Yang recalled this early economic dispute, he scornfully derided those who backed the "little leap" of late 1955-early 1956, noting that its proponents wanted only socialism and viewed capitalism as the enemy, but were nonetheless more than willing to fill up on the peasants' produce.[23]

Conflict and Soul Searching

In August 1958, on the eve of the high tide of the Great Leap Forward, Yang Xianzhen received an assignment that appeared routine but was to

[21]This interpretation of Mao's comments was spelled out in a footnote by the editors of his *Selected Works*, vol. 5 (Beijing: Foreign Languages Press, 1977), p. 93.

[22]Ai Siqi, "A Rebuttal of Comrade Yang Hsien-chen's 'Composite Economic Foundation Theory,'" *Renmin ribao* [People's Daily], November 1, 1964, p. 6; in JPRS Translations of Political and Sociological Information on Communist China (hereafter JPRS) 27414, no. 212 (November 17, 1964).

[23]Bai Ye, "Fang Yang Xianzhen," p. 6.

prove a watershed in his political life. Chen Boda, who lived upstairs in the Party school apartments, ran into Yang and asked him to write a refutation of the explanation of the term "identity" in the Soviet *Concise Dictionary of Philosophy*.[24] Yang was to defend Mao's view of the identity of contradictions as expressed in his *On Contradiction,* which the dictionary indirectly "slandered" as Hegelian. In November 1957 in Moscow, Mao had discussed his views on dialectics and then initiated study of the subject in China; in March 1958, at the Chengdu conference, he specifically mentioned the problem of the dictionary's jab at him.[25] Chen was soliciting Yang's article for the Party's theoretical journal, of which he was the newly appointed chief editor, replacing Ai Siqi. The concurrent change in the journal's name from *Study* to *Red Flag* in May 1959 also reflected the changing times.

In drafting his defense of Mao, entitled "On Two Categories of Identity," Yang argued that the dictionary distorted Mao's views due to a misunderstanding of dialectics.[26] Yang explained that the meaning of identity varied according to context. When materialists like Mao spoke of the identity of contradictions, they were referring to the mutual connections between opposites. Materialists, Yang claimed, would never subscribe to Hegel's view of identity as absolute sameness, which was inherent in the idealist term "identity of thought and existence."

In drafting these judgments, Yang was well aware that he was arguing one side in a philosophical dispute of several years standing. *Study* had been publishing articles since January 1958 claiming that the term "identity of thought and existence" could be accepted by both idealists and materialists, a position Ai Siqi had taken in private disputation with Yang since the early 1950s. Yang no doubt awaited reaction anxiously after he submitted one copy of the article to Chen and one to Kang, keeping a third. His article was not published in October as planned,

---

[24]The following is Yang's account of the episode, provided in an afterword when he published the original draft "without one word revised." "Luelun liangzhong fanchou de 'tongyixing'" [A Brief Discussion of Two Categories of "Identity"], *Xueshu yuekan* [Academic Monthly] 10 (1979):7–16. Yang, "The Destiny of Materialism," indicated that this dictionary entry had been a source of controversy in China as early as 1953, that is, before Stalin's death. Both the dictionary and its Chinese-language version went through several editions in the mid-1950s.

[25]Mao Zedong, "A Dialectical Approach to Inner-Party Unity," November 18, 1957, *Selected Works*, vol. 5, p. 516; and "Talks at the Chengtu Conference," March 1958, in *Chairman Mao Talks to the People: Talks and Letters 1956–1971,* ed. Stuart Schram (New York, Pantheon, 1974), p. 109.

[26]See note 24.

and he heard nothing directly about it until the summer of 1962, when he confronted Chen and forced him to admit that he was backing Ai. In the meantime, debate over the different interpretations was carried on publicly in the academic press by protégés of these higher level officials.

According to Yang's 1981 exposé, he later discovered that Kang Sheng, "that 'theoretical authority' who didn't comprehend theory," misread his article, and using his "Lin Biao-type 'genius,'" concluded that if Yang thought the (absolute) "identity *of* thought and existence" was an idealist conception, then Yang must believe that thought and identity *have* no (dialectical) identity. Using his personal access to the Chairman to his advantage, Kang asked Mao his views as the two of them were swimming. Kang was rewarded with Mao's nod of agreement that "there is identity of thought and existence."[27] Using this cryptic communication, Kang spread rumors of Yang's opposition to the Thought of Mao Zedong. Kang apparently hoped to use Yang's article to discredit him and thus weaken his position in the larger competition over school management policies, which had come to a head in the summer of 1958. Both a Secretariat meeting in June and a national forum on Party school work in August debated the sixteen-character policy without reaching conclusions as to the appropriate mix of theoretical and practical education or the best way to balance studying Mao's works and the (other) classics. From the sparse information available, it seems that Peng Zhen supported Yang, while Deng Xiaoping temporized.[28]

Intellectual Ferment

The personal rivalries at the school were played out against a backdrop of intellectual controversy on many subjects in the context of the de-Stalinization underway in the Soviet Union and Eastern Europe. Increasingly, debate in China focused on the epistemological issue that lay at the heart of the policy disputes leading into the Great Leap Forward: Can the power of the human will be so organized as to overcome material backwardness in expanding production? Yang's philosophical views had already been developed and widely publicized

[27]Yang, "On Kang," p. 55.

[28]For discussions of these meetings, see Kenneth Lieberthal, *A Research Guide to Central Party and Government Meetings in China 1949–1975* (White Plains, N.Y.: International Arts and Sciences Press, 1976), pp. 115 and 120.

in his 1955 lectures and articles on materialism. In responding to a March 1955 Party resolution calling for educational efforts regarding "the relationship between thought and objective reality, in which thought reflects existence," Yang had introduced Engels' exposition of the "number one question in philosophy": whether thought (*siwei*) or existence (*cunzai*) is the primary reality, and what is the relationship between the two.[29] Yang's references, not surprisingly, were taken primarily from Engels' *Anti-Dühring* and Lenin's *Materialism and Empirio-Criticism,* each a polemic against "idealists" of their time.

Yang's lectures strongly emphasized the importance of the first, ontological, issue, and he argued that above all, true materialists must uphold the absolute primacy of material reality. His exposition of the second, epistemological, issue was rather simplistic. He expounded Lenin's "theory of reflection," positing that somehow the human mind, being made of matter, could easily and correctly comprehend the absolute "truth" of external reality, as in a mirror's reflection. Yang's lectures reflected the strong influence of positivism, with its faith that growing knowledge of science and technology inevitably would solve all human problems. This positivism, which was evident in Engels' writings, was a powerful element in the writings of the early Lenin and in the views of Bukharin and other proponents of the Soviet "mechanistic" school, which dominated Soviet schools in the 1920s.[30] Yang was probably already receptive to such thought from his earlier education in May Fourth China, with its faith in science.

[29]Yang Xianzhen, "Siwei dui cunzai de guanxi zheige zhexue shang de jiben wenti ye shi women yiqie shiji gongzuo zhong de jiben wenti" [The Fundamental Question of Philosophy—the Relationship of Thought and Existence—Is Also the Fundamental Question for All Our Practical Work], *Zhexue yanjiu* [Philosophical Research] 5 (1955).

[30]The correlation between Bukharin's views and those of the mechanists, who stressed the "equilibrium" of opposites in a given dialectical relationship, is discussed in Meyer's introduction to Bukharin's *Historical Materialism* and also in Frederic Wakeman, Jr., *History and Will: Philosophical Perspectives of Mao Tsetung's Thought* (Berkeley: University of California Press, 1973), p. 224 ff. But it is quite difficult to determine conclusively the links between these views and Yang's for several reasons. Wakeman traces a convoluted history of polemics in China in which adversaries slandered each other as "Deborinists" and "Bukharinists," with little connection to the substance of opposing positions. Similar charges made in the 1960s against Yang were grossly distorted; he in turn has not addressed them one way or the other. Add to this the fact that Stephan F. Cohen, in his seminal study, *Bukharin and the Bolshevik Revolution* (New York: Knopf, 1973), p. 108 ff., is inconclusive regarding the compatibility of the dialectics of Bukharin and the mechanists.

Although Yang's interpretations were accepted as prevailing orthodoxy in 1955, the intellectual thaw in China in 1956–57 was to spark a
rethinking of his views, by both himself and others, as part of a wider
questioning of theory and policy within the Chinese elite in the wake of
de-Stalinization. The Chinese debates echoed trends in the Soviet
Union and Eastern Europe, as the writings of Western socialists were
made more widely available in China and Chinese philosophers visited
their counterparts in the Soviet bloc. Concern over uniting theory with
reality particularly reflected China's attempts to break away from
Soviet theoretical and economic models and draft a second five-year
plan more suitable for China. In the 1980s, Yang retrospectively linked
the theoretical debates closely with the policy debates: He traced the
source of the heinous concept of the "identity of thought and
existence" to Mao's erroneous criticism in 1955 of those gradualists
with "bound feet" who "trail behind at a snail's pace," followed by
the premature speed-up of "socialization" on all fronts, which in
Yang's view was unsuitable for conditions at the time. This in turn led
directly, according to Yang, to the media themes justifying the Leap,
which in 1958 were termed "spiritual atom bombs."[31]

In this context of intellectual and policy ferment, the publication of
Chinese translations of Marx's early writings and new versions of
Lenin's *Notes on Philosophy*, written when he first studied Hegelian
dialectics, were to have special impact. Throughout late 1956 and
1957, *Study*, under Ai Siqi's editorship, published articles from
schools all over China discussing the issues raised in Yang's 1955
lectures. Most commonly, they used dialectical theory to query whether matter was always primary and thought always derivative or whether
their roles weren't more fluid and relative in the process of learning. In
1979, Yang revealed that he first purchased and read Lenin's writings
on dialectics in 1956, and that this prompted a search for a better
understanding of the subject on his part.[32] He was to claim, however,
that the trend was actually favorable to his original views, since Lenin's
criticism of attempts to "equate" thought and existence became known
for the first time in China when a new version of his *Selected Works* was

[31]Yang Xianzhen, "Siwei ho cunhai de tongyixing lilun ye shi zhongguo gujiu shi
de weixinzhuyi lilun" [The Theory of the Identity of Thought and Existence Was
Also an Idealist Theory in Ancient China], *Shehui kexue zhanxian* [Social Science
Battlefront] 3 (1984):1–9.

[32]Yang Xianzhen, "Guanyu 'he er er yi' de wenti" [On the Question of "Combining Two into One"], *Zhexue yanjiu* [Philosophical Research] 5 (1979):33–36.

published in Chinese in 1957. These "embarrassed" Ai Siqi, but did not change his thinking, according to Yang. And indeed, the tenor of the articles published in *Study* in 1958 propagated an activist view of the role of consciousness in reshaping the external environment. An article published in January 1958 in the journal *Philosophical Research* was a stalking horse for Ai's position, blatantly challenging Yang's views.[33]

Economic Disaster

In late August 1958, Yang Xianzhen received a telephone call from a Propaganda Department official attending the Beidaihe conference, which launched the high tide of the Leap.[34] He was directed not to open the next school session, even though students were already arriving. Students—all fairly high-level local officials—were to be sent back to their units and the staff sent to work in factories or in the countryside. Yang himself was a "little hot-headed," as he now admits, and he chose to send the staff of the Philosophy Education-Research Institute, under Ai Siqi's supervision, to the "progressive" province of Henan. The next January, Yang visited the group, stopping first at provincial headquarters for briefings. He became puzzled by talk there about a need for "magnifying" the reporting of production statistics. He became even more confused by inconsistencies in comments by his staff members during a formal report meeting in the field, attended by provincial and local officials. Only at night, when his staff came to him in private, did he begin to learn the truth—there was no food. Thoroughly shocked, given national press coverage of the leaps in production gained in Henan, the home of the original commune praised by Mao, Yang nevertheless believed his staff, who were thoroughly experienced in local work themselves and had been working in four separate areas of the province. Lacking boldness, he later confessed, he told them to say nothing for the sake of relations with their hosts.

Yang's recent reminiscences have pointed to this visit as an important turning point in his personal and professional attitudes. They

[33]Guo Yuezheng, "Siwei he cunzai de tongyixing wenti shi zhexue jiben wenti de di'er ge fangmian" [The Question of the Identity of Thought and Existence Is the Second Aspect of the Basic Problem of Philosophy], *Zhexue yanjiu* 1 (1958).

[34]The following episode is recounted in Yang Xianzhen's afterword to his article, "Jianchi shishi qiushi zuofeng; hen hen pipan weixinzhuyi" [Uphold the Work Style of Seeking Truth from Facts; Resolutely Criticize Idealism], *Xueshu yuekan* [Academic Monthly] 9 (1981):1–6.

include particularly scathing remarks about Wu Zhipu, the Henan
Party secretary whose article, "The Philosophy of the Great Leap and
a Great Leap in Philosophy," was published in *Philosophical Research*
in June 1958 and reprinted widely. According to Yang, if the article had
been accurate, the rocks moved by peasants doing rural construction
projects in Henan would have circled the earth several times over.[35]

Yang's reticence to speak up at the time may well have been related
to Kang Sheng's own involvement with developments in Henan. Recent
articles on Kang have charged that in 1957 he praised a group of Henan
peasants for studying philosophy as "real learning" as well as for their
"militant philosophy," which Kang and others were to preach during
the Cultural Revolution.[36] Kang also allegedly praised a Henan
teachers' college for covering a three-year course in ten days and
defined true "scientific experiment" as "bold outrages allowed under
the guidance of the Thought of Mao Zedong." Kang's promotion of
spontaneous Marxism—sprung from "sheds and factories, not books
and concepts"—was integral to his efforts to enhance his personal
reputation as an authority on theory.

Disagreement between Kang and Yang over their respective "mass"
and "bookish" approaches to studying theory became bound up with
much more serious matters during the course of 1959. Yang was not
careful enough, it appears. In March, according to Red Guard sources,
Yang made some comments critical of the concept of "mass
philosophy."[37] In June, according to Yang's own later account, he felt
compelled by his conscience to speak freely in private to a visiting
delegation from the Henan Party school, not expecting that they would
print and distribute his remarks.[38] Yang opened the conversation by
blasting the use of simplistic Great Leap slogans, a number of them
linked with Mao. He attacked phrases like "Practice equals theory;
study equals dogmatism"; "the greater the population, the greater the
output"; "don't fear being *able* to act, just fear the inability to *think* of
acting"; and "catch up with Germany, America, and the Soviet

---

[35]Ibid. See Wu Zhipu, "Yuejin de zhexue yu zhexue de yuejin" [The Philosophy of
the Leap and a Leap in Philosophy] *Zhexue yanjiu* 6 (1958):15–22.

[36]Hu Ruquan, "Commenting on Kang Sheng's 'New Philosophy,'" *Guangming
ribao,* December 18, 1980, p. 4, in Foreign Broadcast Information Service Daily
Report: People's Republic of China (hereafter FBIS), January 6, 1981, p. L2.

[37]Liaison Station. Hu Ruquan tends to confirm this by citing a March 1959 statement by Yang urging "systematic study of Marxist philosophy." Ibid.

[38]Yang, afterword to "Jianchi shishi qiushi zuofeng."

Union." Yang criticized the epidemic of fradulent production statistics in 1958, such as the claim by a Henan county to have produced 7,320 *jin* of grain per *mu*. "The title of the article reporting that claim, 'The Riddle of 7320 Disclosed,' should have been changed to '7320 Lies Concealed,'" Yang commented. He was particularly exercised about the call to "slight the past," for example by not reading *Das Kapital*, and to "stress the present," by pursuing what Yang called "little kids' philosophy." Yang exclaimed, "I read that some counties have organized philosophy lecturing troupes of a thousand people. At first, when I heard the youngest philosophy lecturer was six years old, I thought that child must be talented. But later I heard that there was a five-year-old lecturer!" Yang concluded his tirade by admonishing his visitors that "When you speak of materialism you must link it with Party character. If an individual practices idealism, that individual will be cursed; if the whole Party practices idealism, then the Party will collapse."

That fall, when school resumed and the staff returned from Henan, they told Yang of their meeting with the Henan provincial authorities upon departure. They had been told, "Our faults are many; we have had a bit too much romanticism." Even though the recent dismissal of Peng Dehuai after the Lushan Plenum had cowed bolder men, apparently Yang couldn't hold back a scornful laugh, remarking "They shouldn't be so modest! They did not just have a *bit* too much romanticism. They practice '99 percent romanticism and 1 percent realism'!" All of these incidents were reported to Kang Sheng and entered into his growing file on Yang. Kang's golden opportunity came when Peng Dehuai was assigned to study at the Party school, under the charge of Secretariat member Yang Shangkun and Yang Xianzhen, two of Peng's closest associates from Jin Cha Ji.[39]

Political Struggle and "Academic" Debates

Beginning in November 1959, Yang has recalled, he and more than sixty others at the school were "struggled against" for over nine months. Kang's wife raised the charge of collaboration between Peng and Yang, accusing them of representing the military and the literary circles respectively, one at the top of Lushan and one at the foot,

[39]Ibid., and Yang, "On Kang."

opposing the "three red banners" of the Leap.[40] Four years passed
without a mention of Yang's name in the press, as a subterranean
struggle for control of the Party school and a public "academic
debate" over Yang's theoretical views reflected the general seesawing
of political forces. In early 1961, Yang was labeled a right opportunist
and Ai Siqi apparently became acting head of the school as vice-
president; in September, the school's security official, Wang Congwu,
was appointed president.[41]

During this period, Kang Sheng was finally able to push through his
approach to theory education at the school and further develop the cult
of Mao. At a December 1959 school meeting, Kang announced that
"The Thought of Mao Zedong is the Marxism-Leninism of a new
historical period." His opponents tried in vain to stop him by citing
Mao's early injunction to respect and not presume to surpass Marx.
According to Yang later, Kang required all teachers to use Mao's works
as the key link or shortcut to the study of the classics, with Mao's works
listed first on all reading lists. He justified this by claiming that they
were "the pinnacle of Marxism . . . the supreme criterion, the final
criterion." This concept was further developed by Kang in collaboration with Lin Biao, who eventually recommended adoption of the term
"Mao Zedongism" in May 1966.[42]

Anyone who questioned or opposed this trend at the school was
persecuted. Yang later recalled asking himself,

> Who is Chairman Mao? One might think it ridiculous for an old man
> like me to ask such a childish question. . . . But in the preface to the
> *History of the Ming: Biographies of Crafty Sycophants* there is this
> sentence: "Such people, though heavenly works come out of their
> mouths, tyrannically abuse their power, so that the literati and offi-
> cialdom on earth have to follow their direction." Just as with
> "enlightenment" in Buddhism, I had at last discovered that in the
> Central Party School, *"Kang Sheng was Chairman Mao."*[43]

[40]Yang, "On Kang."

[41]There is conflicting evidence based on public appearances, regarding the exact titles held by top officials at the School through the early 1960s, reflecting ongoing
struggle.

[42]Yang, "On Liu," p. 42, and Ma Zhongyang, "Kang Sheng's Theory of
'Development' and Modern Superstition," *Hongqi* 18 (1980), in FBIS, October 10,
1980, pp. L24–30.

[43]Yang, "On Kang," p. 57.

In October 1959, just before the struggle sessions against Yang began at the school, the essential contents of Yang's 1958 article were published in *Guangming Daily* under the name of Yang's student, Yu Shicheng.[44] Perhaps this was an effort to obtain evidence of public support for Yang's group. In the debate over its contents that followed were reflected all the tensions over economic, social, and educational policies generated by the Great Leap, centering on the role of the mass movement in development. The controversy, which has continued in various guises into the 1980s, has centered around different interpretations of an ambiguous passage in Engels' *Ludwig Feuerbach:* "In what relation do our thoughts about the world surrounding us stand to this world itself? . . . This question is called the question of [whether or how there is] 'identity of thinking and being,' and the overwhelming majority of philosophers give an affirmative answer to this question."

Ai Siqi's group interpreted Engels to mean that there was identity between thought and existence and that it could be interpreted either idealistically or materialistically.[45] According to Ai's group, idealists like Berkeley and Hegel viewed thinking and being as "absolutely identical" in substance (*tongyi* 同一 *dongxi*). But for materialists, "identity" lay in the fact that subjective thought could achieve "consistence" (*jiehe* or *heyi*), "conformity" (*yizhi*), and "unity" (*tongyi* 统一) with objective existence. This occurred in the process called "practice," not in an instantaneous, complete, and error-free "reflection" of reality in consciousness. Ai's group stressed that for Marxists, *tongyi* (同一) has the same meaning as *tongyi* (统一) or *yizhi* or *heyi*, as Mao had explained in *On Contradiction*.

The point of all this quibbling over semantics became clear in the further discussion of Mao's views on dialectical identity. Mao had criticized "mechanistic materialists" who thought that in the contradictions between productive forces and the relations of production, between practice and theory, and between the economic base and the superstructure, the first in each pair always played the principal and decisive role. Whereas this was generally true, Mao admitted, under certain circumstances the reverse could be true. According to Ai's group, this view of the mutual interconnection and mutual

[44]Yu Shicheng, "'Siwei he cunzai de tongyixing' shi weiwuzhuyi de yuanli ma?" [Is the "Identity of Thought and Existence" a Materialist Principle?], *Guangming ribao,* October 11, 1959.

[45]Guo Yuezheng, "Siwei he cunzai de tongyixing wenti."

transformability between contradictions applied as well to thought and existence.

Yang and his group totally disagreed with this broad, loose definition of "identity," claiming that Engels (followed by Lenin) had viewed the concept of the "identity of thinking and being" as purely idealist and not open to a materialist interpretation. To get this point across, Yang's student Yu Shicheng, had cited Lenin's own polemical argument that "this theory of the identity of social being and social consciousness is *sheer nonsense* and an *absolutely reactionary* theory." Relying heavily on Lenin's *Materialism and Empirio-Criticism*, Yang's group reasserted Lenin's rather simplistic theory of "reflection" as a means of countering what they saw as degeneration into idealism. They consistently used the Chinese characters that are closer to unity than to absolute identity in meaning to discuss the relationship between thought and existence, thus implicitly assigning a purely secondary, reflexive role for the mind. Although they always spoke approvingly of the "activist, revolutionary theory of reflection" that would unite theory and practice, they described that process as rather passive, stressing that thought first must completely and correctly reflect reality and then, through practice, could be translated into human activity. They emphasized the importance of exactly and completely aligning thought with reality so as painstakingly to avoid "left" or "right" deviations.

Wang Ruoshui, a member of the *People's Daily* staff with earlier ties to the Institute of Philosophy, wrote an article in the institute's journal, *Philosophical Research*, in January 1960, when Yang was being "struggled" against in the school.[46] Opening his criticism of Yang's approach precisely on these weak points, he argued that only a complex process of interaction between thought and existence could possibly explain the achievement of either correct thought or social change. He tried to prove that the categories of idealism/materialism related only to the ontological problem, which was not in dispute; the categories relevant to epistemology were dialectics/metaphysics. In an article in June, Wang turned to the heart of the debate—the mutual transformability of thought and existence. Quoting extensively from Mao's *On Practice* and from Lenin's notes on dialectics, Wang criti-

---

[46]Wang Ruoshui, "Siwei he cunzai meiyou tongyixing ma?" [Don't Thought and Existence Have Identity?], *Zhexue yanjiu* 1 (1960). At the time, Wang's position at the paper was not known publicly. According to *Zhongguo zhexue nianjian 1983*, p. 345, Wang joined *Renmin ribao* at the end of 1950 as an editor in the theory department. He resumed work there in the early 1970s and by 1978 was a deputy editor-in-chief in charge of theory.

cized "old-style materialists" who refused to accept Mao's dictum that "The subjective can be transformed into the objective."[47]

Although Wang softened his view with the caveat that "people cannot unconditionally create anything," he stressed that humans were increasingly coming to understand and therefore to control the laws of nature. With the "realm of necessity" giving way to the "realm of freedom," Wang insisted, human "subjective initiative" (*zhuguan nengdongxing*) was manifesting itself as never before. Guan Feng, a young theorist at the Party school who was to become an editor for *Red Flag* during the Cultural Revolution, elaborated on the latter concept, calling for the human *creation* of the necessary conditions for "early" progress.[48]

In late July 1960, the controversy was elevated to the pages of *People's Daily* as Ai Siqi weighed in to support Wang's arguments. Ominously, he linked "right opportunism" with (Soviet-style) "revisionism," warning that

> those who deny the dialectical identity of thought and existence, who can't see the mutual relations and mutual transformation of the two, who can't see the subjective dynamism of the people that . . . can enter into the mass movement and transform [it] into [a] great material force that can move heaven and earth, such people can make right opportunist mistakes.[49]

Strong circumstantial evidence from this period and into the 1980s suggests that Wang Ruoshui was a protégé of Ai Siqi and Guan Feng was a protégé of Kang and supports Yang's contention that these individuals worked closely together in this period to persecute him just as he was trying to defend himself in struggle sessions.[50]

[47]Wang Ruoshui, "The Problem of the Identity of Thought and Existence," *Hongqi* 11 (1960), in JPRS-RF 3814.

[48]Guan Feng, "On the Identity of Opposites," *Hongqi* 15 (1960), in JPRS-RF 3929.

[49]Ai Siqi, "Engesi kendingle siwei yu cunzai de tongyixing" [Engels Affirmed the Identity of Thought and Existence], *Renmin ribao*, July 21, 1960.

[50]Yang, "Weiwulun de mingyun." Ai supported Wang in the early 1960s polemics; Wang was one of the few younger members, along with Guan Feng, of Ai's prestigious funeral committee, according to *Renmin ribao*, March 23, 1966, p. 2; and Wang has stoutly defended Ai's reputation in the 1980s. Fan Ruoyu, "Origin of the Polemic," p. 112, described Guan as a "trusted follower" of Kang and implicated *Renmin ribao's* theory department in the frameup of Yang. Perhaps most damaging are the claims in 1973, in *Three Major Struggles*, that Kang was behind Ai and the "others."

As the public polemic went against Yang and rightist "caps" were handed out at the school, only a few persisted in opposing the trend, especially in the face of accusations that they were opposing Lin Biao, if not Mao himself. Upon demotion, Yang took Ai's place as head of the Philosophy Education-Research Institute and continued to lecture. According to Red Guard accusations, he also continued to question idealism and leftist revisionism in theoretical circles.[51] He no doubt placed his hopes in his powerful backers, who began working toward his rehabilitation after Mao's (still unpublished) self-criticism in June 1961 for his errors during the Leap. Peng Zhen and the Propaganda Department under Lu Dingyi warned against simplification and vulgarization in the study of Mao's works; Chen Yi in September called for a general relaxation in intellectual circles.[52]

Mao himself in early 1961 had called for "a year of investigation," as the extent of famine began to emerge during the winter and the economy approached collapse.[53] Yang, like many officials, spent months on inspection tour. Not surprisingly, he chose to visit Henan. Upon returning to Beijing in the fall, Yang gave a lengthy, formal report before the assembled Party school body in which he cited evidence of local famine and quoted extensively from the dismal findings of Communist Youth League Director Hu Yaobang's inspection tour of Liaoning as evidence that his own findings were typical nationwide. Yang blamed the "subjective idealism" and false reporting of local officials (who made up most of the student body congregated before him) for the disaster. He cited an old Chinese saying, "When the people are rich, the country is rich," and warned that the widespread fear of allowing the people to get rich stemmed from an unwarranted distaste for capitalism. This situation suggested a need for extensive reeducation of local cadres, in Yang's view.[54] According to leftist

[51]"Thoroughly Castigate Renegade Yang Hsien-chen's Awful Crimes," *Progressive Forces Daily*, Union Research Institute (U.R.I.) Collection.

[52]Liaison Centre for Thorough Criticism of Liu-Teng-T'ao, Tungfanghung Commune, China University of Science and Technology, Red Guard Congress, "Counter-Revolutionary Revisionist P'eng Chen's Towering Crimes of Opposing the Party, Socialism, and the Thought of Mao Tse-tung," June 10, 1967, in SCMM 639 (January 6, 1967). See also Lieberthal, *Research Guide,* pp. 172–74, on current discussions on education, and p. 171 on Mao's self-criticism.

[53]Lieberthal, *Research Guide,* pp. 169–70.

[54]Yang's account is from his afterword written for the publication of "Zenyang zongjie lishi jingyan, jiaoyu ganbu, tigao ganbu" [How to Summarize Historical Experience, to Educate and Improve Cadres], in his collection, *Zunzhong weiwulun; zunzhong bianzhengfa* [Respect Materialism; Respect Dialectics] (Hubei Renmin Chubanshe, 1980), pp. 93–157.

articles published by the school in 1973, Yang formally called for a review of his case in November 1961 and encouraged his followers to work for his rehabilitation by writing academic articles defending his theories.[55]

At the January 1962 "7,000-cadre conference," Mao was clearly on the defensive regarding the Leap, and Liu Shaoqi was able to reopen the cases of those linked with Peng Dehuai. By mid-year, the verdict on Yang was reversed and the school's Party Committee criticized Kang Sheng's "sham Marxism" as well as his administrative policies, including the excessive involvement of students in movements rather than study. The sixteen-character policy was restored, and an investigation begun into Kang's frameup of Yang. But according to Yang, before the review was complete, Kang counterattacked, accusing the school's leadership of "right-wing reversal" and persisting in his accusation that Yang opposed the Thought of Mao Zedong. Thus, as Yang put it, matters came to a draw.[56]

During the period of Yang's disgrace, the debate on his views had entered a lull, with Wang Ruoshui claiming that a "basic unanimity" had been achieved.[57] But it began to heat up again in the general thaw of late 1961–62 as Yang and other "right opportunists" made a comeback in all fields. Hundreds of learned articles discussed a myriad of issues related to dialectics. Yu Shicheng, Wang Ruoshui, and Guan Feng (under the pen-name of Sa Renxing) ranged over the whole history of Western philosophy in their "academic" discussions into 1963; increasingly, however, bitter accusations of "idealism" or "metaphysics" crept in. In 1982, Yang was to cite incriminating references from Wang, both in 1961 and 1965, that stressed the political rather than academic nature of the debate.[58] Under a political cloud, Yang was prevented from writing in his own defense even after his "right opportunist" cap was removed. Events around the time of the Tenth Plenum in September 1962 go a long way toward explaining the growing tension evident in the public forum. An "academic" intervention by Ai Siqi supported Wang Ruoshui and criticized Yang's views just as Mao redefined right opportunism as revisionism and discussed the need for reemphasizing class struggle. Kang Sheng's group was

---

[55]*Three Major Struggles*, p. 40.

[56]Yang, "On Liu."

[57]Wang Ruoshui, "The Understanding and Application of the Concept of Identity," *Renmin ribao*, June 4, 1961, in *Survey of Mainland China Press* (hereafter SCMP) 2521 (June 21, 1961).

[58]Yang, "Weiwulun de mingyun."

later to claim in the 1970s that Kang had openly criticized Yang Xianzhen at the plenum, but there is no corroborating evidence of this.[59]

Yang Xianzhen's Alternative to Maoism

The well-known purge of Yang in 1964–65 on the charge of raising the slogan of "combining two into one" to oppose Mao's "dividing one into two" was in many ways the mere playing out of the substantive disagreements and power struggles between Yang and his competitors, which had been growing increasingly antagonistic since the late 1950s. This was clear at the time, although critiques of Kang Sheng in the 1980s, including Yang's own exposés, have provided more detailed accounts of Kang's orchestration of the attack, culminating in Yang's removal from the Party school in December 1965 at Mao's insistence.[60] In the 1960s, however, there were only a few hints available regarding the sources of these competing slogans. By now, Mao's evolving use of "dividing one into two" has become somewhat more clear, and in 1979, Yang revealed a fascinating story regarding his own search into classical Chinese philosophy for a better understanding of dialectics.

As early as the Yan'an period, in his rough essay on "Dialectical Materialism," Mao spoke of knowledge "splitting into two aspects."[61] A Chinese-language collection of excerpts from Marx, Engels, and Lenin published in Moscow in 1950 included some of Lenin's "On Dialectics," using the traditional Chinese phrase "one dividing into two" in translating a reference to "the division of an entity into two parts" as "the essence of dialectics."[62] Mao followed suit in Moscow in November 1957 in a lengthy discourse on the unity of opposites, which was clearly intended to address the problem of growing friction within the socialist camp. "One divides into two—this is a

[59]Bai Ye, "Fang Yang Xianzhen"; Mao's speech in Schram, *Chairman Mao Talks to the People*, pp. 188–96; Ai Siqi, "Further Discussion of Engels' Affirmation of the Identity of Thought and Existence," *Zhexue yanjiu* 5 (1962), in JPRS 16752.

[60]Fan Ruoyu, "Origin of the Polemic." See note 80 on Mao's intervention.

[61]Dennis Doolin and Peter J. Golas, "*On Contradiction* in the Light of Mao's Essay on 'Dialectical Materialism,'" *The China Quarterly* 19 (July-September 1964):40–46.

[62]Xue Zhen, "Conflicting Views on 'One Dividing into Two' and 'Two Combining into One,'" *Zhexue yanjiu* 8 (1979), in JPRS 74526, 30 (November 6, 1979):36.

universal phenomenon, and this is dialectics.'' He spoke of the presence at all times, in socialist as well as capitalist societies, of contradictions—the unity of opposites—and called for extensive propaganda in China regarding this concept, specifying that dialectics should move from the small circle of philosophers to the broad masses of the people.[63] Despite Kang Sheng's efforts to fulfill this mandate, and the reams of articles on philosophical issues after 1957, Mao still complained in May 1963 that no one in China had yet bothered to study his comments on dialectics even though the Moscow Declaration found it appropriate to incorporate them.[64]

Also in May 1963, in comments that were to become part of the "early ten points" guiding the Socialist Education campaign, Mao again called for the liberation of philosophy from the classroom and addressed the epistemological issue at the heart of the debate involving Yang. He stressed the mutual transformability of matter and spirit and the primary importance of struggle as the mechanism promoting change in the relationship between any two opposites. Just over one year later, Mao pointed out that these words ''touched the soft spot of some people who thereupon came out with 'combining two into one' to oppose me,'' and he personally approved publication of the articles criticizing Yang Xianzhen by name.[65] Clearly, Mao was led to believe that Yang was defying him. A number of articles both then and in 1979 also seemed to confirm that he was, for they explained that Yang had proposed ''combining two into one'' as the best way to characterize the Marxist world-view summed up in Lenin's ''unity of opposites,'' while Mao's ''dividing one into two'' best described the Marxist methodology for analysis of the world, thus implicitly relegating Mao's slogan to a secondary, methodological role.[66] Yang Xianzhen, however, has persistently denied these charges. Rather convincingly, Yang dates his first interest in traditional Chinese dialectical concepts to a nonpolitical event—his first reading of Lenin's ''Notes on Philosophy,'' newly

[63]Mao, *Selected Works*, vol. 5, p. 516. Zhai Sishi, ''Dividing One Into Two and Thoroughly Negating the 'Cultural Revolution,' '' *Hongqi* 17 (1984):18–21, in FBIS, September 28, 1984, p. K5, identifies Mao's Moscow speech as his first pointed and elaborate discussion of this slogan.

[64]Mao, ''Speech at the Hangchow Conference, May 1963,'' in *Miscellany of Mao Tse-tung Thought 1949–1968, Part II*, JPRS-61269-2, February 1974, p. 321.

[65]Ibid., ''Talk on Sakata's Article, August 24, 1964,'' p. 398, and ''Talk on Problems of Philosophy, August 18, 1964,'' p. 396.

[66]See Xue Zhen, ''Conflicting Views,'' for example.

published in Chinese in 1956. Seeing Lenin's references to Heraclitus and Philo, Yang wondered whether ancient Chinese philosophers had also chanced upon the dialectical "laws" of nature. In the hospital in Xian in the summer of 1961, while in disgrace, he borrowed some county records for reading and noticed references to Song studies of Laozi's views on being and nonbeing. The similarities to Hegel's concepts were striking to Yang, who began more systematic research in histories of Chinese thought. He often ran across phrases like "one dividing into two," but was particularly taken with the works of the Ming thinker Fang Yizhi, author of *Dongxi jun* [The Equality of Opposites], first published in 1652 and republished in 1963. Yang has cited the following passage as the heart of Fang's thought:

> Insubstantial and substantial, activity and repose, yin and yang, form and air, the way and implements, day and night, dark and light, life and death, throughout space and time all constitute two. In heaven and earth all things meet and all combine into one. They are mutually opposed and mutually causative, therefore they are equals, yet truly they are neither two nor one.[67]

Yang was delighted to discover such examples of ancient Chinese who understood the "indivisible unity of two things in a larger relationship"— the unity of opposites.

In using Fang's concept of "combining two into one" in major addresses at the school in November 1963 and April 1964, Yang has claimed, he had no intention of opposing the concept of "dividing one into two," since he had always viewed them as two ways of saying the same thing. Moreover, he has argued, he never intended to use Fang's concept to promote a philosophy of pure harmony, since both struggle and harmony exist together in any dialectical relationship. As support for this view, Yang in 1979 quoted phrases from Marx, Engels, and Lenin analogous to "two into one," as well as passages from Mao on the need for both unity and struggle in united front work.[68]

Yang's defense is a bit disingenuous. True, he has not "opposed" Mao, but through the years, as in the 1979 example, he has consistently cited the early Mao of the 1940s united front period to call the later Mao

[67]See Note 32. The title of Fang's book uses the terms for East and West to connote (complementary) opposites, of which this quotation gives other examples.

[68]Ibid. Extensive quotes from the 1963–64 lectures have become available (see Hamrin, "Alternatives within Chinese Marxism," pp. 333, 374–75, 381, 390, 399), and the full texts may be contained in a volume by Yang, *Wode zhexue "zuian"* [My Philosophic "Crimes"] (Beijing: Renmin Chubanshe, 1981), but I have been unable to obtain a copy.

back to his former self. Thus in Yang's apologies for the establishment way over the years, he has revealed his real offense—insistence on a balanced approach and gradual, moderate change at a time when Mao and his cronies were pressing a very unbalanced emphasis on struggle and radical change.

Yang's professional explorations, as well as the political motivation behind them, were echoed in the work of other scholars in the early 1960s, individuals with whom Yang had no institutional or personal ties. The historian Liu Jie, for example, argued at a conference on Confucianism in 1962 that China's history, unlike that of the West, was not governed by class struggle. The philosopher Feng Youlan systematically developed the view that the Confucian concept of humanitarianism (*ren*) was an example of a moral value that, having been developed in a period of transition when a new, progressive class sought to incorporate the interests of other oppressed classes in order to seize power, took on characteristics of universal validity. The Marxist theoretician Feng Ding explored both of these ideas and boldly posited that all social history, regardless of class differences, is at bottom the pursuit of happiness. In aesthetics, the democratic party figure Zhou Gucheng discussed the validity of art as the expression of "ordinary human feelings." Many of these intellectuals drew on united front theory and the "unity of opposites" as justification for entering a phase or stage of development in China in which harmony rather than struggle between classes was promoted. They were accused of anti-Party collusion and discredited along with Yang after 1964 in an attack on humanism in its various forms—liberal bourgeois, traditional Confucian, and socialist.[69]

By 1963, Yang Xianzhen's theoretical views were bringing him high-level attention. A reference in Propaganda Department Deputy Director Zhou Yang's well-known speech of October 1963, which used Mao's "one into two" slogan to attack unnamed Chinese who echoed the revisionist views of certain Soviet philosophers, was likely aimed in part at Yang; Yang's introduction of the "two into one" slogan one month later, in a lecture on the difference between formal and dialectical logic, may well have been his defense.[70]

[69]For a detailed discussion of the trends in other fields that were linked with Yang's views in 1964–65, see Hamrin, "Alternatives within Chinese Marxism," ch. 6. There is no evidence of direct collusion between these intellectuals.

[70]Zhou Yang, "The Fighting Task Confronting Workers in Philosophy and the Social Sciences," *Peking Review* 7, 1 (January 3, 1964):12 and 17, criticized M. B. Mitin and P. N. Fedoseyev for advocating "overcoming" opposites by "merging" or "uniting" them; he also criticized views based on concepts of humanism and alienation.

The Negation of an Establishment Intellectual

Through 1963 and into early 1964, Yang continued to have high-level support. In May 1963 Lin Feng, an associate of Peng Zhen, became president of the school, and in October Peng reportedly visited the school and approved continuing its work under the sixteen-character policy.[71] Following Peng Zhen's call for continued academic discussions in all fields early the next year, two of Yang's students published an article in *Guangming Daily* introducing to the public the concept of "combining two into one."[72] One week later, in early June 1964, the paper published a riposte. Kang Sheng asked Jiang Qing to show both of them to Mao. Debate ensued both in the press and inside the school. On June 17, *People's Daily* published an article revealing that Yang Xianzhen was the originator of the theory; allegedly written by a student, in fact it was drafted under Kang's direction by the paper's theoretical department.[73]

Yang Xianzhen's downfall was assured in mid-August, when Mao gave several talks on philosophy. He approved the campaign against Yang's views and praised Ai Siqi's critique of Lenin's *Materialism and Empirio-Criticism* (Yang's "Bible") for dwelling solely on materialism and neglecting the problem of cognition. Mao used the example of the Chinese civil war to criticize Yang:

> When the Kuomintang troops came, we swallowed them up piece by piece. This is not Yang Xianzhen's theory of combining two into one; it is not a synthesis of peaceful coexistence. They do not want peaceful coexistence, they want to eat us up. . . . But all their rifles, artillery, and troops were "synthesized" by our side. . . . One eats the other and the big fish devours the smaller; this is synthesis. . . . Yang Xianzhen came out with his "combining two into one," saying that synthesis is the linking together of two inseparable things. What kind of link is there in the world that cannot be separated?[74]

[71]See Liaison Station and Liaison Center. These Red Guard groups also claimed that Yu Shicheng at this time wrote a letter to the Central Committee defending Yang and accusing Ai Siqi of revisionism.

[72]Ai Hengwu and Lin Qingshan, "'Dividing One into Two' and 'Combining Two into One,' Some Realization Gained in the Study of Chairman Mao's Thought in Materialist Dialectics," *Guangming ribao*, May 29, 1964, in *Current Background* 745 (December 2, 1964).

[73]Fan Ruoyu, "Origin of the Polemic."

[74]*Miscellany*, pp. 392–93, 397.

Mao at the same time criticized the concept of "negation of negation," arguing that it implied that historical change consists of a series of stages, or equilibriums, and not a constant dynamic change in which equilibrium and disruption coexist simultaneously. His comments no doubt were directed at the "humanist" views discussed above.

Since his rehabilitation in 1979, Yang has indirectly revealed his disdain for Mao's philosophizing. In interviews, he has spoken of his imprisonment as his "negation" and triumphantly cited his return as proof of the validity of the concept of "negation of negation."[75] Yang has pointedly cited the Party's offer in 1979 to negotiate peaceful reunification with Taiwan as an example of the appropriate use of "uniting two into one" instead of "dividing one into two," thus echoing his earlier view that there is a time for unity as well as for struggle. Even though direct, detailed evidence regarding Yang's views on specific policies toward Taiwan or the Soviet Union is not available, there can be little doubt that he thought the crisis of the Leap years called for unity and stability, not struggle, both at home and abroad. Yang's most open criticism of Mao came in his afterword to a collection of his articles *On Party Character*, penned in December 1980: "I never dreamed that our Party's highest leader would repeat Stalin's mistakes and create disaster for our people and our socialist construction. We must learn from that and study Marxism-Leninism and unite it with reality."[76]

After Mao's intervention against Yang in the summer of 1964, Wang Ruoshui and Ai Siqi joined in the general attack with some of their more voluntarist and polemical articles. In the *People's Daily* of October 16, 1964, Wang insinuated that Yang was an "agent of the bourgeoisie donning the cloak of Marxism," linking him with Trotsky and Bukharin. He cited Mao's 1963 comments to complain that Yang neglected the "more important" concept of mutual transmutation of opposites in order to stress their mutual dependence and coexistence. According to Wang,

This is tantamount to providing a philosophical basis for the theory of class compromise. . . . We must not only recognize struggle, but also recognize the use of one side to eliminate the other through struggle;

[75]Bai Ye, "Fan Yang Xianzhen," p. 2.

[76]Yang, "Regarding Problems on 'Merging Two into One,'" p. 41; and afterword to *Lun dangxing* [On Party Character] (Henan Renmin Chubanshe, 1982, revised and expanded edition), p. 226.

this [process] is a "leap," not mere transmutation. It is necessary not only to recognize struggle, but also to recognize the solving of contradictions through struggle and the acceleration of the transmutation of things.

Ai Siqi's article in the *People's Daily* of May 20, 1965 was more of the same.[77]

During this period of accelerating attack, apparently Yang's patrons abandoned him, perhaps in hopes of forestalling further attacks. Peng Zhen, Lu Dingyi, and others criticized the "dogmatism" at the Party school as well as at the People's University, pointing to Yang as one of those who, Mao had warned, were "sliding to the brink of revisionism."[78] Red Guard sources later claimed that this was a convoluted effort to save these targets by implying that they were not *yet* revisionists, while at the same time redirecting attention to other (Maoist) types of dogmatists.[79] If so, Yang himself may not have appreciated the niceties; his reminiscences in the 1980s never mention Peng Zhen, despite the obvious long-time connection. In any case, efforts to stem the tide of the Mao cult failed by the end of 1965.

In December, at Mao's direction, Yang was demoted. He became deputy director of the Institute of Philosophy at the Academy of Sciences under Guo Morou, whom Yang has remembered favorably in recent writings.[80] But this proved a temporary reprieve. At the height of the Cultural Revolution, in early 1967, Yang was again taken to struggle sessions, suffering physical injuries, in the search for evidence against the "prison cadre." With Bo Yibo and others, Yang's Party

---

[77]Wang Ruoshui, "A Criticism of Comrade Yang Hsien-chen's Views on Contradictions," *Renmin ribao*, October 16, 1964, in JPRS 27529, 215; Ai Siqi, "Bu rongxu yong maodun diaohelun he jieji diaohelun lai touhuan geming bianzhengfa" [Surreptitious Substitution of the Theory of Reconciliation of Contradictions and Classes for Revolutionary Dialectics Must not Be Permitted], *Renmin ribao*, May 20, 1965.

[78]Revolutionary Rebellion and Barrel of the Gun Combat Teams, Third Red Guard Headquarters, Metropolitan Red Guard Congress, "The National Conference on Political Theory Class is Iron-clad Proof of Liu-Teng's Opposition to the Thought of Mao Tse-tung," *Doupigai* [Struggle-Criticism-Transformation] 1 (May 15, 1967), in SCMM Supplement 19 (March 4, 1968).

[79]Ibid.

[80]Mao, "Speech at Hangchow, 21 December 1965," in Schram, *Chairman Mao Talks to the People*, p. 239. Yang's appointment to the CAS was not known at the time, but was revealed recently in *Zhongguo zhexue nianjian 1983*.

membership was rescinded and he was imprisoned in Beijing from May 18, 1967 to May 19, 1975.[81]

Yang's name was dragged through the mud once again in articles written in late 1970 through 1971 by the Party school's radical writing group. Their articles appeared to be aimed at recalling Kang Sheng's past service to Mao, perhaps as part of an effort to disassociate Kang from Chen Boda and Lin Biao, who were on the way out.[82] Upon Lin's demise, Yang was allowed reading material other than Mao's works, which he had memorized by then, but still no pen and paper. In 1973, radicals once again tried to extort a confession from Yang. The political context for this is unclear, but others have recounted brave resistance on Yang's part, even in the blackest of times. According to one anecdote, Kang's lackeys forced Yang to admit in writing that he had entertained some Soviet experts who were actually spies, but Yang aborted the exercise when he insisted on mentioning the fact that Kang's wife had introduced them to him.[83] Released from prison and put under house arrest in exile in Shaanxi in 1975 as Kang Sheng lay dying, Yang began drafting articles arguing for his rehabilitation.

Negation of Negation: The Search for a New Synthesis

Through 1979 and 1980, following Yang's reappearance in public, discussion of his case, as with so many others, was intended to help Deng Xiaoping undercut political competitors and open up policy options. In late May 1979, *Guangming Daily* proclaimed that Yang had been framed, a verdict reiterated in August by *People's Daily*. In October, *Red Flag* rendered an apology to Yang for its part in the frameup, written by the author of the joint *People's Daily/Red Flag* attack of August 31, 1964. (The relatively terse commentary on Yang in the Party paper, which fell far short of an apology, may have reflected the bad blood between Yang and Wang Ruoshui, by then the paper's

---

[81]Tai Huaiji, *Tiandi you zhengqi*, p. 142 ff., recounts the March 1967 interrogation. Bai Ye, "Fan Yang Xianzhen," p. 7, cites Yang's prison dates.

[82]For a discussion of these episodes in the 1970s, see Hamrin, "Alternatives within Chinese Marxism," pp. 462–65.

[83]Ruan Shanqing, "What Role Did Kang Sheng Play in the Great Proletarian Cultural Revolution?" *Dongxiang* [Trend] (Hong Kong), March 16, 1980, p. 74. The article mentions that Fan Ruoyu was also present at this meeting. Tai Huaiji, *Tiandi you zhengqi*, pp. 144–45, quotes self-defenses by Yang and others on the 1930s prison issue during an investigation in July 1975.

deputy editor-in-chief responsible for theory.)[84] Other articles in the press all described the various polemics involving Yang as reflections of an idealist, ultra-leftist trend in theory that had led to disaster in all fields. In April 1980, two months after key supporters of Hua Guofeng had been criticized indirectly for dogmatic Maoism and removed from the Politburo and Liu Shaoqi had been rehabilitated, *Red Flag* published Yang's personal eulogy for Liu.[85]

Later, in the summer of 1980, as political momentum gathered behind Deng's reform program, discussion turned to Yang's theories of political economy. Yao Bomao, a long-time colleague of Yang's, defended Yang's mid-1950s' view that China should foster the growth of an "integrated economic base" by developing not only the state and collective sectors but also the private capitalist sector for some time to come. Yao made it clear that Yang had been arguing on behalf of proposals by Chen Yun and Liu Shaoqi that were overruled by Mao. Stressing that this eagerness to establish a "unitary economic base" led to disastrous "premature leaps" into communism, the article implied that Mao was wrong as early as 1955.[86]

By late 1980, the process of rehabilitating Yang and his views and discrediting Maoist ultra-leftism came to a head. In early November, Kang was ousted posthumously from the Party and Yang's Party membership was restored. His past performance at the Party school was praised at a schoolwide rally. *Red Flag* in January 1981 published Yang's lengthy exposé on Kang, apparently written on the basis of secret files that contained information Yang had not previously been aware of, including from the period after he had lost his freedom.[87] This development coincided with rumors that Hua Guofeng had effectively lost his post as Party chairman to Hu Yaobang, a decision formalized in June 1981 at the Sixth Plenum. Clearly, the rehabilitation of Yang and veterans like him had served Deng Xiaoping well.

---

[84]Jin Rui, "Reassessing the Polemic on the Question of 'Combining Two into One,'" *Guangming ribao*, May 31, 1979, in FBIS, June 12, 1979, pp. L2 ff; Correspondent's Report, "Criticism of the Concept of 'Combining Two into One' is a Political Frameup," *Renmin ribao*, August 21, 1979, in FBIS, August 21, 1979, p. L1 and August 23, 1979, pp. L4 ff.; Fan Ruoyu, "Origin of the Polemic."

[85]Yang, "On Liu." Hua Guofeng's supporters were Wang Dongxing, Wu De, Chen Xilian, and Ji Dengkuei.

[86]Yao Bomao, "Reevaluating the 'Theory of an Integrated Economic Base,'" *Guangming ribao*, July 3, 1980, in FBIS, July 24, 1980, pp. L2–8.

[87]Yang, "On Kang."

Tensions Within the Deng Camp

Although Yang Xianzhen was happy to serve as a stalking horse against Maoists, he gradually took on a second role that was perhaps less welcome—as a defender of ideological orthodoxy and policy realism against more radical views on reform by others in Deng's broad coalition. Tensions in philosophical circles emerged early. A lengthy review of post-1949 disputes in philosophy, which was published in *Philosophical Research* in late 1978, upheld the Cultural Revolution verdicts against Yang.[88] It was written by Wu Jiang, a prominent theorist close to Deng from the early 1960s (when he had written articles criticizing "revisionist" Yugoslav theorists). In 1979 and 1980, Yang and some of his former associates from the Party school reprinted their former works and wrote letters to *Philosophical Research* in an effort to rebut Wu. This dispute, like the earlier polemics themselves, reflected much more than abstract theorizing. It no doubt affected the direction of the post-Mao reconstruction of the curriculum at the Party school as well as of theory classes in higher level schools nationwide. As of 1979, the competing works of Yang and Ai Siqi were both prominent on reading lists on theory.[89] Yang, as the school's chief adviser, and Wu Jiang, as assistant dean, both would have had influence in the reshaping of the minds of China's officialdom.[90]

This public academic discourse also had to do with the issue of Yang's access to the media. Through the early 1980s, just as in the 1960s, Yang had trouble breaking into print in *Philosophical Research*, published by the Institute of Philosophy, and in *People's Daily*; Wang Ruoshui was on the staff of both organs. Other than the two memorial articles on Liu Shaoqi and Kang Sheng published in *Red Flag*, Yang's voice was heard primarily in *Guangming Daily*, as well as in forewords or afterwords to collections of his early articles and essays published in Henan and Hubei, his home bases.

[88]Wu Jiang, "Zhexue shang liangtiao zhanxian de douzheng" [The Two-Line Struggle in Philosophy], *Zhexue yanjiu* 1–2 (1978):41–65. One of Wu's best-known early articles was "Dialectics Is the Algebra of the Revolution," *Hongqi* 11 (1960), in *Beijing Review* 3, 46 (November 15, 1960):6–16.

[89]Information from personal conversations with students from Beijing Foreign Language Institute and Foreign Ministry officials in August 1979.

[90]Wu Jiang, editorial note to "It Is Necessary to Wage Two-Front Struggle, and at the Same Time Oppose Two Kinds of One-Sidedness," *Renmin ribao*, December 11, 1981, p. 3, in FBIS, December 22, 1981, p. R1.

Wang Ruoshui, in his mid-1979 foreword to a collection of his own pre-Cultural Revolution writings, apologized to Yang for his part in the 1964–65 polemic, which he repudiated; his 1964 attack on Yang was not included in the collection. Wang also confessed the romanticism of some of his pre-Cultural Revolution views. But he defended his general record, claiming that he too had been oppressed by Guan Feng. In particular, he stood by his (and Ai Siqi's) early 1960s views on the relationship between "thought and existence."[91] In June 1980, Wang wrote a letter to *Red Flag's* internal publication recommending continued discussion of the "still useful" concept of the "identity of thought and existence."[92]

The age-old disagreements and animosities thereupon became caught up in post-Mao political ebbs and flows, as the leadership vacillated, undecided whether merely to restore the theories and policies of the early 1960s or to move on to more fundamental reform of the system.[93] The year 1980 was marked by a surge of reformist thinking in all circles, as the purge of Maoist Politburo members in February led to Hua Guofeng's replacement as premier and the opening in the fall of the public trial of Mao's widow and her associates as well as Lin Biao's. A burst of free thinking raised new criticisms of Mao and calls for reform of Chinese Marxist theory. Wang Ruoshui was one of the most outspoken of Chinese officials to advocate outside controls on the Party, including basic-level elections and recall of cadres; like Chen Boda in the late 1960s, Wang pointed to the Paris Commune model discussed by Marx as a precedent.[94]

This reference was symbolic of a more general similarity between the views of the more radical reformers in Deng's camp and earlier Maoist thinking. Certain antibureaucratic and populist strains that prompted Mao's periodic efforts to revamp the Party have reemerged,

---

[91]Wang Ruoshui, preface (dated June 11, 1979) to *Zai zhexue zhanxian shang* [On the Philosophy Front] (Beijing: Renmin Chubanshe, 1980), pp. i-iv, translated by David A. Kelly in *Chinese Studies in Philosophy* 16, 3 (Spring 1985). This section of my chapter has benefited from personal communication with Mr. Kelly. See his chapter on Wang in *Chinese Intellectuals and the State,* ed. Goldman, Cheek, and Hamrin.

[92]Yang Xianzhen, "Weiwulun de mingyun," revealed a series of internal letters and publications by Wang and himself in 1980–82.

[93]For a detailed analysis of the policy disputes in this period, on which I base much of the following discussion, see my article, "Competing 'Policy Packages' in Post-Mao China," *Asian Survey* 24, 5 (May 1984):487–518.

[94]Wang Ruoshui, comments to American scholars at the office of *Renmin ribao,* June 20, 1980, unpublished transcript.

as well as the totalistic view that sweeping cultural transformation, especially in patterns of economic organization, is necessary to break through the severe constraints on rapid economic growth.

These tendencies among some of Deng's supporters have annoyed his more orthodox allies. At a work conference at the end of 1980, Chen Yun reviewed the history of the Chinese economy and insisted on tabling reform of the economic and political system for the sake of reasserting social discipline and readjusting economic imbalances. All work was to be pursued within the context of upholding Party leadership and improving the economy. The year 1981 saw a return to ideological orthodoxy and policy gradualism. During the following year, Yang Xianzhen published three collections of his earlier writings, which stressed the importance of social conformity and internal Party discipline rather than external controls for improving cadre behavior.[95]

On March 2, 1981, Yang Xianzhen published an article praising this same work conference for proceeding from a full understanding of China's national conditions. This article revealed the policy implications of his theoretical views:

> National conditions mean: Being is primary; the line, principles, and policies, namely, thinking, are secondary. . . . At present, our country has serious economic disproportions and dislocations and also has financial deficits. These are objective facts and current national conditions. We have to admit these facts and conditions which determine the current necessity of carrying out readjustment. . . . Many comrades and particularly some senior cadres still do not have a clear understanding of this point.[96]

Yang went on at length to criticize the idealism and romanticism of Great Leap policies as well as the similar ''impracticable and overambitious objectives and slogans'' of the 1977–78 period. Such comments and those in other media articles in 1981 implicitly criticized radical reform proposals as well for being unrealistic. Yang blamed the residual ''leftist'' attitude of being ''overanxious for quick results.''

Circumstantial evidence suggests that foreign as well as domestic policy may have been at stake in 1981. During the Cultural Revolution,

[95]Yang Xianzhen, *My Philosophic "Crimes"*; *Respect Materialism, Respect Dialectics*; and *On Party Character.*

[96]Yang Xianzhen, ''Adhere to the Principle of the Basic Question of Philosophy; Study the Documents of the Central Work Conference,'' *Guangming ribao*, March 2, 1981, in FBIS, March 23, 1981, pp. L11 ff.

Yang was linked with Chen Yun and several prominent foreign policy specialists as advocates of a moderate foreign policy aimed at cutting back on foreign aid so as to conserve all possible resources for civilian economic development.[97] Specifically, both in the early 1960s and again in the early 1980s, the point appeared to be the desirability of reducing tensions with the USSR through negotiations. In fact, in 1979, when Chen Yun joined the Politburo's Standing Committee and Yang and others were rehabilitated, China moved to reopen talks with Moscow on normalization of relations; in 1981, when this group again received media prominence, there was a warming trend in unofficial contacts with Moscow after a temporary chill due to the Soviet invasion of Afghanistan. At both times, this moderate approach was explicitly identified with Lenin's NEP policies of conciliating capitalists at home and enemies abroad.[98]

Yang's March 1981 article linked theory and policy by asserting that the new retrenchment policies required rectification of errors in theoretical and propaganda work. He accused unnamed theorists of persistently trying "unconventional or unorthodox things" in philosophy over the years, creating incidents that shook people's faith. Yang's target—Wang Ruoshui—was obvious to anyone in the know.[99]

The feud between Yang and Wang became increasingly bitter over the next few years. They exchanged accusations in letters to *Red Flag*, published internally.[100] In one exchange in an academic journal, Yang stated flatly that the current debate, like earlier ones, "is inevitably

[97]Wang Jiaxiang, director of the Party's International Liaison Department in the 1960s, was attacked during the Cultural Revolution for advocating a policy of "three liquidations and one reduction" [eliminating struggle against American imperialism, Soviet social imperialism, and other reactionary governments, and reducing aid to insurgencies]. An editorial in *Hongqi* 8 (1966), in *Beijing Review* 25 (June 17, 1966):9, criticized Yang Xianzhen for providing the theoretical underpinnings for this approach. An account of Liu Shaoqi's crimes in SCMM 652 (April 28, 1969):23 linked Chen Yun as well as Liu with the policy.

[98]For articles praising the late Wang Jiaxiang upon his posthumous rehabilitation and defending the validity of his foreign policy proposal, see Zhu Zhongli (his widow), "Firmly Holding Premier Zhou's Concern for Comrade Wang Jiaxiang," *Gongren ribao* [Worker's Daily], April 5, 1979, in FBIS, May 4, 1979, p. L13 ff.; and Wang Zhen, Liao Chengzhi, Xiao Jingguang, Wu Xiuquan, Fu Zhong, Fang Jiang, and Zhong Ziyun, "Recollections and Inheritance—In Memory of Comrade Wang Jiaxiang," *Gongren ribao*, February 4, 1981, in FBIS, February 26, 1981, pp. L3 ff.

[99]Yang, "Adhere to the Principle of the Basic Question of Philosophy," FBIS, March 23, 1961, p. L14.

[100]Yang, "Weiwulun de mingyun."

linked with politics" and "is of great practical significance." Unre-
lenting, he twisted the knife by reminding Wang of his writings during
the Great Leap (which Wang has admitted were left leaning), and
implied that Wang's well-known interest in humanism was linked
closely with an "idealist" epistemology.[101]

Yang's boldness in thus criticizing a top figure at the Party newpaper
to the point of implying that his writings were antisocialist no doubt
reflected the gains the conservatives had made in 1981. *People's Daily*
was on the defensive for resisting the campaign to criticize the "bourgeois liberalism" of writer Bai Hua. In this favorable atmosphere,
Yang cooperated with like-minded officials to press their advantage.[102]
And yet into 1983, these types of inconclusive disputes continued in a
generally academic atmosphere.[103] At the Twelfth Party Congress in
September 1982, Yang regained more of his former prestige when he
joined other conservative veterans, most of them former Central Committee members, on the Central Advisory Commission.

As the radical reformers, however, led by Hu Yaobang and Zhao
Ziyang with Deng's backing, began to use the momentum of the congress to press again for far-reaching reform in 1983, tensions again
rose within central officialdom. At the Second Plenum in October,
which launched a Party rectification campaign, the conservatives managed to convince Deng Xiaoping to approve criticism of "rightist"
proponents of "spiritual pollution" as well as remaining leftists. In the
weeks following, conservatives at all levels used this green light to
expand the campaign into a more general critique of radical reform
policies.[104]

[101]Ibid.; and Wang Ruoshui, "Bianzhengfa de mingyun" [The Destiny of
Dialectics], *Shehui kexue zhanxian* 3 (1981):1–19.

[102]For example, Yang wrote to the Party school attached to the Ministry of Culture,
encouraging those who worked in culture to follow the advice given to historians by
another conservative thinker, Hu Sheng—they should all study more dialectical materialism so that the contending of "100 schools" would be based on a common
foundation and reach a common conclusion. Report in *Guangming ribao*, June 24,
1982, p. 1, in FBIS, July 9, 1982, p. K7.

[103]*Guangming ribao* published a report on the Yang-Wang exchange on "destiny"
on March 27, 1982, p. 3, and an article by Wang Ruoshui, "Deguo gudian zhexue
jiandande 'zongjie' le ma?" [Did German Classical Philosophy Simply 'End'?],
Guangming ribao, April 24, 1982, p. 3. The latter has been translated by David A.
Kelly in *Chinese Studies in Philosophy* 16, 3 (Spring 1985).

[104]For an excellent account of this campaign, see Thomas B. Gold, "Just in Time!
China Battles Spiritual Pollution on the Eve of 1984," *Asian Survey* 24, 9 (September 1984):947 ff.

Within theoretical and cultural circles, factional competition again burst into the open. Zhou Yang was criticized and Wang Ruoshui and his boss Hu Jiwei lost their posts at the *People's Daily* for their prominent roles in publicizing "heterodox" views of humanism and alienation. This development preempted publication of some of Wang Ruoshui's internal post-Cultural Revolution writings, which allegedly were anti-Mao and antisocialist, a development that no doubt pleased Yang Xianzhen among others.[105] In late November, the new leadership of *People's Daily*, now under closer supervision by Propaganda Department Director Deng Liqun and other conservatives, sponsored a forum of veteran cadres to discuss the plenum's decisions. Yang Xianzhen and a number of his former associates, including Bo Yibo, attended. Not surprisingly, the participants found particular fault with "some theoretical workers [i.e., Zhou and Wang] who have regarded idealism as materialism and metaphysics as dialectics. Following the footsteps of the bourgeois scholars, they have prattled about abstract humanism and have given enormous publicity to 'alienation.' It is high time for us to solve these problems."[106]

In late December 1983, with his nemesis out of the picture, Yang broke into print in the Party paper with an article commemorating Mao on the ninetieth anniversary of his birth, a development that contained double and triple servings of irony. He praised Mao for "correctly" integrating the "universal truth" of Marxism with real conditions in China. Patently twisting the views of the "early Mao" to sound remarkably like Yang Xianzhen, Yang claimed that the leader held that "in philosophy, upholding the materialist line of existence being primary and thinking being secondary *is* to uphold the ideological line of seeking truth from facts" and that the content of the "dynamic revolutionary theory of reflection is that thinking is the *reflection* of existence." Yang similarly quoted extensively from the early Mao in defending a number of sensitive historical decisions by the Party that more radical reformers had been calling into question.[107] Yang's arti-

[105]Deng Liqun in conversation with Stuart R. Schram on April 17, 1984, cited in "'Economics in Command'? Ideology and Policy Since the Third Plenum, 1978–84," *The China Quarterly* 99 (September 1984):442–44.

[106]Report in *Renmin ribao*, November 26, 1983, p. 4, in FBIS, December 1, 1983, p. K7.

[107]Yang Xianzhen, "Advance along the Path of Integrating Marxism-Leninism with the Reality of the Chinese Revolution—in Commemoration of the 90th Anniversary of Comrade Mao Zedong's Birth," *Renmin ribao*, December 23, 1983, p. 5, in JPRS 84–008 (January 24, 1984):7–17.

cle and others like it appeared to serve an effort by Party conservatives to hold Deng Xiaoping to the Eighth Party Congress policies extolled in the 1981 resolution on Party history and thus woo him toward more moderate reform prescriptions.

In the process, Yang did not refrain from kicking his favorite heterodox theoretician while he was down. He explicitly attacked a 1981 collection of Wang's articles printed with the character for "man" writ large, as an example of "some of our Party members who live in the 1980s but peddle the reactionary theory of 'genuine socialism' and 'humanism' that was buried by the Communists in the 1840s." Yang's discussion of the imminent rectification campaign, in which he warned against leniency on the grounds of a cadre's "good intentions," made clear his advocacy of a thorough housecleaning of free thinkers like Wang in theoretical and cultural circles, explicitly including the Party school but logically extending to all research and media organs. The school sponsored a number of activities pressing this view; in January 1984, Yang praised one forum for attacking "the view that because the so-called alienation continuously occurs in socialism, we must 'continuously carry out revolution,'" pointing out that it "is similar to the 'theoretical basis' of the 'Great Proletarian Cultural Revolution.'"[108]

While the virulence of commentary in theoretical circles by 1984 reflected the personal animosities and rivalries involved, the perennial nature of the issues under discussion was symptomatic of more chronic, systemic problems that have faced Chinese leaders in pursuit of modernization. It is particularly unsurprising that the transitional post-Mao period, with its rapid changes in intellectual climate and policy experimentation, should engender fierce debate. Yet the archaic language of the disputes involving Yang and Wang, and the incredible semantic intricacies requiring retranslations and explications of German, English, Russian, and Chinese terms, were testimony to the poverty of thought forms imposed on Chinese theorists by outmoded orthodoxy.

It was encouraging in late 1984 to see some new explorations, without tendentious efforts to square the circle in nineteenth-century Marxist-Leninist terminology, into the fundamental issues raised in these debates—how to guarantee realistic formulation and implementation of policy and how to legitimate and then protect the political-economic interests of the various non-Party social groupings in China. Nevertheless, it had become abundantly clear in the decade without Mao that interlinked disputes over theory, power, and policy from his era had survived him.

[108]*Xinhua* in Chinese, January 31, 1984, in FBIS, February 1, 1984, p. K17.

DENG TUO
A Chinese Leninist Approach
to Journalism

Timothy Cheek

> Any political activity that relies on one's own subjective desires,
> seeks to look good on the surface, takes credit for what would have
> occurred anyway, and lacks any real results is essentially the "Poli-
> tics of Simpletons."
>
> Deng Tuo, "Discard the 'Politics of Simpletons,' " May 1957

Deng Tuo was a politically active intellectual in People's China—in the
Communist movement before 1949 and in government organs in
Beijing during the People's Republic.[1] He was a scholar-official in
Mao's China whose life, and untimely death in 1966 at the beginning of
the Cultural Revolution, can help us understand the role of intellectuals
in China today.

In many ways he is representative of his cohort, the founding generation of establishment intellectuals in the People's Republic. He and
his establishment brethren stand in stark contrast to the radical intellectuals who participated in their purge in 1966, and both exist today in an
uneasy relationship with rising generations of establishment intellectu-

---

I would like to thank the following people for their detailed criticisms, which have
improved this chapter: Merle Goldman, Carol Lee Hamrin, Roderick MacFarquhar,
Mei Jing, and David Ownby. Naturally, the mistakes remain my own.

[1]Bonnie S. McDougall has distinguished politically active intellectuals and professional writers in the People's Republic according to their political participation. See
"Writers and Performers, Their Works, and Their Audiences in the First Three
Decades," in *Popular Chinese Literature and Performing Arts in the People's Republic of China 1949–1979*, ed. Bonnie McDougall (Berkeley: University of California Press, 1984), pp. 269–301, esp. 270–71.

als. This chapter seeks, in part, to use Deng Tuo's story to help explain the past role and current status of intellectuals in the Chinese government, but the life and struggles of the man, Deng Tuo himself, are a story worthy of record. A talented intellectual of renowned integrity, Deng Tuo saw communism not as a challenge or compromise to intellectual integrity but as its fulfillment. That the system to which he dedicated his life turned on him and drove him to death is a human tragedy that overshadows academic analysis.

Deng Tuo was, however, a notoriously complex man who is virtually uncategorizable. Deng Tuo's commitment to the Chinese Communist Party entailed several instances of what would appear to us as intellectual compromise with arbitrary political power, yet his criticisms of Party policy in the 1960s did appear to his detractors in the Cultural Revolution and to Western observers as an independent stance at odds with Party rule.[2] Deng certainly was at odds with "the Party" by 1966. When he was denounced that spring in the national press as the anti-Party leader of "The Three-Family Village," the fifty-four-year-old Deng Tuo followed the precedent set by countless other "loyal ministers" since Qu Yuan in the third century B.C.: he wrote a letter professing his loyalty to his leaders and sealed it with his life on the night of May 17, 1966. Since 1979, when Deng Tuo and thousands of other Party cadres were rehabilitated, the Chinese press has proclaimed Deng Tuo a loyal servant whose actions were invariably taken on behalf of "the Party" and whose death at least reflects the abuse of Party power by usurpers, currently called the "gang of four," and perhaps indicates a heretofore unrecognized movement in the dialectic of history that made the political abuses of the Cultural Revolution unavoidable.[3]

[2]This chapter discusses his compromises; the archetypal attack is Yao Wenyuan, "Ping 'Sanjia cun'—'Yanshan yehua,' 'Sanjia cun zhaji' de fandong benzhi" [Criticizing the Three-Family Village—The Reactionary Nature of *Evening Chats at Yanshan* and *Notes from a Three-Family Village*], *Wenhui bao* [The Literary Gazette], May 10, 1966; translated in *Current Background* 792:22–44. Representative Western studies are Merle Goldman, "The Unique 'Blooming and Contending' of 1961–62," *China Quarterly* 35 (1969):54–83, and *China's Intellectuals: Advise and Dissent* (Cambridge: Harvard University Press, 1981), pp. 25–32; Joachim Glaubitz, *Opposition gegen Mao: Abendgespräche am Yenshan und andere politische Documente* (Freiburg: Breisgau, 1969), pp. 8 and 35–37; Bung-joon Ahn, *Chinese Politics and the Cultural Revolution* (Seattle: University of Washington Press, 1976), pp. 69–74; and Peter Moody, *Opposition and Dissent in Contemporary China* (Stanford: Stanford University Press, 1977), pp. 176–77.

[3]Deng's final letter, which was addressed to Peng Zhen, Liu Ren, and the Beijing Municipal Party Committee, is mentioned in Ding Yilan, "Yi Deng Tuo" [In Memory of Deng Tuo], in *Yi Deng Tuo*, ed. Liao Mosha (Fuzhou: Fujian Renmin, 1980), p. 17; and Deng Yun, "Huiyi wode baba Deng Tuo" [Remembering My Father

From the 1930s onward, Deng Tuo served the Party as an intellectu-
al committed to the goals of a Marxist-Leninist revolution in China.
Yet, long before he was denounced in 1966 there were signs that Deng
Tuo did not interpret that commitment in ways that satisfied others in
the Party, particularly Mao Zedong. There were contradictions. The
picture that emerges brings to mind another journalist, Liang Qichao.
Both men strove to popularize foreign doctrines (nineteenth-century
European liberalism, for Liang) that they hoped would renew China.
Liang was struggling in the last years of the Qing dynasty to break free
of a crumbling tradition; Deng Tuo, some thirty years later, was struggling to join a new tradition in the People's Republic. The contradiction for Liang, according to one biographer, Joseph Levenson, was that
he was emotionally attached to his tradition (in this case, the
"Confucian" past) but intellectually alienated from it. For Deng Tuo,
it was the reverse: he was intellectually attached to his new tradition
(the emerging socialist society) but emotionally alienated not only from
its abuses, which he called "the politics of simpletons," but from the
vulgarization of daily life that appeared as an unintended consequence
of championing "proletarian culture."[4]

Evening Chats at Yanshan, which Deng published under the pen-
name Ma Nancun in 1961 and 1962 in the *Beijing Evening News*, is an
appropriate starting point for understanding the man, his conflicts, and
his role in Chinese politics. This is not only because these articles,
which were published in book form in 1963, became the object of
heated attack in the Cultural Revolution and have become icons of
intellectual loyalty to the Party since 1979 or because previous Western
analysts have emphasized these writings. *Evening Chats* and Deng
Tuo's articles in *Notes from a Three-Family Village* published around
the same time are Deng Tuo's mature pronouncements on what is
wrong in socialist China and what is to be done. What he said, who let
him speak, and what happened to all of them in the name of what was
said in *Evening Chats* throw much light on the role of establishment

---

Deng Tuo], in *Yi Deng Tuo*, pp. 244–45. A current interpretation is Su Shuangbi,
"Ping Yao Wenyuan de 'Ping Sanjia cun'" [Criticizing Yao Wenyuan's "Criticizing
the Three-Family Village"], *Hongqi* [Red Flag] 2 (1979):41:48; translated in JPRS
073304 (April 25, 1979), pp. 73–87, and *Chinese Law and Government* 16, 4 (Winter 1983–84):92–98. Liao Mosha explores the historical materialist roots in "Dai
Xu" [By Way of Introduction], *Yi Deng Tuo*, pp. 4–6.

[4]Joseph Levenson, *Liang Ch'i-ch'ao and the Mind of Modern China*, 2d ed. (Berkeley: University of California Press, 1970), p. 219. My thanks to Merle Goldman for
suggesting this inverted parallel.

intellectuals in China. This search for clarity will view his entire career but will focus on his journalism. As the founding editor of *People's Daily,* Deng Tuo both influenced and reflected the goals and norms of socialist journalism held by the Party establishment.

Deng Tuo's Chinese Leninist Approach to Journalism

Deng Tuo's approach to politics in general, and to his profession— journalism—in particular, can be called a Chinese Leninist one. This approach to public life was a combination of traditional Chinese humanism and Confucian literati aspirations, of May Fourth ideals about the role of science in the transformation of culture and the elite role of intellectuals, and of Marxist-Leninist discipline that resulted first and foremost in the support of the Party according to the rules of collective leadership, minority rights, and democratic centralism. Deng Tuo's personal synthesis of these three strains was unique to himself but falls within the shared outlook of the scholar-officials discussed in this book.

Born to the family of a Qing dynasty degree-holder near Fuzhou in Fujian province in 1912, Deng Tuo spent his early years in the milieu of the traditional scholar-official, practicing his calligraphy and memorizing the traditional texts. The cataclysmic changes of the May Fourth period soon affected him, however, as his father allowed him to read many of the new radical periodicals that circulated in the late 1920s. He studied economics and English at universities in Shanghai, but by the 1930s he had spent time in jails in Shanghai, Fuzhou, and Kaifeng because of his agitation work for the Communist Party, which he had joined in 1930. Deng Tuo's scholarship merged with his political commitments in several lengthy historical articles and a long Marxist treatise, *A History of Famine Relief in China* (Shanghai, 1937). When writing history the young Deng Tuo revealed a detailed understanding of Marxist historical materialism and a positive faith that Marxism could save China.[5]

From the time he began Party work in the "white area" behind Japanese lines in the Jin Cha Ji (Shanxi-Chahar-Hebei) Border Region

[5]He published these works under his real name, Deng Yunte. See "Deng Tuo," in *Zhongguo wenxuejia cidian: xiandai di er fence* [Dictionary of Chinese Writers: Modern Period, Vol. 2] (Chengdu: Sichuan Renmin, 1982), pp. 110–12. Details of his early life are given by Wang Bisheng, "Deng Tuo tongzhi de shengping he wenxue huodong" [Comrade Deng Tuo's Life and Literary Activities], *Xin wenxue shiliao* [Historical Materials on New Literature] 4 (1981):71–76; Liao Mosha, ed., *Yi Deng Tuo*, pp. 220–33.

in the autumn of 1937, Deng Tuo served primarily as a journalist and editor of periodicals intended as propanganda tools in the true sense of the term: to propagate the true belief. As the prestigious Yan'an *Liberation Daily* editorialized in August 1942 during the rectification campaign, "We already know that newspapers not only report the news, they are also sharp weapons in constructing our nation and Party and in reforming our work and our lives."[6] Deng Tuo's journalism consistently fit this mold.

For the next twenty years, Deng Tuo served consecutively as chief editor of two of the most important Party newspapers—the *Jin Cha Ji Daily* and, after 1949, the *People's Daily*. Throughout this time Deng Tuo gave authoritative speeches on the professional and political aspects of journalism, which revealed several aspects of his approach to journalism. In addition, he engaged in a wide range of cultural activities, which he clearly regarded as an integral part of his public life. During these years Deng Tuo stressed the need for individuals to align their interests with the needs of the Party; later, after the Great Leap, he would be more concerned with changes the Party needed to make.

Acceptance of Orthodoxy

Deng Tuo edited the first *Selected Works of Mao Zedong*, published in May 1944 in Jin Cha Ji.[7] In his introduction Deng Tuo wrote, "The thought (*sixiang*) of Comrade Mao Zedong represents the Chinese proletariat and their political party. . . . Historical practice has fully demonstrated that Comrade Mao Zedong's thought is the only correct thought."[8]

Throughout his life Deng Tuo viewed this adherence to Mao's writings as no obstacle to maintaining personal integrity or interests. In a speech to graduating high school seniors in 1961, he made this assumption explicit. "Under this socialist system of ours," he said, "the interests of the nation, of the collective, and of the individual are unified. . . . Furthermore, there are no sharp contradictions between the interests of the present young students and the interests of the state and collective."[9] This hopeful expectation of harmonious unity of

---

[6]Reprinted in *Xinwen gonzuo zhinan* [Guidelines on Journalism], vol. 1 (Kalgan: Jin Cha Ji Xinhua Shudian, 1946), p. 57.

[7]*Mao Zedong xuanji* (Jin Cha Ji Ribaoshe, 1944).

[8]"Bianzhe de hua" [A Word by the Editor], in ibid., p. 1; Deng's introduction is cited as one of the earliest examples of the use of the term "Mao Zedong Thought" in an article by Chen Wenyuan in *Red Flag* 8 (1981), inside back cover.

[9]From *Zhongguo qingnian* 9 (1961), translated in *Survey of China Mainland Magazines* (SCMM) 246, pp. 22–23.

intention and practice by individuals and the state contrasts with the "alienation" theories stressing the potential for divergence of these interests, which emerged in Eastern Europe in the 1950s and in China after 1980.[10] Deng Tuo's approach did not admit to the possibility of differences between personal and Party interest, once they were rightly understood by both parties. Thus, he saw no need for political institutions independent of the Party and never suggested them.

Public Education and Mobilization

Throughout his career Deng Tuo used journalism as a form of public education, particularly to mobilize his readers to act. In a 1944 speech on journalism Deng said, "Because real life struggle is developing, our news reporting methods must be able to reflect and lead the whole process of that struggle's development."[11] This use of journalism as an inspirational tool continued through Deng's writings in the 1960s. The first essay in *Evening Chats*, "One Third of Life," was written expressly to motivate young intellectuals to study at home to become better specialists.

In the same 1944 speech on journalism, he covered aspects of correspondence work and news reporting that needed to be reformed according to the new Party "mass line" recently promulgated in Yan'an. He directed his listeners to eschew Western grammar and flowery traditional Chinese prose. Reporters were to live among the masses and encourage ordinary people to write for themselves. Deng Tuo used the concept of "key reporting," in which a key issue—usually an aspect of current policy—formed the guiding theme and central content of all forms of newspaper writing, including news items, correspondents' reports, essays, and editorials. In this way, Deng said, all the most important aspects of a key issue would be concentrated and therefore better understood by the readers.[12] This style of key reporting continues to this day in Chinese journalism.

Deng continued his loyal popularization of changing Party lines as editor of the *People's Daily* after 1949, penning dozens of editorials on

[10]See D. A. Kelly, "The Emergence of 'Alienation': Wang Ruoshui and the Party of Philosophy," in *Chinese Intellectuals and the State: The Search for a New Relationship*, ed. Merle Goldman, with Timothy Cheek and Carol Hamrin (forthcoming).

[11]"Gaizao women de tongxun yu baodao fangfa" [Reform Our Correspondence and Reporting Methods], *Xinwen gongzuo zhinan*, p. 54.

[12]Ibid., pp. 50–51, 53–54.

Party policies, including the 1951 rectification of intellectuals and the criticism of Hu Feng in 1955.[13] His writings in other forums echoed the same approach. Even during the Great Leap, about which he almost certainly entertained grave doubts and which he later bitterly criticized, Deng loyally produced one after another propaganda article on the glories of the communes and "red" work styles.[14]

Professional Standards

Deng Tuo brought the highest professional standards he could muster to his journalism. He is credited with building the *People's Daily* and constantly working through the 1950s to improve its style and layout. He required that every letter from a reader be answered, and he instituted a regular newsletter to the employees of the paper, who had grown from about 200 in 1950 to over 10,000 in early 1951. Shortly after the establishment of the paper, Deng Tuo changed the organization of the editorial board and the format of the paper from those that had prevailed in base area publications during the 1940s. Party periodicals then had been organized functionally according to activity: editing, interviewing, reporting, research, etc. Deng changed to a topical organization: agriculture, industry, Party life, literature, etc., in order to focus the paper's reporting efforts.[15]

The rehabilitation literature on Deng Tuo since 1979 abounds with somewhat hagiographical stories of his profound commitment to the paper. Most former colleagues recall his friendly personal style and his admonitions to do research every day—to read, read, read, but also to spend at least a third of their time on the streets, "out of the editorial room," talking with the general public and seeing for themselves what daily life for others was like.[16] Deng Tuo's concern that younger

---

[13]Some thirty-two editorials from the *People's Daily*, such as from June 25, 1951 and June 10, 1955, were identified specifically as Deng Tuo's by Ding Yilan, his widow (personal communication). They are to be published in a volume of Deng's political writings.

[14]These are discussed in Timothy Cheek, "Deng Tuo: Culture, Leninism and Alternative Marxism in the Chinese Communist Party," *China Quarterly* 87 (1981):467–77, 479–80.

[15]Yan Ling, "Fenming feimeng yi feiyan—huiyi Deng Tuo tongzhi zai Renmin ribao" [Clearly Neither Dreamy nor Foggy: Remembering Comrade Deng Tuo at the *People's Daily*], *Xinwen yanjiu ziliao* [Research Materials on Journalism] 5 (1980):111–13.

[16]Ibid., p. 114; *Yi Deng Tuo*, pp. 104–108.

journalists develop professional standards as well as orthodox ideas is a constant theme in articles on him. Nie Rongzhen, once military commander of Jin Cha Ji and currently a member of the Politburo, has praised as one of Deng Tuo's greatest contributions, "the great number of propaganda cadres he nurtured and trained."[17]

Elite Cultural Pursuits

Deng Tuo saved time and energy for cultural pursuits and publications that strongly resemble the pastimes of the traditional Chinese scholar elite. He was proud of China's heritage of high culture, including painting, poetry, and antiques, and he encouraged others to enjoy them. He was an art collector of some renown.[18] He also wrote traditional-style poetry and practiced calligraphy throughout his life, often putting these arts in the service of the Party, as in writing an ode to Mao's "On New Democracy" or penning artistic characters for the "Great Leap" (*Da yue*), but most of his poems were simply lyrical or expressed personal concerns.[19] They were printed in the *People's Daily*, *Guangming Daily*, and the Beijing Party Committee's theory journal, *Frontline*, from 1958 under the pen-name Zuo Hai. Several of his poems were written with traditional-style paintings by other artists in "complementary pairs."[20]

Deng Tuo also wrote numerous lyrical essays (*sanwen*) and general essays on art history of only indirect political relevance. His aesthetics, however, included a political concern for the future of Chinese traditional landscape painting in socialist society, the proper role of the calligraphic arts, and the proper class analysis of poetry and paintings of natural scenery in socialist society. These paralleled Wu Han's concerns over the proper role of traditional

[17]*Yi Deng Tuo*, p. 6.

[18]Wang Bisheng, "Deng Tuo he wenwu" [Deng Tuo and Cultural Artifacts], *Wenwu tiandi* [The World of Cultural Artifacts] 3 (1983):36–37, photographic page 2 has photos of Deng and some of his collection.

[19]*Deng Tuo shi ci xuan* [A Selection of Deng Tuo's Poetry] (Beijing: Renmin Wenxue, 1979) contains 160 of his poems; the "New Democracy" poem is on p. 10. A twenty-eight-page booklet reprints some of his calligraphy, with the "Great Leap" on pp. 14–15. See *Deng Tuo shufa xuan* [A Selection of Deng Tuo's Calligraphy] (Beijing: Renmin Wenxue, 1980).

[20]Some examples in *People's Daily* are from page 8 on September 1, 1958, September 4, 1958, September 10, 1958, January 1, 1959, and March 15, 1959; two poem and painting *shi hua pei* appear in *Qianxian* [Frontline] 17 (1961) and 20 (1961).

morality and Jian Bozan's thoughts on the role of the history profession.[21]

Public Commentary

Aside from his editorials in the *People's Daily* and *Frontline*, which naturally conformed to the letter of Party policy, Deng Tuo wrote many *zawen*, or miscellaneous essays, which offered political and social commentary on the issues of the day. Although his *Evening Chats at Yanshan* and his contributions to *Notes from a Three-Family Village* in the early 1960s are the best known, his essays in this style did not begin there. Such essays expressed Deng Tuo's personal opinions, sometimes at variance with parts of the current Party line—usually when the line had strayed from his Leninist faith.

The tone of Deng Tuo's *zawen*, however, was far less hostile than that of Lu Xun, who made the genre famous in the 1920s, nor in content did they challenge the dominant role due the Leninist Party, as did those of the Hundred Flowers period. They were simply, as the Chinese term can be interpreted to mean, "essays of miscellaneous impressions."[22] In Deng Tuo's hands, Lu Xun's old blade was hammered into a plowshare to plant knowledge among the masses, to cultivate a sense of self-confidence and pride among intellectuals, and to root out specific excesses of the leadership.

His use of pen-names for these essays reflected Deng Tuo's orthodoxy. Pen-names did not hide the identity of an author from the authorities; there was always a Party propaganda official on any legal editorial board in China. Rather, the use of a pen-name preserved the image of Party unity and allowed a member to air his or her opinions without violating Leninist dicta. It also indicated at what level of authority an article was to be understood by the reader. That is, Deng Tuo, as editor

---

[21]Zuo Hai [Deng Tuo], "Zhongguo shanshui hua chuang xinde daolu" [Chinese Landscape Painting Creates a New Road], *Qianxian* 7 (1964):9–11; Zuo Hai, "Ni kan shanshui fengjing meibumei" [Do You Think the Natural Scenery Is Beautiful or Not], *Qianxian* 6 (1961):12–13; Ma Nancun [Deng Tuo], "Jiangdian shufa" [On a Few Points on Calligraphy], *Yenshan yehua* [Evening Chats at Yanshan], 2d ed. (Beijing: Beijing Chubanshe, 1979) [hereafter *Evening Chats*], pp. 375–78. Several of these types of essays are reprinted in *Deng Tuo sanwen* [Deng Tuo's Lyrical Essays] (Beijing: Renmin ribao, 1980). See Tao Hai in *Chinese Literature* (Beijing: Foreign Languages Press), issues 8 (1963), 9 (1963), 1 (1964), and 3 (1964).

[22]In other words, *zagan wen*. This is Niijima Atsuyoshi's interpretation of *zawen* in Yan'an. See "En'an seifu undo—sono katei, riron, igi" [The Rectification Movement in Yan'an—Its Process, Theory, and Significance], *Toyo bunka* 32 (May 1962):42.

of the *People's Daily*, wrote or spoke with the authority of the Party. Ma Nancun as a citizen, however, could speak more freely and was understood to be less than authoritative. Finally, use of a pen-name could also reflect the personal aesthetic style of the author or simply be a small joke or remembrance.[23]

The most important example of this type of public commentary by Deng Tuo before the early 1960s is a short satirical piece, "Discard 'The Politics of Simpletons,'" published in the *People's Daily* under the pen-name Bu Wuji during the Hundred Flowers campaign in May 1957.[24] Deng bemoaned the bureaucratic structure that "we ourselves have created" and lampooned activists who used political sloganeering simply to make themselves feel important as "the politics of simpletons." His solution, buttressed with a quote from the Song dynasty poet Lu You, was to advise cadres to listen to specialists and to exercise "certain degrees of noninterference" in daily life and work.

Deng Tuo's public commentary became more strident and more frequent after the Great Leap, primarily due to the changes in the political atmosphere rather than a shift in his own approaach. The social world from which Deng Tuo spoke and the changing political climate beginning in the late 1950s help explain why this minor arena of his journalism became, for a short while, major.

Social and Political Context, 1956–1966

Deng Tuo is remembered as a polymath whose interests spanned a broad range of activities. While Deng Tuo considered himself an intellectual and spoke as one inside the Party and in the press, he spoke first for the Party and tried to harmonize the interests and needs of his social group secondarily to that. This balancing act became increasingly difficult beginning in the mid-1950s as Party policy under Mao Zedong strayed farther and farther from the intellectual side of Deng Tuo's life.

Social Context

Deng Tuo was deeply involved in central Party politics, but never as a

---

[23]These reasons are covered by Deng Tuo himself, writing as Ma Nancun, in "Ni zancheng yong biming ma?" [Do You Approve the Use of Pen-names?], in *Evening Chats,* translated in *CLG,* pp. 61–63.

[24]"Feiqi 'yongren zhengzhi,'" *People's Daily,* May 11, 1959, translated in *CLG,* pp. 31–33.

leader. He never sat on the Central Committee, much less its higher organs. His one brush with such opportunity was at the Eighth Party Congress in 1956 when he declined nomination to the Central Committee for unspecified reasons.[25] Deng held several Party posts outside the realm of journalism. In 1946 he became director of the Policy Research Office of the Party's North China Bureau and director of the Economic Group of the Party's Central Policy Research Office, maintaining both jobs into the 1950s. In 1949 he also became director of the Beijing Policy Research Office. In 1960, he was appointed an alternate secretary of the Secretariat of the North China Bureau (under Peng Zhen).[26] With these posts came the usual government responsibilities as delegate to the first three National Peoples' Congresses and the first Chinese Peoples' Political Consultative Conference. These positions reflect Deng's lesser known role as a back-room boy advising the Party on policy matters.

Professionally, Deng Tuo was always a journalist. He helped found the All China Journalists Association in 1949 and served as its president until March 1960. In 1954 he led a delegation of Chinese journalists to Moscow. In March 1956 he attended a meeting of the Communist International Organization of Journalists held in Warsaw and was elected its vice-chairman.[27] Deng's most important job, of course, was as founding editor of the *People's Daily*.

He lost his position in the *People's Daily* in the summer of 1958, however, and moved to the Beijing Party organization where he became the founding editor of its theory journal, *Frontline* (*Qianxian*). Deng wrote nearly every one of the bimonthly editorials in the six years that the journal operated. In addition, he had administrative control of the *Beijing Daily* and the *Beijing Evening News*.[28]

Deng Tuo spent much time and effort outside Party work. In 1950 he lectured on economics at Beijing University, and from 1956 he was a member of the Chinese Academy of Science's Department of Philosophy and Social Sciences and its History Research Institute. He carried out detailed research projects on Ming-Qing history, helped

[25]There is some indication that Deng was concerned that his brother's service in the Nationalist Party in Kaifeng in the 1930s would arouse opposition to his election.

[26]Information on Deng Tuo's appointments comes from ''Deng Tuo tongzhi zhuidao hui zai Jing longzhong juxing'' [A Memorial Meeting for Comrade Deng Tuo Solemnly Held in Beijing], in Liao Mosha, ed., *Yi Deng Tuo*, pp. 1–4, translated in FBIS-CHI, September 6, 1979, pp. L1-L3, and *Zhongguo wenxuejia cidian*, p. 111.

[27]Union Research Services (Hong Kong), *Biographical Service* 777, May 28, 1963.

[28]*Yi Deng Tuo*, pp. 101, 103.

organize the National Museum in Beijing, published poetry and calligraphy, was a member of the Chinese Writers Association, collected
antiques, authenticated ancient paintings, joined with noted painters in
joint projects, and much more.[29]

Political Context

Beginning in the mid-1950s, Deng Tuo's approach to his work began to
clash with the demands of his office. A complex mix of personal,
professional, and policy conflicts led eventually to his dismissal from
the *People's Daily*.

Liu Binyan, a noted journalist in China today, traveled with Deng to
Moscow and Warsaw in the 1950s and later recalled Deng's life as
editor of the *People's Daily*. Numerous leaders gave him orders, says
Liu, and Deng had to publish articles that "didn't say anything" and
which he knew his readers did not care for. More importantly, Mao did
not like Deng Tuo, perhaps in part due to jealousy of Deng's erudition,
and Liu Binyan implies that Mao's famous derogation of the paper—
"The *People's Daily* is really the *Dead Daily*"—was pointed at its
cautious editor.[30]

Personal tensions between Deng Tuo and Chairman Mao began to
surface in 1956 when it became common knowledge among high-level
cadres that Mao was dissatisfied with Deng Tuo. At one point in a Party
working session, when Deng returned to his seat, reserved for the
editor of the *People's Daily*, Mao suggested that he not bother and
proceeded to announce to the meeting that Comrade Deng Tuo had
"depreciated" over his eight years as editor and really wasn't worth
much anymore. Everytime the masses reported new, larger harvests,
Mao went on, Comrade Deng Tuo insisted on lowering the figures.[31]

Deng Tuo's experience during the May 1957 Hundred Flowers
movement is an example of the compromises and dangers that many
establishment intellectuals faced. It certainly contributed to his dismissal from *People's Daily*. Lin Xiling, the well-known student activist
of that period, has recalled that Deng Tuo encouraged her criticisms of
bureaucratism in the spring of 1957 when she met him as a reporter for
the *China Youth* newspaper. Deng was her "backstage support" when

[29]See *Shehui kexue zhanxian* [Social Science Battle Front] 3 (1928):72; *Yi Deng
Tuo*, pp. 158–64.

[30]AFP Newswire (Paris), April 21, 1983, translation by James Feinerman.

[31]Personal communication.

she made her famous criticisms of the Party, but when she was attacked by the Party that summer he could not defend her and shifted the blame, naming the already doomed Tan Xiwu as her secret supporter. Nonetheless, says Lin Xiling, Deng Tuo was demoted during the anti-Rightist campaign in 1957. This time Deng took the fall—for a superior on the Politburo.[32]

Deng's dismissal from the *People's Daily* was masked at first, when he was "kicked upstairs" with a series of higher managerial titles, beginning in the summer of 1957 and lasting into 1960. His move to the Party offices in Peng Zhen's Beijing administration in August 1958 and the startup of *Frontline* that fall marked the break. These circumstances strongly suggest that Deng Tuo was dismissed from the *People's Daily* at Mao Zedong's behest, but that Deng had the support of Peng Zhen and others to mitigate his fall from grace.[33] Although Deng moved to his new job under a cloud, significantly, it was only a partial cloud. He had a prestigious new journal to edit and retained cordial relations with his successor at the *People's Daily,* Wu Lengxi. In fact, General Secretary Deng Xiaoping personally attended the going away party for Deng Tuo at the paper in February 1959 and praised the editor. Since 1979, Deng's dismissal has been officially blamed on "mistaken criticism from Party leaders."[34]

Deng Tuo's political work after 1958 was undertaken in a house

---

[32]Lin Xiling, interview at Harvard University, February 3, 1984; see also Jean Leclerc de Sablon and Ba San, "Chine: Souvenirs d'une idealiste incorrigible," *L'express* (Paris), November 10, 1983, p. 154. Roderick MacFarquhar, *The Origins of the Cultural Revolution I: Contradictions Among the People 1956–1957* (New York: Columbia University Press, 1974), pp. 192–95, describes Deng Tuo's role in the resistance to Mao's push for public rectification of the Party in the spring of 1957 and Deng's support for Peng Zhen's approach. Thus, the Politburo member for whom Deng Tuo took the fall was probably Peng Zhen, who quickly gave him a new job.

[33]Li Jun, "Deng Tuo tongzhi yu *Qianxian* zazhi" [Comrade Deng Tuo and *Frontline* Magazine], in *Yi Deng Tuo,* pp. 101–102; Wang Bisheng, "Deng Tuo shengping," p. 79; MacFarquhar, *Origins of the Cultural Revolution I,* p. 282, notes Deng's 1957 dismissal, but on p. 312 and p. 397 note 55 he acknowledges he still "continued to run the paper much as before," with Wu Lengxi, his nominal replacement, doing layout work for the first few years, and he concludes that Mao apparently had the power to dismiss Deng but not to disgrace him.

[34]Chen Kehan and Li Jun, "Zhandou zai sixiang lilun de zui qianxian—dao Deng Tuo tongzhi" [Fighting at the Forefront of the Ideological and Theoretical Front—In Memory of Comrade Deng Tuo], *People's Daily,* August 6, 1979, p. 3, translated in FBIS-CHI (August 15, 1979), p. L23; and "Houji" [Postface], *Deng Tuo sanwen,* p. 199.

divided. But there is no evidence that he worked for revenge. He loyally supported the Great Leap in public and generally worked to heal the growing split in the Party in his many editorials—aimed at the cadres of Beijing—in *Frontline*. In his most questionable activity, at Peng Zhen's behest in the fall of 1961 he took charge of a team set up to conduct in secret a review of documents from the Leap period with the express purpose of finding out what led to the disaster. It was later known as the Chang Guan Lou review from the name of the building in which it was carried out. Despite bitter accusations in the Red Guard press during the Cultural Revolution that this was a secret factional preparation for a Khrushchev-style attack on Mao, it was in fact held according to the letter of the current Party policy following the Ninth Plenum in 1961 to investigate the Leap, if not entirely in the spirit of open discussion— something few were willing to do lightly since the purge of Peng Dehuai.[35] Deng Tuo outlined their mission:

> Many shortcomings, mistakes, and problems have emerged in work these few years. What are the reasons? Natural calamities are not the most important. The fundamental problem was detachment from the masses and subjectivism. In short, the objective law has been contravened and mistakes in line have been made. . . . From where did the tendency to exaggerate things spring up?

The review group submitted a long report to Peng Zhen in December 1961. In conclusions that essentially confirmed the views of Peng Dehuai, the report said the mistakes of the Leap were the result of left deviation, not right opportunism (Mao himself had admitted this), that the Party's decisions had been uninformed and divorced from economic law and thus led to waste, that the Leap's excessive emphasis on individual initiative amounted to subjective idealism, and that the Central Committee changed policies so frequently that mass confusion ensued, with nobody daring to tell the truth.[36]

[35]See Frederick C. Teiwes, *Politics and Purges in China: Rectification and the Decline of Party Norms, 1950–1965* (White Plains, N.Y.: M. E. Sharpe, 1979), pp. 491, 384–440. Mao had declared 1961 an "investigative research year" to discover the source of errors in the Great Leap. See *Liushi niandai guomin jingji tiaozheng de huiqu* (Beijing, 1982), p. 184, cited in Nina Halpern, "The Economists," in *Chinese Intellectuals and the State*, ed. Goldman, with Cheek and Hamrin.

[36]Taken from a Red Guard report, "Before and After the Chang Guan Lou Counter-Revolutionary Incident," April 1967, translated in SCMM 640, pp. 23–27, quote from p. 23.

The January 1962 7,000 Cadres' Work Conference immediately following this review witnessed Mao's famous self-criticism and opened up a time of more open policy debate. This was the political context of Deng Tuo's public commentary in the Beijing press, and the themes outlined in the Chang Guan Lou report were echoed in his *Evening Chats*. But even though Mao had been forced to admit to some errors in the Leap and to call for more moderate policies, this trend probably only exacerbated Mao's distaste for his critics and raised further his suspicions about his colleagues and their servants.

Professional Work

Despite his dismissal from the *People's Daily*, Deng Tuo was still a highly placed and active official in Beijing during the early 1960s. Li Jun, who worked with Deng on the journal *Frontline*, recalls that if not for Deng Tuo it would not have its distinctive merits. These merits are summed up in Deng's wish that the journal would continue "on behalf of the former *Study (Xuexi)* magazine." [37] *Study* had been replaced in 1958 (after a brief period of overlap) by the more radical *Red Flag*, under Chen Boda, Mao's former secretary, as the official theory journal of the central Party. Thus, Deng's journal in Beijing was intended from the very beginning as a mouthpiece for the alternative establishment approach. His editorials, the many special columns he established—such as *Notes from a Three-Family Village*—and the regular articles, such as Li Jun's on sparetime cultural activities for the masses, all reflected the approach of Deng and his patrons. [38] The journal argued for an ordered, moderate, and flexible implementation of Party policies.

Deng Tuo's other professional activities similarly served the Party bureaucracy. In the spring of 1961 he was directed by Lu Dingyi, head of the Propaganda Department, to lead a work team sent to the journalism department of People's University to convey the principles of "truthfulness, objectivity, and fairness in reporting." He stressed Liu Shaoqi's call for reporters to maintain links with current reality while keeping an objective distance from it, to avoid sensationalism. [39]

[37] Li Jun, "Deng Tuo tongzhi yu Qianxian zazhi," in *Yi Deng Tuo*, pp. 101, 105.

[38] Ibid., pp. 101–10; Li Jun, "Lun qunzhong yeyu wenhua huodong de chedi geminghua" [On the Complete Revolutionization of the Sparetime Cultural Activities of the Masses], *Qianxian* 3 (1964):9–11.

[39] *Carry the Great Revolution on the Journalism Front Through to the End* (Beijing: Foreign Languages Press, 1969), p. 34.

Deng Tuo's increasing concern for finding a remedy to the mistaken policies of the Great Leap was also echoed in his activities outside the sphere of journalism. For example, in a speech he gave to the Beijing History Association in 1960, which was later published in *Historical Studies*, he used Mao's writings from his more moderate Yan'an corpus to refute the radical historiography of the Great Leap period, which stressed simplistic class analysis of historical figures and events.[40] "Historical facts and Marxist theories must be combined together into an organic unity," Deng said, if one wants to write proper history. This concern for a strong grasp of the details of Chinese history was hammered home repeatedly:

> Only after mastering the characteristics of Chinese history can one apply Marxism-Leninism to the solution of practical problems in the Chinese revolution, in the manner of shooting an arrow at a set target. Otherwise, though one may be full of praises for the good arrow that is Marxism-Leninism, one cannot hit the target in the Chinese revolution with it. And, what is the use of that?[41]

Here Deng used Mao's political metaphors, the arrow and target, not to laud the Chairman's genius and to ferret out class enemies, but to promote standards of historical scholarship compatible with Deng's own approach. Significantly, Deng made no calls for professional autonomy from Party dictates; rather, in his view, Party control—exercised properly—could only improve the standards and enhance the social contribution of historical studies.

The political import of Deng Tuo's cultural pastimes is reflected in some of his poetry, which gives an insight into his personal feelings in this key period following the Great Leap. In 1960 while recovering from one of his chronic illnesses, Deng visited the Yangze River region in Central China. In powerful imagery, he wrote about the role of the intellectual in politics. Visiting the home of the famous Dong Lin (Eastern Wood) Academy in Wuxi, just west of Shanghai, Deng praised the orthodox political critics of the early seventeenth century for their fortitude and martyrdom in the cause of reforming the moral decadence

---

[40]"Mao Zedong sixiang kaipile Zhongguo lishi kexue de daolu," *Lishi yanjiu* 1 (1961):1-12; translated in SCMM 264, pp. 1-13; discussed in Cheek, "Deng Tuo," pp. 481-82. On the radical historiography and establishment rebuttals, see Clifford Edmunds, "Jian Bozan and the Politics of Historiography," in *Chinese Intellectuals and the State*, ed. Goldman, with Cheek and Hamrin.

[41]"Mao Zedong sixiang," p. 6.

and political misdirection of the Ming court.

Passing by Dong Lin Academy

The Dong Lin discourses followed Master Yang Shi,
In all things showing concern between heaven and earth.
None can say writers chatter emptily,
When blood stains where their heads rolled.

Asking Gao Zi to Still the Waters

With strength defying powerful traitors, with wills unmoved,
The Dong Lin was a generation of such fine men!
Gao Panlong's moral fortitude, all ages will know,
Each word stirs the heart from a martyr's verse.[42]

Deng implied that such politically active scholars were still needed and might still have to suffer the political fate of Gao Panlong. Later in *Evening Chats*, Deng gave a short history of the Dong Lin and made clear that their class limitations did not detract from their more general qualities still worthy of emulation. "The truly learned scholar," he concluded, "absolutely must take concern in politics. The learning of a scholar who is completely ignorant of politics, no matter what, is incomplete."[43] Deng appeared to take comfort from his camaraderie with previous scholar-officials who were demoted for their orthodox outspokenness in the central government. Yet, as with his 1957 critique of radical political mobilization and bureaucuratism, the poems in 1960 did not mark a break in Deng's service to the Party, but rather expressed the Chinese side of his approach to political life: loyal criticism and a sense of the historic mission of intellectuals.

By 1963 Deng and his patrons had to contend with the growing power of the radical Maoists—in particular Jiang Qing. Shanghai was for her what Beijing was for the establishment intellectuals—a local haven from which to push ideas on the central leadership. She tried to enlist Deng Tuo in her efforts to popularize her "revolutionary operas." He declined not only to write for her but to see her or to have

---

[42]Zuo Hai, "Gechang taihu—'Jiangnan yincao' zhi san," *Guangming ribao*, September 7, 1960, reprinted in *Deng Tuo shi qi xuan*, p. 79. The reprint deletes three of the original poem's ten stanzas.

[43]"Shishi guanxin" [In All Things Show Concern], *Evening Chats*, p. 158, translated in *CLG*, p. 43.

anything to do with her. Peng Zhen delegated the onerous task of rebutting the artistic theories of Madame Mao to Li Qi, deputy director of the city's Propaganda Department. The current rehabilitation literature on Deng Tuo suggests that Jiang Qing's anger over this incident was "not unrelated" to circumstances precipitating his subsequent death.[44]

The increasing power of the radical Maoists, due mainly to the shift of the Chairman's own views, curtailed Deng's commentaries in the press. *Evening Chats* and *Notes from a Three-Family Village* had been written when Mao was "welcoming" criticism and suggestions and the leadership was calling for open discussion of failures during the Leap years. *Three-Family Village* did continue to publish a few critical articles, among several noncritical ones, into 1964, reflecting the confidence of the establishment leadership in pressing their views through the Socialist Education movement. That confidence faded in the summer of 1964. *Three-Family Village* ceased publication in June precisely when the attacks on other intellectuals, such as Yang Xianzhen and Feng Ding in philosophy and the writer Zhao Shuli, began under Kang Sheng's direction, and with Mao's approval.[45] This was the beginning of the end for establishment intellectuals like Deng Tuo and their political patrons. With its hand forced, the Beijing press reluctantly joined the criticism.

Public Commentary in Socialist Journalism

In the context of Deng Tuo's broad range of activities outlined above, the meaning of his famous articles, his essays in *Evening Chats at Yanshan* and *Notes from a Three-Family Village,* becomes more clear. They were primarily part of an official effort at public education through regular channels. The bulk of the essays presented themes familiar from the 1950s, although specific topics and the style of presentation were clearly influenced by the establishment's critical

---

[44]Chen Kehan and Li Jun, "Zhanzai sixiang," reprinted in *Yi Deng Tuo*, ed. Liao Mosha, p. 14.

[45]Su Shuangbi and Wang Hongzhi, "Wu Han," in *Zhonggong dangshi renwu zhuan* [Biographies of Chinese Communists], vol. 7 (Xian: Shaanxi Renmin, 1983), pp. 288–89.

response to the failures of the Leap.[46] Thus the uproarious lampoons of officials gone amuck present in Deng Tuo's essays did not represent a disenfranchised dissent as his Cultural Revolution critics claimed, but one aspect of the Party's attempt to cope with not only a charismatic leader tending toward egomania but also a volatile, semiliterate corps of lower level cadre ill-trained for rational bureaucratic administration. The great bulk of Deng's essays in fact were directed to lower levels and thus were often a little patronizing and paternalistic in tone. In the process, Deng flaunted his classical scholarship in a fashion that still arouses admiration among Chinese intellectuals, regardless of their political leanings.

Certainly, a portion of the Party did not appreciate Deng Tuo's efforts or what he represented. That portion, however, was in the minority despite its being headed by the supreme leader, Chairman Mao. Thus, in looking at the themes in Deng's famous commentaries, the image that emerges is one Deng himself chose in his poetry—the loyal scholar-official, on the one hand braving death to remonstrate his ruler in the name of orthodoxy and on behalf of the "outer court" (the bureaucracy) and on the other hand taking time to admonish errant subordinates for their vulgar behavior.

A balanced selection of these essays would produce a small encyclopedia on the glories of Chinese culture and a handbook of tips on how to be a good intellectual or cadre in the service of the Party. Of the 175 essays by Deng in the two collections, two-thirds are on cultural matters. Their political significance is only apparent from their context—they are not the simple peasant culture that Mao insisted upon. Of the 49 other essays in *Three-Family Village,* those by Wu Han were much more concerned with history—the revisions of the *Draft History of the Qing* or the use of the traditional school primer, the *Three-Character Classic*—and those by Liao Mosha were much more "Party line" in nature—popularizing various slogans and encouraging diligent study. Again, the very normality of these educational texts as we flip though their reprints today was their political significance. They did not rant about class struggle or pander to peasant needs; they did glory in exercise of the intellect and assume the status quo of life in 1962. In short, they asserted the dominance of the Party and an important role

---

[46]See Deng's "Feiqi 'yongren zhenzhi,'" and Liao Mosha's 1956 series of *zawen* in *Xin guancha* [New Observer], "Luantan zaji" [Report on What Comes Handy], under the pen-name Wen Bi. On how *Evening Chats* was published, see *Yi Deng Tuo,* pp. 111–15 and *CLG,* pp. 9–12.

for the intellectual. It was primarily this elitism that drove Mao to denounce Deng Tuo and similar establishment intellectuals in 1966. Yet, there was a tone of concern in these essays not limited to specific policy issues. Several themes reappeared constantly, and they all pointed to the need for the Party and individual officials to align themselves better with reality. These themes represent an addition to Deng's approach to public life based on his troubled experience in the years before 1961 and stand as his last sustained discussion of it.

Humanism and Cultural Enjoyment

The economic crisis following the Leap led Deng to criticize the abuse of state power and to remind his readers to respect the value of the individual. "We should take inspiration from the experiences of the ancients and pay more attention to treasuring labor power in every area and thereby treasure every individual's labor and the fruits of every labor."[47]

Deng's humanism strongly resembled traditional Confucian concerns not only in his desire to improve the economic welfare of the people, but in his approval of elite cultural pleasures. On a purely quantitative count, the importance of individual cultural enjoyment was the most prominent characteristic of *Evening Chats* and the dominant flavor of the entire *Three-Family Village* collection. In the latter, Wu Han's essays provided most of the cultural excursions, but Deng, too, had essays on calligraphy and on the role of actors in drama and dance.[48] In *Evening Chats* Deng's frequent discussions of poetry, old books, interesting vignettes, flowers, even pieces of tile all implied a legitimate role for private life—individual talent and interests, hobbies, family concerns—in socialist society. These reflected his own rich lifestyle and diverse cultural activities.

Cosmopolitanism

Deng Tuo reflected a cosmopolitan attitude through time (respect for the past) and through space (open to foreign influence). This is what contemporary anthropologists call a "culture-open" approach. It is a

---

[47]"Aihu laodong li" [On Treasuring Labor Power], April 30, 1961, in *Evening Chats*, p. 62, translated in *CLG*, p. 46.

[48]*Sanjiacun zhaji* [Notes from a Three-Family Village] (Beijing: Renmin Wenxue, 1979), pp. 35–37, 52–54.

syncretic attitude that critically selects relevant aspects of these "other" cultures or societies. Consistent with Deng's artistic activities elsewhere, his calligraphic introduction to *Evening Chats* and constant reference to ancient texts in both columns reflected his belief that ancient habits from the "feudal" past, despite their limitations, remained worthwhile in his day. Like the famous historian Jian Bozan, Deng was obviously proud of his heritage as a Chinese. In "On Treasuring Labor Power" he reminded his readers of the Chinese wisdom in the ancient *Book of Rites* in order to commment on the state's responsibility in preparing for famine relief. When this was published in 1961—the last of the "three bitter years" of famine following the Great Leap—no one needed further explanation: the leaders of the Leap had contravened ancient Chinese wisdom on statecraft. Yet, Deng did not rest his arguments simply on ancient texts. He suggested that his conclusion—that one should carefully assess one's abilities before commiting oneself to act—"is something everyone has learned through experience in daily life."[49]

Deng Tuo was concerned, too, that the slogan, "achieving without a teacher," from the Great Leap had become an excuse for ignoring lessons from abroad. We need to consult the ancient books of China and foreign scientific texts, wrote Deng, in order not to waste time recreating the wheel as we build socialism. Since construction cannot be done in a day, he said, "this requires the relevant newspapers and journals to select and introduce to readers in a timely fashion the quintessence of our ancient books or foreign scientific materials which they badly need today, in order to increase guidance in various areas of study."[50]

Intellectualism

Deng Tuo had a deep reverence for book knowledge as well as practical experience. As H. C. Chuang noted in his terminological study of *Evening Chats*, Deng's repeated use and praise of "knowledge" (*xuewen*) is one of the most striking aspects of the collection.[51] In "Welcome the 'Miscellaneous Scholar,'" Deng made this claim ex-

---

[49]See note 47.

[50]"Xuexi yuyao zhidao" [Study Needs Guidance], April 25, 1961, in *Sanjiacun zhaji*, p. 45.

[51]H. C. Chuang, *Evening Chats at Yenshan, or the Case of Teng T'o* (Berkeley: Studies in Chinese Communist Terminology, 14, 1970), p. 16.

plicit: "No matter what sort of leadership or scientific research work we do, we need to have both specialized scholarship and extensive knowledge." And specialists, he added, should base themselves on a well-rounded intellectual base.[52] Later, in *Three-Family Village*, Deng derided the vulgar simplification of Chinese characters he had seen on signboards in Beijing and reminded his readers that language reform should proceed acording to the rules set up by specialists.[53] These admonitions revealed the object of the texts: a particular social class— intellectuals. In his introduction to the first volume of *Evening Chats*, Deng wrote that it was his desire "to satisfy properly the needs of the masses of workers, peasants, and soldiers who have a relatively high cultural level."[54]

In all his essays, Deng reflected the traditional self-concept of the Chinese scholar-official, the literatus (*wenren*), with a paternalistic sense of responsibility for the good of the common people that implicitly justified the special status and privilege of establishment intellectuals in general and Party intellectuals in particular.

Paternalistic Authoritarianism

Deng Tuo's elitist faith in the Party led to his demand for obedience to Party regulations in line with the approach of his patron, Peng Zhen. In the essay "Do Nothing Improper," Deng reinterpreted this phrase from Confucius to justify a quasi-military "need-to-know" basis for public discussion that is quite the reverse of an "open society." "No matter what work we do," he wrote, "there should be fixed rules. . . . The highest standard in our society's rules of life is to subordinate the rights of the individual to the rights of the group." The essay revolved around state secrets and how to protect them. In a later essay he emphasized the self-discipline necessary to be a good scholar and good Communist.[55]

[52]"Huanying zajia," March 26, 1961, in *Evening Chats*, p. 11, translated in *CLG*, p. 51.

[53]"Shi jianhua zi haishi cuobie zi ne?" [Are These Simplified Characters or Miswritten Characters?], March 10, 1962, in *Sanjiacun zhaji*, pp. 101–103.

[54]"Liangdian shuoming" [Two Explanations], July 10, 1961, in *Evening Chats*, p. 4, translated in *CLG*, p. 37.

[55]"Fei li wu," August 6, 1961, in *Evening Chats*, pp. 153–55, translated in *CLG*, pp. 47–49; and "Hanyang" [Self-Cultivation], December 3, 1961, in *Evening Chats*, pp. 212–14.

Two of Deng's last three essays for *Three-Family Village* published in the spring of 1964 were concerned with the hierarchy, its proper operation, and cultivation of future members—the youth. "The Load Can Be Shouldered," an open letter to officials who made decisions on job assignments, recommended that they carefully lead their young "apprentices" in experiencing greater professional responsibility. Later, in "What Kind of 'New' Do You Want?" Deng spoke to his generation of their responsibility to educate youth. "What we call 'new,'" said Deng, "is the new of socialism." He derided the false bourgeois "new" of nineteenth-century European literature and declared it inappropriate for China, even as a stepping stone away from feudal literature. We must guide the youth in their reading of new books, he went on, since we cannot really say all new books are good, and we must lead them through the best of the older books, which after all includes the Marxist-Leninist canon![56]

Rationalism and Gradualism

Deng Tuo's emphasis on the immutable laws of nature reflected the influence of Engels similar to that in the epistemology of Yang Xianzhen. Deng's belief in the superiority of cool, rational analysis— much like Peng Zhen's—was clearly evident in his approach to Marxism-Leninism-Mao Zedong Thought. In one of his most famous essays, "To Channel Is Better Than to Dam," Deng took the ancient Chinese flood myth—in which the Great Yu drained the waters after damming them had failed—to demonstrate the need for the government to recognize natural laws that can only be ignored at the cost of disaster. This careful, gradualist approach was evident in "The Kingly Way and the Tyrannical Way." Quoting at length from several Han dynasty histories, Deng made his socialist interpretation of their significance: "That which is called the Kingly Way can be interpreted as the honest ideological work style of a mass line based on practical reality. And that which is called the Tyrannical Way can be interpreted as the blustering ideological work style of willful acts based on subjective and arbitrary decisions."[57]

[56]"Jiantou shi nengtiao danzi de," February 10, 1964, *Sanjiacun zhaji*, pp. 171–73; and "Yao shenma yang de xin," March 25, 1964, *Sanjiacun zhaji*, pp. 180–82, quote from p. 180.

[57]"Duse buru kaidao," April 13, 1961, in *Evening Chats*, pp. 78–79, translated in *CLG*, pp. 73–75; "Wangdao he badao," February 25, 1962, in *Evening Chats*, p. 321, translated in *CLG*, p. 67.

Deng criticized the abuse of traditional Party leadership methods as a means of defending them. In "The Correct Understanding of 'Criticism'" he cited Marx's *A Critique of Political Economy* to argue that criticism was the same as scientific research, and he quoted Lenin on the role of criticism in developing the workers' movement. Without criticism, insisted Deng, dialectical progress—sublation of thesis and antithesis (he used the German, *aufheben*)—was impossible. A realist, Deng acknowledged his readers' concern about unprincipled criticism, which he admitted had occurred in the past. "But, the inability to use critical methods," he stated confidently, "if you look into the causes, still stems from not understanding the correct meaning of criticism." Rightly understood, the system should work.[58] Even in "Great Empty Talk," when Deng placed the heady rhetoric about the "East Wind," which Mao had made famous, squarely in the realm of arbitrary and subjective work style, he admitted the necessity of "empty talk" on occasion in political life; he asked only that it not be the major legacy to later generations.[59]

In June 1963, during the height of the Socialist Education movement, Deng admonished that cadre error "cannot be changed in a day. It must be resolved slowly on the ideological level, relying totally on persuasion, and absolutely not on force." As always, when quoting Mao, Deng Tuo selected from the Yan'an corpus (here "Get Organized!" from 1943) to buttress his demands for careful research and moderation.[60]

Denial of the Chinese Leninist Approach

Along with other establishment intellectuals and their political patrons, Deng Tuo was purged in 1966 and his ideas were castigated as antisocialist and anti-Party. This entailed a radical redistribution of status and power away from the Party and establishment intellectuals to a previously left-out group of their same generation who called on a rising generation of "revolutionary successors" in the name of Chairman Mao. Nearly every point of Deng's approach to public life was negated by Cultural Revolution ideology, and every circle of life in which Deng was active saw a radical change in personnel and content.

[58]"Pipan zhengjie," May 14, 1961, in *Evening Chats,* pp. 92–95, translated in *CLG,* pp. 58–60, quote from p. 60.

[59]"Weida de kong hua," November 10, 1961, *Sanjiacun zhaji,* p. 8.

[60]"Zhongshi qunzhong de jingyan" [Pay Attention to the Experiences of the Masses], June 10, 1963, *Sanjiacun zhaji,* pp. 120–22, quote from p. 120.

Deng Tuo's activities from late 1965 as he came under attack have been covered in several earlier studies.[61] With the information now available, the context and consequences of these can be better appreciated. Deng Tuo was part of the enlarged "Five-Man Cultural Revolution Group" headed by Peng Zhen, which met on July 13, 1965; the majority of this group, over the objections of Kang Sheng who pushed the radical line, tried to co-opt the radicals' forum for public criticism—opera reform. But this effort was unsuccessful, and in November Deng attended the meeting convened by Zhou Enlai that arranged for the belated publication in the *Beijing Daily* of Yao Wenyuan's notorious attack on Wu Han. An accompanying editorial by Peng Zhen tried to limit the scope of criticism to academic rather than political issues. Three weeks later Deng was given the task of convening several public meetings to discuss Wu Han's play.[62]

Deng organized a group of seven people to work on defending Wu Han in December 1965. According to Su Shuangbi, one of the seven, Deng was deeply disturbed that Wu Han's play was being unfairly criticized. Su himself published a defense of Wu Han's portrayal of landlords in the *Beijing Daily* in late December. But it was no use. By February it was clear that they themselves were in trouble. Su recalls that Deng stood by them and did not disassociate himself when they were under criticism. Of the seven men Deng had assembled, most were university professors or graduates.[63] Thus, while Deng was a member of central Party meetings organized to defend establishment interests, he was the organizer of lower level efforts in Beijing. It was to be his last effort in that line of transmission from the top elite to the intellectual leadership.

By March 1966 Deng Tuo had been relieved of his editorship of *Frontline*; Li Jun edited what was to be the last issue of that journal. In early April Deng was under investigation, and the last time Li Jun saw him was at one such scrutiny session on April 6.[64] On April 16, 1966,

---

[61]Byung-joon Ahn, *Chinese Politics*, p. 177; Yung-hung Lee, *The Politics of the Chinese Cultural Revolution* (Berkeley: University of California Press, 1978), pp. 1–25; Merle Goldman, *China's Intellectuals*, pp. 118–33.

[62]Kenneth Lieberthal, *A Research Guide to Central Party and Government Meetings in China, 1949–1975* (White Plains, N.Y.: International Arts and Sciences Press, 1976), pp. 226, 234; Ahn, *Chinese Politics*, p. 177.

[63]Interview with Su Shuangbi at the offices of *Guangming Daily*, Beijing, June 7, 1983; Li Jun, in *Yi Deng Tuo*, pp. 108–109.

[64]Li Jun, in *Yi Deng Tuo*, p. 109.

the *Beijing Daily* printed its criticism of Deng Tuo, for the first time exposing his pen-name and confirming in public that he was the author of *Evening Chats* and contributing editor of *Three-Family Village*. On May 8 "Gao Ju" (Jiang Qing) began the barrage of criticism against Deng Tuo in the national press, beginning predictably in the *Liberation Army Daily*. There followed hundreds of articles in the national and local press, most notably Yao Wenyuan's "Criticizing the 'Three-Family Village'—The Reactionary Nature of *Evening Chats at Yanshan* and *Notes from a Three-Family Village*," which finally appeared on May 11 in the *People's Daily*.

In this long and rambling textual analysis of Deng Tuo's essays, Yao set out to demonstrate that Deng was the antithesis of everything socialist and Chinese. Yao's logic was so fallacious that it is not interesting to refute his assertations on the grounds of logic, though Chinese writers after 1979 have attempted this.[65] In general, Yao indulged in quotation out of context and anachronistic value judgments—i.e., castigating Deng Tuo for advancing opinions with which Mao disagreed in 1966 but that were Party policy in 1962.

Yao's closed-door definition of truth, which he limited to a single proletarian class within modern society, was contrary to Deng Tuo's cosmopolitanism. Yao equated interest in foreign culture or praise of any past figure with the desire to "restore capitalism." He implied the latter was superstitious ancestor worship of "great Bodhisattvas," "feudal die-hards," and "geomancers." Yao concluded his criticism of Deng's "To Channel Is Better Than To Dam" by saying, "Isn't this clearly demanding that we practice bourgeois liberalization?" In analyzing "On Treasuring Labor Power," Yao rejected Deng Tuo's faith that the ancients of the "feudal period" could teach socialists some objective laws about society and concluded that such class enemies were incapable of comprehending any objective laws. He summed up its meaning by asking, "Was this not clearly coordinated with the venomous attacks of U.S. imperialism and modern revisionism of [the Soviet Union]?"[66]

Yao was clearly a revolutionary romantic; the need for a monolithic unity of views meant that criticism in public of the Party or of Mao's habits was never right. Yao fervently believed in the power of positive thinking, and in this he reflected much of the Chairman's philosophical

[65]*Yi Deng Tuo*, pp. 284–88.
[66]Yao Wenyuan, "Ping 'Sanjiacun,'" translated in *CLG*, pp. 82–83.

approach in the 1960s. In 1964, Yao had criticized the novelist Zhao Shuli for his admittedly accurate description of the range of peasant characters in his fiction. Yao denounced this as counterrevolutionary because it required "a fundamental exclusion and suppression of new things which are germinating or developing, and an extension of protection to old things which superficially still exist extensively."[67]

Yao was stridently anti-intellectual, equating academic knowledge with capitalism. He claimed that Deng Tuo, Wu Han, and Liao Mosha used " 'history,' 'learning,' and 'things of interest' to dull the people's revolutionary vigilance, dupe yet more readers, and expand their influence."[68] Here, Yao was trying to redefine the basis for the *legitimate* exercise of power in the public arena. In powerful metaphors, if not reasoning, Yao dubbed academic skill as "landlord" in nature because it continued the hegemony of the literati in Chinese society *similar* to that enjoyed by the scholar-officials in "landlord" times. He lauded the models of Dazhai and Daqing in which peasants and workers espousing Mao's inspiration *took control of their lives*, and this was the rationale for his own claim to legitimate authority—as interpreter of Mao's views. Yao and other radicals could not compete with Deng Tuo or Wu Han in the field of historical knowledge or organizational ability, so they changed the grounds of the debate. Anti-intellectualism served both Mao's utopian goals and their own professional ambitions.

As the basis for legitimacy was turned upside down, the circles of Deng Tuo's life—the intellectual and Party establishment in Beijing— were torn apart and ransacked. In the government Peng Zhen, Liu Ren, and the whole Party Committee were removed. In the journalistic world, Gu Xing, the whole editorial board of the *Beijing Evening News*, and everybody associated with *Frontline* were subjected to the notorious "mass criticism" of 1966. The publications themselves were suspended; the circle collapsed to nothing more than the *People's Daily*, and even Deng's successor there, Wu Lengxi, was purged. The effect in artistic realms was even more personal and reached into Deng's home. The emerging Cultural Revolution elite, despite their public outcry against the "four olds," helped themselves to Deng Tuo's art collections and calligraphy. Kang Sheng in particular selected

---

[67]Goldman, *China's Intellectuals*, p. 102, quoting *Guangming Daily*, December 20, 1964.

[68]*CLG*, p. 84. Mao had similar charges, but against the rightists of the Hundred Flowers in 1957. See *Selected Works of Mao Tsetung*, vol. 5 (Beijing: Foreign Language Press, 1977), p. 442.

the finest pieces of his former associate.[69]

Finally, Deng Tuo committed suicide on the evening of May 17, 1966, after writing his last testimony. His children were kicked out of school, his wife was paraded through the streets of Beijing, and "revolutionary successors" took occupancy of his traditional-style home.

Rehabilitation: Deng Tuo as a Model

The "Three-Family Village" was officially rehabilitated in February 1979, along with hundreds of other establishment intellectuals, following the consolidation of power by Deng Xiaoping at the now famous Third Plenum of the Eleventh Central Committee of the Party in December 1978.[70] Like the other well-known Party loyalists from the 1960s, Deng Tuo has been used posthumously to push the current regime's model for intellectual participation in public life. In addition, each of the professional spheres in which Deng was active has used his good political reputation as well as his professional standards to push its own interests. Finally, literature on Deng Tuo since 1979 has reflected true personal grief over the loss of a friend and teacher that serves to expiate feelings of fellow intellectuals and to honor their comrade in the eyes of history. In all of this Deng Tuo and his ideas and methods have been held up as a model for youth in China today.

The national newspaper for intellectuals, the *Guangming Daily,* produced the first major rehabilitiation article on Deng Tuo, as it did for many others. On January 26, 1979 Zhang Yide's "It Is No Crime to Criticize Idealism, It Is Meritorious to Propagandize Materialism— Refuting Yao Wenyuan's False Charges in 'Criticizing *Evening Chats at Yanshan* and *Notes from a Three-Family Village'* " lived up to its title and praised Deng Tuo for his "clearcut views, resourceful knowledge, vivid examples, and fine literary style." But Zhang also was out to use Deng Tuo's past to serve Deng Xiaoping's present; Deng Tuo was acclaimed as a serious model for "integrat[ing] our revolutionary spirit with our scientific approach."[71] Welcome the return of the establishment intellectuals and their professional expertise.

[69] *Yi Deng Tuo,* pp. 157–58.

[70] *Guangming ribao,* February 23, 1979, p. 1. The official rehabilitation article appeared six months later. See Chen Kehan and Li Jun, "Zhandou zai sixiang."

[71] Zhang Yide, "Pipan weixinlun wu zui, xuanchuan weiwulun yougong—tuidao Yao Wenyuan 'Ping *Yanshanyehu, Sanjiacun zhaji'* de wuxian," *Guangming ribao,* January 26, 1979, p. 3, translated in FBIS-CHI, February 9, 1979, pp. E2-E8.

Su Shuangbi's paeon to the "Three-Family Village" and denunciation of Yao Wenyuan and the "gang of four" two days later was more or less repeated in the authoritative central Party theory journal, *Red Flag*, in February 1979. Su, as the editor of the history supplement of *Guangming Daily*, has emerged as a major spokesman for rehabilitated cadre, particularly his old teacher Wu Han, and propagandist for current Party intellectual policy.[72] Su's major concern was to remind his readers that Deng Tuo was attacking ultra-leftism, not the Party itself. This analysis stands up to a close reading of the original texts in *Evening Chats*, but Su did sidestep the issue of Deng's lampoons of Chairman Mao. He did not deny the possibility, but it has not been politic for a Party loyalist to broach that topic.

As Su's disinclination to deal with Deng's jibes at Mao indicates, these rehabilitation aritcles are not dispassionate reassessments of history. Like Yao's 1966 attacks, they are propaganda for their political patrons. Unlike Yao Wenyuan's essays, Su's and Zhang's are not guilty of gross misrepresentation, but they still paint Yao as implacably evil, out to "usurp Party and state power," and a "literary rascal." Nothing Yao ever said or did was good. Finally, in parallel with the Cultural Revolution denunciations of Deng Tuo as a leader of an organized plot (the "Three-Family Village") to take power, Su, too, tars his subject as a member of the noted fiction, the "gang of four."

In this process of official political rehabilitation, journalism circles, of course, have relied most heavily on Deng Tuo as a model. His widow Ding Yilan's "Commemorating Deng Tuo" appeared in *News Battlefront*, the major journalism journal, in February 1979.[73] And *Guangming Daily* published a book review of the new edition of *Evening Chats* on February 10, 1979, which strongly defended the critical commentary on current social issues embodied in Deng's 1960s essays.[74] Several hundred articles over the next three years spelled out in meticulous detail just what standards and practices Comrade Editor

[72]Su Shuangbi, "Ping Yao Wenyuan de 'Ping *Sanjiacun*,'" *Hongqi* [Red Flag] (1979):41–48, translated in JPRS 073304 (April 25, 1979), pp. 73–87. See Su's essays attacking radical historiography, *Jieji douzheng yu lishi kexue* [Class Struggle and the Science of History] (Shanghai: Shanghai Renmin, 1982).

[73]"Yi Deng Tuo," *Xinwen zhanxian* 2 (1979), reprinted in *Yi Deng Tuo*, pp. 17–28.

[74]Wang Zhen [nb. not the Politburo member], "Dui pipan Lin Biao, 'Siren bang' zuoqing jihuizhuyi luxian you zhongyao yiyi—*Yanshan yehua* jijiang chongxin chuban" [Of Great Significance in the Criticism of the Opportunist Line of Lin Biao and the 'Gang of Four'—*Evening Chats at Yanshan* Will Soon Be Republished], *Guangming ribao*, February 10, 1979, p. 2.

Deng Tuo had advocated and explicitly linked them with how newspapers and journals should be run today.

This pattern was repeated in historical circles. Deng's associates, such as his student Liu Yongcheng, were appointed to the Academy of Social Sciences. Deng's works in history were republished with praise, and finally he was enshrined in the first of the new *History Almanacs* in 1979 along with Fan Wenlan, Guo Moruo, Wu Yuzhang, Jian Bozan, and Wu Han.[75]

In artistic circles, *A Selection of Deng Tuo's Poetry* was published in December 1979 with a laudatory preface by Nie Rongzhen, and *A Selection of Deng Tuo's Calligraphy* came out in February 1980, followed by a volume of *Deng Tuo's Lyrical Essays*. Finally, the *Collected Works of Deng Tuo*, a five-volume set to include his editorials and other political writings in addition to bringing together the volumes mentioned above, is planned for publication in 1985. Zhou Yang's preface to the *Collected Works* appeared in the *People's Daily* in December 1983.[76]

In each of these publications, the relevance of Deng Tuo as a model of culturally rich but politically orthodox intellectual and professional life has been stressed. Since 1981, national press stories on Deng Tuo, as for other rehabilitated establishment intellectuals, have tapered off. There is, however, a lively cottage industry in specialized journals and local publications that reflect more "local" uses of Deng within the broad rubric on what he is allowed to "mean" as set at the national level. Of particular interest has been the response of youth—China's future establishment intellectuals. Letters by "youth" now well into their thirties have declared Deng's beneficial influence on them in the 1960s or have appologized for wrongfully criticizing him during the Cultural Revolution.[77] The success of efforts by writers and editors to popularize Deng Tuo's essays and ideas as models of inspiration for the youth of today is hard to judge now, but based on the picture of youth in David Ownby's chapter in this volume, it would appear that many find

[75]Jin Chengji, "Jianchi lishi kexue geming zhendi de douzheng jilu—du Deng Tuo tongzhi de *Lun Zhongguo lishi de jige wenti*" [A Record of Upholding the Revolution in Historical Sciences—On Reading Comrade Deng Tuo's *A Few Questions in Chinese History*], *Guangming ribao*, January 30, 1979, p. 4; *1979 Zhonghuo lishixue niangjian* [1979 Chinese History Almanac] (Beijing: Sanlian Shudian, 1980), pp. 315–18.

[76]Zhou Yang, "Deng Tuo wenji xu" [Preface to the *Collected Works of Deng Tuo*], *Renmin ribao*, December 22, 1983, p. 8. See also note 19.

[77]*Yi Deng Tuo*, pp. 213–15, and *Suibi* [Jottings] 8 (1980):34–45.

both his scholarship hard to match and his orthodoxy difficult to embrace.

Conclusions

We return now to the question raised at the beginning of this chapter: Who is "the Party"? Deng Tuo's case shows clearly that various groups have competed for that authority, and that the question of legitimacy has been answered by the current leaders of China in favor of establishment intellectuals such as Deng Tuo.[78] His Chinese Leninist approach to public life represented but one variation of the synthesis of Marxist-Leninist ideas with Chinese cultural assumptions in the Party, but it was one that was compatible with the establishment of the People's Republic until 1966 and is declared to be so today. Deng never really articulated his views until after the Great Leap because his assumptions were standard operating procedure. Only with the challenge of the Great Leap and its radical ideology did Deng Tuo articulate his ideas. His commmentaries in *Evening Chats* were not only a call for rectification—a return to the standard operating procedures of the 1950s—but a plea to further humanize Party rule. A committed Communist, Deng brought the moral concerns of his Confucian heritage and the public outspokenness of the May Fourth intellectual world to his journalism in the 1960s.

Deng Tuo's activities as a poet and callligrapher were characteristic of what Joseph Levenson has described for scholar-painters in late imperial China as "the amateur ideal."[79] This parallel is significant in judging the nature of such traditional cultural interests among establishment intellectuals in China. Deng Tuo clearly shared the eclecticism and connoisseurship of the Ming Dynasty literati, but his aesthetic delight did not extend to their formalism and in no way impeded his commitment to modern values of science and rational bureaucratic organization.[80] Deng's approach was more like that of a Jesuit—culturally urbane, paternalistic, and humane but also orthodox and tireless in

---

[78]Carol Hamrin has detailed the mechanism used in this competition among Party elites. See "Competing 'Policy Packages' in Post-Mao China," *Asian Survey* 24, 5 (May 1984):487–518.

[79]Joseph Levenson, *Confucian China and Its Modern Fate*, vol. 1 (Berkeley: University of California Press, 1972), pp. 15–43.

[80]See Deng's criticism of such formalism in the study and practice of calligraphy in "Jiangdian shufa" [A Few Points on Calligraphy], in *Evening Chats*, p. 376.

his efforts to serve the institution that he believed served the people. This public-minded elitism contrasts with Mao Zedong's populist approach. For all his mistakes, Mao was concerned that China's working masses learn to speak for themselves in politics. The question remains whether Deng Tuo and other establishment intellectuals operating in an unelected bureaucratic state could or will adequately represent the interests of China's peasant majority.

Deng Tuo only criticized the Party when Mao led it away from its established rules of operation. When push came to shove in 1965 Deng Tuo had to choose, as did everyone else, between loyalty to Mao or to the collective leadership; Deng Tuo chose the latter and was purged with them. The tragedy of Deng Tuo, and the natural concern of establishment intellectuals today, is that the institution he served, the Communist Party, was turned against its loyal servant and drove him to suicide. Until some guarantee of security is given to establishment intellectuals, whether by Peng Zhen's socialist legal code or by other means such as institutional checks on the Party as advocated by Wang Ruoshui, the ghost of Deng Tuo will haunt the halls of power in China.

III. Establishment Scholars

SUN YEFANG

Toward a Reconstruction of Socialist Economics

Barry J. Naughton

> It never occurred to me that an old Communist Party member like myself could be thrown into a Communist prison! But prisons are one thing, and ideas another thing altogether. I will not change my ideas.
>
> Sun Yefang, mid-1970s

Sun Yefang joined the Chinese Communist Party at the age of sixteen and worked actively for the Party for sixty years until his death in 1983. For those sixty years, Sun maintained an unswerving commitment to Marxism and to the Chinese Communist Party, in spite of a prolonged prison term ordered by Party officials. As an intellectual and economist, Sun developed the rudiments of an independent theory of the economics of socialism that marked a distinct break with Stalinist orthodoxy. In spite of the attack that he sustained for his ideas, Sun survived, maintained his viewpoint, and played an important role in the revival of theoretical discussion in post-Mao China. He ended his days amidst a chorus of praise for his theoretical contributions, and for the personal integrity with which he upheld them.

The following discussion of the evolution of Sun Yefang's ideas and influence places them within the framework of his personal biography.[1]

[1]David Bachman, Nina Halpern, and Dorothy Solinger read and provided detailed comments on an earlier draft of this essay and provoked significant changes. In addition, I owe a special debt of gratitude to the editors of this volume for their constant encouragement and enthusiasm, without which this essay would never have seen the light of day. Tim Cheek helped locate certain of the early pieces by Sun cited in note 11. Remaining errors and omissions are solely my responsibility.

During Sun's long career as a Communist Party member, he was shaped by many of the same forces that influenced the Chinese Communist movement as a whole: contact with the Soviet Union; the period of war and revolutionary struggle; the construction of socialism during the 1950s; and the bitter political divisions of the 1960s and 1970s. Sun responded to these experiences by developing a flexible, cosmopolitan approach to Marxist theory that enabled him to make some genuinely original contributions to the problem of applying Marxism to the economic problems of socialist countries. The events to which Sun Yefang was subject required a personal as well as an intellectual response: although thousands of Chinese intellectuals have suffered extreme reversals of fortune during the past thirty years, few others have sustained such a concentrated, virulent assault during the bad years, nor reached such heights of official acclaim during the good. In his response to these events, Sun demonstrated a degree of personal integrity that cannot help but elicit our admiration.

The biographical format requires a selective and somewhat compressed treatment of Sun's economic theories. This deficiency is particularly regrettable since a thorough account of Chinese economic debates does not yet exist.[2] Luckily, Sun's biography is particularly rich.

Soviet Training and United Front Experience

Sun Yefang was born in Wuxi, Jiangsu, on October 24, 1908.[3] His father was a clerical employee in a small silk factory, and though the family was "of modest means," they were able to send young Sun to

[2]A start has been made. See Cyril Lin, "The Reinstatement of Economics in China Today," *The China Quarterly* 85 (March 1981):1–48; *JPRS Economic Affairs*, February 15, 1980, translation of Sun Shangqing et al., "An Appraisal of the Discussion on Socialist Commodities and Prices in China's Economic Circles in the Past 30 Years," originally appearing in *Jingji yanjiu* [Economic Research] 10 (1979); and Joint Editorial Boards of *Jingji yanjiu* and *Jingjixue dongtai* [Trends in Economics], eds., *Jianguo yilai zhengzhi jingjixue zhongyao wenti zhenglun* [Major Debates in Political Economy since 1949] (Beijing, Caizheng Jingji, 1981). The major drawback of these works, each excellent in its own terms, is that they fail to connect theoretical debates with real developments in China or related discussions in other socialist countries.

[3]Sun Yefang is a pseudonym: his real name is Xue Eguo. The account of Sun's life is drawn primarily from Deng Jiarong,"Woguo jingjixuezhe Sun Yefang" [Chinese Economist Sun Yefang], *Dagong bao* [Impartial Daily] (Hong Kong), June 30, 1981, p. 15; July 1, p. 19; July 2, p. 15; and July 3, p. 13; and He Jianzhang, "Sun Yefang," *Jingjixue dongtai* 2 (1981):37–40.

school with the financial assistance of friends and relatives. By the end of 1924, Sun had already made two decisions that set him on his lifelong course: he had joined the Socialist Youth Corps and subsequently the Communist Party, serving as the secretary of the Wuxi Party branch; and he had begun studying economics at the Wuxi Industry-Commerce Middle School. Sun's entrance into the Party was doubly precocious: not only was he only sixteen years old, but the Party itself was still in its infancy, having enrolled fewer than 1,000 members by the spring of 1925.[4] Sun was sent to Moscow in 1925, where he enrolled in Sun Yatsen University to study economics. He graduated in 1927 but remained in Moscow until 1930 working as a translator at the school, renamed the University of the Toilers of the East.

Sun received a Marxist education from a very early age. Moreover, he was in Moscow during the period of the New Economic Policy, a complex and intellectually stimulating time. On the one hand, Russian economists were making seminal contributions in several areas of economic thought, and the Soviet "industrialization debate" raised fundamental questions about the nature of socialist development policy; on the other hand, this was also the period when Stalinist orthodoxy was beginning to be imposed in the field of economics, and doctrinal uniformity gradually extinguished fertile discussion. What effect did these powerful intellectual currents have on the young student? One might suppose that Sun later introduced into China ideas that had their origin in these rather open discussions.

In fact, it appears that Sun was influenced very little by the diverse currents in Soviet economics of the 1920s. By his own testimony, Sun was simply too young, and too accepting of the rapidly forming Stalinist orthodoxy taught him in school, to have been receptive to the heterodox opinions then still circulating.[5] In later works, Sun occasionally refers to Soviet economists of this period, but always to criticize some of the fundamental tenets of his own orthodox education, particu-

---

[4]Lyman P. Van Slyke, *Enemies and Friends: The United Front in Chinese Communist History* (Stanford: Stanford University Press, 1967), p. 22. Large-scale recruitment into the Party began after the May 30th incident in 1925.

[5]Sun Yefang, *Shehuizhuyi jingji de ruogan lilun wenti* [Some Theoretical Problems of Socialist Economics] (Beijing: Renmin, 1979), p. 290. This work collects Sun's published and unpublished works from the period 1956–1964, as well as three short essays from 1977–78. It is the basic source for the development of Sun's views. However, it must be used with some caution since some earlier works have been edited to remove references to Soviet economists and details of practical policy disputes.

larly the "natural economy" standpoint of the war communism of
1918–1920, recapitulated in Stalinist theory. In later years he came to
see this view—echoed in the assumptions of the Great Leap Forward in
China—as a particularly pernicious influence on the economic theory
of socialism.

According to the natural economy standpoint, a fully developed
socialist economy will resemble a "natural" economy in that all goods
will be directly distributed to users. Money and markets will be elimi-
nated, and political economy will be replaced by engineering solutions
to production problems. Sun came to see the natural economy
viewpoint as the result of a misplaced emotional hostility toward money and economic calculation, a hostility which was itself the result of
the relatively low levels of economic development in both Russia and
China as they embarked on socialist construction.[6] Although Sun attacked this standpoint consistently from the 1950s until the end of his
life, there is no evidence that he developed these criticisms at an early
stage of his education, or that he shared more than an indirect affinity
for views associated with Bukharin.

Sun's early education in the Soviet Union clearly had another, more
direct impact on his development. In the first place, because Sun left
China at such an early age, he never received a thorough classical
Chinese education. Compared with the other intellectuals discussed in
this volume, Sun was old enough to be a revolutionary intellectual of
the May Fourth generation; but Sun's approach to problems does not
spring from a particularly Chinese sense of predicament, nor does his
prose reflect the penchant for classical Chinese allusion that sometimes
marks the writing of his contemporaries. Instead, Sun's writing is
relatively technocratic, and influenced by Western (Russian) linguistic
patterns. Sun's stay in Moscow removed him from distinctly Chinese
intellectual influences and apprenticed him to a distinct tradition of
Marxist scholarship. Sun's intellectual background is Marxism, and
more particularly Soviet Marxism; in this respect, Sun is more like
younger intellectuals who joined the Party in the war years.[7] Moreover,
in later years, as Soviet economics regained the diversity it had lost
under Stalin, Sun was to show himself thoroughly familiar with different trends of thought within Russian economics. This familiarity is also
part of the legacy of Sun's early education.

[6]See Sun Yefang, *Some Theoretical Problems*, pp. 175–78; 140; 150.
[7]I am indebted to Dick Kraus for helping me clarify this point.

Sun returned to Shanghai from Moscow in 1930, at approximately the same time the "28 Bolsheviks" were also returning to take up the leadership of the Chinese Communist Party, though there is some evidence that Sun was already out of favor with their leader, Wang Ming.[8] Sun was initially assigned to the practical task of labor organizing in Shanghai, under the overall leadership of Liu Shaoqi. This was the period when the Party apparatus stressed the development of independent Communist labor unions to the exclusion of other kinds of activity.[9] Sun worked with rickshaw drivers, even pulling a rickshaw himself for a period. However, as the Party gradually moved to the advocacy of united front tactics with the Nationalists against Japanese imperialism, Sun was transferred to propaganda work. After the "September 18 (1931) incident," when Shenyang was occupied by the Japanese, Sun began writing for the *The China Forum* (*Zhongguo luntan bao*), edited by Agnes Smedley. Sun's writings stressed the difficult lives of urban workers. In 1933, he moved on to participate in the formation of the most effective front group the Communist Party was to establish in intellectual circles, the Chinese Rural Economy Research Society.

The Rural Economy Research Society was organized by Chen Hanseng, an American-trained economist of considerable ability and an underground Party member. It included as active members men who were destined to be among the most influential economists in the People's Republic, such as Xue Muqiao, Luo Gengmo, and Qian Junrui, as well as Sun himself.

Several of these men, including Chen Hanseng, Sun, and Sun's distant cousin Xue Muqiao, as well as the famous rural anthropologist Fei Xiaotong, came from the same area in Jiangsu. Thus this group may well have shared emotional ties and ways of viewing things. Circumstantial evidence suggests, too, that they had the sympathetic ear of Party elder Chen Yun, who came from the same locale and has been close to Xue Muqiao in particular. Xue and Sun both achieved special

[8]During the Cultural Revolution Sun was accused of being a follower of this group of Soviet-oriented Communists. Deng Jiarong, going to some length to deny this charge in his account of Sun's life, recounts Wang Ming's suspicion that Sun was heading a "Jiangsu faction" among Chinese students in Moscow.

[9]See Van Slyke, *Enemies and Friends*, pp. 42–56. Van Slyke spends some time searching for the beginning of Party commitment to united front policies and is unable to find unambiguous evidence before 1935. However, the career of Sun and others indicates that Party members were being instructed to engage in united-front-type propaganda work as early as 1932.

prominence in the early 1960s and in the post-Mao period, when Chen oversaw the economy. Nevertheless, there does not appear to have been a consistent, tightly knit faction in economic work based on these associations. For the most part, this group passed through quite different careers.[10]

For nearly ten years in the 1930s, the Rural Economy Research Society published *Rural China* (*Zhongguo nongcun*), publicizing the plight of China's peasantry, while simultaneously propagandizing for a united opposition to imperialism as the crucial first stage of social revolution. This influential journal—to which Sun was a regular contributor—did much to lay out the theoretical justification for a policy of collaboration with the Nationalist Party, a policy which was an integral part of the strategy that ultimately brought the Communist Party to power.

Sun Yefang made important contributions to the elaboration of the theory of the united front in China, which itself was based on the writings of Lenin, Bukharin, and Mao. The core argument rested on the assertion that China was not a capitalist country, but rather a semifeudal, semicolonial economy. Penetration of China by powerful merchants and industrialists backed by imperialist powers meant that indigenous Chinese capitalism had had little chance to develop. Instead, Chinese "capitalists" were actually compradors and collaborators with foreign merchants, a dependent, stunted version of a bourgeoisie; and this same political structure also served to prop up the "feudal" landlord class, which otherwise would have collapsed under the impact of growing bourgeois influence. The conclusion was that native Chinese entrepreneurs and intellectuals were not the primary enemy of social revolution, since they also suffered from the oppression (and competition) of imperialism and international capitalism. Chinese leftists should therefore ally with as large a portion of the nation as

[10]Chen Hanseng attended Pomona College, subsequently doing graduate work at the University of California and Harvard. Author of a number of high quality studies of Chinese village economies in the 1930s, Chen achieved an additional measure of influence in the United States through his affiliation with the Institute for Pacific Relations. See Zhang Xichang, "Chen Hansheng," *Jingjixue dongtai* 9 (1980):36–38; and John N. Thomas, *The Institute of Pacific Relations* (Seattle: University of Washington Press, 1974), pp. 22, 26, 83–84. The surviving members of the society (nearly all living in Beijing) assembled in 1983 to inaugurate a Sun Yefang prize for economic work upon the suggestion of Qian Junrui. See *Jingjixue dongtai* 8 (1983):11–12. Nina Halpern has pointed out to me that Red Guard publications charged during the Cultural Revolution that the Rural Economy Research Society *did* form a faction.

possible to oppose the primary enemy—imperialism—all the while maintaining their separate identity and principles.[11]

In the course of thus propagating the "Party line," Sun argued with considerable force and subtlety against alternative approaches to China's problems. With equal vigor he attacked "reformist" approaches and "leftist" (or Trotskyist) solutions. His analysis drew the conclusion that the dominant present task was to struggle for "bourgeois democracy," and he argued that although the peasantry was the main revolutionary force in China, it must moderate its demands (and call for rent reduction rather than land redistribution) and unite with all "national" forces.[12] It is reasonable to link Sun's views as expressed in the 1930s with those he advanced later: he consistently advocated cooperation with bourgeois intellectuals and the removal of obstacles to capitalist development as a transitional stage in the building of socialism, while retaining a commitment to Marxist categories of analysis and communist goals. While these views were the Party line during the 1930s, being elaborated by Mao Zedong, among others, it could be argued that Sun continued to hold these beliefs after others—notably Mao—had abandoned them, out of a commitment to a moderate version of Marxist socialism. In any case, the argument put forward by Sun and others at this time was extremely effective in encouraging China's intellectuals to abandon the Nationalist Party and collaborate with the Communist Party, a shift of forces that stood the Communist Party in good stead around 1949.[13]

In 1937, with the outbreak of war, many in the group of economists in Shanghai dispersed to different parts of China. Sun stayed in Shanghai doing underground work until 1940; he was then ordered to Yan'an, but on the way he was diverted to the northern Jiangsu base area where the New Fourth Army, under Liu Shaoqi and Chen Yi, was establishing itself. For the next nine years, Sun lived the life of the guerrilla, though his responsibilities remained those of the intellectual and economist. He lectured in the guerrilla school, and his primary job

---

[11]Sun Yefang, "Caizheng ziben de tongzhi yu qianzibenzhuyi de shengchan guanxi" [The Dominance of Finance Capital and Precapitalist Relations of Production], *Zhongguo nongcun* [Rural China] 1, 12 (1935):15–50; "Minzu wenti he nongmin wenti" [The National Question and the Peasant Question], *Zhongguo nongcun* 2, 7(1936):23–30; and " 'Zibenzhuyi wansui' he 'Dadao zibenzhuyi' " ["Long Live Capitalism" and "Down With Capitalism"], *Zhongguo nongcun* 2, 11 (1936):35–41.

[12]Sun Yefang, "The National Question and the Peasant Question," pp. 25, 28–29.

[13]See Suzanne Pepper, *The Civil War in China: The Political Struggle, 1945–49* (Berkeley: University of California Press, 1978).

was organizing illicit economic contacts between the Communist base area and merchants in Shanghai. By this period, if not before, Sun had come to the favorable attention of Liu Shaoqi, who praised him for what was to become Sun's hallmark—his close attention to theroetical, not just practical, economic research.[14]

Sun's practical work in Shanghai continued and broadened after the Communist takeover in 1949. He was made head of the heavy industrial bureau of the East China Military Commission, taking charge of the confiscation and management of the heavy industrial enterprises owned by capitalists linked with the Nationalists and by Japanese nationals and collaborators. Subsequently Sun served under Wang Daohan as vice-head of the East China Industrial Bureau, a post he held until 1954. During this period, Communist success in maintaining and expanding economic activity in Shanghai played a crucial role in the ability to consolidate power in the early years of the regime. For the first years of the People's Republic, the city of Shanghai alone contributed fully one-third of the infant government's budgetary revenues. In 1954, Sun was transferred to Beijing to serve under Xue Muqiao as deputy director of the State Statistical Bureau, and he was to remain in Beijing thereafter. Not surprisingly, these activities kept Sun quite busy, and we have no writings from him dating from this period. Sun began to write again for public consumption in 1956, but by then Communist parties all over the world were undergoing unprecedented changes, and the Chinese Party was no exception. These changes brought Sun Yefang to national prominence as an economic theoretician for the first time.

The "Law of Value" and Economic Reform

De-Stalinization in the Soviet Union shook the socialist bloc to its foundations. After the Twentieth Congress of the Soviet Communist Party in February 1956, the prestige of the Stalinist model was weakened severely and it became possible to consider alternative paths to the development of socialism. In economic circles, de-Stalinization kicked off bloc-wide controversy over the economic institutions appropriate to a socialist society, while at the same time making the possibility of

[14]During this period, Sun must have worked directly with Liu Shaoqi for Liu wrote to Sun (who was then using the pseudonym Song Liang) agreeing with his suggestion that greater stress should be given to theoretical work. See Liu Shaoqi, "Reply to Comrade Song Liang" (July 13, 1941), *Selected Works of Liu Shaoqi* (Beijing: Foreign Languages Press, 1984), pp. 217–21.

diverse national forms of socialism seem both legitimate and desirable. Nowhere were these possibilities seized on more rapidly than in China, for China was in the midst of a period of fundamental change.

During the winter of 1955–56, China had completed the nationalization of industry and the collectivization of agriculture. It had thus taken the fundamental steps toward the creation of a Soviet-style economic system just at the moment when the legitimacy of that system was thrown open to question for the first time. Until 1956, China's economic planners had operated a "mixed" economy, in which a large and growing state sector coexisted with a significant capitalist industrial sector as well as an agricultural sector based on private, small-holder production. During this period, economic planners had had little choice but to operate with a combination of direct administrative controls and indirect economic measures such as price, purchasing contracts, and taxation policies. Although the government had possessed and used numerous "extra-economic" means to force capitalist entrepreneurs to comply with its wishes, it could not simply ignore questions of market equilibrium, appropriate incentives, or proper prices. Inattention to these questions would have caused serious disruptions in economic production. Moreover, the legitimacy of markets, money relations, and price policy could hardly have been repudiated during this period, since the social system was recognized to be in the transitional phase of "New Democracy" (which implied a mixed economy), with the construction of socialism still lying in the future. With the speed-up of collectivization of agriculture in 1955 and of nationalization of industry in 1956, socialism, it would seem, had been created virtually overnight. And yet exactly what type of socialism would be most appropriate for Chinese conditions was still undecided.

The first response of the leadership to the new liberalism in international Communist politics was to initiate a campaign against "reckless advance." The target of this slogan was the overly rapid pace of economic construction that for a few months in early 1956 followed collectivization—a miniature "leap forward" that had strained the nation's resources, and particularly supplies of grain and other consumer goods. Although this opposition to "leaping" would later be criticized by Mao, a period of relaxed controls in all areas of domestic policy unfolded, continuing through the rest of 1956 and the Hundred Flowers period in the first half of 1957. In the field of economics, a number of pragmatic proposals were advanced by Chen Yun, designed to let markets play a somewhat greater role in the production and distribution of consumer goods. Reform of the economic system was on the agenda of the top political leadership, and China's economists were called on to explore the economic principles that would guide the design of this reform.

Chinese economists, including Sun Yefang, were in agreement with economists in other socialist countries in identifying the "law of value" as one of the principles of socialist economics that should serve as a basis for changes in the economic system. In Poland, in a speech soon well known in other socialist countries, Oskar Lange discussed a dichotomy between administrative and economic methods of directing a socialist economy and advocated reliance on the latter. In practice, this meant using "value" categories like prices and taxation as "economic levers" to direct economic activity. In the Soviet Union, discussions that had been carried on among economists underground for many years burst into the open in December 1956 with publication of an open debate on the "law of value" under socialism.[15] At the same time, Sun wrote two articles on the subject. With their publication in early 1957, Sun emerged as the most prominent advocate of the law of value in China. In his most famous article, "Place Planning and Statistics on the Basis of the Law of Value," Sun criticized voluntarism, a clear critical reference to the "reckless advance" of 1956.[16] To the day of his death, Sun remained identified with this advocacy of the law of value, arguing in later years that it was the most fundamental of all economic laws under socialism.

Yet the law of value remains one of the most confused—and confusing—topics ever discussed in the socialist world. Years of sometimes heated debate eventually served to demonstrate that socialist economists were operating with so many different and contradictory definitions of this "law" that it was impossible to come to any real agreement on its proper role.[17] Sun's position can best be understood by placing it within a range of possible interpretations of this elusive law.

[15] Maurice Dobb, "The Revival of Theoretical Discussion among Soviet Economists," in *Capitalism, Development and Planning* (New York: International, 1967), pp. 140–63, especially p. 150; also, George Feiwel, *The Soviet Quest for Economic Efficiency* (New York: Praeger, 1967), pp. 158–68.

[16] "Ba jihua yu tongji fangzai guilü de jichu shang," in *Some Theoretical Problems*, pp. 1–14. See also *Major Debates*, pp. 165–69.

[17] The best survey of this question, emphasizing both its importance and the incomplete and contradictory nature of the debate, is Wlodzimierz Brus, *The Market in a Socialist Economy* (London: Routledge & Kegan Paul, 1972), originally published in Polish in 1961.

One extreme interpretation of the law of value has been advanced by economists who hold that all production in a socialist economy is production for the market, i.e., it is "commodity production." In the marketplace, prices perform an essential role in allocating goods, including the crucial investment goods that will determine the direction of the economy's future development. Therefore, if planners wish to enforce their priorities on society they must do so by manipulating prices and taxes, much as Chinese planners did on a pragmatic basis before 1956. The ideas that Oskar Lange advanced in 1956 were close to this conception, and a bold and independent expression of similar ideas was put forward around this time in China by Gu Zhun, an economist with experience in the Ministry of Finance in Shanghai. In Gu's formulation, planners would no longer allocate supplies and issue orders to enterprises, but should rather guide their activity through manipulation of economic incentives.[18] But Gu's path-breaking ideas found few supporters in China. Another interpretation of the law of value, more popular in China in 1957, held that the law of value played a limited role in regulating exchanges between the state-owned sector and the agricultural collectives, as well as coordinating the population's demand for consumer goods with available supplies.[19] The law of value was therefore something that planners had to "make use of," but within the state sector planners would make decisions independently of the influence of the law of value.[20]

What these two views, otherwise quite opposed to each other, have in common is the acceptance of a certain dichotomy between planning through administrative orders and the market mechanisms operating through the law of value. It was this dichotomy that Sun rejected. In Sun's view, the law of value continued to operate within the planned sector of the state-owned economy. To Sun, this meant that planners had an absolute responsibility to account accurately for the true social costs of all production. If planners neglected a detailed and accurate accounting of production costs, economic growth would be retarded and the development of the economy would suffer from inefficient deci-

[18]"Shilun shehuizhuyi zhidu xia de shangpin shengchan he jiazhi guilü" [A Tentative Discussion of Commodity Production and the Law of Value in a Socialist System], *Jingji yanjiu* 3 (1957). This article is discussed by Cyril Lin at length.

[19]This was also the position advanced by Stalin in 1953 in his *Economic Problems of Socialism in the U.S.S.R.*

[20]See, for example, Xue Muqiao, "Zailun jihua jingji yu jiazhi guilü" [Once Again on the Planned Economy and the Law of Value], *Jihua jingji* [Planned Economy] 2 (1957).

sion making. Sun's stress on the law of value in this period was thus part of an attack on arbitrariness in planning, and an assertion that planners are subject to immutable economic principles. However, since Sun did not specify the mechanisms through which the law of value exerts control over planners (except for efficiency losses in the long run), his writings on this subject have an almost moralistic cast. That is, if planners act in an arbitrary fashion, the law of value will take revenge on them by depriving them of the economic results they so urgently desire. In a companion piece to his famous article, "On the Gross Value of Output," Sun developed a similar argument regarding the types of targets, or success indicators, that are used to evaluate enterprise performance.[21] He argued that judging enterprises by their total output value causes them to neglect costs and to produce unneeded and substandard goods in order to fulfill their plan targets. In this case, Sun's argument was on stronger grounds, for he could specify the process through which the law of value affects economic outcomes: enterprises react in certain definable and inefficient ways to the requirement that they fulfill targets specified in terms of total output value.

Sun laid such stress on the law of value because he saw it as the guiding principle for the whole range of activity in a socialist economy. Yet precisely because its operation was seen as being pervasive, the question of what form the economic management system should take was not directly raised. Gu Zhun linked the law of value directly to the operation of markets and thus called for rapid steps toward the creation of a kind of market socialism. But Sun Yefang denied that the law of value was necessarily related to the operation of markets (to the "commodity" nature of production); he could therefore continue to uphold the role of planning and did not feel compelled to argue for the introduction of markets. In effect, Sun argued that, if only costs, prices, and enterprise incentives could be set perfectly, then a socialist economy could be operated without inefficiency, either through planning or through markets.

Sun's views on the law of value were identical to those advanced by a group of Soviet economists headed by I. Malyshev, V. Sobol, and Z. Atlas.[22] Not accidentally, Malyshev was also Sun's direct counterpart

---

[21]"Cong 'zhongchanzi' tanqi," in *Some Theoretical Problems*, pp. 24–41.

[22]Richard W. Judy, "The Economists," in H. Gordon Skilling and Franklyn Griffiths, eds., *Interest Groups in Soviet Politics* (Princeton: Princeton University Press, 1971), p. 234n; Gregory Grossman, "Gold and the Sword," in H. Rosovsky, ed., *Industrialization in Two Systems* (New York: Wiley, 1966), pp. 211–12, 229.

in the bureaucracy, serving as the vice-head of the Soviet Central Statistical Administration, with which Sobol was also affiliated. Sun had visited the Soviet Union as head of a statistics delegation in mid-1956, and he had extensive contact with these men, particularly Sobol. In early 1958, Sobol was in turn invited to lecture in China by Sun and the two had extensive discussions on a broad range of topics.[23] Sun's affiliation with the views of these Soviet economists raises two important questions. The first has to do with the source of Sun's ideas, and the second with the implications of these ideas.

The ideas of Malyshev and Sobol should not be taken as representative of a Soviet as opposed to Chinese interpretation of economics. Though these men were influential, their viewpoint remained a minority one within the Soviet Union. Sun's adherence to views like theirs should be taken not as a sign of Soviet origin for Sun's thought, but rather as a sign that Sun was participating in a general discussion of economic principles that cut across national boundaries and engaged economists throughout the socialist world. Indeed, it is most likely that Sun contributed to the development of these ideas, and it might be more appropriate to speak of a Malyshev-Sobol-Sun Yefang school of thought. In this respect, Sun's early education in Russia may have been important in giving him a familiarity with Russian intellectual life that allowed him to locate and draw on theoretical developments there that were congenial to his own thinking. In this perspective, if Sun emerges as somewhat less original as a theorist, he nevertheless appears very much a cosmopolitan thinker, in touch with intellectual currents in the socialist world as a whole. At the same time, Sun and nearly all the Chinese economists advocating a greater role for the law of value had undergone a common apprenticeship: the socialist takeover of Shanghai industry. The difficulties of managing the sprawling but economically vital industrial base in Shanghai—the most developed and most capitalist area in China—had convinced these economists of the impossibility of subjugating all market forces to the direction of the central plan. Thus, Sun and others combined this uniquely Chinese experience with the intellectual currents abroad in the socialist world in an attempt to guide a Chinese program of economic system reform.

Clearly, the positions advanced by the Malyshev-Sobol-Sun Yefang group left many questions unresolved. In the Soviet Union, Malyshev

---

[23]Dong Furen, *Lun Sun Yefang de shehuizhuyi jingji lilun* [On Sun Yefang's Theory of Socialist Economics] (Wuhan: Wuhan University Press, 1983), pp. 3–5. I am indebted to Nina Halpern for bringing this work to my attention.

and Sobol attempted to develop their ideas by advocating the principle of "production prices," an advocacy joined by Sun Yefang by 1959. The concept of production prices, which later became the focus of controversy between Sun Yefang and his opponents, draws from the analysis of capitalist production put forward by Marx in the third volume of *Das Kapital*. Prices formed according to the production price principle would include a uniform rate of return on capital, and their advocacy in a socialist economy is extremely controversial since it seems to imply that capital, and not just labor, can produce "value."[24] For Malyshev and Sobol, as for Sun Yefang later on, production prices were a concrete way to implement their views on the law of value. By charging accurately for capital, planners would come closer to the ideal of full accounting for social costs that was required for the proper functioning of the law of value in a planned economy. Yet even such advocacy did not directly address the question of what type of economic management system is appropriate to socialism, for production prices can be regarded as an appropriate pricing system either under planning or under a market-type system. In the Soviet Union, debate progressed gradually beyond the question of price-setting to the problem of the economic management system as a whole, and in particular to the role of the individual enterprise within that system.[25] At this point the ambiguities remaining in the Malyshev-Sobol school became apparent and the group of production-price advocates split into two groups, one favoring thorough marketizing reforms and the other advocating increasingly sophisticated mathematical planning techniques, a planners' "computopia."[26] Although Sun was eventually to tend toward the first group, the logical development of the argument was interrupted in China by the tremendous upheavals associated with the Great Leap Forward. In 1956–57, these ambiguities remained unresolved in Sun's writings. Yet he had established himself as a major Chinese economic theoretician, and he clearly stood with the moderate camp in the concrete deliberations of the period. Events were soon to bring Sun to the center of controversy and to force him to address the ambiguities in his position and the policy implications.

[24]See Francis Seton, "The Question of Ideological Obstacles to Rational Price Setting in Communist Countries," in Alan Aboucher, ed., *The Socialist Price Mechanism* (Durham: Duke University Press, 1977).

[25]See Charles Bettelheim, *The Transition to Socialist Economy* (Atlantic Highlands, N.J.: Humanities Press, 1975), p. 185.

[26]Judy, "The Economists," pp. 234, 238–39, 246–47, shows changing opinion groups by institutional affiliation.

Sun's Response to "Leaping"

Throughout 1957, work proceeded on economic reform in China, culminating in a government document of November 1957 that reduced the power of central planners and gave industrial enterprises the right to retain a portion of their profits. In mid-1957, Sun was appointed acting director of the Economic Research Institute, a position to which he was ideally suited, combining as he did familiarity with diverse trends of thought in the socialist world with a detailed knowledge of Chinese conditions.

But by the winter, the political atmosphere in China was undergoing a decisive shift, and under the direct influence of Mao, the earlier period of relaxed control was brought to a close. The slogan opposing "reckless advance" was repudiated, setting the stage for the Great Leap Forward. In intellectual circles, restrictions on discussion rapidly led to attacks on non-Party intellectuals. According to one account, Sun barely escaped being attacked for taking a position in statistical theory that contravened one of Mao's dicta.[27] In spite of this close call, however, Sun—an experienced and loyal Party member—managed to survive and even prosper at this time.

In 1958, the Research Institute was brought more directly into the policy-making arena by having it report both to the State Planning Commission headed by Li Fuchun and to the Academy of Sciences, to which it was directly subordinate.[28] In a difficult political atmosphere, but now having direct contact with policy makers, Sun continued discreetly but forcefully to advocate his ideas. There is little question that Sun opposed the excesses of the Leap, although his position at its inception is not known since only one document is available from the late 1957-early 1959 period.

A talk by Sun in March 1958 (not published at the time) at a meeting of economists held to commemorate the first anniversary of Mao's speech "On the Correct Handling of Contradictions among the People" indirectly but clearly revealed his negative opinion of the

[27]Huang Hai, "Sun Yefang dui tongji renyuan de zhufu" [Sun Yefang's Exhortation to Statistics Personnel], *Tongji yanjiu* [Statistics Research] 6 (1983):18.

[28]Nina Halpern, "China's Economic Decision-Making Specialists' Participation and Party Attitudes," unpublished manuscript, March 1984. I am indebted to Professor Halpern for permission to cite this work. Halpern shows in this work that new channels were established in 1958 to permit economists' input into policy making. I find her demonstration convincing, but I differ slightly in my interpretation of these developments.

Leap.[29] Sun began with fullsome praise for Mao's philosophical contributions, but he soon shifted the focus of discussion to his own concerns. Mao's stress on contradiction is brilliant, Sun declared, and in economics the primary contradiction is between people and things, manifested in the struggle to raise the productivity of labor. While overtly praising many aspects of the Leap, Sun came to the crux of his argument: "To divorce oneself from economics in order to talk about politics, and substitute the mass line and 'politics in command' for objective economic laws . . . is not only philosophical idealism; it is also lazy economic thinking." Ultimately, this single sentence of pungent criticism outweighed the paragraphs of praise in Sun's talk.

The contents of Sun's talk certainly would suggest that in his contributions to an April 1959 conference on economic theory, and to a draft speech that Bo Yibo, as part of his responsibilities for industry, planned to present at the summer Lushan Conference, Sun would have strongly recommended reining in the Leap. The fact that Bo decided not to present the speech once he perceived the highly charged political atmosphere at Lushan tends to confirm this. Sun's views were indirectly criticized by Mao at Lushan, however, through another set of circumstances. Two researchers from the institute contributed to an investigation report by the Chinese Academy of Sciences that was highly critical of the public dining halls set up during the Leap. Mao labeled the report rightist and the authors were demoted, not to be rehabilitated until several years later. Sun's response to this development was characteristic, revealing his strong personal integrity. He said that although the report had been circulated without his review, "If I had read the report then, I would have agreed with what it said." None of these documents is yet available, no doubt reflecting the sensitivity of this period even in the 1980s.[30]

Yet another set of circumstances hints at Sun's critical attitude toward the Leap. After Lushan, when Zhang Wentian, general secretary

[29]"Yao dongde jingji bixu xue dian zhexue" [It's Necessary to Study a Little Philosophy in Order to Understand Economics], in *Some Theoretical Problems*, pp. 42–69, quote from p. 58.

[30]Kenneth Lieberthal, *A Research Guide to Central Party and Government Meetings in China, 1949–1975* (White Plains, N.Y.: International Arts and Sciences Press, 1976), p. 137, discusses the April conferences; Roderick MacFarquhar, *The Origins of the Cultural Revolution, 2: The Great Leap Forward 1958–1960* (New York: Columbia University Press, 1983), p. 218, discusses Bo's speech; *JPRS Economic Affairs*, no. 315, translates Lin Yushu, "Shoulders of Iron Bearing Justice," originally published in *Guangming ribao*, January 17, 1983.

of the Party in the mid-1930s and vice-foreign minister in the 1950s, was demoted for his joint attack on the Leap with Peng Dehuai, he joined the Economic Research Institute where Sun used his talents in a serious manner. This development may have reflected former personal ties, since Zhang is also from the Shanghai region, was close to Chen Yun (who introduced him to Party membership in 1925), and was in Moscow at the same time as Sun. The Cultural Revolution charges against Sun for alleged ties with the "28 Bolsheviks," of whom Zhang was one, may have pointed to this relationship.[31]

By 1960, it had become apparent that the Great Leap Forward, combined with drought and flooding, had led China into an unprecedented economic disaster. Beginning in 1961, China's planners developed a series of emergency measures to cope with the crisis situation. Millions of urban workers were sent back to the countryside to grow food, in an attempt to ameliorate the famine conditions that had developed across China. Investment projects were terminated in an attempt to divert resources back to consumption, and factories across China, unable to get raw materials from the devastated agricultural sector, shut down or suspended production. Suddenly, central planners were open to any ideas that might help them to deal with the crisis situation: ideological respectability counted little.

In economic circles, this situation led to a revival of the relatively free discussion of economic principles that had been cut off during the Leap. There was general agreement that the economic collapse was due to a failure to respect "objective economic laws" and to understand what these laws implied. From Sun Yefang's perspective, he had been vindicated in arguing that the law of value was a principle that planners had to take into account. During 1961 and 1962, a relatively free discussion unfolded in economic circles, and particularly at the Economic Research Institute. However, whereas in 1956–57 important parts of this discussion had been carried on publicly, this was not the case in 1961–62. Open discussion might have revealed to the outside world the magnitude of the disaster that had befallen China as well as the widespread disagreement about how to repair the damage, and so discussion was confined to internal channels. It is only with the publication in 1979 of Sun Yefang's internal reports from this period that we can reconstruct the positions that were advanced during these years.[32]

[31]Lin Yushu, "Shoulders of Iron," pp. 48–49, discusses Zhang at the institute.

[32]Ironically, these were preserved because they were circulated during the Cultural Revolution to aid in the criticism of Sun.

These reports show Sun Yefang at the center of creative theorizing, boldly advancing the basic elements of an entirely independent conception of a proper socialist economic management system.

Inside: Sun's Proposals for Reforming the System

From 1961 to 1963, Sun Yefang wrote a series of reports and delivered several talks on his ideas about economics. From the very first of these reports to which we now have access, it is apparent that Sun's thinking had developed considerably since 1957. It is as if Sun, recognizing that his advocacy of the law of value led inevitably to the question of what economic management system was appropriate for China, had spent three years trying to resolve the problem. Sun began by stating that the question of enterprise authority was the central question of the entire management system of the national economy.[33] He then proceeded to sketch out a program for drastically expanding the scope of independent authority that the industrial enterprise should exercise.

The cornerstone of Sun's approach was to divide the activity of the enterprise into two parts. One part he called "expanded reproduction," following Marxist terminology; a Western economist might term this "net new investment." This portion of economic activity would continue to be directly and entirely controlled by central planners. That is, all decisions about new factories and major expansion of existing factories would be made by central planners. The other portion of economic activity Sun labeled "simple reproduction"; a Western economist might describe this as current operating decisions, plus replacement investment. Sun suggested that all responsibility over simple reproduction be granted to the individual enterprise.

Even so, it is clear that Sun did not actually advocate turning the factories loose to produce whatever they wanted. Instead, he called for planners to fix—permanently—the type of output a factory could produce, as well as that factory's suppliers and customers. Moreover, central planners would continue to set prices for virtually all products. These obligations would cement the enterprise firmly into the edifice of the planned economy but allow it to control fully all remaining decisions. Thus, the enterprise would decide on the basis of contracts it signed with its suppliers and customers how much output was to be produced and which production techniques and raw materials were to

[33]*Some Theoretical Problems*, pp. 138–42.

be used. Factories were also to be given greater financial independence, in particular by allowing them control over their own depreciation allowances, so that they could manage their own fixed capital as they saw fit, replacing and upgrading equipment as the need arose and financial resources permitted. The primary responsibility of the enterprise to the state would be its obligation to turn over profit to the state budget. The more profitable an enterprise was, the more successful it should be judged to be, as long as it had not deviated from the prices and production relationships set by the planners.[34]

This was a bold and original program. It is similar, in its stress on the division between simple and expanded reproduction, to the theoretical proposals being developed at about the same time in Poland by Wlodzimierz Brus, proposals which in turn served as the inspiration for Hungarian economic reforms begun in 1968. Yet, in this case, there are no indications that Sun was directly influenced by Brus's ideas. On the contrary, every indication is that Sun developed these ideas completely independently, and as such he can be credited with at least joint authorship of one of the most important and interesting theoretical developments in socialist economics in the post-Stalin era. Ultimately, Sun's claim to be remembered as an independent theoretician rests on this bold and yet fairly simple proposal.

At the same time, there are a number of serious problems that remained to be worked out in this proposal. For example, the whole framework assumes that relationships between enterprises are regular and repeated, so that they can be established by central planners. Yet at the same time, enterprises are given responsibility for a portion of investment (replacement and modernization investment). To carry out this investment, which by its very nature is intermittent and irregular, the enterprise must purchase goods from other state enterprises with which it does not normally do business, and which have also had their coordination relationships established by central planners. If enterprises are not operating freely in a marketplace, how can they select the appropriate suppliers for their investment projects? Furthermore, if enterprises are linked to single suppliers and customers, how can they avoid being subject to various kinds of pressures created by the monopolistic relationships that confront them on either end of their production process?

More fundamentally, Sun did not fully confront the relationship

[34]Ibid., pp. 145–46, 277.

between his proposal and the individual material interests of the workers in a given enterprise. Enterprises were to produce profits because they were instructed to do so by central planners, not because it was to their benefit to do so.[35] Furthermore, because Sun continued to hold that the operation of the law of value was not directly linked to markets (commodity production), he did not specifically advocate a greater role for markets in determining what would actually be produced. As a result, he seemed to be advocating a form of market socialism without markets, and it is extremely difficult to understand the relationships among social needs, planners' preferences, and enterprise activity that would be implied by this proposal. However, it is difficult to hold Sun Yefang totally responsible for these failings. Answers to these questions, if such answers exist, required a prolonged period of public discussion and years of practical experience: they could not be provided by the genius of a solitary individual. This discussion and practical experience were not forthcoming in China. Instead, Sun Yefang's theorizing was cut short, and he was never able to address the further questions raised by his proposal for economic reform.

Outside: The 1960s "Production Prices" Debate

While Sun Yefang was advancing his ideas in internal memoranda and closed-door sessions with other economists, a closely related discussion, on a much more restricted topic, was developing in the pages of publicly circulated journals. This topic was the question of production prices, which were mentioned above in the discussion of the ideas of Malyshev and Sun Yefang. Sun did not publish any articles during this period: although there is one pseudonymous article from this period included in his collected works, it was written by a protégé, not by Sun himself.[36] Sun had advocated production prices, however, in an article published in 1959, and so he could be identified generally with the positions advanced.[37] Moreover, the authors of the articles on production prices were mainly young economists who would have been widely

---

[35]Ibid., pp. 258–67, also p. 3, where he criticizes this shortcoming but accepts it as his genuine position at the time.

[36]The article now in *Some Theoretical Problems,* pp. 217–37, was written under the pseudonym "Fang Qing." This can be interpreted as a kind of pun on "Sun Yefang qing-nian," i.e., Sun Yefang youth, or one of Sun's protégés. The article was actually written by Zhang Zhuoyuan but, of course, reflected Sun's views.

[37]Ibid., p. 132. It was advocated in passing at the end of a very long article.

recognized as Sun Yefang's students. These young economists served to broach tentatively Sun's ideas to a larger public, and in turn they became the first targets once a decision had been made to attack Sun Yefang's "revisionist" economics.

During 1962, when Sun Yefang's theory on management had already been boldly expressed in private forums, the public discussion in the press on profitability and production prices began, though in an extremely tentative fashion. He Jianzhang, Sun's protégé, published an article arguing that profit was the most appropriate standard to use in evaluating an enterprise's performance.[38] He did not argue that profit should be the only standard for evaluation, but he argued that it was the most important indicator because it could comprehensively reflect all aspects of an enterprise's performance, including efficiency of operation as well as volume of sales. Moreover, the author specifically argued that the *rate* of profit, in relation to capital, could be used to compare enterprises in different branches of industry: the higher the rate of profit, the more praiseworthy the enterprise. Such a procedure, he claimed, was essential if planners were to be able to determine that capital was distributed efficiently between different branches of industry.

Although He Jianzhang did not say so in this initial article, his argument requires that prices be set according to the production-price formula. According to this formula, prices will be set so that the average rate of profit (on capital) will be the same in each branch of industry. If prices can in fact be accurately set in this fashion, then the rate of profitability that a given enterprise reaches can be used to measure its performance. In late 1963 and early 1964, two articles appeared specifically advocating the production-price procedure for setting prices. One was by Yang Jianbai, an older economist not closely linked to Sun Yefang; the other was by He Jianzhang and Zhang Zhuoyuan, both known as followers of Sun.[39] These two articles almost immediately elicited an outpouring of criticism.

The development of the argument on production prices in the public

[38]He Jianzhang, Gui Shiyong, and Zhao Xiaomin, "Guanyu shehuizhuyi qiye jingji hesuan de neirong wenti" [On The Question of the Content of Economic Accounting in Socialist Enterprises], *Jingji yanjiu* 4 (1962).

[39]Yang Jianbai, "Guomin jingji pingheng he shengchan jiage wenti" [National Economic Balance and the Question of Production Prices], *Jingji yanjiu* 12 (1963); He Jianzhang and Zhang Ling [Zhang Zhuoyuan], "Shilun shehuizhuyi zhong de shengchan jiage" [A Tentative Discussion of Production Prices in a Socialist Economy], *Jingji yanjiu* 5 (1964).

journals was extremely curious, since it seemed to proceed in a direction precisely opposite to what was happening in discussions behind closed doors. We have already seen that in 1961–62, Sun was freely expressing his ideas in private conclaves, and these ideas broadly included the set of issues raised in connection with the production-price discussion. Beginning in September 1962, however, after the Tenth Plenum when Mao called for attention to class struggle, the atmosphere of discussion internally began to change. At the Tenth Plenum of the Party Central Committee, held in that month, Mao Zedong specifically criticized the notion of individual material self-interest, and in particular any stress on profits and profit-seeking behavior.

As a result of this development, although internal discussions continued, the atmosphere became increasingly tense, and most individuals became afraid to discuss profits.[40] Sun Yefang defied this indirect pressure: in his internal reports he continued to advocate expanded authority for the industrial enterprise, profit targets, and price reform. As "Libermanism" (advocacy of material incentives) came under attack in 1963, Sun wrote in September an unpublished report differentiating his views on profit from Liberman's theories and protesting the unhealthy, tense atmosphere.[41] In the face of repeated warnings that it would be more prudent to tone down his advocacy, Sun thus became, if anything, more outspoken. But it is apparent that he was an increasingly isolated figure: the internal discussion was narrowing, with the circle tightening around Sun Yefang. Yet at this very same time, the public discussion seemed to be expanding.

And yet, this was illusory. He Jianzhang, Zhuo Zhouyuan, and Yang Jianbai clearly were increasingly handicapped in their discussion of production prices precisely because they were unable to discuss openly the question of individual incentives. Normally, advocacy of production prices would include the provision that enterprises would pay some kind of interest charge on capital (thus giving the production-price formula a firm basis in the costs an enterprise was charged), so that enterprises would have an incentive to economize on the economy's scarce capital stock. Because Sun's protégés were unable to discuss this aspect of the production price system, they also were unable to answer

[40]*Some Theoretical Problems,* pp. 266–67, and retrospective comments, pp. 294–96. Also, Zhang Tianlai, "Lotus Blossoms on a Snowcapped Mountain," *Guangming ribao,* January 16, 1983, translated in *JPRS Economic Affairs,* no. 315, p. 37.
[41]Ibid.

many of their critics' charges. Why should there be a uniform rate of profit, their critics asked, if central planners allocate capital between branches of industry anyway? Uniform profitability comes about under capitalism because of competition between capitalists, but how can there be free competition in a planned economy?[42] Zhuo, He, and Yang were accused of wishing to put "profits in command" and dismantle the apparatus of the planned economy. They could not answer these charges without reference to larger issues regarding the structure of the economic system and the nature of incentives. Since discussion of these issues had already been crippled, the debate on production prices was effectively stillborn.

Sun Under Attack

During 1964, the advocates of production prices became the object of an increasingly virulent attack, although Sun Yefang was not mentioned by name in the press. A Party work team was sent to the Economics Research Institute as part of the Socialist Education campaign. On August 10, a conference was convened at the institute to criticize Sun's views; on August 18, Mao gave the green light for criticism of Sun, at Kang Sheng's instigation.[43] Sun was "struggled against"—subjected to sustained public criticism sessions—twice weekly, for a total of thirty-nine times. Throughout this ordeal, and indeed for the rest of his life, Sun refused to recant or even modify his views. In the face of enormous psychological pressure and almost without support from other senior economists, Sun continued to defend

[42]These points were made in a bitter attack on production-price advocates by Wang Ya'nan, in what was the last intellectually honest contribution to the debate. See "Dangqian zhengzhi jingji zhanxian jiazhi pai he suowei shengchan jiage pai de lilun douzheng" [The Current Theoretical Struggle on the Political Economy Front Between the So-Called Production-Price School and the Value School], *Zhongguo jingji wenti* [Problems of Chinese Economics] 11 (1964):1–11.

[43]It is possible that in the complex politics of 1964, the criticism of Sun by some of his close colleagues was actually part of an ill-starred effort by the Liu Shaoqi faction to save Sun from a worse fate, as some Red Guard reports claimed. Zhang Tianlai, "Lotus Blossoms," p. 39 of translation discusses events at the institute. Zhang states explicitly that the attacks on Sun and on Yang Xianzhen at the Party school were designed to be simultaneous and symmetrical. See Stuart Schram, *Chairman Mao Talks to the People: Talks and Letters 1956–1971* (New York: Pantheon, 1974), pp. 215–16, on Mao and Kang Sheng.

his ideas.[44] Indeed, a number of the "lectures" included in his collected works are actually records of his self-defense, a fact which goes some distance to excuse occasional inconsistencies in his argumentation. As Sun himself wrote later on: "Before Lin Biao, Chen Boda, and the 'gang of four' implemented their 'all-around' dictatorship, it was still permitted at criticism or struggle meetings for the person being criticized or struggled against to speak, as long as he dared to uphold the things he believed to be true."[45]

Sun dared. Defending his ideas in every particular, he attacked in return the ideas of his opponents and refused to promise to remain silent in the future. Sun's "personal arrogance" later became one of the charges leveled against him.

Sun Yefang was removed from his position as head of the ERI, and at the end of 1964 the entire institute was sent to Zhoukoudian locality to serve in their turn as a work team carrying out the campaign. Sun went with them, but he was under the "supervision" of the other members. For two years the entire institute remained in this rural setting, carrying out ordinary political work. They returned to Beijing in 1966 but were not to remain for long, for in 1968 the entire institute was sent to rural Henan to "reform their world views" through a prolonged period of agricultural labor. This time Sun did not go with them, for on April 5, 1968, he had been thrown into prison. He was to remain there for seven years and five days.

Return to Work—1978

Sun Yefang was released from prison in 1975 and returned to public prominence in 1978. His activity until his death on February 22, 1983 was significant in three respects. First, he played a crucial role in reviving economic research and discussion and broadening the permissible scope of discussion. Second, the ideas that Sun continued to advocate in the field of economics still retain some importance. Finally,

---

[44]Zhang Tianlai, "Lotus Blossoms"; Deng Jiarong, "Woguo"; see also *Some Theoretical Problems,* pp. 291, 293, and 296–97, which are part of Sun's verbal defense. It is apparent that Sun was not receiving assistance from colleagues such as Xue Muqiao, Yu Guangyuan, and Xu Yi. Moreover, Yang Jianbai had by that time been forced to agree not to discuss production prices again, if he had not actually recanted his views.

[45]*Some Theoretical Problems,* p. 268.

the respect, verging on adulation around the time of his death, accorded to Sun by the regime clearly marked him as an ideal type of Communist Party intellectual.

Sun Yefang reemerged into the public eye not just as a former victim of the Cultural Revolution, but as an active participant along with his close associates in economic discussion of the post-Mao era. His former protégé, He Jianzhang, contributed a crucial early article on the position of the enterprise and the need for systemic reform.[46] At first, a number of works were produced that consisted generally of reaffirming and developing ideas that had originally been put forward in the early 1960s, including the concept of production prices.[47] Sun himself was quite active in propagating ideas he had developed earlier: he continued to attack the "natural economy" viewpoint and its pernicious influence; argued in favor of production prices and stressed the importance of profit; and again advocated giving enterprises control over all "simple reproduction." Especially through 1980, Sun's advocacy of these positions played an absolutely fundamental role in reestablishing the grounds for meaningful economic discussion and pushing back the limitations that had choked off economic debate during the Cultural Revolution. Sun helped to raise the general economic issues that underlie all discussions of specific socialist economic problems; he stressed the interrelatedness of all aspects of the economic system and the consequent need for system-wide reform.[48]

Many of the specific positions advocated by Sun, however, bear only a limited relationship to the most important questions being discussed in China, particularly since 1981. In theoretical discussions, today's economists have begun with the assumptions that commodity relations and individual and enterprise material self-interest persist under social-

[46]He Jianzhang, "Woguo quanmin suoyouzhi jingji jihua guanli tizhi cunzai de wenti he gaige fangxiang" [Existing Problems in the System of Planned Management of the State-Owned Economy in China and the Orientation of Reform], *Jingji yanjiu* 5 (1979):35–45.

[47]He Jianzhang and Zhang Zhuoyuan, *Lun shehuzhuyi jingji zhong de shengchan jiage* [On Production Prices in a Socialist Economy] (Harbin: Heilongjiang Renmin, 1981); Lu Nan, "Shehuizhuyi zhidu xia gongyepin an shengchan jiage dingjia wenti" [The Question of Setting Prices of Industrial Products According to Production Prices in a Socialist System], *Jingji yanjiu* 5 (1980).

[48]Sun Yefang, "Guanyu gaige woguo jingji guanli tizhi de jidian yijian" [A Few Opinions on the Reform of the Economic Management System], in Jingji Yanjiu Editorial Board, ed., *Guanyu woguo jingji guanli tizhi gaige de tantao* [An Exploration of the Reform of Our Economic Management System] (Jinan: Shandong Renmin, 1980).

ism. Thus, in today's radically altered environment, a number of the positions associated with Sun seem like artifacts from an earlier historical period. For instance, Sun's concept of the law of value has been subjected to friendly criticism from other reform economists for slighting the role of markets.[49]

The question of production prices, which once seemed so inflamatory, is now readily accepted on theoretical grounds. Consider the casual way in which one recent writer has dismissed what were once the most contentious ideological issues preventing reasonable discussion of this problem:

> As everybody knows, the reason that commodity production persists under socialism, even between enterprises owned by the state, is the persistence of separate material interests of individuals and collectivities. . . . Thus, competition is not necessary to establish production prices; the impact of the organic composition of capital on the material benefit of producers must be accounted for; and adjusting individual rewards to account for external factors is precisely equal to the demand of capital for equal return.[50]

Moreover, the focus of current discussion on prices has shifted to include limited price flexibility (prices "floating" within a limited range determined by market conditions) and sophisticated "dual track" pricing schemes.[51]

In recent years, China's central planners have been clearly unable to control total investment—expanded reproduction—so that Sun's stress on expanding enterprise authority up to the limits of simple reproduction has also seemed a little dated. These changes have led Sun to declare that, "In the past I was a 'revisionist,' but now I seem 'conservative,' or even a little 'left.' But those labels don't matter: we should all read a little more of *Das Kapital.*"[52] Such characteristic

[49]Ma Jiaju, "A Pioneer Work on Economic Reform," *Social Sciences in China* (Beijing) 1 (1980):222–24.

[50]Shen Shuigen, "Shilun shengchan jiage zai shehuizhuyi jingji zhong de keguan biranxing" [On the Objective Necessity for Production Prices in a Socialist Economy], in *An Exploration*, ed. Jingji Yanjiu, pp. 192–99.

[51]Lu Nan, "Gaige jiage tixi he guanli banfa ying zunxun de yuanze" [Principles that Should Be Followed in the Reform of the Price System and Management Procedures], *Caimao jingji* [Finance and Trade Economics] 1 (1983):16–20.

[52]"Ye tan lilun lianxi shiji he baijia zhengming wenti" [Again on Uniting Theory with Practice and a Hundred Schools Contending], *Caimao jingji congkan* [Digest of Finance and Trade Economics] 6 (1981):2.

good humor and receptiveness (combined with a consistent personal dedication to Marxist analysis) have given Sun Yefang an importance in current discussions that goes well beyond the relevance of the specific ideas with which he is identified.

Sun has played an important role in rebuilding the institutions that carry on economic research in China. As early as April 1978, he went to Sichuan and Yunnan to preside over the drafting of a long-range plan for economic research, a plan which resulted in the establishment of independent economic research institutes in both provinces. These two new institutes have been quite important in formulating reform proposals and carrying out research in recent years.[53] Moreover, nearly all the younger economists participating in economic discussions owe some kind of debt to Sun Yefang. Although, in a sense, all the members of the central institute can be considered students of Sun Yefang, it is possible to single out three who were his special protégés. These three are Liu Guoguang, its current director; He Jianzhang, deputy director of the research institute attached to the State Planning Commission; and Zhang Zhuoyuan, head of the Institute of Finance and Trade Economics. They played an important role in Sun's struggles of the 1960s, and all three have been at the center of innovative developments since 1978.

Sun's personal receptiveness to diverse currents of thought has continued to play a progressive role in broadening the terms of economic debate. One of the "crimes" Sun was accused of during the Cultural Revolution was passing on to his students ideas "indistinguishable from" the standard Western microeconomics textbooks by Henderson and Quandt.[54] In recent years, Sun has continued to welcome a discriminating borrowing of concepts and methods from Western economics.[55] Sun's commitment to open-mindedness has included a commitment to democratization. In one of his recent talks, Sun told of receiving a letter from a young man who opposed expanded authority for enterprises on the grounds that this would only give more power to patrimonial basic-level cadres who were already bleeding the populace. Sun rebutted the young man's postition, but then conceded his larger

---

[53]Lin Ling, "Huiyi Sun Yefang tongzhi xinan zhi xing" [Remembering Comrade Sun Yefang's Trip to the Southwest], *Shehui kexue zhanxian* [Social Science Front] 1 (1984):48-50.

[54]Gong Wensheng, "Bo Sun Yefang de xiuzhengzhuyi 'jingji gangling'" [Refute Sun Yefang's Revisionist 'Economic Principles'], *Renmin ribao* [People's Daily], August 10, 1966.

[55]Sun Yefang, "Again on Uniting Theory," p. 3.

point: "Economic democratization must be ensured by political demo-cratization. After the expansion of enterprise autonomy, there must be legal guarantees of the masses' democratic authority in order to prevent arbitrary use of power by cadres. The experience of Hungary and Yugoslavia proves this to be true."[56] Sun's recognition of this prob-lem, and his willingness to raise it, clearly put him in the most pro-gressive camp of Chinese intellectuals. In economic debates, Sun has tried to establish norms of direct, "comradely" criticism, to overcome past practices of indirect criticism with ulterior motives.[57]

In recent years, Sun has consistently been accorded a degree of respect almost unequaled among Chinese intellectuals. "In every re-spect, Comrade Yefang is a model we intellectuals should study."[58] On his deathbed, Sun was visited by Premier Zhao Ziyang, and apprecia-tions of the man and his work reached a crescendo. But the respect shown by Zhao had begun much earlier. During Sun's visit to Sichuan in 1978, then First Party Secretary Zhao invited Sun to speak to the provincial leadership. Instead of the usual practice of the leadership assembling around the podium, the entire leadership sat in the audience to display their respect for Sun as a teacher.[59] A flood of reminiscences and appreciations of Sun have appeared since his death.[60] Such appre-ciations are a traditional Chinese literary form, but the current exam-ples occasionally verge on hagiography and have the same purpose—the inspiration of faith among readers.

In particular, Sun has been put forward as a model for disillusioned young people, presented as a dedicated worker who devoted nearly forty years of selfless service to the Communist cause, was thrown into prison and subjected to innumerable indignities, and yet never lost his faith in Marxism or the Communist Party. To the end of his days he was urging young people to read *Das Kapital* and intensify their commit-ment to Marxism in China. How can you young people claim to be demoralized or disillusioned, the question is asked, in the face of this man's refusal to succumb to despair? It is not accidental that much of

[56]Sun Yefang, in *An Exploration,* ed. Jingji Yanjiu, pp. 2–4.

[57]Sun Yefang, "Again on Uniting Theory," p. 2.

[58]Tang Xianglong, "Dui Sun Yefang tongzhi de pianduan huiyi" [A Fragment of Reminiscence of Comrade Sun Yefang], *Shehui kexue zhanxian* 1 (1984):52.

[59]Lin Ling, "Huiyi Sun Yefang," p. 48.

[60]Several pieces of this literature have been cited: Lin Yushu, Zhang Tianlai, Lin Ling, and Tang Xiaglong.

the anecdotal literature about Sun stresses his commitment to young people and his support for their questioning attitude toward socialist society.[61]

Sun has also been put forward as a model for current establishment intellectuals, especially as a model practitioner of democratic dialogue among intellectuals. In this respect, one key fact stands out—Sun never recanted. In praising this aspect of Sun's career, the current leadership implicitly has given its approval to a role for intellectuals that includes a greater scope for personal integrity. The Leninist norm has required ritual self-criticism for specific errors. During the Cultural Revolution, individuals had been expected to "remold" their thought and change their opinions wholesale. There was no scope left for individual conscience. But in praising Sun, the current reformist leadership seems to be broadening the conception of the intellectual. Even when a position has been rejected by the leadership, intellectuals are to be allowed to retain their private opinions without harrassment. Xue Muqiao is alleged to have said that he learned one major lesson from Sun Yefang— never retreat from ideas that you personally believe in. In earlier years, Xue was frequently willing to abandon minority positions for the sake of consensus.

The legitimation of a larger realm of individual conscience should not, however, obscure the fact that intellectuals are still expected to restrain the expression of their opinions according to a definite set of principles. Discussion of topics is subjected to an informal tripartite classification. Some topics are open for genuine public discussion, as the regime seeks to resolve problems and come up with a consensus. For other topics, on which a party position has already been taken, public discussion must include an affirmation of the party position, and internal criticisms must be subtly phrased. Finally, some topics are open only for internal discussion because especially contentious issues, or state secrets, are involved. Sun Yefang repeatedly demonstrated his willingness to abide by these principles. During the early 1960s, he would not openly publish his views until some kind of Party consensus emerged on how they should be viewed, i.e., until they were moved from the third category of topics

---

[61]In addition to the sources cited in the previous note, see Wang Wu, "How Much I Want the New Pine Trees to Grow More Than a Thousand Feet Tall—The Story of Sun Yefang Helping the Young People," translated in *JPRS Economic Affairs*, no. 315, pp. 51–56; originally published in *Guangming ribao*, January 28, 1983.

into either the first or second category.[62]

The writings published by Sun's protégés during that early period clearly fell within the parameters approved by the regime. Sun's refusal to remain silent in 1964, in turn, must be seen as his response to the violation on the part of his attackers of accepted norms governing internal party discussion. According to the principles of "democratic centralism," it was impermissible to attack Sun for ideas he had advanced during a period when such ideas had been declared open for internal discussion.

We should keep these limitations to discussion in mind when we evaluate published material from the People's Republic today, for the disappearance of issues from public discussion may simply mean that debate continues in internal forums. In considering Sun Yefang as a model establishment intellectual, we should remember his service to the regime and willingness to abide by rules of discussion as well as his personal integrity and consistency. Economists, like other technocratic intellectuals, have much greater freedom in China now than in the past, but they still must cope with a complex set of restrictions on their personal expression. Sun Yefang demanded that these restrictions be impartially applied, but he indicated that he himself was willing to comply when they were.

Sun's Place in History

Sun Yefang will be remembered for his contributions to the economic theory of socialism. His outline of a reformed economic system giving much greater scope for profit, the "law of value," and the authority of the enterprise was an important and creative contribution to economic thought. Like all really major innovations in a field, Sun's contributions are not the product of a solitary genius. Rather they come from his understanding of, and modification of, ideas that have their roots in the common experience of socialist countries, and to which Sun was exposed, especially during the 1950s. In the long run, Sun may be remembered even more for his openness to different currents of thought and for his role in establishing and expanding the grounds for intellectual discourse in China than for his theoretical contributions. Sun Yefang was a cosmopolitan Marxist, struggling to find the principles

[62]*Some Theoretical Problems,* p. 156. Also note his care not to criticize in a public source an article by Yu Guangyuan until he ascertained it was also public. See "Comrade Sun Yefang's Speech," p. 3.

within Marxism—as well as selectively to incorporate non-Marxist ideas—that would be of most benefit to China's economic development. The consistency with which he pursued this aim in the face of nearly constant upheaval must be considered an expression of his exemplary personal character. His intellectual contributions, personal integrity, and service to the cause of Marxism combined to mark him as an ideal Communist Party intellectual in the eyes of the current Chinese leadership. It would be difficult for us not to share at least some of their admiration.

WU HAN

The "Upright Official" as a Model in the Humanities

Tom Fisher

[We] see an intellectual who had been struggling for many years in unpredictable political storms. He had the good intention of working for the Party and the people, did his work carefully, and tried his best not to make mistakes and to draw a clear demarcation line between himself and all those who made mistakes. Yet he was always accused of making mistakes.

Li Shu, February 1, 1979

From at least the Yuan dynasty onward, the "upright official" (*qing guan*) has been perpetuated as a model for the ideal government administrator through popular literature and theater. The Chinese term connotes a constellation of qualities, including a concern for the welfare of

I wish to thank the School of Humanities of La Trobe University and the East Asian Studies Department of the University of Melbourne for research funds; Lily Hu of the East Asian Collection of Baillieu Library (University of Melbourne) and Y. S. Chan of Menzies Library (Australian National University) for help in obtaining materials; Su Shuangbi of the *Guangming Daily* for sending me copies of his publications on Wu Han and answering some questions by mail; and Lau Mang Lye, Shen Gensheng, Robert Irving, and Rosemary Clark for research assistance. Earlier versions of this chapter were presented to the Melbourne China Study Group and the Oriental Studies Department of the University of Sydney. Bruce Jacobs, Fred Teiwes, and Jane Leonard offered penetrating criticism of these drafts, as did the editors of this volume to whom I am especially grateful.

the general populace, impartiality toward the more favored social groups, a personal life style beyond reproach, and frank criticism of the shortcomings in the practices of the political system combined with absolute loyalty to its basic principles and its ruler. The actual historical actions of officials thus designated may be difficult to assess, but the power of their popular image was so strong that in some cases they gained the status of local deities. In recent times Mao Zedong himself sponsored the model in the wake of the failure of the Great Leap Forward, and the actions of an important group of Beijing-based Party intellectuals manifest a self-understanding consistent with many *qing guan* characteristics.

Wu Han, leading historian, cultural popularizer, and deputy mayor of Beijing, became the man most closely associated in recent times with the image of the upright official. At the Party's direction, he produced a series of writings on the Ming official Hai Rui, one of the best-known *qing guan* in Chinese history. These include a modern Beijing opera, popular essays of varying length, and the definitive scholarly edition of Hai Rui's collected works. Moreover, Wu Han himself, although working within the framework of a modern Leninist Party, exhibited qualities reminiscent of the *qing guan* of the past. In his position as a member of the Chinese Communist Party well-placed in the Beijing Municipal administration and with access to both local and national organs of communication, he used his skills as a literary publicist and historian to attack privilege, dogmatism, and abstract theory and to promote popular education, reasoned debate, and action based on concrete experience and the principles of Marxism-Leninism. Like outspoken scholar-officials of the past, he died a martyr to his cause, and like them he has been posthumously rehabilitated. Since 1979 the Party has made him a model for a new generation of post-Cultural Revolution intellectuals.

Wu Han Before 1958

Wu Han was born in 1909 into the family of a Zhejiang school teacher and landowner who was well-off by local standards but did not support his son's advanced education.[1] Wu's adult life falls roughly into four

---

[1] The most complete biographical sources for the life of Wu Han are two studies by Su Shuangbi and Wang Hongzhi: ''Wu Han,'' in *Zhonggong dangshi renwuzhuan* [Biographies in the History of Chinese Communism], vol. 7 (Xian: Shaanxi Renmin, 1983), pp. 244–95, and ''Wu Han xueshu huodong biannian jianpu'' [Sim-

periods. During the first phase in the 1930s and early 1940s he devoted himself to the study of Chinese history. From 1943 until 1949 he also engaged in essay writing and political activity. Directly following Liberation he plunged into cultural administration and political work with Beijing intellectuals. Finally, after his acceptance into the Party in 1957, he concentrated heavily on literary work, primarily in popular history and *zawen,* or light essay, composition.

Wu Han's first steps along the path to professional history were guided by the towering figure of the American-trained empiricist Hu Shi, who was principal of the Shanghai China Institute which Wu Han attended from 1928 to 1930. Wu Han then followed Hu Shi to Beiping, selling his first piece of historical writing to finance his trip. Hu Shi not only arranged a part-time job so the impoverished student could attend Qinghua University, but he also encouraged his bent for rigorous textual studies.[2] Moreover, Hu Shi put Wu Han in touch with the eminent textual scholar Gu Jiegang and with Jiang Tingfu, the well-known liberal historian of modern China, who encouraged Wu to study Ming history, a field in which Wu became one of the leading scholars of his generation. Wu's passion for the study of history was such that his classmates dubbed him "the Grand Historian."[3] He also was active in university literary life, publishing more than forty essays during his third year of university alone, thereby injecting much-needed cash into his precarious economic existence. After graduating from Qinghua in 1934, he rejected a job with the more prestigious Academia Sinica to take a better-paying position in Qinghua's history department. During the next three years he published over twenty scholarly articles, some

---

plified Chronicle of Wu Han's Scholarly Activities), in *Wu Han de xueshu shengya* [Wu Han's Scholarly Career], ed. Su Shuangbi (Hangzhou: Zhejiang Renmin, 1984), pp. 124–234. This latter work arrived too late for me to make extensive use of it. See also Li Youning, *Wu Han zhuan* [Biography of Wu Han] (Hong Kong: Mingbao, 1973) and Howard Boorman, ed., *Biographical Dictionary of Republican China*, vol. 2 (New York: Columbia University Press, 1967), pp. 425–30. Su Shuangbi has informed me that his book-length *Wu Han zhuan* was to be published toward the end of 1984, and other materials will appear in the wake of a memorial conference on Wu Han in October 1984.

[2]Hu Yuzhi and Li Wenyi, "Kuairen kuaiyu, gandan zhaoren: shenqie huainian Wu Han tongzhi" [Straightforward Talk from a Straightforward Person, Utter Devotion to Friends: Deeply Cherishing the Memory of Comrade Wu Han), *Renmin ribao* [People's Daily], October 3, 1979, p. 3.

[3]Xia Nai, "Wo suo zhidao de shixuejia Wu Han tongzhi" [The Historian I Knew, Comrade Wu Han], *Shehui kexue zhanxian* 2 (1980):24. This essay has been reprinted in *Xueshu shengya*, ed. Su.

of which became standard references on Ming history. He also worked on the preconquest Manchu period and began a lifelong interest in the Korean *Veritable Records of the Yi Dynasty*.[4]

Wu Han's outlook changed significantly during the latter part of the War of Resistance against Japan (1937–1945). At first, after moving to Kunming to teach at Yunnan and Southwest United Universities, he continued his prolific scholarly life. By 1943, however, his writing indicates a growing political awareness critical of the Nationalist government. For example, his semipopular biography of the first Ming emperor pointed to the despotism of Ming Taizu as a direct analogy to the autocratic rule of Chiang K'ai-shek.[5] Also in 1943 Wu Han joined the local branch of the China Democratic League, to which the Party had recently sent a team of organizers. League academics organized a study group, writing papers that combined scholarship with topical concerns. Wu Han's contributions included "On Corruption," "A Chapter in the History of Corruption," and "On the Gentry."[6]

From then on Wu played an increasingly important role in the League, organizing both faculty and students in political activity and eventually becoming the editor of the Kunming *Democratic Weekly*. A compelling speaker as well as inspiring writer, Wu also addressed public meetings. With the end of the war, the level of political activity on the university campus rose sharply. Clashes between the Nationalist Party and university staff and students culminated in the "December First" incident of 1945, when police opened fire on student demonstrators, killing four. In response Wu Han helped organize mass protest meetings and penned a series of vitriolic articles with titles like "What Kind of Personal Freedom Is This?" "Rank and File Soldiers, Put Down Your Guns and Batons," and "Protest Against the Illegal Military Interference with the Freedom of Assembly." Political action

[4]Su and Wang, "Wu Han," pp. 248–50 and 254; Xia, "Wo suo zhidao de shixuejia Wu Han tongzhi," p.25; Zheng Tianting, "You xueli, you nengli, you poli de lishi xuejia: zhuinian Wu Han tongzhi" [A Scholarly, Capable, and Daring Historian: Reminiscing about Comrade Wu Han), *Guangming ribao*, September 18, 1979, p. 3.

[5]See Su and Wang, "Wu Han," pp. 255–59. For a discussion of the writing of *From Monk's Begging Bowl to Imperial Power*, see my "Wu Han, the Cultural Revolution, and the *Biography of Zhu Yuanzhang*: An Introduction," *Ming Studies* 11 (Fall 1980):33–43.

[6]Su and Wang, "Wu Han," pp. 259–60, 262; Hu and Li, "Kuairen." Wu Han's essays were reprinted in Wu Han, *Lishi de jingzhi* [The Mirror of History] (Chongqing: Shengsheng Chubanshe, 1945) and *Touqiang ji* [Javelins] (Beijing: Zuojia, 1959).

became more dangerous. Only a month after Wu Han left Kunming in 1946, his close friend and associate in the League, the poet Wen Yiduo, was gunned down after giving a press conference.[7]

The process of Wu Han's radicalization accelerated after his return in August 1947 to Beiping, where he resumed teaching at Qinghua. Although in early 1946 he had joined his colleague Fei Xiaotong in writing to General George Marshall to support the American attempt at mediation between the Communists and the Nationalists, like so many other intellectuals with democratic predilections, he found himself driven increasingly toward the Communist camp.[8] He became a leading figure in the Beiping Democratic League, gaining a position on the standing committee, and was particularly active in political organization at the university level. He continued to produce both political essays and scholarly articles, some of which drew parallels between the past and present, like his well-known study on the oppressiveness of early Ming education.[9] By 1947 Wu Han's cooperation with the Communist Party was quite direct. In February 1947, after peace talks between the Communists and the Nationalists had broken down, Communist delegates had to leave Beiping. On the eve of their departure, delegation heads Ye Jianying and Xu Bing invited leading members of the league, including Wu Han, to a farewell banquet. Later Xu gave Wu a radio, through which Wu stayed in touch with the Communists, frequently helping students escape to Communist-held areas.[10]

In October 1947 the Nationalist government declared the League illegal, and in August 1948 Wu and his wife fled behind Communist lines. Shortly thereafter, at Xibopo, Hebei, Wu Han met Chairman Mao, who is said to have questioned the accuracy of a description of the fate of a rebel leader mentioned in the revised edition of Wu's biography of the Ming dynasty founder. Somehow, amidst the turmoil of the pre-Liberation struggle, Wu had found time to revise thoroughly his earlier popular study, doubling it in length and turning it into what has

---

[7]Su and Wang, "Wu Han," pp. 268–76; Li Youning, *Wu Han zhuan*, pp. 27–33. On Wen Yiduo and Wu Han, see Wang Yi [Xu Shiqian], "Wen Yiduo yu Wu Han," *Guangming ribao*, March 17, 1973, p. 3.

[8]Boorman, ed., *Biographical Dictionary*, p. 246.

[9]Su and Wang, "Wu Han," pp. 276–77; Boorman, ed., *Biographical Dictionary*, p. 426; Wu Han, *Dushi zhaji* [Reading Notes on History] (Beijing: Sanlian, 1956), "Houji" [Afterword].

[10]Su and Wang, "Wu Han," pp. 277–78.

been called "the best biography written in modern Chinese."[11] At the end of January 1949 Wu Han returned to Beiping as a representative of the Communists' Military Control Commission, with a special brief to help in the takeover of Beiping University and guide the reorganization of Qinghua.[12]

During the next decade Wu Han's academic activities were sparse.[13] He spent most of his time on public administration as deputy mayor of Beijing in charge of culture, education, and health, a post he held from November 1949 until the Cultural Revolution. In addition he occupied many other public and scholarly positions, including vice-chairman of the National Youth League, delegate to the National People's Congress, chief editor of *Xin jianshe* [Reconstruction], editorial board member of *Lishi yanjiu* [Historical Studies], member of the Academy of Science's History Institute, and founding president of the Beijing Historical Association.[14]

At the same time he continued his involvement with the Democratic League. Although nominally independent, the League worked under the guidance of the Communist Party, and today the Party praises Wu for his close adherence to its directives in movements like land reform, thought reform of intellectuals, and the Three-Anti and Five-Anti campaigns. Wu's special responsibility concerned the mobilization of intellectuals, and during the aftermath of the Hundred Flowers campaign and the Great Leap Forward, when their morale was low, he convened meetings to rekindle their enthusiasm.[15]

In March 1957, during the Hundred Flowers campaign, the Party finally granted Wu Han's long-standing request for membership, though it did not publicize the matter.[16] His admission followed by six years that of his wife, Yuan Zhen, whose personal ties with eminent

[11]Boorman, ed., *Biographical Dictionary*, p. 426; Su and Wang, "Wu Han," p. 279; Fisher, "Biography of Zhu Yuanzhang," p. 36.

[12]Hu and Li, "Kuairen."

[13]Some of his historical work is covered in Su and Wang, "Jianpu," pp. 197–200, and Xia Nai, "Wo suo zhidao de shixuejia Wu Han tongzhi," p. 27.

[14]Su and Wang, "Wu Han," pp. 281–83; Zhang Youyu, "Mao zhuxi, Zhou zongli jiaodao women zuohao tongzhan gongzuo—huiyi yu Wu Han tongzhi gongshishi de yijian wangshi" (Chairman Mao, Premier Zhou Instructed Us to Do Our Best in Making a United Front—A Recollection from When I Worked with Comrade Wu Han), *Dangshi yanjiu* 4 (1980):60–62; Li Youning, *Wu Han zhuan*, p. 48.

[15]Hu and Li, "Kuairen."

[16]Zhang Youyu, "Mao zhuxi, Zhou zongli," p. 62; Su and Wang, "Wu Han," pp. 283–84.

Party members dated back to the early 1940s. In June, he demonstrated his new commitment by initiating criticism of his erstwhile league superior Luo Longji and former academic colleague Lei Xiaotong during the anti-Rightist campaign.[17] The following year he became vice-chairman of the reformed League. Wu Han had become a full-fledged member of the establishment.

Party Lines and Model Officials

After Wu Han's entry into the Party his writings once again began to appear in large numbers. In 1956 he had already published *Notes on Reading History*, a collection of some of his major scholarly writings from the 1930s and 1940s. Between 1959 and 1965, however, an average of almost one major work a year by him came out in print. The relationship between Wu Han's acceptance into the Party and the resurgence of his publishing career does not seem coincidental. Between 1949 and 1957 the publishing industry became increasingly centralized and probably began to exhibit many of the features that characterized it in more recent times, such as the Party Committee as the "leading body" in publishing enterprises, a national registry of publications, a unitary distribution network (though this now has been modified), and remuneration based on a combination of quality, length, and the number of copies printed, with collections of previously printed articles in book form counting as new publications.[18]

Clearly, Party concerns and officials have dominated the publishing industry and restricted access to print, which may be used as an incentive or material reward. Prior to his entry into the Party in 1957, Wu Han had published merely a handful of articles and one collection of pre-Liberation scholarly essays. In 1959, however, not only did two collections of earlier writings appear as books, but he also began to write prolifically for the current press. Major newspapers carrying his work included the national organ of the Party, the *People's Daily*; the national paper for intellectuals, the *Guangming Daily*, which is official-

[17]Roderick MacFarquhar, *The Origins of the Cultural Revolution I: Contradictions Among the People* (New York: Columbia University Press, 1974), p. 271; Hu and Li, "Kuairen." Wu's *Renmin ribao* attack on Luo is reprinted in *Chuntian ji* [Spring] (Beijing: Zuojia, 1961), pp. 63–75.

[18]G. Raymond Nunn, *Publishing in Mainland China* (Cambridge: M.I.T. Press, 1966), p. 16; *Zhongguo chuban nianjian 1980* [China Publishing Yearbook, 1980] (Beijing: Shangwu, 1980), pp. 627, 633; *Zhongguo chuban nianjian 1981* (Beijing: Shangwu, 1981), pp. 386–89.

ly under "Party direction"; and three publications directly under the control of the Beijing Party apparatus, the *Beijing Daily,* the *Beijing Evening News,* and *Frontline.*[19] Furthermore, many of these articles were reprinted in two subsequent books published in 1960 and 1961.

After entering the Party Wu Han also continued his work as a professional historian, initiating the reprinting of several important Ming texts and resuming work on his own massive compilation of materials in Korean sources relevant to Chinese history. In addition, he organized several large-scale historical popularization projects, gave a series of lectures on Ming history to the Party school (later published in book form), and revised his biography of the Ming founder once again.[20]

On Hai Rui

Between 1959 and 1962 Wu Han devoted a good deal of attention to the subject of the Ming official Hai Rui, known in both official historiography and folklore as an incorruptible, outspoken, and popularly acclaimed champion of justice.[21] At a Central Committee work conference in Shanghai during April 1959, Mao promoted the model of Hai Rui after having seen a play in which the character of Hai Rui appeared. Mao allegedly consulted a standard biography of the official and was impressed by the combination of his outspokenness and loyalty to the ruler. Vice-Minister of Culture Qian Junrui then broadcast the Chairman's interest in Hai Rui among cultural and artistic circles. Hu

[19]*Zhongguo xinwen nianjian 1982* [China Journalism Yearbook, 1982] (Beijing: Zhongguo Shehuikexue, 1983), pp. 197, 199–200.

[20]On his historical writing, see Zheng Tianting, "You xueli." On popularization see three articles by Zhang Xikong: "Wu Han Tongzhi he *Zhongguo lishi xiao congshu"* [Comrade Wu Han and the *Collection of Short Books on Chinese History],* *Xinhua wenzhai* 3 (1979):255–57, reprinted from *Beijing Daily,* February 17, 1979; "Yiwei rexin puji gongzuo de lishi xuejia" [A Historian Who Worked Enthusiastically at Popularization], in *Wu Han he "Hai Rui baguan"* [Wu Han and "Hai Rui Dismissed from Office"] (Beijing: Renmin, 1979), pp. 73–84; and "Wu Han de zhixue daolu ji qi dui puji lishikexue de gongxian" [Wu Han's Pursuit of Study and His Contributions to the Popularization of Historical Science], in *Xueshu shengya,* ed. Su, pp. 95–111. See also Wu Han, *Mingshi jianshu* [Simplified History of the Ming] (Beijing: Zhonghua, 1980), and *Zhu Yuanzhong zhuan* [Biography of Zhu Yuanzhang] (Beijing: Sanlian, 1965, 1979).

[21]Tom Fisher, " 'The Play's the Thing': Wu Han and Hai Rui Revisited," *The Australian Journal of Chinese Affairs* 7 (1982):8–9. A thoroughly nontraditional portrait of Hai Rui is contained in Ray Huang, *1587, Year of No Significance* (New Haven: Yale University Press, 1981), pp. 130–55.

Qiaomu, deputy director of the Propaganda Department with specific responsibility for the press, subsequently contacted Wu Han, who less than two months afterward published "Hai Rui Upbraids the Emperor" in the June 16, 1959 issue of *People's Daily*. The Xinhua Bookstore was instructed to bring out an edition of Hai Rui's collected writings and engaged Wu Han as editor, publishing the work in 1963.[22]

At the same time another Propaganda Department deputy, Zhou Yang, journeyed to Shanghai to encourage the Beijing Opera Troupe of Shanghai to produce an opera on the theme of Hai Rui's remonstration with the emperor. The company performed "Hai Rui Sends a Memorial" as part of the festivities to commemorate the tenth anniversary of the founding of the People's Republic of China that October.[23] In addition to this play and the one later written by Wu Han, Hai Rui also was the central figure in at least two other plays. A number of historians also contributed scholarly and popular articles on the Ming official, and the revised edition of a book-length study about him appeared in 1959.[24]

Wu Han contributed to the Hai Rui enterprise in three different literary genres: the scholarly collection of the Ming official's writings mentioned above, historical *zawen*, and the Beijing opera. Wu Han's popular historical essays of the time generally focused around a single text, excerpts of which he translated from classical Chinese into the vernacular. Through this medium he entered into a number of historical debates, including the relevance of the past to the present, the appropriate evaluation of progressive premodern figures like "upright officials," and the relationship between historical plays and history.[25] Hai Rui provided a focus for all three topics. In "Hai Rui Upbraids the Emperor" Wu Han concluded that even though Hai was an official of "feudal" times, his example was relevant to the present because of his ability to discern right from wrong and to combat "the powers of

---

[22]This account is now standard, but it is most detailed in Guo Xinghua, "*Hai Rui baguan* shi zenmayang xiechulai de" [How *Hai Rui Dismissed from Office* Was Written], *Xueshu shengya*, ed. Su, pp. 112–14.

[23]Tao Xiong, "Chenyuan shi'erzai de wenziyu" [The Gross Injustice of Twelve Years of Literary Persecution], in *Hai Rui shangshu* [Hai Rui Sends a Memorial], ed. Xu Siyan (Shanghai: Shanghai Wenyi, 1979), pp. 76–80.

[24]Fisher, " 'The Play's the Thing,' " p. 23, and Jiang Xingyu, *Hai Rui* (Shanghai: Renmin, 1957, 1959). Zhongguo Shehuikexue Yuan Lishi Yanjiusuo Mingshi Yanjiu Shi, ed., *Zhongguo jin bashi nian Mingshi lunzhu mulu* [Bibliography of Works on Ming History in the Past Eighty Years] (Zhenjiang: Jiangsu Renmin, 1981), p. 262.

[25]Fisher, " 'The Play's the Thing,' " pp. 13–16.

darkness,'' qualities that won the approval of the masses.[26] Three months later, in September 1959 Wu published "On Hai Rui," which eventually appeared as the introduction to his *Collected Writings of Hai Rui*. This more detailed portrayal, also printed in the *People's Daily*, clearly placed the Ming official within the confines of a "feudal" period he did not transcend. Wu described him as siding with the people against the exploitive bureaucracy and the large landlords, thus gaining popular support, but still as a patriotic official loyal to the emperor. Wu Han had drafted "On Hai Rui" prior to the August 1959 Lushan Plenum where Chairman Mao "dismissed" Peng Dehuai. During the meeting Peng, to whom Mao evidently had earlier presented a copy of Hai Rui's biography, attempted to present his criticisms of the Great Leap Forward in conformity with the *qing guan* model of candor and loyalty, and he explicitly identified himself with the Ming official. There ensued a discussion of "left" and "right," "real" and "false" Hai Ruis, which Hu Qiaomu, who had a copy of the draft article, duly reported back to Wu Han. Wu then added a disclaimer, distancing himself from "rightists" who "falsely" claimed the sanction of Hai Rui. Through this addendum and a reference to the play that inspired Mao's original interest in Hai Rui, Wu signalled his loyalty to the Party line, whatever personal misgivings about the Peng affair he might have had.[27]

Later in 1959 and again in 1960 Wu Han returned to the topic of Hai Rui. Deepening his historical analysis, he turned his attention to Hai Rui's reforms as a regional and local official in the lower Yangtze area. He also related some of the popular stories that circulated in Ming times about Hai Rui's frugality and plain living. Wu compared him to other famous Ming reformers and concluded that while their deeds actually benefited the large landlords, Hai's did not, with the result that the emperor honored the others but deprived Hai Rui of his position.[28] In all these articles Wu Han closely followed the *Ming History* biography of Hai Rui and demonstrated particular skill in translating

---

[26]*Renmin ribao*, June 16, 1959, p. 8.

[27]"Lun Hai Rui" [On Hai Rui], *Dengxia ji* [Under Lamplight] (Beijing, Sanlian, 1960), pp. 146–68; Guo Xinghua, *"Hai Rui baguan,"* p. 113. Guo's account, which must have been released with the approval of Hu Qiaomu, contradicts the Red Guard version, which states that Hu had requested Wu to write another article on Hai Rui *after* the Lushan Plenum. See also Su and Wang, "Jianpu," pp. 210–11, and Fisher, " 'The Play's the Thing,' " p. 11.

[28]*Hai Rui de gushi* [Stories about Hai Rui] (Beijing: Zhonghua, 1959).

classical texts into the vernacular, while keeping much of the original spirit of the material.

Meanwhile Ma Lianliang, the head of the Beijing Opera Troupe of Beijing, asked Wu Han to write an opera on the theme of Hai Rui. Despite Wu's inexperience with the genre, he agreed to undertake the challenge. Altogether he wrote seven drafts, some of which he circulated in mimeographed or printed form to a number of leading Beijing writers and actors and to Hu Qiaomu, who saw at least the first version.[29] "Hai Rui Dismissed from Office" is a morality play in which the outgunned good guy, the reformist official Hai Rui, confronts the bad guys, the local landlords with official ties, and gets cashiered for his efforts. The action revolves around the brutalization of a peasant family by a son of a retired grand secretary and the rectification of the situation by Hai Rui. Firmly siding with the victimized peasants against the exploitative landlords and their hireling local officials, Hai Rui executes the Grand Secretary's son and only then gives up his seal of office to a replacement sent by the poorly advised emperor, whom Hai never criticized. The play closed after a short run in Beijing, despite some favorable reviews, but it seems to have been performed at a dozen or more venues over the next two years.[30] Mao himself is said to have personally congratulated Ma Lianliang after seeing the opera.[31]

The relationship of history to the theater was one of Wu Han's major preoccupations during the period 1959–1962. A new genre of drama known as "newly arranged historical plays," which took themes from history but served contemporary society, had emerged in the late 1950s. By the early 1960s major companies had staged more than a

[29]*Hai Rui Dismissed from Office*, trans. C. C. Huang (Honolulu: University of Hawaii Press, 1972), pp. 30–33; Guo Xinghua, "*Hai Rui baguan*," p. 114.

[30]James R. Pusey, *Wu Han: Attacking the Present Through the Past* (Cambridge: Harvard University Press, 1969), pp. 36–37. Pusey notes that favorable reviews appeared in the Beijing Party press, as does Xuan Mo, *Zhonggong wenhua dageming yu dalu zhishi fenzi* [The Cultural Revolution and Mainland Intellectuals] (Taipei: Zhonggong Yanjiu Zazhi She, 1973], p. 86. Other reviews appear in Su and Wang, "Jianpu," pp. 212–13. Nevertheless, there is a negative evaluation in Zhao Cong, *Zhongguo dalu de xiju gaige* [Drama Reform on the Chinese Mainland] (Hong Kong: Xianggang Zhongwen Daxue, 1969), p. 154, and conversations and correspondence with Chinese intellectuals, including one Beijing opera expert, have echoed that opinion. Red Guard sources, however, indicate that it did play outside of the capital for quite a while. "*Hai Rui baguan* chulong de qianqian hou hou" [The Complete Story of the Appearance of *Hai Rui Dismissed from Office*], *Beijing xin wenyi*, June 8, 1967, p. 1.

[31]Su and Wang, "Wu Han," p. 286.

dozen such plays, including ones by such well-known playwrights as Tian Han, Cao Yu, and Guo Moruo. Some of these new plays treated themes quite clearly related to debates then current among historians, such as the reevaluation of certain historical figures, while others were based on traditional stories.[32] Historians very quickly became involved in discussions about the new plays, as leading academics and theoreticians participated in conferences called to discuss historical plays. A major theater journal ran a series of articles under the heading "Historical Truth and Artistic Truth," in which discussion focused on questions like the proper use of the past, the criteria for the evaluation of "feudal" ruling class heroes, and the portrayal of the masses in prerevolutionary times.[33]

Wu Han not only wrote his own play, but he also entered the debate on historical drama both as a theater critic and a theorist, presenting papers at major conferences and contributing reviews, articles, and interviews to the periodical press. He argued that true historical plays must be rooted firmly in verifiable historical texts, but he recognized that authors must be selective in their treatment and must employ dramatic techniques to "heighten reality." He maintained that playwrights must portray their characters within the confines of the spirit of the times in which their plays were set, not that of the present-day world. Thus, he pointed out, the Song general Yue Fei (1104–1142) cannot be depicted in terms of the People's Liberation Army; nor should premodern peasant rebellions be shown effecting a program of equal land distribution.[34]

Wu Han's zawen

Between early 1959 and mid-1964 Wu Han also published at least one hundred zawen, or light essays. In 1959 he concentrated on historical themes, writing more than thirty pieces covering an impressive range of topics and periods, including the origins of Chinese commerce, overseas trade, cotton production, techniques and strategies in premodern warfare, clothing, historical drama, and individual figures

[32]Fisher, " 'The Play's the Thing,' " p. 22.

[33]Xijubao, nos. 10, 11, 15, 20, 21, 22 (1959); Su and Wang, "Jianpu," pp. 213–17.

[34]"Tan lishiju" [On Historical Plays], Chuntian ji, pp. 265–70; "Zai tan lishiju" [More on Historical Plays], Chuntian ji, pp. 148–60; Lu Mei, "Wu Han tongzhi tan lishiju," Xijubao 9–10 (1969):23–28.

from the past. His output in the following year was much lower, probably because he was writing "Hai Rui Dismissed from Office." In 1961 he published over twenty articles, and between January and September 1962 more than thirty.[35] His *zawen* of the early 1960s still frequently drew on Chinese history and historical plays, but in more general terms than his earlier essays, while they embraced a far greater variety of subjects, from personal reminiscences to ghost stories, and from academic methodology to personal behavior and morality.

The period between 1959 and 1962 was a heady one for Chinese intellectuals, especially those associated with the Beijing Party establishment. Despite Mao's treatment of Peng Dehuai, he had to acknowledge the failures of the Great Leap and called for frank assessments of the situation. Specialists contributed their opinions not only in the economic sphere, but in the areas of culture and education as well. Liu Shaoqi, Deng Xiaoping, Lu Dingyi, Zhou Yang, and others convened meetings, dispatched investigation teams, and reassessed the role of the Party, criticizing the undisciplined excesses of the Great Leap and emphasizing the need for a return to regular procedures. As part of this effort Mayor Peng Zhen ordered the Beijing Party organization to carry out its own review, entrusting Deng Tuo with supervision of this work. This period ended with the Tenth Plenum in September 1962, which after two years of energetic debate legitimated most of the post-Great Leap adjustment policies but acceded to Mao's view that criticism should cease.[36]

The early 1960s atmosphere of relative open-mindedness and frank exchange of opinions encouraged the *qing guan* approach of loyal remonstrance that Mao had inspired in 1959. In addition to writing numerous essays by himself, which appeared in national and local Party publications, Wu Han also collaborated with other Beijing writers on two *zawen* series. The Beijing Party journal *Frontline* asked him to join its editor Deng Tuo and Liao Mosha in "Notes from a Three-

[35]See *Chuntian ji*, *Dengxia ji*, and *Xuexi ji* [Study] (Beijing: Beijing Chubanshe, 1963).

[36]See Merle Goldman, "Party Policies Towards the Intellectuals: The Unique Blooming and Contending of 1961–2," in *Party Leadership and Revolutionary Power in China*, ed. John Wilson Lewis (Cambridge: Cambridge University Press, 1970), pp. 268–303, and Byung-joon Ahn, "Adjustments in the Greap Leap Forward and Their Ideological Legacy, 1959–62," in *Ideology and Politics in Contemporary China*, ed. Chalmers Johnson (Seattle: University of Washington Press, 1973), pp. 257–300.

Family Village," and the *People's Daily* invited him to get together with Liao, Xia Yan, Meng Chao, and Tang Tao on "The Long and the Short" (*Changduan lu*). "Three-Family Village" first appeared in October 1961 and lasted until July 1964, while "The Long and the Short" ran only from May to October 1962. Apparently the Beijing Party journal was less constrained by Mao's criticism of writers at the Tenth Plenum than the national journal, which stopped its *zawen* column shortly after the meeting.

Lu Xun had made the *zawen* style famous in the 1920s and 1930s, using it as a vehicle for sharply criticizing the society and government of Nationalist China. Mao, however, in his "Talks on the Yan'an Forum for Art and Literature" in 1942, had explicitly attacked the medium as unsuitable for a situation in which a revolutionary government already held power. Nevertheless, by the early 1960s both regional and national periodicals were printing *zawen*.[37] In 1962 Wu Han faced this question directly. In "Writing Some More *Zawen*" he acknowledged the history of the form, but he claimed it was still appropriate. Of course, the target of *zawen*, he stated, was no longer a government that oppressed the people, but rather mistakes in work style, due to residues of past feudal and capitalist behavior patterns. Furthermore, he cautioned, people must offer their views in a straightforward way, not by analogy or insinuation, and take criticism as constructively offered.[38] Wu Han's contributions to "Three-Family Village" and "The Long and the Short" thus emphasized reasoned and informed debate, the concrete rather than the abstract, and a view of the past that recognized both change and continuity.

Wu Han saw both benefits and drawbacks in the atmosphere of "contending" that followed the Great Leap Forward. Although he recognized the value of meetings in formulating and disseminating policy, he lamented the number of useless meetings that had no clear purpose and lacked adequate preparation. He preferred instead "meetings of immortals," attended by well-informed and well-prepared participants who could deal effectively with the issues at hand. He saw the stridency of contentious meetings and the emphasis on empty theoriz-

[37]Timothy Cheek, ed. and trans., "The Politics of Cultural Reform: Deng Tuo and the Retooling of Chinese Marxism," *Chinese Law and Government* 16, 4 (Winter 1983–84):10–11.

[38]"Duoxie yidian zawen," *Wu Han zawen xuan* [Wu Han's Selected Light Essays] (Beijing: Renmin Wenxue, 1979), pp. 23–24.

ing as intimidating to many and thus counterproductive.[39] Elsewhere Wu Han concluded:

> We must be careful about the manner of [such] contention: first, everyone has an equal right to reason; second, this reasoning must be scientific if it is to convince others; third, [there must be] a common vocabulary and a unanimous approach; and fourth, the reasoning must be thoroughly discussed and the attitude must be correct.[40]

"Seek truth from facts," a phrase much in favor since Mao's death, appeared frequently in Wu Han's *zawen* and underlay much of his thinking. Two generals from the Warring States and Han periods, Wu noted, failed in battle because their strategy was taken from theory rather than experience. Conversely, a Ming general noted for his effective coastal defense against the "Japanese pirates" was even more successful on the northern landward frontier because he did not mechanically apply his earlier approach, but flexibly took into consideration the differing aspects of his new situation.[41] Wu Han also lauded the practical sense of the masses, who defied interdictions from successive feudal governments by cremating the dead rather than wasting valuable land by interring their bodies.[42]

Wu Han criticized a history conference on peasant rebellions at which many talked about contradiction with appropriate citations from "classical authors" but gave little indication of how the concept related to the historical phenomenon under consideration. Such an approach, Wu maintained, was contrary to the tenets of Marxism-

[39]"Lun kaihui" [On Meetings], Wu Nanxing, *Sanjiacun zhaji* [Notes from A Three Family Village] (Beijing: Renmin Wenxue, 1979), pp. 41–43. This is the only essay from *Sanjiacun zhaji* not reprinted in *Xuexi ji*. "Shenxianhui he baijia zhengming" [Meetings of Immortals and the Contention of One Hundred Schools], *Xuanji*, pp. 184–90.

[40]"Zhengming de fengdu" [The Manners of Disputation], *Changduan lu* [The Long and the Short] (Beijing: Renmin ribao, 1980), pp. 10–12. The current edition of *Changduan lu* omits the concluding paragraph of this article. For the full text see Robert Tung, ed., *Proscribed Chinese Writing*, Scandinavian Institute of Asian Studies Monograph Series no. 21 (London: Studentlitteratur/Curzon Press, 1976), pp. 95.

[41]"Zhao Gua he Ma Su" [Zhao Gua and Ma Su], Wu Nanxing, *Sanjiacun zhaji*, pp. 23–26; "Qi Jiguang lianbing" [Qi Jiguang Trains His Soldiers], *Changduan lu*, pp. 52–54.

[42]"Tan huozang" [On Cremation], Wu Nanxing, *Sanjiacun zhaji*, pp. 72–74.

Leninism and the Thought of Mao Zedong.[43]

Wu Han also identified aspects of the past that transcended the context of feudalism to be relevant to contemporary Chinese life. In two *zawen* that even before the Cultural Revolution attracted critical attention for advocating "supraclass," humanist values, Wu Han contended that although morality tends to reflect the interests of the ruling class, there are virtues from the past, like loyalty, filial piety, integrity, diligence, and courage, that are relevant to life today.[44] In these and other such pieces Wu Han recognized the gulf that separates the feudal past from the socialist present but argued for the critical assimilation of the past to the present.

As a self-acknowledged intellectual Wu Han showed concern with study, writing, and research, and he often drew his topics from his own educational and historical activities. He offered advice on how to study and how to write that emphasized the combination of broad and narrow approaches and the necessity for serious commitment.[45] Modesty, rather than arrogance or the fear of making mistakes, he said, was the hallmark of a genuine search for knowledge, and teachers must combine research with their pedagogical work.[46] Perhaps with his own life experience in mind, as well as the dilemmas facing young graduates, he wrote that a balance must be struck between individual wishes and the needs of society. Though one may not have the opportunity to do exactly as one pleases, one can cater to one's own interests in his spare time or acquire new interests more appropriate to one's changed situation.[47] He also twice addressed the topic of village histories, a concern which accompanied the Socialist Education movement's emphasis on rural life. He warned would-be historians of China's villages to base their work on hard evidence, to seek comprehensiveness and balance,

---

[43]"Taolun de chufadian" [The Starting Point of Discussion], Wu Nanxing, *Sanjiacun zhaji*, pp. 27–31.

[44]"Shuo daode" [On Morality] and "Zai shuo daode" [More on Morality], Wu Nanxing, *Sanjiacun zhaji*, pp. 49–51, 66–68. See also Merle Goldman, "The Chinese Communist Party's 'Cultural Revolution' of 1962–64," in *Ideology and Politics*, ed. Johnson, pp. 224–26.

[45]"Tan dushu" [On Reading] and "Tan xueshu yanjiu" [On Scholarly Research], Wu Nanxing, *Sanjiacun zhaji*, pp. 13–15, 192–94; "Tan xie wenzhang" [On Writing Articles], *Changduan lu*, pp. 21–23.

[46]"Shuo qianxu" [On Modesty] and "Shuo xueshu yanjiu" [On Scholarly Research], Wu Nanxing, *Sanjiacun zhaji*, pp. 57–59, 132–34.

[47]"Tan xingqu" [On Interests], Wu Nanxing, *Sanjiacun zhaji*, pp. 141–43.

and to write with a mass audience in mind.[48] Citing "Mao's Talks at the Yan'an Forum," Wu Han maintained that all effective writing must be anchored in concrete experience from life and a long-term and unconditional commitment to the subject matter, in this case the masses.[49]

Wu Han's *zawen*, like his work on Hai Rui, were part of mainstream intellectual life in China between 1959 and 1962. The focus of Wu Han's light essays had shifted from Chinese history in 1959 to encompass a variety of social and intellectual problems in subsequent years. They appeared in major publications under the direct control of the national and Beijing Party propaganda apparatuses. They were by and large not blatantly satirical, but rather quite straightforward, often resting on explicit historical analogy. He identified problems openly and proposed solutions that often combined traditional wisdom and socialist consciousness. He opposed dogmatism, abstract theorizing, and fruitless confrontation, preferring instead reasoned debate and careful study. Like the *qing guan* remonstrators of the past, Wu Han questioned not the policy but its execution. Even so, he apparently cut back his *zawen* production after the Tenth Plenum and increased the prominence of socialist theory and current political policy in his writings of 1963–64. His later pieces on theater, for example, have a cautious ring, stressing the need for reform and the importance of political content.[50]

Wu Han under Attack

Wu Han nevertheless became the first public target of the Cultural Revolution. The attack against him focused on his play "Hai Rui Dismissed from Office," though it reached his *zawen*, popular education efforts, and *Biography of Zhu Yuanzhang*. The campaign against the play began in late 1965, more than four years after the work had first been performed, with the publication in a Shanghai cultural journal of an article by Yao Wenyuan that had taken months of secret work

[48] "Tan xie cunshi" [On Writing Village History] and "Zai tan bianxie cunshi" [More on Compiling Village Histories], Wu Nanxing, *Sanjiacun zhaji*, pp. 154–56, 166–70.

[49] "Tan yu zuo" [Writing and Doing], Wu Nanxing, *Sanjiacun zhaji*, pp. 177–79.

[50] "Lun xiju gaige" [On Reform of Theater] and "Tan yanxi" [On Putting on Plays], Wu Nanxing, *Sanjiacun zhaji*, pp. 123–25, 183–85. The only essays from this period collected in book form are his last eleven from the "Three-Family Village." Su and Wang also mention none in "Jianpu."

to prepare under the guidance of Jiang Qing. Though it may have had its roots in Jiang Qing's personal antipathy for Wu Han and Peng Zhen, which had surfaced two years earlier, it was expressly approved by Chairman Mao himself.[51] Wu Han's portrayal of Hai Rui is easily recognizable from the *Ming History*, which depicts him as a savior of the people and dispenser of justice, but Yao criticized Wu on a variety of issues, both historical and theoretical. He castigated the historian for failing to show his protagonist acting in the interests of his own class and therefore for perpetuating the antiquated point of view of the landlord class and the bourgeoisie. He singled out the theme of ''returning the land'' (*tuitian*) as criticism of the commune system that had been launched shortly before the play had been written, and he labelled the work a ''poisonous weed.''[52] Despite the vehemence of the attack, Mao believed it had not gone far enough. Claiming that Yao's article ''did not hit the crux of the matter,'' Mao himself introduced the analogy of the dismissal of Defense Minister Peng Dehuai: ''The Jiajing emperor dismissed Hai Rui from office. In 1959 we dismissed Peng Dehuai from office. And Peng Dehuai is Hai Rui too.''[53]

Both of these major charges against Wu Han lack substantiation. *Tuitian* is a term that existed in Ming times and appears in correspondence between Hai Rui and Grand Secretary Xu Jie.[54] It thus is historically verifiable, and critics of the play would have to employ more than Yao Wenyuan's rhetoric to draw a convincing analogy between Hai Rui's attempt to force large landholders to return land acquired by force and advocacy of the dismantling of the commune system. On the other hand, since Peng Dehuai did in fact equate himself with Hai Rui, Mao's contention was accurate, but it was not valid because Wu Han's original interest in Hai Rui, prompted by Mao himself, predated the Lushan Plenum.[55] Furthermore, by adding to his subsequent articles

[51]Byung-joon Ahn, ''The Politics of Peking Opera, 1962–1965,'' *Asian Survey* 12, 12 (December 1972):1069, 1074.

[52]Yao Wenyuan, ''On the New Historical Play *The Dismissal of Hai Rui*,'' *Chinese Studies in History and Philosophy* 2, 1 (Fall 1968):39–40.

[53]Stuart Schram, ed., *Chairman Mao Talks to the People* (New York: Pantheon, 1974), p. 237.

[54]*Hai Zhongjie gong quanji* [Complete Works of Hai Rui], vol. 5 (Taibei: Hai Zhongjie Gong Quanji Jiying Weiyuan Hui, 1973), p. 38.

[55]Fisher, '' 'The Play's the Thing,' '' pp. 12–13. For the terms ''accurate'' and ''valid,'' see Lowell Dittmer, ''Death and Transfiguration: Liu Shaoqi's Rehabilitation and Contemporary Chinese Politics,'' *Journal of Asian Studies* 40, 3 (May 1981):469–70.

the disclaimers about contemporaries claiming the sanction of Hai Rui, Wu had demonstrated an uneasiness that current events had overtaken history. However, with the encouragement of high-ranking members of the Propaganda Section and the support or the Beijing political and cultural establishment, he had felt safe in continuing his work on the Ming official.

The Beijing Party at first attempted to protect Wu Han. Peng Zhen's committee to investigate this incident and related cultural matters tried to restrict debate to purely nonpolitical terms. The municipal Party Committee declared that Wu and Peng Dehuai had neither a personal nor a working relationship. Beijing newspapers, which initially had refused to print Yao's article, finally did so under pressure, but they added commentaries that reminded readers to "seek truth from the facts." A number of historians publicly defended Wu Han. Beijing Second Party Secretary Liu Ren even pointed out that Mao had suggested the topic, and in March 1966 First Secretary Wan Li sent Wu to the suburbs, where the danger was less.[56] Nevertheless, the Shanghai-based campaign ground relentlessly on, switching from Wu Han to other prominent Beijing establishment intellectuals, eventually implicating Peng Zhen and bringing down Liu Shaoqi. Wu Han was arrested, tortured, and subjected to a public "struggle" rally. After almost two years of imprisonment and further physical abuse, he died on October 11, 1969, at the age of sixty.[57]

The Cultural Revolution portrayal of Wu Han as "anti-Party" is a clear case of the "manufacture of deviance." In such situations the social control agencies themselves largely shape and sustain the deviance they purportedly try to suppress.[58] The "deviance" contained in Wu Han's officially published texts of the late 1950s and early 1960s had not itself changed in the intervening period. Rather, the Party, at least as defined by the grouping known as the "gang of four," had transformed itself and was making a retrospective judgment using new criteria. The meaning of published literary texts is public and therefore

[56]Li Shu, "Yige weijian zhishifenzi de da yinmou: ping Yao Wenyuan dui *Hai Rui baguan* de piping" [A Big Conspiracy to Encircle and Destroy the Intellectuals: Evaluating Yao Wenyuan's Criticism of *Hai Rui Dismissed from Office*], *Renmin ribao*, February 1, 1979, p. 3. A translation appears in SWB FE/BII 2–4 (February 8, 1979). Su and Wang, "Wu Han," pp. 290–91; Li Youning, *Wu Han zhuan*, pp. 92–93; MacFarquhar, *Origins of the Cultural Revolution I*, p. 402 n.125.

[57]Fisher, "'The Play's the Thing,'" p. 5.

[58]Walter D. Conner, "The Manufacture of Deviance: The Case of the Soviet Purge, 1936–1938," *American Sociological Review* 37 (August 1972):403–13.

exists independently of authorial intention. As environmental circumstances change to alter the connotations of what is designated in the text, so does its meaning, that is, the way in which people understand the text. Thus many readers, both Chinese and Western, not surprisingly found the attack on Wu Han believable, if not compelling. Although the common understanding of the term "propaganda" stresses its emotive aspects, much modern propaganda is in fact quite rational.[59] Whether or not the criticism of Yao Wenyuan and others was sincere, it was in many cases heavily documented and persuasively argued. Wu Han had operated within the framework of remonstrance acceptable at the time of his writing "Hai Rui Dismissed from Office" and other texts, but a group within the Party itself had broken with accepted norms of behavior at a later date.[60]

"Reversing Verdicts": The Rehabilitation of Wu Han

The posthumous rehabilitation of Wu Han has accompanied the attack against the "gang of four" and the promotion of the "four modernizations," campaigns which have emphasized the importance of mental production and the "reversal of verdicts" of intellectuals victimized by the Cultural Revolution. Scholars, journalists, and veteran cadres have linked the case of Wu Han to the "gang of four's" drive to power, their systematic persecution of intellectuals in general, and the prostitution of the discipline of history to political expediency during the Cultural Revolution.[61] To describe the process of the victimization of Wu Han and others, they have revived the expression *wenziyu*, or "literary persecution." This term, designating the practice of using written texts as political pretexts, had hitherto been used only in describing imperial practices. Perhaps the most damning condemnation of the way in which Wu Han was treated has been the reprinting of

[59]A.P. Foulkes, *Literature and Propaganda* (London: Methuen, 1983), p. 11.

[60]Fredrick C. Teiwes, *Politics and Purges in China: Rectification and the Decline of Party Norms* (White Plains, N.Y.: M.E. Sharpe, 1979), part 3.

[61]Li Shu "Yige weijian zhishifenzi de da yinmou''; Su Shuangbi, "Ping Yao Wenyuan 'Ping xinbian lishiju *Hai Rui baguan'*'' [Criticizing Yao Wenyuan's "Criticism of the Newly Arranged Historical Play *Hai Rui Dismissed from Office*''], *Guangming ribao*, November 15, 1978, p. 3; Zhang Menggen, "Yao Wenyuan 'Ping xinbian lishiju *Hai Rui baguan'* zaocheng de zhongzhong yuanyu'' [On the Various Unjust Charges Created by Yao Wenyuan's "Criticism of the Newly Arranged Historical Play *Hai Rui Dismissed from Office*''], *Renmin xiju* 2 (1979):33-55.

thirty-year old reflections on Wu Han and Wen Yiduo with an editorial note drawing a parallel between Wu's death and Wen's assassination by the Nationalists.[62]

The Man

The public rehabilitation of Wu Han started with an article in the November 15, 1978 issue of the *Guangming Daily* by Su Shuangbi, deputy editor of the theory section and editor of the history page.[63] Shortly thereafter, "Hai Rui Dismissed from Office" was restaged and reprinted. In the next two years most of Wu Han's major writings reappeared, and his collection of Korean materials on Chinese history was finally published in 1980.[64] An official memorial ceremony convened in September 1979 confirmed this reversal of verdicts. Leading political and cultural officials in attendance heard that Wu had been a "good member of the Party and a staunch revolutionary fighter."[65]

Writers both in specialist publications and in the official press have praised Wu as "red and expert." Historians have extolled his professionalism. The 1979 *Historical Studies Yearbook*, for example, contains a biographical sketch of him. Xia Nai, head of the Academy of Social Sciences' Archaeology Institute, endorsed his former classmate's "extensive reading and extensive copying" of primary sources as sound method. Historian Chen Wutong lauded Wu's *Biography of Zhu Yuanzhang* for its "outstanding scholarship" and "conspicuous merits in writing style," and senior colleague Zheng Tianting emphasized both Wu's links with the textual tradition of the past and his success as a popularizer of history.[66]

---

[62]Wang Yi, *Guangming ribao*, March 27, 1979, p. 3. Fei Xiaotong makes the same comparison in his "Xindeguo de ren—yi Wu Han tongzhi" [A Trustworthy Man—Remembering Comrade Wu Han], in *Wu Han he Hai Rui baguan*, p. 18.

[63]Su, "Ping Yao Wenyuan."

[64]*Chaoxian Lichao Shilu zhongde Zhongguo shiliao* [Chinese Historical Materials in the Korean *Veritable Records of the Yi Dynasty*] (Beijing: Zhonghua, 1980).

[65]"Wu Han tongzhi he Yuan Zhen tongzhi zhuidao hui zai jing juxing" [Memorial Meeting Held in the Capital for Comrades Wu Han and Yuan Zhen], *Renmin ribao*, September 15, 1979, p. 2.

[66]Su Shuangbi, "Wu Han," in *Zhongguo lishixue nianjian 1979* (Beijing: Sanlian, 1980), pp. 324–27; Xia Nai, pp. 25–56; Chen Wutong, "Chongping Wu Han tongzhi de *Zhu Yuanzhang zhuan*" [Reevaluating Comrade Wu Han's *Biography of Zhu Yuanzhang*], *Guangming ribao*, December 31, 1978, p. 4. This text has been translated in *Ming Studies* (Fall 1980); Zhang Tianting, "You xueli."

Other writers have stressed Wu Han's political commitment. Su Shuangbi and Wang Hongzhi have accentuated Wu's close links with the Party from 1943 onward, while Li Wenyi, one of the Party members sent to Kunming in 1943, and fellow Democratic League stalwart Hu Yuzhi have praised Wu for "fully understanding and implementing Party policies toward intellectuals" and skillfully managing the "dialectical relationship between red and expert, between politics and professionalism."[67] Former Beijing Vice-Mayor Zhang Youyu has recalled how Chairman Mao and Premier Zhou Enlai took a personal interest in Wu Han as part of their united front policy in the early 1950s, and others have reiterated many of these same themes.[68] Moreover, discussions on Wu Han's work on Hai Rui clearly point to the role of Mao and other Party officials in promoting the subject and specifically clear Wu of the charges of distorting history and using the Ming official to discuss the dismissal of Peng Dehuai.[69]

Professional Concerns

The resurrection of Wu Han has been evident not only in the rehabilitation of his person and republication of his writings, but also in the attention given to the areas of his greatest concern. In popular history, for example, the *Collection of Short Books on Chinese History*, of which Wu had been founding editor-in-chief, has reprinted old titles and added new ones. At the end of 1982 it comprised nearly 200 volumes, making it the largest historical series published since 1949.[70] The *Collection of Short Books on Foreign History*, also founded by Wu Han, has been revived too, along with several other collections of popular history. "History Stories," a radio series, is on the air again, and a new magazine called *Wenshi zhishi* [Knowing Literature and History] has recently appeared.[71]

[67]Su and Wang, "Wu Han," pp. 255ff.; Hu Yuzhi and Li Wenyi, "Kuairen."

[68]Zhang Youyu, "Mao Zhuxi, Zhou Zongli"; *Wu Han he "Hai Rui baguan,"* passim.

[69]See especially Guo Xinghua, "*Hai Rui baguan* shi zenmayang."

[70]*Zhonghua shuju shumulu, 1949–1981* [Catalogue of Books Published by Zhonghua Shuju, 1949–1981], pp. 147–59; Zhang Xikong, "*Zhongguo lishi xiao congshu*," p. 256.

[71]Liu Danian, "Tan xue lishi" [Speaking of Studying History], *Guangming ribao*, November 16, 1983, p. 3; Tang Tao, "Xuexi lishi, jianshe shehuizhuyi jingshen wenming" [Study History to Build a Spirit of Enlightened Socialism], *Guangming ribao*, January 11, 1984, p.3.

Historical plays have undergone a renaissance, too. By mid-1979 both the general press and specialist drama periodicals began to call for a revival of newly arranged historical plays, and discussion on the subject has continued through the early 1980s.[72] The *Guangming Daily* stated that there is nothing inherently wrong with using historical subjects, and a writer in *Juben* [Playscript] advocated the revival of plays like "Hai Rui Dismissed from Office" and the creation of more such plays.[73] Another cited with approval the classic formulation of the second Tang emperor, who himself has become the subject of a number of plays: "Using [burnished] copper as a mirror we can adjust our clothes and hats; using the past as a mirror we can know about growth and decay [of the country]."[74] By the end of 1979 newly arranged historical plays accounted for 25 of 151 plays listed in *Playscript*'s survey of the year's new productions, and in 1980, 232 of 2,209 plays staged had historical subjects.[75] Some of these of course have tenuous roots in history, being primarily the literature of the reversal of verdicts, but clearly historical themes were on their way back.

Post-Cultural Revolution discussions on the subject of historical plays have dealt with many of the points raised in the exchanges of the early 1960s. Critics and playwrights generally have advocated somewhat less stringent historiographical standards than those for which Wu Han had argued.[76] Such writers, however, have explicitly attacked the "historiography of insinuation" on the stage, which has led even foreigners to ask, "Whom does this character allude to?" or "What does this phrase imply?"[77] One type of newly arranged historical play that

[72]For example, see *Juben* (April, May, and August 1982), and Wang Gui and Wang Peigong, "Shiju siti" [Four Questions about Historical Plays], *Wenyi bao* 11 (1983):61–64.

[73]*Guangming ribao*, June 12, 1979, p. 4. "Jianchi 'shuangbai' fangzhen, fanrong xiju chuangzuo" [Uphold the Guiding Principles of the "Two Hundreds," Promote the Writing of Plays], *Juben* 6 (1979):2–4.

[74]Zhang Zhen, "Lishi ticai dayou kewei" [Historical Subjects Are Well Worth Doing], *Juben* 7 (1979):56–58.

[75]*Juben* 12 (1979):94–96. *Zhongguo xiju nianjian 1981* [Chinese Theater Yearbook, 1981] (Beijing: Zhongguo Xiju Chubanshe, 1981), pp. 300–302.

[76]See, for example, Hou Guangfeng, "Xinbian lishiju ying gei ren yi zhengque de lishizhishi" [Newly Arranged Historical Plays Ought to Impart a Correct Knowledge of History], *Guangming ribao*, December 18, 1979, p. 3; and Bei Huai, "Lishiju de lishihua yu feilishihua" [The Historicization and Nonhistoricization of Historical Plays], *Xiju yishu* 1 (1981):86–98.

[77]Wang Gui and Wang Peigong, "Shiju siti"; Hu Shigang "Ping 'sirenbang' de yingshe shixue," [Criticism of the "Gang of Four's" Historiography by Insinuation], *Renmin ribao*, December 23, 1977, p. 3; Kong Li [Chen Kongli], "Lun lishi

has been affirmed since 1978 is, not surprisingly, that about upright officials. The earlier plays about Hai Rui have been restaged and some reprinted, and at least two new plays about the Ming official have been written.[78] Plays about similar historical personages, most notably the Tang official Wei Zheng, also have appeared, and a number of writers have discussed the issue in serious and well-informed terms.[79]

A substantial body of literature on the question of upright officials also has appeared. It broadly follows Wu Han's viewpoint but contains some debate. Wu Han, while recognizing the historical limitations of such figures, also stressed their positive contributions to their society and their appropriateness as models for present-day bureaucrats. Some writers, however, caution against overenthusiasm for the feudal model. Xu Lianda, a history professor at Fudan University who once attacked Wu Han's portrayal of the Ming dynasty founder Zhu Yuanzhang, was rather muted in his praise for *qing guan*. While criticizing the Cultural Revolution approach, he concluded that because such officials upheld the interests of the landlord class in general, it is inappropriate to see them as "bearing in mind the interests of the people" and "not hesitating to sacrifice their posts." Another historian noted that the positive role of *qing guan* was only localized and temporary, so their importance should not be exaggerated.[80]

Some of this ambivalence is evident also in the work of one of Wu Han's biographers, Su Shuangbi. Su has lauded the "spirit of Hai

---

leibi yu yingshe shixue'' [On Historical Analogy and the Historiography of Insinuation], *Guangming ribao*, June 1, 1978, p. 4.

[78]In addition to Wu Han's play, "Hai Rui Sends a Memorial" and "Hai Rui the Tracker" have been restaged. See *Renmin ribao*, October 3, 1979, and SWB FE/6039/BII/13 (February 10, 1979). The new plays are "Hai Rui xunhu" [Hai Rui Tames the Tiger], which appeared in *Juben* 11 (November 1980):54–76, and "Hai Rui sougong" [Hai Rui Searches the Palace], *Renmin xiju* 297 (February 18, 1982), inside cover.

[79]FBIS 392 (February 16, 1983), p. 57; Li Ping, "Shilun qing guan de jiji yiyi" [Some Thoughts on the Positive Meaning of Plays about Upright Officials], *Guangming ribao*, November 14, 1978, p. 4; Guo Hancheng and Su Guorong, "Lun qing guan he qing guan xi" [On Upright Officials and Plays about Upright Officials], *Wenxue pinglun* 3 (1979):80–87; Wu Naifu and Wang Hongye, "Lishishang de qing guan Kuang Zhong" [The Upright Official Kuang Zhong in History], *Guangming ribao*, June 5, 1979, p. 4; "Lishishang de Bao Zheng" [The Historical Bao Zheng], *Renmin ribao*, February 25, 1980, p. 5.

[80]Xu Lianda, " 'Qing guan' 'tanguan' youlie lun" ["Upright Officials" and "Corrupt Officials"—a Discussion of Good and Evil], *Xinhua wenzhai* 1 (1979):82; Wang Sizhi, "Zai lun 'qing guan' " [More on Upright Officials], *Guangming ribao*, September 15, 1978, p. 4.

Rui," as shown in his "courage to tell the truth," resistance to despotic power, opposition to the "village hypocrites," and strict enforcement of the law, all virtues which should be promoted in contemporary China.[81] Nevertheless, because of their class loyalty, fear of the masses, and limited vision, *qing guan* never "succeeded in establishing themselves as the dominant social force . . . to attain the hoped-for results of reforming society," for they aimed simply to moderate class contradiction in order to maintain the development of the productive forces in society.[82]

Other articles on upright officials, both scholarly and popular, have been more fulsome in their praise. The respected historical journal *Research on Chinese History* printed a fairly detailed discussion of Hai Rui's local reforms and reminded readers not to judge his achievements according to present standards but to view his reforms as basically progressive, for they enhanced the people's productivity.[83] Literary critic Pan Renshan wrote an "Appeal for the Rehabilitation of Upright Officials" attacking the Cultural Revolution slogan that "upright officials were not upright" and enumerating such basic *qing guan* characteristics as loyalty to the country and political system without blind obedience to the throne, courage to act against the rich and powerful, strict enforcement of the laws, and promotion of what is beneficial to the people and elimination of what is harmful. Though they were protectors of the "feudal" system and not "the saviors of the people," upright officials nevertheless can be used as a mirror with which to look at contemporary cadres.[84]

Wu Han's Colleagues

Many of the authors of the rehabilitation literature themselves had been linked with Wu Han or were otherwise persecuted during the Cultural Revolution. They include old political associates like Li Wenyi and Hu

[81]"Shilun Hai Rui jingshen" [Preliminary Discussion on the Spirit of Hai Rui], *Xinhua wenzhai* 3 (1979):46–48.

[82]"Jieji douzheng yu qing guan" [Class Struggle and Upright Officials], in Su, *Jieji douzheng yu lishi kexue* [Class Struggle and Historical Science] (Shanghai: Shanghai Renmin, 1982), p. 144.

[83]Liu Zhongri and Cao Guilin, "Qing guan Hai Rui" [The Upright Official Hai Rui], *Zhongguoshi yanjiu* 3 (1979):29–43.

[84]"Wei qing guan zhaoxue" [For the Rehabilitation of Upright Officials], *Xinhua wenzhai* 1 (1979):78–81.

Yuzhi of the Democratic League and Zhang Youyu, Beijing deputy mayor who along with local Second Party Secretary Liu Ren provided the formal introduction of Wu Han to the Party.[85] Su Shuangbi had been academic secretary to the Beijing Historical Society when Wu Han was president.[86] Li Shu, now deputy director of the Academy of Social Sciences' Modern History Institute, had defended Wu in May 1966, and Guo Xinghua worked with Wu Han for many years.[87] Beijing University Professor Zheng Tianting had been Wu's department chairman in Kunming and a member of the editorial board of the *Collection of Short Books on Chinese History*.[88] Other *Collection* contributors who have written rehabilitation articles include Jiang Xingyu, author of a book on Hai Rui and historical adviser to the production team of the opera "Hai Rui Sends a Memorial," editor Zhang Xikong, and Chen Kongli, whose manuscript on Qing "literary persecution" had been suppressed.[89] This list also includes editorial board member Ma Shaopo, who also had seen early drafts of "Hai Rui Dismissed from Office," and Zhang Menggeng and Guo Fei, who were both linked to the play.[90]

[85]Donald W. Klein and Anne B. Clark, eds, *Biographical Dictionary of Chinese Communism*, vol. 1 (Cambridge:Harvard University Press, 1971), pp. 385–86; Wolfgang Bartke, *Who's Who in the People's Republic of China*, trans. Franciscus Verellen (Armonk, N.Y.: M.E. Sharpe, 1981), pp. 534–25; 665; Zhang Youyu, "Mao Zhuxi, Zhou Zongli," pp. 60–62.

[86]Personal conversation with Mr. Wang Qianghua, deputy editor-in-chief, *Guangming ribao*.

[87]Wolfgang Bartke, *Who's Who*, p. 679; *Who's Who in Communist China*, vol. 1 (Hong Kong: Union Research Institute, 1969), p. 394; Su Shuangbi, *Xueshu shengya*, foreword.

[88]Zhang Youren, "Lieshi danxin, shijia bense: shenqie huainian Wu Han jiaoshou" [Loyal Heart of a Martyr, True Qualities of a Historian: Profoundly Cherishing the Memory of Professor Wu Han], *Shehui kexue zhanxian* 2 (1980):30. The author had been a student at Southwest United University during the war. Su Shuangbi, *Xueshe shengya*, foreword; Li Youning, *Wu Han zhuan*, p. 52.

[89]Jiang Xingyu, "Hai Rui, Hai Rui xi, Hai Rui jingshen" [Hai Rui, Plays about Hai Rui, and the Spirit of Hai Rui], in *Hai Rui shangshu*, ed. Xu Siyan, p. 89. Xu Siyan was the principal author of the play. Zhang Xikong, "Puji gongzuo," pp. 81–82; Su Shuangbi, *Xueshu shengya*, foreword; Li Youning, *Wu Han zhuan*, p. 52; Kong Li [Chen Kongli], "Lun Qingdai de wenziyu" [On the Qing Dynasty Literary Persecutions], *Zhongguoshi yanjiu* 3 (March 1979), p. 129. The original work has now appeared in the *Zhongguo lishi xiao congshu* series as *Qingdai wenziyu* [Literary Persecution in the Qing Dynasty] (Beijing: Zhonghua, 1980).

[90]Li Youning, *Wu Han zhuan*, p. 52; "*Hai Rui baguan* chulong," p. 2. Ma has recently written a play entitled "Ming jing ji" [Record of a Bright Mirror]. See *Juben*

The rehabilitation of Wu Han clearly indicates the power of his legacy in post-Mao China. Writers in both the popular and specialized press have consistently praised his abilities as a scholar and popularizer of Chinese history. They have lauded his political commitment, especially in dealing with fellow intellectuals and placing his scholarship in the service of the Party, and they have portrayed him as the victim of an inner-Party coup. Those interested in the theater have reasserted the importance of intellectually responsible historical plays. Most importantly, the current image of the traditional upright official is positive, though there are varying degrees of reservation about exactly how relevant such figures from the past are to the contemporary world.

The rehabilitation materials, regardless of the sincerity of the author's intentions, generally contain elements of propaganda in that they express "the values and accepted power symbols of a given society." The force of these texts, within the context of their publication, has shown a gradual swing from agitational to integrative.[91] The propaganda of agitition sought above all to discredit the "gang of four" and to mobilize public opinion, especially that of intellectuals, against their remaining power bases. Writers attacked the "gang's" abuse of Wu Han as the first step in their drive to power and showed how they twisted both the historical record and Wu's own words to perpetrate "literary persecution" on a mass scale, resulting in the complete intimidation of the intellectual class. The propaganda of integration, on the other hand, has stressed the *qing guan* elements of the life and thought of Wu Han that are useful to the post-Mao reconstruction of China. Politically inclined writers have emphasized united front policies and Wu Han's work with non-Party intellectuals; writers on historical drama have argued that a handful of the traditional elite did possess virtues relevant to contemporary China. These include a genuine concern for the living and production conditions of the people, unservile behavior toward the rich and powerful, combined with loyalty to the political system, a frugal life style, strict adherence to the law, and the reversing of unjust verdicts.

---

7 (July 1980):37–55; Zhang Menggeng, "Yao Wenyuan," p. 33; Guo Fei, "Cong *Hai ba* tan zhengming" [Speaking of "Contending" from the Point of View of *Hai Rui Dismissed from Office*], *Wen hui bao*, February 2, 1979.

[91]Foulkes, *Literature and Propaganda*, pp. 3, 11.

Ramifications of the *Qing Guan* Model

The rehabilitated image of Wu Han, like that of the traditional *qing guan*, portrays him as a scholar-official loyally serving the existing polity. As Mao himself pointed out, a major characteristic of upright officials like Hai Rui was their combination of frank remonstration with devotion to the political system. Thus Hai Rui, imprisoned for criticism of the Jiajing emperor (r. 1522–1567), shed tears upon hearing of the death of his ruler, even though it meant his own liberty. Political leadership at any given moment may go astray, as it did in the late Ming and the Cultural Revolution, but the legitimacy of authority, be it the Son of Heaven or the Party, remains unassailable. The Cultural Revolution leadership prohibited the expression of critical but loyal opinion within the Party's institutional framework and retrospectively attacked what earlier had been encouraged. In rectifying the situation after the death of Mao the Party once again has encouraged intellectuals to offer their expertise and points of view to create a modern, socialist China.

> Only a sound system of democratic centralism, which puts state and Party leading organs under the supervision of the whole country and the entire Party membership, can effectively prevent and shatter in good time the conspiratoral activities by the careerists to make a comeback. This is the conclusion we should draw from redressing the case in which Comrade Wu Han was wrongly accused for his writing of "Hai Rui Dismissed from Office."[92]

The current regime has exposed the historiography of insinuation and cautioned historians and dramatists against basing their work on specific contemporary figures or policies. Nevertheless, the past must continue to serve the present, and it may be appropriate to employ historical analogy within the framework of scientific historiography.[93] Moreover, although post-Mao writers have claimed that "art should not be subordinate to politics," it must still "serve the people."[94] The overwhelming majority of the rehabilitation writers have not questioned the subservience of art to the concerns of the people as deter-

[92]Li Shu, "Yige weijian."

[93]Kong Li [Chen Kongli], "Lishi leibi."

[94]Jia Hongyuan, "Wenyi buying congshu yu zhengzhi" [Literature and Art Should Not Be Subordinated to Politics], *Juben* 10 (1982):15–16.

mined by the Party. Instead they have leveled their attack against the "gang of four's" abuse of that principle. One drama critic, in contrast to this dominant trend, however, has argued that political interference has been subverting historical drama ever since liberation. The first example of what he terms such "antihistoricism" occurred in the 1950 campaign against the movie "The Biography of Wu Xun," in which critics accused the protagonist, a former poor peasant who had founded a school for peasants, of selling out to the imperial system instead of trying to overthrow it. "Stemming from the undue emphasis placed on the political duty to the proletariat," maintained this writer, "the creation of historical plays has been channeled to a great extent along the track of willfully distorted history that serves as an illustration of politics and makes use of the past to praise or attack the present."[95]

Like the *qing guan* of the past, Wu Han worked from within the established bureaucracy, though he was far more dependent on patronage from above. His outspoken condemnation of dogmatism, abstract theorizing, and privilege resulted from general Party-wide dissatisfaction with the Great Leap Forward[96] and was a response to central Party initiatives. It is thus difficult to see him as a dissenter. Even the term "permitted dissent" is inadequate. Although it describes views "published in the journals of official institutions" as seen, for example, in the context of the post-Stalin thaw in the Soviet Union, it stands in some degree of tension to proclaimed policy and may be cut off abruptly by the central authority.[97] In the case of Wu Han, however, between 1959, when his *zawen* first started to appear, and the Tenth Plenum in September 1962, when the post-Great Leap policy of responsible remonstration was modified, his writings do not appear to have exceeded the boundaries commonly accepted by editors and publishers. Even afterward, as strains between the Beijing establishment and the Maoists

[95]Zheng Liping, "Ping lishiju chuangzuo de fanlishizhuyi qingxian" [Comments on Antihistoricist Tendencies in the Creation of Historical Plays], *Xinhua wenzhai* 5 (1981):148. For a short discussion of the Wu Xun campaign, see Merle Goldman, *Literary Dissent in Communist China* (Cambridge:Harvard University Press, 1967), pp. 90–91.

[96]For a reference to Wu Han's shock at post-Great Leap living conditions, see Fang Mu, "Wu Han de beiju" [The Tragedy of Wu Han], *Guanchajia* 50 (January 1979):35–36. This has been confirmed in a private conversation with one of Wu Han's colleagues.

[97]Dina Spechler, "Permitted Dissent in the Decade after Stalin: Criticism and Protest in *Novy Mir*, 1953–1964," in *The Dynamics of Soviet Politics*, ed. Paul Cocks et al. (Cambridge: Harvard University Press, 1976), pp. 28–50.

mounted, it is arguable whether the group around Mao either consciously permitted or even had the power to prohibit writings like the "Three-Family Village," which continued well into 1964. It was only when the views of that faction finally became orthodox that the work of Wu Han and similar writers *retrospectively* became dissent.

Today, some within the Party clearly believe the positive re-evaluation of the *qing guan* has gone too far. *Red Flag* theoreticians, for example, have explicitly attacked the reemergence of an "upright official ideology" as fostering the expectation that the people will be saved by outside heroes rather than through their own actions.[98] This concern is not necessarily misplaced, as illustrated by the parallels between the *qing guan* of traditional folklore and modern-day "upright officials" in recent Chinese fiction. In "Manager Qiao Assumes Office" and its sequel, for example, a dynamic and technically skilled manager relinquishes his comfortable higher level administrative job to turn a troublesome machinery factory into a modern unit capable of producing goods that are internationally competitive. Despite corruption and factionalism he finally succeeds in winning the confidence of the workers, who oppose his "dismissal."[99] Another well-known story from the "scar literature" era conludes that the only way of removing corrupt officials is through the intervention of upright ones: "Our nation has been ruined by deadbeats like him. Framing and false accusations are stacked as high as mountains. It's almost hopeless. China needs people like Bao Gong and Hai Rui."[100]

[98]JPRS 77051 (December 23, 1980), pp. 40–51.

[99]"Manager Qiao Assumes Office" and "More About Manager Qiao," in *Prize-Winning Stories from China, 1978–1979* (Beijing: Foreign Languages Press, 1981), pp. 218–301. I am indebted to Kam Louie for the analogy.

[100]Li Yanhua and Wang Jingquan, "Cries from Death Row," in *Stubborn Weeds*, ed. Perry Link (Bloomington: Indiana University Press, 1983), p. 113.

IV. On the Fringe of the Establishment

BAI HUA

The Political Authority of a Writer

Richard Kraus

> I appeal for courage! No courage, no breakthrough; no break-
> through, no literature!
>
> Bai Hua, speech at Fourth National Congress
> of Literature and Art, November 1979

No matter what Bai Hua's future literary accomplishments may be, the fifty-five-year-old dramatist and short story writer is assured a place in the history of China's cultural politics for the "Bai Hua Incident" of 1981. A national campaign to criticize Bai's screenplay, *Unrequited Love*, broke the momentum of a post-Mao trend toward fewer political restrictions on the arts. *Unrequited Love* dealt with the frustrated patriotism of a painter who returned to his native China, only to be misunderstood and ill-treated by Maoist cultural revolutionaries. "Bourgeois liberalism" was the label attached to the screenplay, and although Bai continued to enjoy a prominent career after making a public self-criticism, the atmosphere for the arts in China has not yet returned to the comparatively freewheeling mood of 1979 and 1980.

The circumstances in 1981 have led to a perception of Bai as a kind of liberal critic of state-controlled culture, but a review of Bai's career in art and in politics leads to quite a different assessment.[1] Bai's fusion

---

[1] It is impossible to reconstruct Bai Hua's career from official Chinese sources alone. Within China, much of the political impact of Bai's positions is transmitted through informal communication, rather than published articles. Much of this literary and political gossip makes its way to Hong Kong, where it has been reproduced in a lively but not always accurate political press. Information about Bai and other

of art and political activism actually continues a very ancient Chinese pattern of literati involvement in affairs of state. Although Bai Hua is a twentieth-century Communist, his conception of the role of the artist and intellectual is shaped by the pattern of his mandarin predecessors, who assumed that the writer could draw upon a certain political authority, traditionally vested in the intellectual elite, to influence state policy. And in contrast to those who would interpret the "Bai Hua Incident" merely as a reimposition of political control over the arts, it appears that Bai's conflict with the Chinese state has been critical in an ongoing effort to fashion a new, and less tumultuous, relationship between artists and politicians in the People's Republic.

Bai Hua's Career as a Politically Engaged Artist

Bai Hua was born Chen Youhua in Xinyang, Henan, in 1930, the younger twin brother of Chen Zuohua, who under the pseudonym of Ye Nan also is a professional writer for the armed forces.[2] After a rough childhood, during which his merchant father was buried alive by the Japanese and he was expelled from secondary school for political activism, Bai joined the Red Army, where he worked in a propaganda unit. In the later 1940s, on the battlefield in East China, he became a member of the Communist Party.

Moving southward with the army, Bai took part in the takeover of Yunnan and remained there, where his career in army cultural work flourished. He wrote extensively on military and minority themes,

---

controversial figures has been selectively leaked to the outside. It is striking for instance, that no account has appeared providing details of Bai's activities during the Hundred Flowers movement, or during the Cultural Revolution. Such lacunae in Bai's recorded career are so blatant that they must have political origins. Nevertheless, the dozens of Hong Kong articles about Bai Hua have been consistent in the facts they do present, reinforcing the impression of a carefully managed release of information.

[2]Information on Bai Hua's career until the Cultural Revolution is found in the following sources: Tao Yin, "Wo suo renshi di Bai Hua" [The Bai Hua That I Know], *Zhengming* [Contending], Hong Kong, 67 (May 1983):28–33; Ding Wang, "Fenxi Bai Hua di daibiaozuo 'kulian' " [Analyzing Bai Hua's Representative Work, 'Unrequited Love'], *Dangdai* [Contemporary Age], Hong Kong, 9 (May 15, 1981):14–23; Zhou Yushan, "Bai Hua shijian" [The Bai Hua Incident], *Feiqing yuebao* [Bandit Affairs Monthly], Taibei, 12 (June 1981):54–63; Wang Zhangling, *Bai Hua di "lu"* [Bai Hua's "Road"] (Taibei: Li Ming Cultural Enterprises Co., 1982); Hong Min, "Wo suo renshi di Bai Hua" [The Bai Hua That I Know], *Zhengming* 44 (June 1981):28–29.

experimenting in several genres: poetry, short stories, and movie screenplays. At the same time, Bai was politically active. In 1952 he served for a period as secretary to the celebrated General He Long, and the following year he participated in the Second National Congress of Literature and Art, a singular distinction for a seemingly obscure young author. In 1955, Bai was promoted to a post as a writer in the General Political Department, the central bureaucracy for propaganda and cultural work within the People's Liberation Army.

This swift professional ascent came to a halt in 1957. Along with so many other intellectuals, Bai had joined in the Hundred Flowers movement, responding to Mao Zedong's call for helpful criticism by which the Party might rectify its increasingly bureaucratic ways. Bai's complaints about the administration of cultural work within the Kunming Military District, his former base, were not well received, and he was dismissed from both the Party and the army during the anti-Rightist campaign.

Bai's fate, while bitter enough, was milder than that of many of the other intellectuals labeled "rightist elements." He was not sent to labor reform camp, nor was he exiled to a remote village. Instead, following the intervention of Marshal He Long and General Xiao Hua, a leading official in army political and cultural affairs, Bai was permitted to work in Shanghai. By one account, this was in part from consideration for the illness of his wife, actress Wang Bei, who worked for a Shanghai film studio. Although Bai was no longer able to write, he did find employment at the fringe of the cultural world, as a worker in the military's "August First" Movie Equipment Factory.

By 1961, the cultural climate had loosened; Bai's rightist label was removed and he was permitted to resume his former craft as a writer for the Haiyan Film Studio of Shanghai. As part of the Socialist Education campaign, he spent much of 1963 among the poor and lower-middle peasants near Shaoxing. This episode, however, appears not to have been punishment, but a prelude to Bai's reacceptance into the mainstream of cultural life, for he was fully rehabilitated the following year. With his Party membership and military status restored, Bai was assigned as a writer for the Wuhan Military Region Drama Troupe, once more through the patronage of Xiao Hua, who in 1964 had become the head of the army's General Political Department.

But this rehabilitation was cut short by the Cultural Revolution, not a happy time for most of China's artists. Those who earlier had been classified as rightist elements were typically subjected to renewed political abuse for words they had uttered a decade before. Bai's exact fate is not clear. One Hong Kong article did say, without elaboration, that he was criticized by name by Mao's wife, Jiang Qing, in 1967.[3] Nonetheless, Bai's supporters in recent years have not claimed that he was singled out for special victimization, although he did engage in physical labor as a janitor and handyman for the Hubei Art Academy, which had been placed under military supervision and occupied by a Wuhan Military Region "cultural work team." Bai was considered an "object of dictatorship" and thus had no access to internal documents or any right to participate in political meetings. In 1973, when many disgraced officials were "liberated" across China, Bai was permitted at last to rejoin his family.[4]

Although Bai had been inactive as an artist, he had certainly observed closely a cultural regime of which he thoroughly disapproved. In 1974, he was offered an opportunity to act upon his convictions. Bai was approached by He Jiesheng, the daughter of his old patron, He Long. Although He Long was dead, those once associated with him, most notably Deng Xiaoping, were militant in their opposition to the radicals who surrounded Mao. He Jiesheng asked Bai to join an investigation to gather materials about problems in literature and art that might be used against Jiang Qing, Yao Wenyuan, and others. Bai agreed, and he interviewed people from the movie industry who had been involved in the production of "Haixia" and "The Pioneers," films that the radicals had criticized severely. He also spent much time with painters whose work had been collected for humiliating display as negative examples in the notorious Black Art Exhibition of 1974.[5] In

---

[3]Jiang said, "This Bai Hua is a bad person. Where is he? How did he slip into the army?" according to Tao Yin, "Wo suo renshi di Bai Hua," p. 32. Despite the reference to the army, it is possible that Tao confuses Bai Hua with a Tianjin propaganda official of the same name, who was criticized by central leaders in 1968 for his involvement in producing a play, "The Madman of the Modern Age." This Bai Hua from Tianjin was rehabilitated to become director of the Municipal Propaganda Department in 1979. See "Speeches of Comrades Zhou Enlai, Chen Boda, Kang Sheng, Jiang Qing, Yao Wenyuan at Reception for Members of the Tianjin Revolutionary Committee and Representatives of the Tianjin Revolutionary Masses," in *Jiang Qing tongzhi lun wenyi* [Comrade Jiang Qing Discusses Literature and Art], n.p., May 1968, pp. 187–202.

[4]Tao Yin, "Wo suo renshi di Bai Hua," p. 32.

[5]They included Huang Yongyu, Huang Wei, and Li Kushan. See Wang Yiyao, "Bai Hua fan Jiang Qing di yi duan mishi" [The Secret History of Bai Hua's Opposition to Jiang Qing], *Zhengming* 44 (June 1981):30–32; Wang Zhangling, *Bai Hua di "lu,"* pp. 5–6.

undertaking the investigation, Bai certainly came to the attention of Deng Xiaoping, although it is possible that the two had also had prior contact while Bai worked as He Long's secretary.

Bai's investigation work was incorporated into a lengthy report that was submitted first to cultural official Hu Qiaomu and then to Deng Xiaoping, who used it as a basis for arguing with Mao that cultural policy should be reformed. And in fact, Mao did criticize the radical policies, with "pungent remarks" in July 1975:

> Model operas alone are not enough. What is worse, one comes under fire for the slightest fault. No longer are a hundred flowers blossoming. Others are not allowed to offer any opinion; that's no good. . . . People are afraid to write articles or produce plays. There is nothing in the way of novels and poetry. . . . There should be some readjustments in the Party's policy on literature and art, and the performing arts should gradually enlarge their repertories in a year or in two or three years.[6]

The purge of the most militant radicals after Mao's death in 1976 marked a major turning point in Bai Hua's career. Bai had assumed significant risk by gathering materials against them; had the "gang of four" prevailed in the power struggle that followed Mao's death, Bai would have been vulnerable to retribution. Instead, he was promoted to deputy director of the Political Department of the Wuhan Military Region and became an editor for its Drama Troupe.[7] Bai resumed writing, entering a period of great productivity. One personal debt was repaid through his art: he wrote a screenplay eulogizing his old patron, He Long. The old marshal had been disgraced during the Cultural Revolution, and *Shuguang* [The Light of Early Dawn] accompanied his posthumous rehabilitation in 1977.[8]

In other writings, Bai began to assume the public posture for which he is now known in China—the militant voice for rehabilitated artists against old-line cultural administrators. This is evident in his television screenplay, "A Story of 'Looking Forward.'" "Looking Forward" was a slogan put forth in 1979 by propaganda officials unhappy with the widespread rehabilitation of rightist writers and artists, as well as with

---

[6]Hua Guofeng, "Political Report to the Eleventh National Congress of the Communist Party of China," *Peking Review* 20, 35 (August 1977):50–51.

[7]Wang Zhangling, *Bai Hua di "lu,"* p. 7.

[8]Hong Min, "Wo suo renshi di Bai Hua."

the embittered messages often borne by their art. Better to "look forward" toward the future, they argued, than to harp constantly on past unhappiness, as many writers were then doing with stories full of rage toward the Cultural Revolution. Bai's response to the slogan was to create a story about a naive woman novelist, visiting the countryside to gather material for her work. Bai used this tale about swine breeding to teach his young novelist that if one does not remain vigilant toward past enemies, they will again do one harm. The political message is tough, uncompromising, and thoroughly unforgiving toward Bai's political and cultural adversaries.[9]

At the same time, Bai's political activism became open, even ostentatious. Following Deng Xiaoping's political victory at the Third Plenum in December 1978, further movement away from Maoist policies was encouraged. Bai became a cultural gadfly, pestering the regime to loosen former restrictions in the arts. Wherever there was controversy, there too was Bai Hua. He made a dramatic speech at the Fourth National Congress of Literature and Art in late 1979, offering a battlecry: "No courage, no breakthrough; no breakthrough, no literature!"[10] He involved himself with "deviant" art, including the "Little Star" exhibition of unofficial painters and sculptors in Beijing.[11] He gave a speech at the ceremonial unveiling of the murals at the new Beijing International Airport, which became a subject of scandal because of the inclusion of nude figures, a taboo subject for art during the Cultural Revolution.[12] And Bai gained additional notoriety for his enthusiasm for the ill-fated "democracy" movement of 1979: "Comrade poets, we would rather sing the praises of a brick in the democratic wall. Never should we again sing the praises of any savior."[13]

[9]Bai Hua, " 'Xiang qian kan' di gushi" [A Story of 'Looking Forward'], *Renmin wenxue* [People's Literature] (September 1979), reprinted in *Zhongguo xin xianshizhuyi wenyi zuopin xuan* [Anthology of China's New Realist Literature], ed. Li Yi (Hong Kong: Qishi niandai zazhi she, 1980), pp. 125–35.

[10]Bai Hua, "No Breakthrough, No Literature," *Chinese Literature* 4 (1980):101.

[11]Jiang Youbei, "Beijing jietou neizhan di fengbo" [Disturbance Over Beijing Street Art Exhibit], *Zhengming* 25 (November 1, 1979):50.

[12]Bai's remarks urging cultural officials to follow the example of the civil aviation bureaucrats who commissioned the airport's artworks may be found in "Beijing guoji jichang bihua zuogong jiemu dianli jianghua zhaiyao" [Summary of the Speeches at the Ceremony Unveiling the Completed Murals at the Beijing International Airport], *Guanchajia* [Observer], Hong Kong, 34 (August 20, 1980):32–33.

[13]Quoted in Yuan Fang, "Unrequited Love and Intellectuals' Patriotism," *Hongqi* [Red Flag] 9 (May 1, 1981), in *Joint Publications Research Service*, no. 78425, July 1, 1981, p. 48.

Bai was criticized for his stance by Maoist officials, but he was given special protection by the editor of the prestigious *Literary Gazette,* Feng Mu. Feng had been Bai's superior in the Kunming Military Region in the 1950s. The Kunming alumnae included other strident voices of the post-Mao era, such as Gong Liu and Peng Xingfeng, all of whom were provided an important measure of protection by the influential Feng Mu.[14] The utility of the old link was demonstrated when Bai's screenplay, "Tonight the Starlight Glistens," an account of the Red Army's Huaihai campaign, aroused angry feelings among some military leaders. They felt that Bai's description of fear in battle belittled China's warriors. At a national military political work conference in January 1980, some officials demanded that Bai be given anew his rightist label. The anger of these soldiers was no doubt intensified by the knowledge that Bai was their fellow army worker.

At the same time, Bai's status as a military writer may have provided the army's cultural establishment a rationale for expressing broader discontent with the relaxation of cultural and social policy under Deng Xiaoping's administration. The screenplay was criticized in *People's Daily* by the radical head of the Shanghai Party Propaganda Department, Chen Yi (not to be confused with the former Red Army leader and foreign minister, although this Chen Yi was once head of cultural work in the army). It was Feng who defended Bai in print in both *Cinema Art* and *Beijing Evening News,* thereby forestalling more strenuous criticism of the nettlesome author.[15]

During all this controversy, little note was made of Bai's publication in 1979 of a screenplay, *Unrequited Love,* which appeared in a leading literary monthly.[16] Party leaders became alarmed only when Bai's screenplay was in fact made into a motion picture for a mass audience. It was never released. After the film was shown on a limited, internal basis to selected officials, final editing was aborted in 1981 by a

[14]Sun Wu, "Wusi di yuanding caihua hengyi di wenyi pinglunjia" [A Selfless Gardener, a Literary Critic Overflowing with Talent, Part I], *Jingbao* [The Mirror], Hong Kong, 3 (March 10, 1980):34–35.

[15]See Ji Chongyi, "Dichihao wenjian di chongji" [The Conflict over Document No. 7], *Dongxiang* [The Trend], Hong Kong, 30 (March 1981):4: T. S. L., "Rang qizimen bu zai chiyou" [Not Allowing Wives to Worry Again], *Jingbao* 8 (August 10, 1980):15–17; T. S. L., "Nandao jen you xie chouyi ma?" [Is It Really Possible That There Is a Whiff of Autumn in the Air?], *Jingbao* 10 (October 10, 1980):18–19.

[16]Bai Hua, "Kulian" [Unrequited Love], in *Zhengming* 44 (June 1981):82–98; reprinted from *Shiyue* [October] 3 (September 1979). The title is also often translated as "Bitter Love."

campaign against "bourgeois liberalism," of which the prime example was Bai Hua.[17] This was the first political campaign directed against an artist since the death of Mao five years earlier.

The initial public attack on *Unrequited Love* was made by a special commentator in *Liberation Army Daily* on April 18, 1981.[18] Some, but not all, of China's civilian press soon joined the campaign. Bai's tale was both melodramatic and militantly anti-Maoist: a patriotic artist returns from America to China after the Communist victory, only to encounter savage political harassment from narrow-minded radical officials. More broadly, Bai's comparisons of the painter's sorrows under Nationalist and Communist rule (to the relative advantage of the former!), as well as his failure to distinguish the policies of the "gang of four" from those of the Communist Party, were held up as examples of his "bourgeois liberalism." Bai was accused of opposing the Party.[19]

Three parts of the film were frequently identified as problematic. One was a scene in which a blackened Buddha was described as dirtied by the smoky incense of its worshippers. This was taken as an attack upon Mao Zedong. A second offending scene contained the inflammatory line addressed to Ling, the old painter, by his daughter: "You love your country, but does your country love you?" This scene was held to question China's treatment of intellectuals. The third controversial scene was the conclusion, in which Ling, physically weakened from living in the wilderness to avoid apprehension by radical mobs, dies in the snow, his body forming the point to a question mark that he has carved from the snow. This was held to be a negative judgment on China's socialism.

[17]A film from Bai's screenplay was made and distributed in Taiwan, where the "Bai Hua Incident" was given considerable publicity.

[18]The special commentator is believed to have been Liu Baiyu, head of cultural work in the army's General Political Department. The article, "Si ding jiben yuanze burong weifan" [The Four Basic Principles Must Not Be Betrayed], was reprinted in *Jiefangjun wenyi* [Liberation Army Literature and Art] 5 (May 1981):7–12, along with other articles from the army critical of Bai. A translation may be found in *Foreign Broadcast Information Service* (hereafter *FBIS*), May 21, 1981, pp. K6–K14.

[19]Specifically, Bai was charged with violating the "Four Basic Principles," set forth by Deng Xiaoping in March 1979, which require support for the socialist road, the dictatorship of the proletariat, the leadership of the Communist Party, and Marxism-Leninism and Mao Zedong Thought. See *Deng Xiaoping wenxuan 1975–1982* [Selected Works of Deng Xiaoping] (Hong Kong: Joint Publishing Co., 1983), pp. 150–51.

The fact that the campaign against Bai was mounted at all aroused considerable anxiety among the Chinese intelligentsia. Perhaps for that very reason, it was limited in scope. While *Unrequited Love* was roundly denounced, the campaign was not extended to include Bai's other works or other reform-minded writers associated with Bai, which would have been the normal course in earlier campaigns. Nor was there public discussion of Bai's past political difficulties, not even his old rightist label, another departure from the past pattern. As if to underscore the campaign's limited nature, in its midst, the Chinese Writers' Association awarded Bai a national prize for poetry.[20]

The campaign thus did not turn into a second Cultural Revolution nor even a full-blown anti-Rightist campaign. It ended with Bai's letter of self-criticism in November 1981, addressed to *Liberation Army Daily* and *Literary Gazette* (one the publication of his adversaries, and the other of his defenders). Bai apologized for a "lack of balance" in *Unrequited Love* and for failing to recognize the power of the Party and the people to overcome obstacles in Chinese society.[21]

Bai was not in public view during the next year. He passed the early part of 1982 revisiting the site of his early army career, the Yunnan frontier, which had become the front line in the conflict with Vietnam. By the end of the year, he had completed four novelettes. His continued respectability was demonstrated when the Ministry of Culture invited him to participate in a Shanghai conference on film scripts, in January 1983.[22]

Bai was next in the public eye in May, when the Beijing People's Art Theater mounted a major production of his new historical play, "The King of Wu's Golden Spear and the King of Yue's Sword." The play, set in the ancient Spring and Autumn period, deals with a once virtuous ruler who has become self-indulgent. Since it can be read as an

[20]Bai is a member of the Council of the Writers' Association. His poem, "Spring Tide in Sight," was honored on May 25, 1981. A prize was also given to Liu Binyan, another outspokenly reformist writer, for his controversial "People or Monsters?" *Beijing Review* 24, 30 (July 27, 1981):30. The Writers' Association may well have decided to give prizes to Bai and Liu to demonstrate the resistance of its members to the campaign against "bourgeois liberalism." It is also possible that top political leaders allowed this action to signal that this limited campaign was different from earlier ones. This message was reinforced when Bai's twin, army writer Ye Nan, received a Golden Rooster award for the screenplay of "Bahan Night Rain," judged the best movie of the previous year.

[21]"Bai Hua Criticizes Himself," *Beijing Review* 25, 2 (January 11, 1982):29.

[22]"Bai Hua: Public Criticism a Good Incentive," *Beijing Review* 26, 6 (February 7, 1983):29.

aesopian criticism of Mao Zedong (and perhaps also of Deng Xiaoping, some suggest), Bai clearly did not interpret his self-criticism as a pledge to foreswear further controversy.[23] Some Hong Kong press articles suggested that this play was criticized privately during the late 1983 campaign against "spiritual pollution." But although some works by other controversial writers were criticized openly and explicitly, Bai Hua apparently was protected against further attack.

Bai Hua and the Mandarin Tradition

Because Bai Hua is such a tenacious fighter, he may initially appear to Westerners as a liberal artist seeking to practice his craft without interference, locked in conflict with a repressive state that seeks to control all artistic expression. But the fact that the Party criticized Bai for being a bourgeois liberal does not make him one; actually, such a characterization fits him poorly. Bai is no battler for liberal values, and he is an unlikely person to press for a kind of Chinese Civil Liberties Union. Bai's conflict with political authority is of a different nature, perhaps best understood in the context of a very traditional interplay between Chinese politics and culture.

What distinguishes Bai Hua's politics from Western liberalism is his profoundly statist approach to cultural affairs. For Bai, the problem of the relationship between art and politics is not the liberal question of how to keep culture free from the power of the state. Instead, it is accepted that the two are inevitably intertwined: the state has the duty to manage cultural affairs well, and the artist has a responsibility to influence the political world according to his or her ideals.

Consider, for instance, Bai's fascination with one of the heroic figures of Chinese literary and political tradition, the poet-official Qu Yuan. Qu, the author of China's oldest signed poetry, remonstrated with his emperor over prevailing policies. When his advice was not heeded, Qu killed himself in sorrowful protest in 278 B.C., becoming

[23]Bai Hua, "Wu wang jinge Yue wang jian," *Shiyue* 2 (1983):64–95. The title is sometimes simplified as "The Story of King Goujian." *Shiyue* is the same journal that published *Unrequited Love* in 1979. For commentary, see Fang Jie, "After Seeing 'The King of Wu's Golden Spear and the King of Yue's Sword,'" *Wenzhai bao* [Press Digest] 109 (November 4, 1983):5; Lin Kehuan, "Lishi yishi yu daode piping" [Historical Consciousness and the Criticism of Morality] *Zuopin yu zhengming* [Writings and Contention] 10 (October 1983):43–45; and Ding Yi, "Buyao weile guannian wangle lishi" [Don't Forget History for the Sake of a Concept] *Zuopin yu zhengming* 10 (October 1983)46–47.

China's most famous political suicide. Qu Yuan's memory has lasted in Chinese cultural tradition as a symbol of the politically engaged artist, willing to stand with patriotic integrity in isolated opposition to unjust policies.[24] Bai Hua very self-consciously places himself in this tradition by quoting Qu at the outset of *Unrequited Love,* as well as by an effort to liken the fates of Qu Yuan and the painter of his screenplay. (The painter, for instance, participates in the April 1976 Tiananmen demonstration bearing a poster inspired by Qu Yuan.)

Even as Bai Hua's political activism draws upon the tradition of the critical mandarin, he also situates himself within another political tradition equally distant from liberal concerns: Stalinism. In Bai's essay, "A Question That Must Be Answered," he asks, "Must literature and art serve politics?" His answer is that it must not, in the sense in which Maoist practice tied art to specific policies, producing bad art as well as bad politics. Yet Bai endorses an equally politicized conception of the artist as an "engineer of the human soul" (he quotes the phrase of Stalin's literary lieutenant, A. A. Zhdanov) who has an obligation to take a political stance in his or her work.[25]

Both in his reference to classical symbols of political involvement and in his use of slogans from modern Communist tradition, Bai makes no secret of his statist orientation. Bai's career shows a deep commitment to *maximize* the political power of artists in order to bring about change, rather than a liberal desire to avoid the entanglement of power and art. How else can one interpret Bai's repeated enthusiasm for the political force of artists, such as his 1980 remark: "We must have faith in our own power. Today, when some comrades are repressed, it shows that we have power. If you have no power, who would bother to repress you? . . . We have won the support of the popular masses."[26]

Because of Bai's concern with power, and his appreciation of the mandarin tradition, it is unsurprising that throughout his career he has

[24]For a recent discussion of the place of Qu Yuan in China's political tradition, see Laurence A. Schneider, *A Madman of Ch'u: The Chinese Myth of Loyalty and Dissent* (Berkeley: University of California Press, 1980). Qu's memory lingers in popular culture through the annual tradition of dragon boat races, especially in South China where Bai has spent his career.

[25]Bai Hua, "A Question That Must Be Answered," in *Perspectives in Contemporary Chinese Literature*, ed. Mason Y. H. Wang (University Center, Michigan: Green River Press, 1983), p. 110.

[26]Bai's remarks were made at a Lushan study class on novel creation for young authors. Quoted in Huang Wei, "Zhongguo zuojia di xinsheng" [The Aspirations of China's Writers], *Guanchajia* 38 (December 20, 1980):25.

repeatedly drawn upon a strong network of personal loyalties. The central place of factional ties of patron to client in Bai's career underscores a classic Chinese approach to power and influence. Critical to Bai's career have been the bonds forged among the military liberators of Southwest China. And three and a half decades after the establishment of the People's Republic, Bai still works for the Wuhan Military Region, an organization initially staffed (along with the Kunming and Chengdu military regions) by the Second Field Army, which conquered the Southwest.[27]

Bai Hua's career as a military official is full of irony. The army plays a complex role in the politics of Chinese culture. For much of the history of the People's Republic, it has assumed the stance of the vigilant conscience of the revolution, stressing such values as purity, austerity, and socialism. The army has its own cultural apparatus, which is influential even in the civilian arena. The army newspaper, for instance, played a leading role in 1965 in launching the Cultural Revolution, just as it initiated the criticism of Bai Hua in 1981.

Many in the army profited from the Cultural Revolution and have been resentful of efforts to purge China of radicalism since Mao's death. Cultural reformers have especially criticized senior military leaders for the abuse of their bureaucratic privileges, and Bai has joined his civilian comrades in raising this topic.[28] Nevertheless, more reformist elements in the army have provided him a measure of sanctuary during some of China's difficult political times. Military units gave him employment and underwrote his 1964 rehabilitation at a time when many rightists were left in the wilderness for another decade or more. And once rehabilitated, Bai was afforded the political protection that accompanied membership in a work unit that was officially subordinate to the radical Lin Biao. This serves to remind outsiders of the complexity of military politics in China, where a supposedly radical institution can give rise to Marshal Chen Yi, who argued strenuously for looser state control over the arts, even as it can sustain a controversial maverick like Bai Hua. Indeed, at the height of the 1981 campaign against bourgeois liberalism, the *Beijing Evening News* printed an article de-

[27]See William W. Whitson, *The Chinese High Command: A History of Communist Military Politics, 1927–71* (New York: Praeger, 1973).

[28]See Bai's story, ''A Bundle of Letters,'' in *Stubborn Weeds, Popular and Controversial Chinese Literature after the Cultural Revolution*, ed. Perry Link (Bloomington: Indiana University Press, 1983): 114–41.

scribing the support given Bai by his Party branch in the Wuhan Military Region.[29]

Bai's ties to the powerful have not only aided his career, but also put it in considerable jeopardy, when his deeds have demonstrated loyalty to patrons out of favor in Beijing. This role of literary retainer to persons of power has been a common one in the politics of China.[30] Thus, although there is no question that Bai has been willing to take unusual personal risks through his public activism, he remains an establishment figure, even when he is out of the political mainstream. Bai is certainly among the more outspoken members of China's literary establishment; nonetheless, he holds a leading post in the Chinese Writers' Union, and his personal ties to Feng Mu, Xiao Hua, He Long, and Deng Xiaoping do not suggest a writer alienated from his society.[31]

Bai's concern with power neither is abstract nor is it purely personal ambition. He has specific goals, which center around displacing the cultural officials who supported the Cultural Revolution and ensuring that it does not recur. Along with many thousands of other intellectuals, Bai regards the Maoist policies in culture as a tragedy, both personally and nationally. Because of his skills, his social position, and his boldness, Bai has assumed a stance of uncompromising militance against those intellectuals and officials who still would adhere to radical ways. He thus has gained a following among those intellectuals who share this interest and support from official reformers who seek to establish safeguards against future mass movements. But he cannot be said to speak on behalf of all intellectuals, as a distinct social group. As Bai has noted, "Jiang Qing seized the opportunity to organize a new literary and art contingent."[32] Bai has made it his business to wage war against that contingent, displacing it if possible and taming it other-

[29]Huai Bing, "'Bai Hua shijian' zai zhonggong yinqi di douzheng" [*The Bai Incident* Raises a Struggle in the Chinese Communist Party], *Zhengming* 44 (June 1981):34–35.

[30]See Merle Goldman, *China's Intellectuals: Advise and Dissent* (Cambridge: Harvard University Press, 1981).

[31]For a very different interpretation of Bai, drawing more upon his writings than his career, which treats Bai as a humanist rather than as a politically sophisticated cultural cadre, see chapter 5, "Resurgent Humanism in Bai Hua's *Bitter Love*," in Michael S. Duke, *Blooming and Contending: Chinese Literature in the Post-Mao Era* (Bloomington: Indiana University Press, forthcoming). Professor Duke generously showed me a draft of this chapter.

[32]Bai Hua, "A Question That Must Be Answered," p. 103.

wise. Since Maoist influence was especially powerful within the political apparatus of the army and among civilian propaganda bureaucrats, it is among these groups that opposition to Bai has been strongest.[33]

Precisely because he has been so clearly identified in China as a spokesman for the interests of the anti-Maoist intelligentsia, Bai takes considerable care to present his case in the most universalistic terms possible, lest he be charged with narrow partiality. One way in which Bai has done this is by constant invocation of "the people" as the cause for which he fights:

> Sometimes I think about a certain question: As a writer, should I be rejected by the people, or should I let those in power reject me? I believe that when there is a contradiction between the two, I can only stand on the side of the people. This is because history is written by the people and the history of literature is also written by the people. There are some works of literature that were rejected by those who held power during the author's lifetime, but then they became immortal classics after they died. Why was that? Because these works were recognized by the people. Therefore we must rely on our own conscience in writing, thinking all the time about the people, forever loyal to the people.[34]

In this passage Bai links the Qu Yuan tradition of a special political authority for the mandarin elite as paternal protector of the people to the Party's familiar Leninist claims to represent the "proletariat." One can easily imagine, however, that there are many in the establishment who are not happy with this, viewing artists' claims to be "serving the people" as competitive with the Party's monopoly.

Although Bai is fond of cloaking himself in the ample robe of "the people," his career in the past decade has clearly been distinguished by activism on behalf of a narrower circle of reform-minded artists, cultural officials, and central politicians. In particular, Bai Hua is linked to thousands of intellectuals who had been labeled rightists in the wake of the failed Hundred Flowers movement in 1957. Many were quite elderly by the late 1970s, a factor which encouraged a generally quiet reassimilation into cultural life. Bai, however, was only twenty-seven

---

[33]These students are officials on leave from their regular posts and include many from propaganda deparments. See Luo Bing, "Liuzhong guanhui hou di Zhongguo" [China after the Sixth Plenum], *Zhengming* 45 (July 1981):10.

[34]Quoted in Micheal S. Duke, "The Second Blooming of the Hundred Flowers: Chinese Literature in the Post-Mao Era," in *Perspectives in Contemporary Chinese Literature*, ed. Wang, p. 35.

in 1957. In many respects he is representative of a group of young writers of 1957 who reentered public life energetically after Mao's death. One thinks of other former rightists such as Wang Meng (criticized for his 1956 story, "A New Young Man Comes to the Organization Department"), who is now a member of the Party Central Committee, or Liu Binyan, China's leading investigative reporter, whose pen at the *People's Daily* is as harsh now as it was before 1957.[35] While these and other leading members of the generation of 1957 (such as Gong Liu and Liu Shaotang) have followed individual paths since the rise of Deng Xiaoping, they share a certain public image. Class struggle is definitely off their agenda, while building a secure environment for patriotic intellectuals is a prime goal. Apparently undeterred by past political difficulties, the leaders of the generation of 1957 seem willing to press the politicians from earlier generations to test and protect the limits of what the system will allow for outspoken artists.

In the jockeying for political position that preceded Mao's death, Deng Xiaoping shared with Bai and other cultural reformers the goal of striking at radical excesses in cultural policy. Deng needed the rehabilitation of veteran bureaucrats to gain political allies. The cultural reformers needed to dislodge Maoists from cultural positions if their own careers were to flourish.[36] Yet neither could happen until the power of the radicals had been blunted. This practical alliance was the basis for the wave of reform in culture that unfolded from the mid-1970s until the 1981 campaign against bourgeois liberalism.[37]

The more the cultural reformers aided Deng in bashing the radicals so that old bureaucrats might be rehabilitated, however, the less it appeared that the Deng camp needed their fiery attacks on the old-line cultural administration. This became especially true as the rehabilitation process restored increasing numbers of cultural officials who had been purged by the Maoists. These officials often had shared bitter

[35]Some of Liu Binyan's recent writings have been translated in Perry Link, ed., *People or Monsters? and Other Stories and Reportage from China after Mao* (Bloomington: Indiana University Press, 1983).

[36]Zi Lin, "Zhao Dan 'Yishu' di fengbo" [The Turmoil over Zhao Dan's "Testament"], *Dongxiang*, Hong Kong, 30 (March 1981):8–11.

[37]For background on arts reforms after 1976, see Sylvia Chan, "The Blooming of a 'Hundred Flowers' and the Literature of the 'Wounded Generation,'" in *China since the "Gang of Four,"* ed. Bill Brugger (London: Croom Helm, 1980), pp. 174–201; Anthony J. Kane, "Literary Politics in Post-Mao China," *Asian Survey* 21, 7 (July 1981):775–94; and Colin Mackerras, *The Performing Arts in Contemporary China* (London: Routledge & Kegan Paul, 1981).

experiences in common with the cultural reformers. Although this provided a sufficient basis for joint opposition to radicals, the two groups had disagreed before the Cultural Revolution, and in the 1980s they increasingly feuded about what Chinese culture should be; thus they could form no long-term alliance. For instance, the 1957 anti-Rightist campaign had dislodged both writers such as Bai and cultural administrators such as Chen Yi, who lost his job as head of cultural work in the army's General Political Department. Both suffered in the 1960s, but following his rehabilitation in the 1970s, Chen became the leading official for Shanghai culture and propaganda, a nationally prominent position from which he consistently resisted tendencies to weaken Party supervision of the arts. Another of Bai's leading adversaries was his nominal superior, Liu Baiyu, who had become head of the army's cultural work in 1977. Liu was an honored military writer, the winner of a Stalin Prize in 1951 and the hagiographer of the army hero, Lei Feng, in 1963. Although he was criticized fiercely in the Cultural Revolution, he has always viewed the role of the artist primarily as propagandist, a vision Bai does not share.[38]

It was during the disintegration of the 1976–79 alliance between Deng's officials and the cultural reformers that Bai Hua became an obvious target for criticism. As Deng Xiaoping chose to make concessions to cultural figures content to work within the resurrected status quo, rather than to the reformers, Bai's unwillingness to stop pressing for further change made him a symbol that required a blow. Apparently, however, given the limited character of the attacks upon Bai in 1981 and the fact that both Chen Yi and Liu Baiyu have since been retired, this criticism was only a temporary sop to Bai's enemies. This suggests that the conservative trend of the early 1980s could yet be reversed.

Does Bai Hua envision himself in a position of higher political leadership, perhaps as a reformist head of the army's cultural department? We have no access to Bai's aspirations, and we can easily imagine that his controversial background would place some appointments beyond his reach. Bai's behavior, however, fits the role of the mandarin at the edge of power, writing memorials urging his emperor to adopt reforms in hopes of enjoying higher appointments from which to advance his cause.

[38]Editorial note to "On the Dusty Road," in Kai-yu Hsu, ed., *Literature of the People's Republic of China* (Bloomington: Indiana University Press, 1980), p. 125. See also Marian Galik, "The Concept of 'Positive Hero' in Chinese Literature of the 1960s and 1970s," *Asian and African Studies*, Bratislava, 27 (1981):34.

Struggles on the Path to Cultural Reform

What is the significance of Bai Hua's career within the broader processes of change in the People's Republic of China? With his fearless joy in controversy, Bai has played a central role in the complicated process in which Chinese artists and officials are coming to a new understanding of the rules by which writers write and censors censor. Bai's efforts in the cause of cultural reform have been repeatedly frustrated, yet the relationship between artists and the state has shifted, if ever so clumsily, in a direction that responds to some of the demands put forth by the reformers.[39] One must understand that complete cultural reform, even on Bai's terms, would not mean the abolition of political influence over the arts and the establishment of an unfettered cultural marketplace. Rather, Chinese reformers are seeking to learn to administer the arts in a way that recognizes the fact that the revolution is over, and that many past methods are ill-suited to a postrevolutionary situation. This process has not been simple, nor has it been harmonious.

The reformers were encouraged by a series of successes after Deng Xiaoping's political victories in late 1978. There was the turbulent excitement of Democracy Wall, followed by the Fourth National Congress of Literature and Art, which was full of enthusiastic promise; a year later, in late 1980, came the trial of the "gang of four." Hua Guofeng was removed from his top posts, and Minister of Culture Huang Zhen, thought to be insufficiently eager for change, was replaced.

Yet during the same period, the fever for cultural reform was cooled by other events. In 1979, literary radicals made a counterattack through their slogan of "looking forward" and Deng Xiaoping stressed the need to uphold Party dominance in all fields. The next year cultural administrators launched a campaign to raise awareness among artists of the "social effects of literature and art," and excitement over the trial of the "gang of four" was dampened by another political trial, for the Democracy Wall activist Wei Jingsheng.

If these evident tensions in the cultural world were to be contained without harsh repression, it appeared that a new way of doing things was necessary. Some of the proposals of the cultural reformers for

[39]This theme is developed more extensively by Tang Tsou, "Political Change and Reform: The Middle Course," in *China: The 80s Era*, ed. Norton Ginsberg and Bernard A. Lalor (Boulder: Westview Press, 1984), pp. 27–69.

greater artistic autonomy began to gain official endorsement. The *People's Daily* editorial on the 1979 Fourth Congress of Writers and Artists repeated Deng Xiaoping's message to that assembly: "Writers and artists must have freedom to choose subject matter and methods of presentation. These can be explored only through their own practice and gradually resolved. In this respect, no outside interference by the leadership will be permitted."[40] Bai Hua's patron, Feng Mu, referred to the allegedly autonomous "laws of art" that must be respected by officials if culture is to develop.[41]

A similar call for limiting Party leadership was published in the Party's own journal, *Red Flag*. Recalling the traditional Daoist injunction to "rule through inaction" (*wu wei er zhi*), Wang Ruowang, an author and coeditor of *Shanghai Literature* (and another former rightist), advocated political detachment from the arts. According to Wang,

> Flourishing periods in literature and art have appeared in China and foreign countries, in ancient and modern times, but they are not the result of the harsh and tedious interference, or the orders, of the leading organs of the state. [It is the state that often issues] blind instructions in violation of the laws of art and applies the methods of leading industrial production to literature and art.[42]

People's Daily published another assault on Party domination—the deathbed testament of popular movie star Zhao Dan: "If art is governed too precisely, it has no hope."[43] The Party's willingness to publicize such views was startling.

Many Party officials were extremely unhappy to have their position challenged so openly. In their eyes, the political environment had

[40]"Greet the New Period of Socialist Renaissance—Warmly Congratulating the Successful Conclusion of the Fourth National Congress of Chinese Writers and Artists," *Renmin ribao* 17 (November 1979), in *FBIS*, November 19, 1979, p. L11.

[41]See Sun Wu, "A Selfless Gardener, a Literary Critic Overflowing with Talent (Part II)," *Jingbao* 4, 10 (April 1980):33.

[42]Wang Ruowang, "On 'Rule Through Inaction' in Literature and Art,'" *Hongqi* 9 (September 1979):47–49; also see Li Jiang, "Wang Ruowang qi ren ji qi zuopin" [Wang Ruowang, the Man and His Work], *Dongxiang* 32 (May 1981):18–20.

[43]Zhao Dan, "Guande tai juti, weiyi mei xiwang" [If Art Is Governed Too Precisely, It Has No Hope], *Renmin ribao*, October 8, 1980. Also see Zi Lin, "The Turmoil over Zhao Dan's 'Testament.'"

shifted too far to the right. To be sure, the "gang of four" had been too harsh on artists, but the boldest reformers were systematically discrediting all of the techniques by which state officials had customarily "nurtured" the development of Chinese culture.

One of the key battlegrounds for the struggle between cultural reformers and their adversaries was the motion picture industry. Movies have a special place in China's politics. Because film is an efficient way to reach a mass audience, the Party has long regarded it as a preeminent propaganda medium and has carefully supervised its production. Thus, the leadership's public indifference to *Unrequited Love* when it was published in 1979 in a literary magazine for a sophisticated readership ended when Bai and his supporters sought to reach a broader audience through film.

With the post-Mao decentralization of artistic censorship, the Film Bureau of the Ministry of Culture began to approve scripts after shooting, rather than before.[44] But the political sensitivity of movies meant that the potentially liberating effects of decentralization often were aborted in practice, as problem films were passed on to higher levels for resolution. Top Party officials often ended up as film censors, with members of the Political Bureau and other leading bodies previewing and discussing troublesome movies. One film was allegedly screened privately in Beijing twenty-six times and still no one could make a decision about it.[45] Indeed, an early hint that Bai Hua's movie might encounter difficulty surfaced in a Hong Kong report early in 1981 that *Unrequited Love* was being screened in Zhongnanhai, the residence of China's central leadership, with no conclusion reached as to its suitability for public release.[46]

In the first ten months of 1980, twelve films were halted in progress, including *Unrequited Love*.[47] And this was in a year when only eighty-

[44]Liu Shao, "Zhonggong dianyingye di nanti he zhangwang" [The Difficulties and Prospects of the Chinese Communist Film Industry], *Dongxiang* 14 (November 16, 1979):44–46.

[45]Guan Ping, "Cong wenyi 'jiancha zhidu' shuokaiqu" [Speaking of "Inspector Systems"], *Dongxiang* 32 (May 1981):51.

[46]Su Jiong, "Zhonggong wentan you guaqile fengqiu" [Another Wind Blows in the Chinese Communist Literary Scene], *Zhengming* 40 (February 1981):27.

[47]Bi Ming, "Chuyu 'shou' feng zhong di dalu wenyijie" [Mainland Literature and Art Circles in the Midst of a "Restrictive" Wind], *Dongxiang* 29 (February 1981):22.

two features were released for distribution.[48] The immediate cause of the rash of unfinished movies was Hu Yaobang's speech at a forum on script writing, held from January 23 through February 13, 1980, which initiated an attempt to tighten leadership over culture through a public discussion of the "social effects" of literature and art. Remnant "leftists" took this occasion to press for restoration of tighter overall political limits in the arts, especially in film making. One of the troubled films of 1980 was about the Lin Biao affair, *In a Twinkling*. After internal screenings for military personnel, a letter of protest from an air force club accused the film of mocking the military, and it was prohibited from distribution.[49]

Amidst such controversy, *Unrequited Love* in celluloid appeared more menacing than it had on paper in 1979. Curiously, the filmed version was retitled as *Sun and Man*. Given the long tradition in modern Chinese politics of using the image of the sun to represent Mao Zedong, the new title was likely perceived as still more inflammatory, suggesting as it did the connection between the cult of Mao and the inhumanity of the Cultural Revolution. The movie was reedited and the three most controversial scenes were removed, and then it was shown privately to officials of bureau chief level and higher.[50] It was during such screenings that sentiment against Bai Hua mounted into a national campaign. Internal screenings of *Unrequited Love* at the Central Party School and among military officials elicited the initial criticism of the movie, in the form of letters to Wei Guoqing (then head of the army's General Political Department) demanding formal censure of Bai.[51]

While it is possible that Bai would not have become the leading "bourgeois liberal" of 1981 if *Unrequited Love* had not been filmed, or if its screening had been timed differently, the attack upon him probably owed more to his activism for cultural reform than to his film work. It is striking, for instance, that there was no criticism during the campaign of the film's director, Peng Ning, who was also coauthor of the

[48]John L. Scherer, ed., *China: Facts and Figures Annual*, vol. 6 (Gulf Breeze, Florida: Academic International Press, 1983), p. 320.

[49]Yu Zi, "Dalu wentan di yi chang da bianlun" [A Great Debate in the Mainland Literary World], *Dongxiang* 26, 16 (November 1980):10–12.

[50]Xu Ming, "Bai Hua shijian yu wentan fan 'you'" [The Bai Hua Incident and Anti-'Rightism' on the Literary Scene], *Zhengming* 43 (May 1981):14–15.

[51]Nai Xin, "Cong Bai Hua shijian kan zhonggong zhengju" [A Look at the Chinese Communist Party's Political Situation from the Bai Hua Incident], *Zhengming* 45 (July 1981):12.

final filmed version.[52] Nor did the campaign use the new film title, leaving attention focused on Bai's original screenplay.

In February, with the launching of the campaign, the Party issued its restrictive Central Directive No. 7. Its nine provisions attempted to bring greater order to cultural affairs:

1. Artists must support the four basic principles.

2. Public criticism of individuals by name must be approved by a higher level of authority.

3. Art should stress the four modernizations, and writers should not leave people sick at heart when dealing with the anti-Rightist campaign of 1957 or the Cultural Revolution.

4. In treating the issue of bureaucratic privilege, artists should not harm the image of the Party.[53]

5. Do not support illegal publications.

6. Develop literary and art criticism. If a leading official takes part, do not interpret this to be the use of clubs and labels.

7. Tighten control over local opera, which has excessive superstition.

8. Art and propaganda must be good at cultivating youth in such qualities as organization, discipline, and courtesy.

9. There are restrictions on exchange and purchase of Hong Kong political magazines, unless approved by a provincial or central propaganda unit.[54]

Only the restriction on criticism by name was a gesture to the reformers. All of the other provisions addressed matters of growing concern to officials who thought that culture had drifted too far to the right. The ban of aid to "illegal publications" referred to the unofficial journals that had appeared during the Democracy Wall movement. Many reformers, including Bai Hua, had encouraged these new publications.[55] Several leftist magazines in Hong Kong had become enthusi-

[52]Peng, a Cultural Revolution-era graduate of the Beijing Cinema Academy and the son of a high official, is a director at Chang Chun Film Company. See Hong Min, "The Bai Hua That I Know."

[53]See Richard Kraus, "Bureaucratic Privilege as an Issue in Chinese Politics," *World Development* 11, 8 (August 1983):672–82.

[54]Ke Xin, "Yin ren guanzhu di zhonggong qihao jiuhao shierhao wenjian" [The Noteworthy Central Committee Documents Nos. Seven, Nine, and Twelve], *Jingbao* 4, 10 (April 1981):7–8.

[55]The Central Committee also issued Central Directive No. 9 of 1981, directed specifically against such unofficial publications. This was apparently in reaction to a November 1980 meeting in Jiangsu to organize a national association of such periodicals. See Xu Ming, "The Bai Hua Incident."

astic supporters of cultural reform and had formed ties with the bolder reformers, who found it politically advantageous to leak information to them. Thus the leadership sought to limit their circulation.

The criticism of Bai Hua cannot be disentangled from this broader discussion in 1981 of how the arts should be run. A *People's Daily* article subsequently justified the campaign against Bai as a correction for insufficient attention to cultural leadership by the Party: "For a certain period of time, while carrying out literature and art criticism, we failed to provide sufficient guidance in certain aspects and no strict demands were set. We also failed to boldly and forcefully criticize wrong ideas. Some comrades detested or rejected any criticism."[56]

It was not initially clear what this new and tougher attitude meant for the more obstreperous writers. Bai Hua's role was instructive to all parties in the controversy. He served as a double example. The national criticism of Bai showed that cultural reformers could no longer write whatever they pleased with impunity. Enormous anxiety was thus aroused among the Chinese intelligentsia, whose conduct quickly became more cautious. But the gentle manner in which the campaign was conducted also demonstrated that criticism of artists need not be a savage trashing of a person's career, family, friends, and life's work. By criticizing a specific work, *Unrequited Love,* without disciplining its author, the leadership indicated that this tightening of control represented a new approach to the arts, rather than a return to customarily rough methods of silencing critics. Even the campaign's first hostile article by *Liberation Army Daily's* special commentator closed by saying: "We hope that after passing through the criticism of *Unrequited Love,* we can raise our army's literature and art workers' awareness of supporting the four basic principles; we also hope that the author of *Unrequited Love* can learn a lesson from this error, sharpen his creative thought, and hereafter write works beneficial to our socialist fatherland and to the people."[57]

The unusually light treatment that followed during the campaign contributed to making Bai something of a celebrity. Articles in the Communist press of Hong Kong revealed that far from being sent to labor reform camp, Bai had just bought a new motorbike, or was

[56]Gu Yan, "Develop a Healthy Literature and Art Criticism," *Renmin ribao*, June 8, 1981, in *FBIS*, June 10, 1981, pp. K4-K7.

[57]See T. S. L., "'Xingguang' zhi zhan wei yi yunniang xin di jiaoliang" [The "Starlight" Battle Is Not Yet Over, a New Round Is Brewing], *Jingbao* 12, 12 (October 1980):16–17.

enjoying working at a seaside resort.[58] During the summer, someone in the central leadership reportedly invited Bai to the capital to live in the Beijing Hotel, and the Propaganda Department had already been asked to approve Bai's next commission, a historical play for the Beijing People's Art Theater ("The King of Wu's Golden Spear and the King of Yue's Sword").[59]

This is not to say that the campaign was not waged in earnest; the issues involved were too vital. Bai and other reformers had been extremely vocal in the preceding two years, and when the campaign put them on the defensive, many voices of resentment were heard. Some thought people like Bai were arrogant for equating the slightist criticism with unfair political attack. (Bai had labeled his critics the "big stick" faction).[60] It was also reported that some were complaining that too much recent writing was ignoring ordinary people, focusing instead upon "five kinds of people": rightists, intellectuals, sons of high-ranking officials, overseas Chinese, and criminals. Some peasants were said to feel that "literature and art had entered the big cities" and no longer addressed their concerns.[61] It was also said that many writers were drifting away from the masses, with innovations such as stream of consciousness writing. *Red Flag* complained that some would rather "create the spring snow for 1,000 people than create the song of the rustic poor for the 800 million people."[62]

The remnant left joined the campaign with enthusiasm. Beijing's *Shidai di baogao* [Contemporary Reportage], run by the army's General Political Department, began to use the phrase "patriotic intellectuals" to indicate those deemed worthy of political support. Such a phrase implied clearly that there were also unpatriotic intellectuals, a formulation that reminded many of the hostility with which intellectuals as a social group systematically were treated during the

[58]Special commentator, *Jiefangjun bao*, p. 12.

[59]"Bai Hua Interviewed in Wuhan," *Wenhui bao* (Hong Kong), May 14, 1981, in *FBIS*, May 14, 1981, p. W2; and "Bai Hua Escapes the Heat at Beidahe, Talks about Two New Works and 'Unrequited Love,'" *Dagong bao* (Hong Kong), July 10, 1981, in *JPRS* 78597, July 24, 1981, p. 39.

[60]Dai Dan, "Liuzhong quanhui hou di wentan qihou" [The Climate in the Literary Scene after the Sixth Plenum], *Jingbao* 16 (August 1981):24–25.

[61]Qun Ming, "Literature and Art Must Serve the People and Socialism," *Wen hui bao* (Shanghai), May 23, 1981, in *FBIS*, June 4, 1981, pp. 06–08.

[62]Ding Zhenhai, "The Question of 'For Whom' Is Still a Fundamental Question— Studying 'Talks at the Yan'an Forum on Literature and Art,'" *Hongqi* 10 (16 May 1981):13–17, in *FBIS*, June 16, 1981, pp. K16-K22.

Cultural Revolution.[63] The department distributed booklets of study materials for the campaign throughout the army. They included the text of *Unrequited Love* as well as critiques of it.[64] There was a feeling elsewhere in the army, too, that there was a growing tendency to slight the Chinese nation.[65]

The defense of Bai was more subdued, but active. A somewhat disingenuous argument was made by Bai's old patron, Feng Mu, who claimed that to exaggerate the social impact of art constituted "subjective idealism" similar to that of the "gang of four." To argue thus that Bai's work really had little impact was of course counter to the reformers' own conviction that art could be a leading force for change. Feng also argued for critical pluralism, asserting optimistically that it is normal to have "different views on a certain book or a certain article."[66] As the campaign went on, others of Bai's defenders conceded that criticism of artists was appropriate, but that there must also be room for "countercriticism."[67]

This round of strife in the Chinese literary scene made it difficult for reformist cultural officials to determine the most politic position to take. Even Zhou Yang, typically a central figure in arts controversies since 1949, attempted to duck the issue (and avoid criticizing Bai Hua and the reformers) by claiming at the height of the controversy that "I have not read many contemporary works."[68] To help resolve the con-

---

[63]"*Shidai di baogao* Criticized," *Dagong bao* (Hong Kong), August 4, 1981, p. 2, in *FBIS*, August 11, 1981, pp. W5-W6.

[64]Yen Kai, "Subjects Ranging from Teng Lichun to the All-Army Criticism of Bai Hua—Part X of Division Commander Luo's Review of National Affairs with This Correspondent," *Zhengming ribao* [Contending Daily] (Hong Kong), July 23, 1981, in *FBIS*, July 27, 1981, pp. W3-4.

[65]For instance, there were complaints from the Kunming Military District about a poem, "The General and the Soldiers." The poem became controversial by contrasting the medals of generals to the blood shed by ordinary soldiers. It was especially resented that people like Bai regarded any criticism as an unfair political label. Ke Qing and Yun Lang, "Some Comments on 'The Generals and the Soldiers,'" *Yunnan ribao*, March 16, 1981, in *FBIS*, April 3, 1981, pp. K10-K12.

[66]Feng Mu, "Writers and Artists Should Heighten Their Sense of Responsibility and Mission," *Renmin ribao*, July 25, 1981, in *FBIS*, August 4, 1981, pp. K12-K14.

[67]Xue Zhongxin, "Criticism Should Not Be Confused with the Stick," *Banyuetan* 15, reported by Beijing *Xinhua*, August 10, 1981, in *FBIS*, August 11, 1981, p. K7.

[68]Zhou Yang, "Award Works According to the Will of the People and Criteria of the Science of Aesthetics—Speech at the National Meeting for Presentation of Awards for the Best Novels, Reportage, and Poems," *Renmin ribao*, June 24, 1981, in *FBIS*, June 29, 1981, p. K10.

flict, the Propaganda Department called a national conference in July, at which Deng Xiaoping's emphasis on the need for criticism and self-criticism was prominent. Hu Yaobang seemed less harsh, stressing the importance of handling the campaign against *Unrequited Love* well, as if he were anxious that this was not being done.[69]

To bring the conflict to a conclusion, the press emphasized the need to relearn the skills of criticism and self-criticism that allegedly had been the Party's glory before the Cultural Revolution. There was considerable attention to the contrast between "proper" methods of criticism and anonymous attacks.[70] In this way, central leaders apparently hoped to reach a consensus and offer something to both sides of the conflict. For the angry cultural officials, there was the reassertion of the Party's right to discipline a maverick. For the frustrated reformers, there was a demonstration that campaigns could be waged in a new and more limited way.

The Ministry of Culture and the Federation of Literary and Art Circles held a forum in Beijing in August in an apparent effort to bring the Bai Hua incident to a close. While many participants made ritual attacks on "bourgeois liberalism," many also continued to point to the need for improved methods of criticism. Two weeks later, Zhou Weizhi, the acting minister of culture, included conciliatory words toward the reformers in his report to the Fifth National People's Congress:

> Improper and excessive criticism and struggle carried out in the past in literary and artistic field [sic] had bad consequences. We must draw a lesson from it and not launch any more political movements. We must try to set the minds at ease of those who have well-meaning concern about the development of our art and literature by reminding them of the fragrant flowers that have already blossomed and the sweet fruits that have already appeared.[71]

[69]"Strengthening Party Leadership Over Ideological Work," *Beijing Review* 24, 36 (September 7, 1980):13–14.

[70]For instance, one *People's Daily* article recalled the harm done by the anonymous criticisms published under the collective pseudonyms of "Chu Lan" and "Liang Xiao" during the early 1970s. Rong Ya, "Pay Attention to the Signing of Articles," *Renmin ribao*, July 12, 1981, in *FBIS*, July 17, 1981, p. K2.

[71]"Achievements and Problems in Cultural and Artistic Work," *Beijing Review* 24, 38 (September 21, 1981):13, 19. Comments from some of the more celebrated participants in the August forum on literary criticism are in the same issue, pp. 14–16. See also "Jiaqiang dui wenyi di lingdao, gaibian huansan ruanruo zhuangtai" [Strengthen Leadership Over Literature and Art, Change and Discard a Weak State of Mind], *Renmin ribao*, September 10, 1981, p. 2.

In September, Party Chairman Hu Yaobang used an address commemorating the centenary of the birth of Lu Xun to continue the theme of developing better criticism, again including words for both extremes in the dispute, but more sternly stating the reasons for carrying out the campaign. Hu complained that many good works received insufficient praise, "nor do certain pernicious works receive forceful criticism and condemnation." Hu admonished those who were "afraid of destroying the renewed flourishing of literature and art" and warned that "if we allow weeds and flowers to grow together, without the requisite struggle, there is bound to be chaos in our literature and art."[72]

In the following month, the reformers began to concede under pressure. *People's Daily*, which had been resisting the campaign, printed an article against Bai, and the *Literary Gazette* published a self-criticism for its early reluctance to enter the campaign.[73] And Bai wrote his own letter of self-criticism on November 25, although he had claimed in May that "no one in the leadership has tried to compel me to make self-criticism."[74] By December, Hu Yaobang was able to declare the Bai Hua affair finished at a reception for delegates to a conference on film creation and to turn attention once more to correcting the more serious misdeeds of corrupt Party officials.

Bai Hua has experienced ample frustration in his career as a reformer. One should not exaggerate the changes that have been made within China's cultural system since Mao's death. Ultimate control of change has not rested in the hands of fully committed cultural reformers, but with more cautious politicians. Deng Xiaoping and Hu Yaobang periodically have responded to pressure from Bai and his fellow warriors, but they have not overhauled the cultural bureaucracy through which China has implemented arts policy since 1949. So far, it has merely been readjusted to prevent the harsh suppression of intellectuals. Thus the campaign against *Unrequited Love* was conventional in the rhythm of its development, even though Bai Hua's career has continued to flourish, while some of his leading critics have lost their positions.

Despite his disappointments, Bai Hua enjoys personal success at the edge of the post-Mao Chinese literary and political establishment, playing a major role in shaping its concerns and continuing to press for further change. There is of course the danger that a future backlash

[72]*Beijing Review* 24, 40 (October 5, 1981):11–16.

[73]Tang Tsou, "Political Change and Reform," p. 40.

[74]Beijing *Xinhua* in English, May 23, 1981, in *FBIS*, May 26, 1981, p. K6.

against reformers will not treat him so gently, and he may yet suffer a bitter fate comparable to that of the protagonist he created for *Unrequited Love*. Bai himself is more optimistic, or at least he was in 1979 as he summed up the experience of the People's Republic in a poem, "Pearl":

> Thirty years have congealed into a huge pearl,
> its name is: awakening.[75]

[75]From *Shikan* [Poetry] 10 (1979), quoted in Shiao-ling Yu, "Voices of Protest: Political Poetry in the Post-Mao Era," *China Quarterly* 96 (December 1983):708.

THE AUDIENCE

Growing Alienation among Chinese Youths

David Ownby

> I am twenty-three this year and should say that I have just begun
> my life, but none of life's mystery or charm will ever again exist for
> me. It seems I've already reached its end. Looking back at the road
> I've traveled, it has been a passage from crimson to gray, a journey
> from hope to disappointment, a process in which the long river of my
> thought began in selflessness and ended in selfishness.
>
> Pan Xiao, letter to *China Youth*, May 1980

One cold evening during the winter of 1981–82, I sat in my dormitory
room at Nanjing University, scanning the evening papers. Noting the
attempt to revive the legacy of Lei Feng, I remarked to a Chinese friend
that the return from the dead of this goody-two-shoes was a sad commentary on the imaginative powers of the Chinese leadership. My
friend, generally accustomed to my cynicism, was this time stunned:
"You don't believe in Lei Feng?" he asked. "How can you believe in a
hero who died unrecognized, and yet left a photographic legacy that
rivals Douglas MacArthur's?" I replied. "Don't make fun of Lei
Feng," my nineteen-year-old friend warned me sternly. "That guy was
really something." "But he was too good to be true," I insisted. "How
can you believe he ever existed?" "Because the *People's Daily* says
so," my friend replied confidently. "Until the *People's Daily* says
otherwise, Lei Feng is a fact."

I was to discover that my friend was an exception among contemporary Chinese youths, a throwback to an earlier, simpler era. The Cultural Revolution had injected a large dose of skepticism into the thinking of those in their teens and twenties. For the older establishment intellectuals, the Cultural Revolution was an unthinkable, often fatal tragedy, but it still was only one phase in lives that had witnessed war and revolution. Many of these intellectuals and their colleagues died during the "ten-year catastrophe"; all suffered incredible mental and physical anguish. But they survived, in one manner or another. Those who could not be recalled from obscurity and humiliation to occupy important positions in Deng Xiaoping's government were rehabilitated posthumously, their works republished and hawked as signposts of legitimacy for a regime seeking to create a modern socialist China through revival of the prematurely discarded ideas of the early 1960s. Thus for these intellectuals, the Cultural Revolution was but a temporary setback. Whether they survived the ordeal or not, their ideas survived, ideas which stress the primacy of Leninist organization and discipline.

Not so for many Chinese youths. The five, ten, fifteen years that the older intellectuals spent cleaning privies and feeding hogs coincided with the childhood, adolescence, and young adulthood of these young people. For them, the Cultural Revolution was not a temporary setback to be endured, but the formative period of their lives. Without historical perspective, they learned not to respect the "right" authority, but to distrust all authority; they learned not to distinguish "leftist truth" from "rightist truth," but to question all prefabricated "truth." By the time they reached the age of twenty-five, many Chinese youths had already experienced "revolutionary primacy" as Red Guards, social reality as sent-down youths, and historical obscurity as Deng Xiaoping and his faction sought to sweep the Cultural Revolution under the rug and forge ahead to a new socialist future—one which largely ignored these unfortunate young people. Whatever the leadership might do, the Cultural Revolution will not disappear for these youths. It will remain the central fact of their lives and will influence their attitude toward authority, toward their future, and toward their children.

The generation gap created by varying perspectives on the Cultural Revolution and by the reemergence of the "capitalist roaders" and their twenty-year-old ideas is a new problem in Chinese Communist society. The picture was different in the regime's early years. In those days, the training and cultivation of revolutionary successors was a much easier matter. Youths accepted and believed in the Party and its demands on them. *People's Daily* published unquestioned truth. The Party's word was law. There were problems, of course: the 1957 explosion of campus demonstrations during the Hundred Flowers movement evidenced dissatisfaction among a vocal minority of youths;[1] the shrinking of opportunity after 1957 led to the policy of resettling youths in the countryside and engendered some opposition.[2] But these were the exceptions that proved the rule. Generally, authorities and youths shared a common understanding of Chinese socialist society, and of youths' role in that society.[3] This shared understanding was shattered during the Cultural Revolution, with profound consequences for the future of the ideas advocated by the present leadership: part of the audience is no longer listening.

The fact of youth alienation should come as no surprise to any student of current Chinese affairs. Reports of illegal, antisocial youth activities appear frequently in Western and Hong Kong journals, and to some extent even in the Chinese press. But most of these accounts focus on either hoodlums who exist on the fringes of orthodox society as petty thieves, black marketeers, pickpockets, and the like, or on the tiny, articulate minority engaged in the "democracy" movement. This chapter, by contrast, examines what might be called "establishment youths," those who still make some effort to work within the system. The data on which this analysis is based comes almost exclusively from the discussion sections of the journal *China Youth*,[4] in which questions of concern to either authorities or youths are discussed and resolved through letters to the editorial section of the journal.[5] No claim is made

[1]See Dennis J. Doolin, *Communist China: The Politics of Student Opposition* (Stanford: Hoover Institution, 1964); Jean Leclerc du Sablon and Ba San, "Souvenirs d'une rightiste incorrigible," *L'express,* November 4–10, 1983, pp. 154–56; and Roderick MacFarquhar, *The Origins of the Cultural Revolution I: Contradictions Among the People 1956–57* (New York: Columbia University Press, 1974), pp. 220–22.

[2]See Thomas P. Bernstein, *Up to the Mountains and Down to the Villages: The Transfer of Youth from Urban to Rural China* (New Haven: Yale University Press, 1977).

[3]Susan L. Shirk, *Competitive Comrades: Career Incentives and Student Strategies in China* (Berkeley: University of California Press, 1982), p. 18.

[4]For an earlier study of *Zhongguo qingnian* [China Youth], see James Roger Townsend, *The Revolutionization of Chinese Youth: A Study of Chung Kuo Ch'ing Nien* (Berkeley: Center for Chinese Studies, University of California, 1967).

[5]For an analysis of letters to the editors of *Renmin ribao* [People's Daily], see Godwin C. Chu and Leonard L. Chu, "Mass Media and Conflict Resolution: An Analysis of Letters to the Editor," in *China's New Social Fabric,* ed. Godwin C. Chu and Francis L. K. Hsu (London: Kegan Paul International, 1983), pp. 175–224.

here that these letters represent the genuine opinion of all Chinese youths; the broader propaganda and control functions of *China Youth*, the official journal of the Communist Youth League, influence the selection and publication of letters and distort what basically may be an accurate reflection of youth attitudes. Realizing this, youths whose ideas diverge significantly from those of the leadership do not participate in these debates. Nonetheless, many youths *do* participate, and these debates have been and remain an important aspect of *China Youth*. Thus, despite their propaganda functions, the contents of the debates, and more particularly their underlying form and language, do reveal something about the kind of youth-authority relationship that actually exists.

An analysis of several discussions from before the Cultural Revolution in comparison with a debate that occurred in 1980 leads to the conclusion that there is a fundamental difference in the tone and character of the debates of the two periods: the earlier discussions revealed a paternalistic, authoritarian leadership and a submissive, obedient readership that accepted this paternalism; the later discussion, by contrast, was characterized by a defensive, unsure leadership and a young readership that was independent-minded, inquisitive, and dissatisfied with its position in society.

Pre-Cultural Revolution Discussions: The Basic Model

The pre-Cultural Revolution debates were characterized first and foremost by a pervasive editorial paternalism. This paternalism took a number of different, yet related, forms. The first was strictness of editorial control. Each discussion was preceded by an editorial introduction that analyzed the ideological content of the letter that was to initiate the debate, selected the pertinent features of the letter that were to be addressed in future discussion, and outlined the correct response to the questions under examination. The editors intervened frequently during the course of the discussion to summarize what had transpired and to indicate the correct course of the debate's future development. They commented on the nature of the letters they received and did not hesitate to criticize those whose viewpoints diverged from their own. At one point they even inserted an editorial correction into the text of a youth's letter when they thought he had misinterpreted an ideological point.[6] Each discussion was concluded by an authoritative essay writ-

6*Zhongguo qingnian* 1 (1956):18.

ten either by the editors themselves or by an outside authority invited by the editors to draft the conclusion, which restated the issues under discussion, reinforced the correct response to these issues, and criticized those who had deviated from the correct line.

The second aspect of editorial paternalism was the zealousness and heavy-handedness with which the editors defended their own position. The editors were not fellow discussants with youths in these debates. They were the fount of all truth and authority. They brooked no questioning of their wisdom, nor did they even make a show of allowing the presentation of conflicting viewpoints. The most significant debate of 1956 did not address concrete youth problems, but instead focused on the letter of a young man who had the temerity to question the editors. In October 1955 Han Yan, an urban youth assigned to work in the countryside, wrote to *China Youth* of his unhappiness there and his desire to return to the city. Staff writer Ma Tieding replied that Han's problems lay not in the hardships of village life, but instead in his ideology and worldview.[7] In early 1956 another youth, Li Nanfeng, wrote in suggesting that Ma had gone too far in describing Han's problems as "thought" problems.[8] This launched the discussion of "Is It Right to Feel Uneasy about Working in the Villages?" After printing Li's letter, which was to be the center of the discussion, the editors announced in the next issue that since those letters that agreed with Li Nanfeng did "not differ significantly from his," *China Youth* would not print them.[9] During the course of the discussion, Li Nanfeng was criticized far more severely than Han Yan, although he himself had nothing to do with the problem ostensibly under discussion.[10]

As a result of this editorial absolutism, most debates followed a standard format: they began with the publication of a "controversial," mildly critical letter, after which followed at most a handful of letters that supported the original critic, and finally a preponderant number of letters that criticized, corrected, and condemned the young comrade whose letter had kicked off the discussion. Thus the debates were redundant to the point of being soporific. The editors "argued" not through logic or reason, but through tireless repetition of the didactic points they had made in their introduction to the debate.

[7]Ibid., 20 (1955):16–19.
[8]Ibid., 1 (1956):17.
[9]Ibid., 3 (1956):17.
[10]See, for example, ibid., 3 (1956):17–18; and 6 (1956):32–33.

Youths seemed to accept their role as children to these stern, fatherly editors. The questions they raised were neither very interesting nor very far-reaching. Sample debate titles included: "Is It Right to Feel Uneasy about Working in the Villages?" "Should Youths Have Hobbies?" and "Is It All Right to Have Special Friends Within the Collective?"[11] There are a number of points to note about these questions. First, youths often found themselves asking editorial permission to do or feel something that they feared might lead them astray of orthodox behavior. This in itself indicates general youth acceptance of the paternalistic role assumed by the editors. Youths recognized their need for guidance and turned to the editors for authoritative counsel. Second, the very triviality of the questions further reinforced the image of youths' acceptance of their inferior status within the socialist collective. No question was too small for editorial attention, no thought or feeling was to be hidden from the editors. And this relates to the third point: no one questioned the basic nature of the system under which he or she lived. Not only were there no direct attacks on Chinese socialism, but even if the implications of an argument led logically to a critique or redefinition of some aspect of the socialist system, youths still refrained from following up this implication. For example, youths "won" the 1956 debate on hobbies: the editors agreed that those cadres who interfered with youths' pursuit of healthy after-hours or extracurricular activities were overstepping their bounds.[12] Because youths were agreeing with one another and sharing experiences rather than attacking some officially designated *bête noir*, these letters were some of the most revealing of the earlier period.[13] Yet no one suggested that this discussion implied there was a sphere of activity that the authorities should not invade; no one followed up the logical conclusion of the editorial sanction for the pursuit of outside hobbies. Instead they thanked the editors for their time, care, and consideration.

The general impression one receives from these discussions is that the authoritarian, paternalistic pattern of youth-authority relations imposed by the editors on the participants was working. Everyone knew and was satisfied with his place. The editors stood at the top of a vertical relationship and dictated orthodox truth to eager listeners. The questions raised by youths indicated acceptance of the society in which they lived, and a desire to fine-tune that society so that it might function

[11]Ibid., 10 (1956):39; 17 (1956):37.
[12]Ibid., 14 (1956):205; 15 (1956):2-4.
[13]See, for example, ibid., 11 (1956):38-40; 12 (1956):30-32.

even more smoothly. The editors gave them the tools to carry out this fine-tuning.

The 1960 Discussion: A Case Study

In March 1960, *China Youth* launched a discussion of "What Is the Ideal Life of a Revolutionary Youth?" with the publication of a letter from a young woman, Xiao Wen, who essentially asked for the freedom to be a socialist and a housewife at the same time. Xiao worked in a government ministry, had been married for four years, had recently given birth to a child, and asked for the time and latitude to enjoy her child and her home life. Xiao insisted that she was perfectly willing to be a cog in the socialist machine, to put in her eight hours a day, six days a week, and to go to the meetings and study sessions necessary to keep her ideological and technical skills equal to the demands of her work. Nonetheless, leadership demands for increased dedication, further study, and struggle robbed her of the time to enjoy her life.[14]

For a time, Xiao had maintained an uneasy balance between her own values, which stressed home and family, and the demands of her work, which required ever more of her precious time. But this balance had begun to tip and Xiao increasingly found herself the object of her comrades' criticisms. She wrote to the youth journal seeking a resolution to her dilemma. She pleaded her case on the basis of a somewhat subtle redefinition of the goals and achievements of the Chinese revolution. First she argued—in complete accord with the nature of contemporary propaganda—that China's revolution had made great strides since the founding of the regime in 1949, and particularly since the Great Leap Forward in 1958. Domestically, national reconstruction had changed the "poor and blank" face of the motherland, and the foundation for the eventual achievement of communism had been laid through the communization of the countryside. On the international front, the "east wind prevailed over the west wind." Second, Xiao argued that since the goal of the revolution was to provide for the happiness of the masses, and since the individual was part of the masses, then pursuit of individual happiness was in accord with the aims of the revolution. This line of reasoning enabled Xiao to request time and latitude to pursue her own goals, even as she remained dedicated to continuing the revolution:

[14]Ibid., 5 (1960):36–37.

Neither my husband nor I has any particular ambition. We have no illusions about making any great contribution and gaining larger compensation from the people and we are certainly not yearning for a luxurious bourgeois lifestyle. I just hope that these comfortable days will get better and better. We believe that tranquility is happiness, that comfort is the greatest enjoyment. Of course, we would not oppose socialist revolution or socialist construction, but the best would be to make revolution smoothly, stably, and to build socialism comfortably.

Prior to the publication of Xiao's letter, the editors printed an introduction to the discussion in which they made their opinion clear even while refraining from outright condemnation of her point of view. They accomplished this first through posing rhetorical, leading questions: "What kind of lives should we revolutionaries lead? Should we be complacent with the current situation, and seek a leisurely, carefree life, or should we throw ourselves into the fires of a struggle, and lead a life of tense combat?" Moreover, the editors implied that the questions posed by Xiao related to questions of philosophy of life and worldview, indicating their doubt whether Xiao was a true revolutionary. They concluded that the "resolution of [Xiao's] questions has an urgent contemporary significance [in our attempts to] raise the ideological consciousness of youths."[15] The editors had no intention of discussing the merits of Xiao Wen's argument or of helping her solve her practical and ideological dilemmas.

Given this editorial introduction, the discussion followed a predictable course. To make the debate somewhat interesting, the editors did print a few letters that supported Xiao Wen and that advanced—however slightly—the argument she had presented. These letters revealed the reemergence of traditional, humanistic Chinese values with their emphasis on family, harmony, and tranquility. After ten years of sacrifice, at least some Chinese youths were beginning to question the prominence of politics, work, and struggle in their lives, and to find the courage to assert that the individual, even if merely a part of the masses, nonetheless constituted an important social unit.[16] Moreover, at least some youths couched their pleas for greater personal space in reasonably sophisticated socialist logic. Some argued that since their revolutionary predecessors struggled for them, and succeeded, then

15Ibid., p. 36.
16Ibid., 6 (1960):38, 39; 7 (1960):23.

they should be permitted to enjoy the fruits of this success.[17] Others argued that history moves forward independent of man's will, and that leisure and personal contentment could not obstruct this process.[18] All suggested that since the individual is part of the masses, and since everything in China is done for the benefit of these masses, then each individual should be allowed to enjoy some of the accruing benefits.

Yet none of these arguments was very penetrating, and none of the youths pushed very hard for a redefinition of the relationship among the state, the individual, and the masses. And in any case, these supporting letters were buried under an avalanche of detracting letters. Published critical responses outnumbered favorable responses three to one. Critics insisted that the individual could realize his happiness and individual fulfillment only within the collective. At China's current stage of historical development, individual happiness was a "trivial matter unworthy of mention."[19] In fact, the critics argued, Xiao Wen and her supporters came perilously close to a relapse into bourgeois thought and life style with their insistence on individualism, and this relapse explained their unhappiness with their current lives. Xiao Wen had forgotten that she could enjoy her family life only because of the success of the revolution. Family and individual love, the critics insisted, were class-based phenomena, not absolute values on which to construct a worldview. In the new society, the Party was the parents, the collective the family.[20]

Finally, the editors invited an outside authority, Wu Zhipu, first secretary of the Henan Communist Party Committee, to draft the conclusion to the debate.[21] Wu did little more than restate the criticisms in the detracting letters already printed. He argued that Chinese society was still characterized by the bitter struggle between socialism and capitalism and that Xiao's bourgeois distaste for labor was the precise opposite of the proletariat's belief that "struggle is happiness." Her hopes for an easy revolution represented "petty bourgeois illusions."

[17]Ibid., 6 (1960):39.

[18]Ibid., 7 (1960):24.

[19]Ibid., 10 (1960):27.

[20]Ibid., 9 (1960):34–35.

[21]One of Mao's students at the Peasant Movement Training Institute in the mid-1920s, Wu also played an important role in launching the Great Leap Forward in 1958. See Roderick MacFarquhar, *The Origins of the Cultural Revolution II: The Great Leap Forward 1958–1960* (Oxford: Oxford University Press, 1983), pp. 42–43, 80–81.

Great victories had been won, Wu conceded, but there was still much work to do. And it was in this work, not in the bourgeois values espoused by Xiao, that true happiness was to be found. Wu concluded by asking that Xiao "seriously consider the majority opinion."[22]

The 1960 debate is a concrete illustration of the composite model presented above. We see youths asking trivial questions—"Is it all right to go to a movie rather than to a meeting?"—and largely refusing to follow up the implications of the questions they raised. We see the strictness and heavy-handedness of editorial control and authority. Moreover, we see in this debate clear evidence of the function of these discussions in Chinese society. Xiao Wen and her supporters based their arguments in large part on the "success" of the revolution. The fact is, however, that 1960 was not a year of marked success. Famines struck many areas of China. People starved. The leadership had lost a great deal of prestige and faced a population that had lost some faith in the party and no longer was highly motivated for continued sacrifice. Discussions such as these in *China Youth* represented a means of coping with this popular dissatisfaction. The strategy was to admit the existence of the problem, but to dress it up in optimistic, revolutionary language, and finally to attack the problem from a doctrinal, ideological point of view. The editors accomplished this through publication, and then criticism, of a letter with slightly negative overtones.

This was Yan'an-style rectification, institutionalized in a "Dear Abby" format.[23] The editors consciously used these discussions to maintain and strengthen the ideal paternalistic youth-authority relationship illustrated in the debates analyzed above. And this editorial consciousness of the function of these discussions supports, rather than undermines, the contention that most youths accepted the paternalistic guidance of the authorities: if the editors were intent on conducting a minipurge through these discussions, then why was the content of the offending letters so pedestrian? The editors could have organized a discussion to examine and resolve virtually any problem—including protocounterrevolutionary tendencies—that they viewed as standing in

---

[22]*Zhongguo qingnian* 11 (1960):9-11.

[23]For an account of the theory and central importance of rectification in the Chinese Communist context, see Frederick C. Teiwes, *Politics and Purges: Rectification and the Decline of Party Norms, 1950-65* (White Plains, N.Y.: M. E. Sharpe, 1979), particularly chapter 1; for an analysis of rectification in action, see Timothy Cheek, "The Fading of Wild Lilies: Wang Shiwei and Mao Zedong's *Yanan Talks* in the CPC Rectification Movement," *Australian Journal of Chinese Affairs* 11 (January 1984):25-58.

the way of their desire to revolutionize Chinese youths. The fact that the problems they chose to address were so trivial reveals the fundamental success of their efforts prior to the mid-1960s. Widespread youth alienation did not predate the Cultural Revolution; it was produced by it.

The 1980 Discussion

In August 1966 *China Youth* went into a thirteen-year hibernation, reappearing in September 1979. Its reemergence coincided with a broader trend to rehabilitate individuals and organizations discarded during the Cultural Revolution and to repair the damage done during the "ten-year catastrophe." Deng Xiaoping and his like-minded colleagues slowly began the enormous tasks of rebuilding a Leninist party and government and generating the public confidence necessary to mobilize the populace to work toward modernizing China.

Deng's attempt to establish the legitimacy of his government in the eyes of the people—as well as to wrest political control from the hands of his rivals—led to a thaw in the Chinese political climate from roughly late 1978 to early 1980. This thaw witnessed the outbreak of widespread questioning of the government, symbolized in the Democracy Wall movement.[24] In May 1980, shortly after the suppression of the Democracy Wall activists, *China Youth* launched its first discussion since the Cultural Revolution. The leadership's motivation was thus superficially similar: as before, it sought to coopt youth dissatisfaction and defuse it through officially sponsored discussion of potentially explosive issues.

But there the similarity ends. The earlier debates were small, well-packaged affairs rarely lasting more than a few weeks and seldom straying from the editorial introduction that kicked off the discussion. In 1980, by contrast, participating letters appeared prominently in every issue from May to December, and by the time the editors drafted their conclusion to the debate in March of the following year, the journal had received some 60,000 letters, of which 111 were published over the course of the discussion.[25] Second, the title of the discussion—

---

[24]James D. Seymour, *The Fifth Modernization: China's Human Rights Movement, 1978-79* (Stanfordville, N.Y.: Human Rights Publishing Group, 1980), pp. 7-21.

[25]*Zhongguo qingnian* 6 (1981):3.

"What Is the Ultimate Meaning of Life?"—indicated that youth questions, as well as editorial willingness to indulge these questions, had expanded considerably in scope. Even after the discussion branched out into various subheadings—"What Is a Scientific, Revolutionary Philosophy of Life?," "How Should One View Current Reality?"—the questions were not phrased in such a way as to imply the answers, as was so often the case before. Moreover, the editors, in significant contrast to their predecessors, went out of their way not to impose answers to the questions under examination. They did suggest an "official" attitude toward the question and tried to ensure that this interpretation not be forgotten or buried under conflicting opinions, but generally speaking, the editors stressed that their view was but one among many possibilities.

In these circumstances, letters contributed by youths revealed a remarkable diversity: some parroted the official line with almost humorous tenacity; some were much more radical than the editors and attacked the opinions of others as peddling the ideology of the exploiting class; other youths were quite bold in expressing views incompatible with the official line or even with socialism itself. In 1980, no negative model emerged for youths to gang up on. No longer did youths thank the editors for their time and consideration in arranging a discussion to address their problems. Instead, most youths ignored the editors completely and responded to other letters directly through the pages of *China Youth*.[26]

Thus for the first time in the history of the journal's discussions, content became more important than form. The editors stepped back from their positions as censorial guardians of orthodoxy to perform more purely editorial functions—the selection and publication of interesting material. Youths responded by providing a wealth of such material. In 1980, *China Youth* presented a genuine, interesting debate on the meaning of life, not a stylized, choreographed rectification through which erring youths were sacrificed to "frighten the monkey." The old model had disappeared. The Abbies of the post-Mao era no longer had the answers, and even if they did, post-Mao youths were no longer listening.

[26]Several of these letters have been translated in Peter J. Seybolt ed., *Chinese Education* 14, 1 (Spring 1981). My translations of representative letters and editorial statements from both 1960 and 1980 appear in *Chinese Sociology and Anthropology* 17, 4 (Summer 1985).

Launching the Discussion: Pan Xiao and the Editors

The letter initiating the 1980 discussion appeared in the May issue. Entitled "Why Does Life's Road Grow Increasingly Narrow?" the letter was the result of the collaboration of two youths: Xiao, a twenty-four-year-old female worker at the Number Five Beijing Woolen Sweater Company; and Pan, a twenty-year-old male student at the Beijing Municipal Economics Institute. The letter—printed under the pseudonym "Pan Xiao"—was not a spontaneous creation. Prior to its publication, the editors of *China Youth* had organized a panel to discuss "Views of Life of Today's Youth" and selected from among the participants in this panel two youths whose views seemed "most representative."[27] The organized nature of the production of this letter reveals at least partial continuity with the editorial approach before the Cultural Revolution.

Pan Xiao's letter, however, would not have been published earlier. Although the letter was not a document of dissent, outlining flaws in the Chinese political system and suggesting means of redress, it did recount the tragedy of her own personal history in a way that implictly questioned not only the implementation of socialist policies but also the basic validity of socialist doctrine. Pan's tale was the familiar one of ideological disillusionment. Like most of her generation, she was taught very early that the purpose of life was to make others' lives more beautiful. In elementary school, she copied passage after passage from *Lei Feng's Diary* into her own and passed restless nights dreaming of the day when she, too, could become a hero in the service of all mankind.[28]

The onset of the Cultural Revolution forced Pan to begin to question her youthful idealism. Youths only slightly older than she—and who had received a similar education—spent their days in armed struggle and violent abuse of human life. After she graduated from junior middle school, trouble invaded Pan's personal life. Her parents, both of whom were Party members, became embroiled in one family quarrel after another and more or less abandoned their daughter. Pan was

[27]Helen F. Siu and Zelda Stern, eds., *Mao's Harvest: Voices from China's New Generation* (New York: Oxford University Press, 1983), pp. liii-liv, 3. Pan Xiao's letter is translated on pp. 4-9.

[28]*Zhongguo qingnian* 5 (1980):3. Subsequent serial references to Pan Xiao's letter are indicated by page numbers in the text.

forced to discard her plans of advancing to senior middle school (pp. 3–4).

Still hopeful, Pan sought to realize her dreams of heroism in work. She found a job in a small collective factory and set to work with high spirits. Nonetheless, she was "once again disappointed." She believed in the organization and raised an honest objection to the factory leadership out of a sincere desire to improve it. Because of this she was for many years denied entrance into the Youth League. Then, a close friend betrayed Pan by reporting to the authorities a "minor error" she had committed during a private conversation. Losing faith in the possibility of self-fulfillment through work, Pan sought solace in love and became attached to the son of a cadre who had been attacked during the Cultural Revolution. In 1976, after the "gang of four" fell from power, the cadre was rehabilitated and Pan's lover abandoned her (p. 4).

This final personal blow was a turning point in Pan's ideological development. She repudiated whatever remnant of faith she retained in her childhood ideals. Not only was there no possibility of becoming a hero, but those around her seemed cruel, evil, and selfish. She began to search for a new philosophy of life. She turned her attention away from books and began to observe how other people lived, hoping to find a new significance in life. No answer seemed satisfactory:

> As for living for the revolution, that seemed empty and off the mark, and anyway I didn't want to hear any more of those sermons. As for seeking fame, that seemed a little too far from most people's experience. . . . Working for the sake of humanity again seemed unrelated to reality. You break your back over a few work points, curse and swear over trifles—how can you even talk about working for humanity? Living simply for physical pleasure seemed equally meaningless.

Many people told her not to worry, to live just to live, but Pan remained obsessed with finding a purpose that would lend meaning to her life (pp. 4–5).

She returned again to her books. She read Hegel, Darwin, Owen, Balzac, Tolstoy, Turgenev, Lu Xun, Cao Yu, Ba Jin, and others, but all of these writers described a world as unappealing as the one Pan had discovered in her daily life. Finally, in Social Darwinism she discovered a truth that enabled her to cope:

> People are people after all! No one can escape the laws of his own

> basic nature. . . . All people are selfish; no one is sublime to the point that he forgets himself. All of that past propaganda was just so much pure imagination. . . . If not, I would like to ask all those stately sages, those learned scholars, honored professors, and respected propagandists—if they dare to examine themselves honestly, how many can escape the law that man struggles to achieve his personal desires?!

This revelation enabled Pan to come to terms with the world around her. She too learned to lie, to cheat, to flatter the leadership in pursuit of more work points and larger bonuses. And when such behavior made her feel common, she consoled herself with the knowledge that she was simply following her basic nature, from which there was no escape (pp. 4–5).

But Pan's embrace of Social Darwinism served only to explain why life was so miserable; it did not provide a prescription for good living, nor did it erase the feeling of emptiness and purposelessness that continued to gnaw at Pan's soul. Gradually she developed a somewhat more positive outlook. She came to believe that one should work subjectively for oneself and do the utmost to develop individual potential, and that the objective result of this enlightened individualism would be service to the people. Pan hoped to complete herself through literature, "not to make any contribution to the people or to the Four Modernizations. I want to do it for myself, for my own personal needs" (p. 5).

Yet even four years after Mao's death, these hopes remained distant goals. Pan's current life seemed monotonous, meaningless, and difficult. Her fellow workers, who talked of nothing but clothing and hairstyles, ridiculed Pan and asked if she was preparing for a life of spinsterhood. Her wages remained so low that she could not afford the books and paper that she needed in order to write. Furthermore, she was still unconvinced that she had literary ability and believed that even if she were to write, her writings would have very little influence on society. Out of desperation, she had secretly attended Catholic church services and had considered becoming a Buddhist nun. She had even toyed with the idea of suicide. Pan closed her letter with the following appeal:

> Comrade Editors, I address this letter to you out of my extreme anguish. In revealing all of this I am not expecting any miraculous cure-all from you. If you dare to publish my letter, I would rather

instead that youths throughout the country read it. I believe that the hearts of youths are one. Perhaps I can obtain help from them. (p. 5)

When the readership of *China Youth*—at first unaware of editorial collusion in the composition of the letter—read Pan's narrative, they saw an account that exemplified many of the problems, ideological and otherwise, common to their generation. First and foremost among these was spiritual emptiness, the absence of any acceptable ideal around which young people might order their lives. Pan's life—as well as that of her readers—had spanned the founding years of the People's Republic, the Cultural Revolution, and the reconstruction that followed the death of Chairman Mao. Self-sacrifice modeled after Lei Feng now struck these young people as impractical, if not impossible. Revolution no longer assumed a concrete meaning in their lives. The post-Mao regime had not filled the vaccuum created by the Cultural Revolution's negation of the hopeful idealism inculcated in Pan Xiao's generation. The fact that this generation was brought up to believe that ideology provided the ultimate meaning to man's thoughts and actions rendered the resulting disillusionment far more painful.[29] This was reflected in two particular expressions of disillusionment. First, Pan Xiao became angry at the authorities and propagandists who had inculcated her with such an unrealistic world view. Note her sarcastic jibes at those "stately sages," those "respected propagandists," and her challenge to the editors of *China Youth* to print her letter. But at the same time, much of her confusion and frustration stemmed from the fact that she could not completely escape from under the weight of an absolutist world view. She moved from a belief that the world is beautiful to an opposite belief that everyone is completely selfish. The second viewpoint is as absolute as the first. Moreover, Pan maintained some hope that her future writings might influence society. Despite her claim that everyone struggles to achieve his own desires, she could not envision her own life without social significance.

Pan Xiao's letter also struck a chord with readers when it took issue

[29]On the various effects of education and socialization on this generation of youths, see Stanley Rosen, "Education and Political Socialization," in *Education and Social Change in the People's Republic of China*, ed. John W. Hawkins (New York: Praeger, 1983), pp. 97–133; and Susan L. Shirk, *Competitive Comrades*. For supporting evidence from other members of Pan Xiao's generation, see Liang Heng and Judith Shapiro, *Son of the Revolution* (New York: Alfred A. Knopf, 1983); and Ken Ling, *The Revenge of Heaven: Journal of a Young Chinese* (New York: G. P. Putnam's Sons, 1972).

with several objective facets of Chinese life that increased her disillusionment and speeded the process of ideological disintegration. The treatment she received when she expressed an opinion to the leadership reflected both the rigidity of the Chinese bureaucracy and the slavish position of the masses vis-à-vis the leadership. Her betrayal at the hands of her close friend and her boyfriend illustrated that political survival often took precedence over personal relationships. And there was no indication in Pan's letter that her situation had improved in any way since 1976. A number of the problems Pan identified were systemic problems, not those created by any specific leadership faction.

The final viewpoint Pan had come to espouse—work subjectively for self and objectively serve others—posed very serious questions to the editors of *China Youth,* and by implication to the leadership of contemporary China. Her views deviated considerably from an official ideology that still called for self-sacrifice for the sake of the nation, the revolution, and the modernization program. Pan did little more than outline her concept of enlightened individualism and did not discuss the proper course to take in the event of a conflict between self and others. But it is clear that it would take more than Marxist diatribes to reconscript her into service of the revolution. The editors were forced to address why, after more than thirty years of socialist construction, Chinese society was characterized by pettiness and selfishness and why the lives of many youths seemed meaningless.

As in earlier debates, the journal's editors prefaced the publication of Pan Xiao's letter with their own introductory remarks. The structure of this introduction was superficially similar to those of the pre-Cultural Revolution discussions. The editors interpreted Pan's letter in such a manner that it invited debate:

> Like Pan Xiao, [the youths of this generation] originally believed that the entire world was good. They were all sincerely willing to sacrifice themselves for the revolution and for their beliefs. Ten years of chaos destroyed all of this: when there exists such a frightening distance between ideals and reality, when the purpose of life is this muddled, who could remain confident?

They tried to place the issue in broader historical context, asserting that a discussion of the meaning of life had preceded ''almost every important social advance in the history of mankind.'' The editors attempted to draw subtle parameters to be heeded by participants in the discussion. They stated that this generation of youth reexamined the meaning of life "with an outlook influenced by the development of modern science" and with "concern for the fate of the motherland and the future of mankind." They declared that despite its disillusionment, "the young generation . . . has not turned its back on the responsibilities of the era but instead is more tenacious than ever." The editors posed questions to which participants in the discussion were to respond: "How should we view society? How should we regard human life? When contradictions arise between ideals and reality, how should one live so as to give meaning to life? Where is the value of an individual existence?"[30]

But in stark contrast to the practices of the pre-Cultural Revolution era, the 1980 editors did not spell out the answers to their own questions or to the specific questions raised by Pan Xiao. Their introductory remarks indicated that they would prefer optimistic and "progressive" replies, but they left the discussion open-ended by declaring that they would "let youths themselves talk about these serious matters." Moreover, the emphasis throughout the introduction, and throughout the entire discussion, was on a "broad, equal discussion." From May to December, while the debate was in progress, the editors did not explicitly express their own opinion about the ideas bandied about in their journal. The conclusion to the discussion, which finally appeared three months after the debate had ceased, in March 1981, was only superficially similar to the hard-hitting, authoritative conclusions that had characterized discussions before the Cultural Revolution.

The broad-based, serious nature of the questions raised by Pan Xiao and the relative lack of editorial guidance combined to produce a discussion of remarkable vitality and diversity. The discussion was so diverse, in fact, that it could not be encapsulated in a simple doctrinal formula or political slogan, a most significant feature indicating that the earlier model had broken down. There were, of course, points shared by many participants. They shared a common experience: whether the writers were old enough to have participated in Red Guard activities or not, virtually all youths recounted their passage from an ideologically motivated childhood to a disillusioned young adulthood. Furthermore, most of the participants in the debate showed themselves to be good rhetoricians: most youths made an effort to provide logical, analytical proof for their conclusions. Third, all of these youths had a desire to share their opinions with others of their generation through the vehicle provided by *China Youth*.

[30]*Zhongguo qingnian* 5 (1980):2–3.

Aside from these points, however, the participants seem to have had little in common. Separate discussion of four fairly broad categories of opinion is required to analyze the diverse viewpoints of the participants: the "official liners" followed or embellished the editorial attitudes expressed in the introduction to the discussion; the "absolutists" resembled Pan Xiao in their inability to cope without a holistic worldview; the "philosophical revisionists" took Pan Xiao's formula—work subjectively for self, objectively serve others—as a starting point for their own defense of a "reasonable" understanding of the relationship between self and others; and the "reformers" argued that problems such as those identified by Pan Xiao could be solved only through reform of China's social, economic, and political structure. These categories are not exclusive, and attitudes overlapped in individual letters.

Official Liners

Those youths who followed the official line (slightly more than half of all letters published) asserted that views such as those expounded by Pan Xiao were ahistorical. Some traced the development of the concept of individual value from primitive times to the present, illustrating man's progressive, but still incomplete, liberation from all forms of bondage.[31] Others retold the story of man's emancipation through an examination of European intellectual history.[32] These youths argued that the achievement of communism would resolve all problems of individual value, with some declaring that the emancipation of the individual was contingent upon the emancipation of all mankind.[33]

To explain China's present situation in light of this historical-materialist argument, the official liners admitted that China's development had been unique. Plagued by more than two thousand years of feudal history, China's capitalist phase of development was by contrast short and incomplete. As such, China's current economic and political problems stemmed from remnant feudalism. The weak economic base and the absence of a bourgeois superstructure normally associated with the capitalist phase of development led to the "madness" of the Cultural Revolution—the complete denial of individual value—and the "gang of

[31]Ibid., 6 (1980):2–3.
[32]Ibid., pp. 13–16.
[33]Ibid., p. 16.

four's feudal fascism.'' When Pan was denied entrance into the CYL for having expressed an opinion, this reflected a ''patriarchal work style'' on the part of the leadership. Pan's betrayal at the hands of her close friend illustrated the ''influence of the gang of four's feudal fascism, inherited from the Ming dynasty's . . . secret police system of purging people.'' Pan's abandonment by her boyfriend reflected that ''scoundrel's feudal idea of proper marriages.''[34] Pan's frustrations were understandable: weaned on socialist idealism, her adolescence unfortunately coincided with the reenactment of some of the worst scenes from China's feudal past.

But if Pan's frustrations deserved sympathy, her solution did not. Her search for personal significance was an advance over ideological rigidity, but her espousal of individualism was anachronistic. Individualism was a useful weapon in the battle between feudalism and capitalism, and it might be helpful in cleaning up feudal remnants still existing in contemporary China, but to take this concept as the base of one's ideology was erroneous and damaging. Despite China's unique history and its recent difficulties, history was still moving forward toward communism, which still represented the final term of human liberation. Suppression of the individual was bad, but so was extreme individualism. To avoid both of these extremes, one needed to realize that fulfillment of individual value occurred only in tandem with the advance of society. The official liners thus stood Pan's formula on its head:

> We can turn things over completely, taking the prerequisites and conditions for the realization of the individual as the standard for our current actions, subjectively thinking more of the welfare of the people and thereby allowing our individual goal (the realization of individual value) to become the natural result of our actions: ''Work subjectively for society, objectively fulfill oneself.''[35]

According to this formula, Pan had come only half way. To realize fully her individual value, she first had to come to understand this value in terms of the collective. It was in increasing the value of this collective and submitting to its leadership that Pan would find her ultimate solution.

[34]Ibid., 7 (1980):8.
[35]Ibid., 10 (1980):17.

Absolutists

Another group of letters was important primarily for revealing the inability of many Chinese youths to cope without the support of a nonrelative worldview. This took three different forms: there were those who were totally cynical or fatalistic (these letters constituted about 5 percent of all letters published); those who took Pan Xiao's discovery of selfishness and turned it into a general virtue, arguing that "only the self is absolute" (there was only one good example of this); and those who reverted to, or perhaps never abandoned, the purist radical ideology on which this generation was raised (two good examples of this were published). None of these youths was able to articulate a relative position that granted the interest of both the individual and the group.

The best example of those who had given up completely in the face of difficult circumstances was a young man who wrote in to say that "man fights against fate, but can never defeat it." China's unique pattern of historical development had produced a current situation so complicated that no one individual could hope to understand it. Pan's problem was that she read too many books, which filled her head with all sorts of ideas not applicable to the morass of contemporary Chinese life. Pan's complaint that life's road was growing increasingly narrow was a "social question, and there is nothing any individual can do about it."[36]

Other youths were less philosophical and more cynical. One young man agreed completely with Pan Xiao: "In current society, if people do not look out for themselves they will be like a car that has run out of gas." Another argued that any talk of "modernization" or of "sacrificing one's life for the liberation of mankind" was a farce. In fact, people worked hard hoping for bonuses; they studied with an eye toward their individual futures. It was, he admitted, a common ideal to strive to realize modernization, "but it is an ideal, not reality, and reality leaves one disappointed."[37] Still another youth averred that hypocrisy and situational ethics were the key to survival. He discovered that in his reports to his local Youth League branch, the more nonsense

[36]Ibid., 7 (1980):21. On the general topic of Chinese youths' belief in fate, see Du Feng, "Tamen weishenma biancheng youshenlun?" [Why Have They Become Theists?], *Zhengming* [Contending] (Hong Kong) 27 (January 1980):40.

[37]*Zhongguo qingnian* 7 (1980):12.

he wrote, the more praise he received.[38] A teacher wrote in to say that there was little point in inculcating youths with a revolutionary worldview when society at large could not accommodate such people. When those who "used the back door" actually found better jobs, one had to be a fool to remain committed to his ideals.[39]

The most extreme letter of the entire discussion was also contributed by one of the absolutists. Entitled "Only the Self Is Absolute," the letter was written by a young college student named Zhao Lin. Slightly older than Pan Xiao, Zhao had received the same sort of education that made him "color-blind" to those elements in society that did not jibe with his idealistic outlook. He experienced the Cultural Revoluton as a Red Guard, assuming a "wild, religious-like fervor . . . and attempt[ing] to strangle [him]self to realize a utopian political ideology." But disillusionment followed quickly for Zhao. He discovered that when he "lived to make others' lives more beautiful," those people treated him like a fool. He became convinced that everyone was selfish at base. Even after passing the university entrance exams in 1978, Zhao remained firm in his belief that the "individual is the center and basis of the world. . . . This concept may be subjective idealism, but I don't care what 'ism' it may be. As long as it is realistic then it is rational."[40]

Unlike for Pan, this realization did not lead Zhao to frustration. He began to read Sartre's existentialism, European surrealism, Social Darwinism, and the philosophy of Nietzsche, all of which directed him toward a "brand-new philosophy of life," one which exalted the self above all else: "According to man's basic nature, selfishness is that which is most sacred and inviolable, it is humanity's most primitive, most legitimate right. Without selfishness, society cannot develop, history cannot advance." Accordingly, Zhao did not attribute China's recent problems to feudal remnants inherited from the past. Instead, all of China's difficulties grew out of a long period of suppression of the basic selfishness of all individuals. The Cultural Revolution was precisely the outcome one could expect from such a distorted worldview: people worshipped others rather than themselves; they fought against themselves and their most basic instincts. Despite improvements since Mao's death, Chinese ideology and propaganda still distorted the natural and proper relationship between the individual and the collective.

[38]Ibid., p. 13.
[39]Ibid., p. 16.
[40]Ibid., 8 (1980):4.

Zhao turned Chinese socialism on its head by declaring that only when individual interests were satisfied could society move forward.[41]

Zhao counselled Pan that the root of her frustration lay in incomplete self-discovery. She should not give in to those elements in society that pushed her toward hypocrisy. Nor should she seek outside herself for a solution: "A discovered self is a vast universe in which you will find countless treasures. . . . All of real society appears tiny and pitiful before an awakened self." Thus while Zhao praised Pan for having abandoned her distorted ideal of serving the people, he felt that she had not gone far enough. The meaning of life lay in realizing the fact of selfishness and striving to fulfill its value.[42]

Also in the absolutist group were two writers who seemed even less willing than the editors to grant the legitimacy of youth grievances and who argued that Pan's mistake was in abandoning the ideology on which she was raised. Both insisted that one could not blend "public" and "private," one could not confuse the individual and the collective: "[Pan Xiao's] extremely erroneous and damaging viewpoints oppose the system of proletarian thought and communist doctrine at the very base."[43] In class society, when the economic base is not advanced to the point where everyone's material needs can be satisfied, even thinking about one's individual welfare necessarily and inevitably led to conflict with the interests of others. If one persisted in the pursuit of selfish goals, one would injure the interests of the collective and become a member of the exploiting class.[44]

Those who talked about "working subjectively for self, objectively serving others" were deluding themselves. Any action taken in pursuit of self-interest weakened the collective. One of the writers asked what Pan would do if she wanted to listen to the radio while others in the dormitory wanted to sleep. Without a willingness to sacrifice to the collective, man became as "cold and weak" as Yang Zhu, the ancient Chinese philosopher-sage who would not sacrifice a single hair of his body to save the world. To strengthen and enrich the Chinese people, to realize modernization, Chinese youths had to maintain "a strong feeling of nationalism . . . and an abundant spirit of self-sacrifice." The meaning of life lay in the individual's rededication to

[41]Ibid., pp. 4–5.
[42]Ibid., pp. 5–6.
[43]Ibid., pp. 7–8.
[44]Ibid., 6 (1980):13.

the interests and desires of the socialist collective.[45]

Philosophical Revisionists

Perhaps the most interesting letters of the entire discussion were those written by youths who believed that one could find some "reasonable" compromise between private desires and public needs, between working for self and serving others, and that one could create a philosophy of life to accommodate this compromise. Most of these philosophical revisionists ostensibly accepted socialism in much the same fashion as the official liners. The difference between the two groups was that where the official liners emphasized the collective and the future, the philosophical revisionists talked about the individual and the present. And they were concerned above all with the idea of "reasonable." One of the absolutists asked what would happen should one person want to listen to the radio while his roommates wanted to sleep. A member of the "reasonable" group queried in reply why the music lover did not go out and buy a set of earphones.[46]

This group attributed the chaos of China's recent history not to remnant feudalism, but to misguided absolutist propaganda and doctrine that distorted the rational, natural relationship between the public and private realms. An overemphasis on service to the collective meant that an individual had no more value than that of a "part in a machine": "It seemed that unless all of man's emotions and desires were directed 'toward the revolution,' then they had no value in existence nor any right to appear." Moreover, the concept of "class" was abstracted to the point that "an individual's emotions, consciousness, words, and actions were all only the direct expression or reflection of his class nature. . . . Class did not assume its social existence in man; the individual instead lived until his death as the mere phenomenal existence of this governing concept."[47] The result of this attempt to force a multitude of varied individuals into the same mold was that everyone assumed a veneer of submission to authority while retreating into his own world to "take care of his own little self."[48]

Submission to this erroneous doctrine had damaging effects in the

---

[45]Ibid., 8 (1980):7–8.
[46]Ibid., 10 (1980):24.
[47]Ibid., 9 (1980):13.
[48]Ibid., p. 14.

political realm as well. Since the public at large had been indoctrinated to accept the definition of public interest formulated by the authorities, this public interest was used during the Cultural Revolution "to maintain the political power of a certain person. . . . Let it be noted: Once we turn 'public' and 'private' into absolute antagonisms, then the private desires of a certain number of people can pass for the public interest."[49] This unreasonable distortion of the relationship between public and private infected both the leadership and the people and produced the frustration and confusion characteristic of Pan Xiao and much of her generation. The same distortion created a leadership group that could not judge objectively the effects of its policies.

To remedy these problems, according to the philosophical revisionists, it was necessary to make both policy and propaganda accord with reality. As a whole, this group still accepted socialism and the movement of history toward the eventual achievement of communist society, but they asserted that at the present stage of China's development, people needed space to develop themselves and pursue their private desires. These youths declared that they were tired of living a "transitional existence" and tired of sacrificing everything for the sake of posterity. They reasoned that "'revolution' should have a realistic content; it most assuredly is not something abstract or intangible."[50]

These revisionists were, moreover, distressed by inconsistencies in the doctrine professed by the current leadership, inconsistencies which worked to limit the frontiers of their existence. Like good Marxists, they based their arguments on economic grounds and claimed that many effective economic policies under implementation—bonuses, higher salaries, and the like—tacitly admitted that most workers were to some extent selfish. They labored not explicitly for the sake of mankind, but to improve their own standard of living. "If we affirm these policies, we should also affirm a moral view consistent [with these policies]. Otherwise, we must admit that these policies increase people's selfishness and thus are revisionist—expedient measures taken to traverse a period of economic difficulty." Should the leadership make such an admission, "there would be no way to guarantee the stability of these policies, and no point in talking about the Four Modernizations."[51] Proper laws and disciplinary measures could pre-

[49]Ibid., p. 10.
[50]Ibid., p. 13.
[51]Ibid., p. 10.

vent this pursuit of self-interest from becoming injury to the collective or outright exploitation; it was unreasonable not to permit the pursuit of reasonable self-interest. Failure to purge current propaganda of unrealistic elements would simply force the people into hypocrisy.

The philosophical revisionists did not spell out the precise nature of the "new philosophy of life" implied by a reasonable understanding of the current situation. They said only that they did not want to be "molded" as in years past. They did not want someone else's future to limit their present.[52] Perhaps this reticence indicated only good political sense; had they taken their argument much further they would have found themselves on treacherous ground indeed. But we should note that their argument aimed precisely to diminish the inexorable force of collectivist logic as well as the authority structure that logic implied. They sought to find and secure a niche for the individual within the socialist collective.

Reformers

The reformers constituted a subset of the philosophical revisionists. Their aim was either to secure the stability of the reasonable freedoms requested by the revisionists or to attack various concrete problems encountered by youths in current society. One poor Shanghai worker declared that given the policies of economic readjustment and the constriction of educational opportunities, he, and many like him, had been discarded with the "gang of four": "The cadres of many units care only about profits and increasing production. They hold out to us models of hard-working youths, but take little interest in our problems and desires." To rectify this situation, the writer argued that the Youth League should be more than a "submissive tool" of the Party; it should be revitalized and transformed into a body that would take a genuine interest in youth problems.[53] Another participant applauded the concern now shown for youths by the Central Committee, but noted that after this concern filtered through the "middle levels" of China's vast bureaucracy, very little concrete action was taken. He suggested that the bureaucracy be reformed so that the people would have direct power to appoint and dismiss particular cadres according to their

[52]*Zhongguo qingnian* 9 (1980):13.
[53]Ibid., 7 (1980):17.

performance.[54] Still another reformer presented a similar case. The electoral reforms implemented since 1976 were not yet complete, he argued. Although the vast majority of those serving in public office did have the interests of the people at heart, there were others who "feel obligated to the Party and the state and do not regard their position as a sacred mission to safeguard the people's interests. And there are quite a few people who have never even laid eyes on their 'electorate.' '' The people still had little control over even basic policy matters and were forced to rely on the "conscience" of the Party and the state.[55] The brunt of the arguments advanced by the reformers was that until appropriate reforms were carried out, youth disillusionment could be expected to continue.

The Editorial Conclusion

In March 1981, the editors of *China Youth* finally drafted their conclusion to the discussion in a twelve-page article entitled "To Those Who Ponder the Meaning of Life." The three-month hiatus between the final publication of letters from the readership on this matter and the appearance of the editorial conclusion suggests some difficulty or even disagreement among authorities as to how to handle this unprecedented discussion.[56] The diversity of opinions expressed in *China Youth* over the course of the debate, published without censorial or disapproving editorial remarks, contributed to the discussion's immense popularity. But this diversity also posed a serious dilemma for the editors: how could they draft a conclusion to a discussion that had achieved no internal consensus without reneging on their own promise to respect individual viewpoints? To write the kind of authoritative, definitive article that marked the conclusion of the earlier debates would have cost the authorities whatever limited confidence among readers had been built up by the debate itself. Yet an inconclusive editorial summation might suggest tolerance of ideological diversity, or even tacit approval of some of the unorthodox opinions expressed during the course of the discussion.

[54]Ibid., 11 (1980):11–12.

[55]Ibid., 8 (1980):10–11.

[56]The issue of factional struggles within the leadership is important to an ultimate evaluation of the significance of the 1980 discussion, but it is far too complex for extensive treatment here. To understand the complexity of the situation, begin with Kjeld Erik Brodsguard, "The Democracy Movement in China, 1978–79: Opposi-

These tensions produced a concluding essay of notable length and subtlety. The editors maintained the pose that they were but fellow discussants with youths in the common search for the meaning of life, and they took pains to try to convince their readership of the correctness of their views through logic and reason, rather than using the "big stick" of authority wielded with such precision and confidence by their pre-Cultural Revolution predecessors. This willingness to explain the logic behind doctrinal standpoints was most clear in the editorial response to Pan Xiao's assertion that an individual should "work subjectively for self, objectively serve others." As we have seen, this nonsocialist contention not only animated Pan and the extreme absolutist Zhao Lin, but also received more subtle endorsement from the philosophical revisionists.

It is obvious that the editors could not sanction without qualification the notion that one's first duty in life was to protect and advance oneself. But the editors' critique of Pan's assertion was well-reasoned. They began with an exposition of Marxist ideas—chiefly from Marx's earlier writings—about the concept of human value. Marx, they argued, was first and foremost a humanist, and his desire to liberate humans from all forms of bondage revealed the extent to which he cherished the idea of human value. This concept, the editors suggested, lay at the heart of all Marxist teachings about society, history, and morality.[57] The editors thus coopted the dissenting opinions expressed by Pan Xiao and her supporters by implying that the desire to elevate individual value was in fact a genuine Marxist concern.[58]

---

tion Movements, Wall Poster Campaigns, and Underground Journals," *Asian Survey* 21, 7 (July 1981):744–74; Victor C. Falkenheim, "Popular Values and Political Reform: The 'Crisis of Faith' in Contemporary China," in *Social Interaction in Chinese Society*, ed. Sidney L. Greenblatt, Richard W. Wilson, and Amy Auerbacher Wilson (New York: Praeger, 1982), pp. 237–55; Carol Lee Hamrin, "Competing Policy Packages in Post-Mao China," *Asian Survey* 24, 5 (May 1984):487–518; and H. Lyman Miller, "The Politics of Reform in China," *Current History* 80, 467 (September 1981):258–62, 273.

[57]*Zhongguo qingnian* 6 (1981):5–6. Subsequent references to this editorial are indicated by page numbers in the text.

[58]On the Chinese "rediscovery" of Marxism and Marxist concepts of alienation, see David A. Kelly, "The Socialist Humanism of Wang Ruoshui and the 'Alienation School,'" unpublished manuscript presented at the New England China Seminar, May 5, 1984; and Ding Wang, "Cong 'muzhong wuren' dao renxing fugui: shehuijuyi de yihualun chutan" [From "No Concern for Man" to the Return of Human Nature: An Initial Exploration of the Theory of Socialist Alienation], *Mingbao* [Ming Daily] (Hong Kong) 19, 1 (January 1984):29–36.

Having established that the arguments of Pan Xiao and her supporters were in reality proto-Marxist, the editors moved easily to the next
step of argumentation, stressing that individual human value is a relative reflection of objective economic conditions at a given time and that
the ultimate realization of individual value must await the liberation of
all mankind. But they were not content simply to evoke the authority of
orthodoxy in persuading youth to move to this "higher plane." Instead, they proceeded to a careful examination of the relationship
between public and private, hoping to convince disillusioned youths
that service to the collective was, in fact, the most intelligent means to
pursue one's individual self-interest (pp. 7–9).

First, they argued that the relationship between public and private
was unified. Working for self and working for others produced essentially the same results:

> In socialist society, where public ownership of the means of produc-
> tion and the system of "to each according to his labor" have been
> basically implemented, the unity of "public" and "private" is no
> longer confined to one class, but instead is expanded to the entire
> society. . . . For example, the people want to improve their own
> lives, and the "private interests" of one billion "individuals" thus
> produce the "common interest" of "enriching and strengthening the
> country." (p. 7)

Nonetheless, the editors insisted, this unity was not absolute; under
certain conditions the relationship between public and private could
produce contradictions and even become antagonistic. They illustrated
this antagonism with reference to the housing problem that plagued
China's urban residents. It was reasonable, the editors admitted, for
every youth to want decent, individual housing on reaching a certain
age. Nonetheless, because the state had other, equally reasonable
priorities, this demand could not immediately be satisfied in all instances. In this case, public and private interests did not exactly coin-
cide. Thus, the editors concluded, both Pan Xiao's desire to "work
subjectively for self, objectively serve others" and her opponents'
contention that "if you serve yourself, you cannot serve others" failed
to deal with the complexity of the relationship between public and
private: "In the final analysis, each is incomplete, unscientific, and
should not be adopted as a guiding principle" (p. 8).

But the editors did not stop here. In a direct reply to the philosophical revisionists who requested the latitude to pursue what they called

"reasonable" self-interest, the editors argued that, in fact, there was no such thing:

> When "public" and "private" became antagonistic, when "working subjectively for self" cannot "objectively serve others," then if you give precedence to "objectively serving others," you must abandon "working subjectively for self"; in actuality, this has already become "working subjectively for others." And if you persist in "working subjectively for self," then you must abandon "objectively serving others," and the situation has now changed to "work objectively for self," which can move toward injury to the public to the benefit of self, and injury to others for one's own self-advantage. (p. 8)

The ultimate conclusion to the editorial argument was obvious: since the socialist system itself sought to "integrate 'public' and 'private' in a reasonable manner," then one's individual interests should be subservient to the needs of the socialist system and to those who defined those needs—the Party (p. 8). Still, this doctrinaire point was not expressed with the same dogmatic insistence witnessed before the Cultural Revolution, nor did doctrinaire fervor overwhelm good Marxist reasoning.

Furthermore, the editors did not insist that every youth immediately cease and desist from all activities not firmly grounded in the public interest. Realizing that they were dealing with a widespread social phenomenon rather than the errant ideologies of a few black sheep, the editors admitted that "under conditions prevailing in current society, it is reasonable that this consciousness [which emphasizes the importance of the pursuit of self-interest] should exist. We should not completely condemn it. Should we condemn it we would run the risk of injuring the proper individual initiative of a significant number of youths" (pp. 8–9). Youth League members and other enlightened elements should help those youths engaged in the pursuit of self-interest to overcome this behavior and move to a higher level of consciousness, but this was to be an evolutionary process, not a violent ideological struggle, and could be completed only as the Party's attempts to readjust the economy and implement reforms took effect.

The editors thus respected the general tenor of the discussion through logical explication of their argument and through congenial phrasing that preserved the fiction that they were but equal participants in the discussion. But this supposed equality was, after all, fictitious. After months of patient silence, the editors finally did attempt to provide guidance to their readership. First, they tried to reduce the significance of the issue under discussion by limiting its historical context. They accomplished this by repeatedly blaming problems on the "gang of four." The editors simply ignored the various other explanations for the contemporary *crise de coeur* of Chinese youths offered during the course of the debate, retreating into the safety of attacking a convenient scapegoat and thus implying that these problems were unusual and temporary.

Second, the editors argued that this discussion, concluding with their essay, had importance primarily as part of the larger movement to "emancipate thought," representing an "important initiation into Marxist theory for young people" (p. 3). By so doing, the editors attempted to deflect attention away from the deep alienation expressed in many letters and from specific concrete problems raised and sought to put an optimistic face on the contents of the debate: "The 60,000 letters [we received] pulsate with the utter innocence of youths' earnest desire to contribute their knowledge and abilities to the great enterprise of the motherland's Four Modernizations." Again, the editors asserted that in the course of the discussion youths "observed the restoration and development of the Party's work style of seeking truth from facts, and felt the kindness and warmth of the Party" (p. 3). The very fact that this sort of discussion could take place in China proved (to the editors) that

> it is entirely correct that the people place their hope in our Party and believe that the Party can perfect the leadership and improve the Party work style. Any tendency that weakens or breaks away from Party leadership violates the wishes of the people. Any design to abolish or oppose the leadership of the Party goes against the current of history and is destined to fail. (p. 10)

Finally, the editors wrapped the entire discussion in the flag, arguing that youths should achieve self-realization not through pursuit of self-interest, but "in the sacred enterprise of the revitalization of the motherland!" (p. 11).

Because this editorial marked the conclusion of the discussion, we have no way of knowing what Chinese youths thought of these editorial assertions. One senses, from the content of many letters, that many youths were probably not convinced by the optimistic orthodoxy with which the editors sought to sway their readership. Nonetheless, this belated editorial attempt to assert their authority as ultimate arbiters of youth opinion should not obscure the truly unique features of the 1980 discussion. A wide-ranging, reasonably open debate about important issues did occur. Diverse, unorthodox opinions achieved a wide audience through the pages of *China Youth*. The authorities kept their promise to allow youths themselves to discuss the issues and added their own viewpoint only three months after the discussion had concluded. The conclusion itself was in general hortatory and expository, rather than absolutist and doctrinaire. Most important, there was no negative model, no mass criticism, no dialectical resolution. There was no rectification.

Conclusions

Before the Cultural Revolution, *China Youth* discussions represented a variety of Yan'an-style rectification applied to non-Party elements of society. The revolutionization of Chinese youths was to be accomplished through the same tool that had proved so effective in forging a unified Party in the early 1940s. These debates often provided the textual material that fueled small-group discussion in the Youth League throughout China, a more concrete, immediate form of rectification.[59]

The success of rectification requires at least two preconditions. First, there must be an articulate political elite whose legitimacy and authority depend heavily on shared ideology. Second, the group undergoing rectification must share a good part of the fundamental concerns and beliefs of the elite. Otherwise, rectification either gives way to physical coercion or evaporates into mass indifference or superficial conversion to elite views. Resort to physical coercion requires either totalitarian power or implementation of a body of law that defines the rights and responsibilities of both the leadership and the led. Acceptance of mass indifference implies abandonment of the idea of revolution from above.[60] The fact that rectification remained a part of youth work in the 1950s and 1960s suggests that in youth-authority relations, these preconditions were met. The revolutionary energy and enthusiasm that marked the Yan'an period and the early years of the People's Republic continued to infect the regime's "revolutionary successors."

Turning to 1980, we see only the skeletal remains of rectification through discussion. We have the "negative model" of Pan Xiao, the leading editorial introduction, the publication of a preponderant num-

[59]*Zhongguo qingnian* 7 (1960):22; 8 (1960):36.
[60]See Teiwes, *Politics and Purges*, ch. 1.

ber of letters from the official liners, and the final editorial conclusion. The form remained; the content was absent. The editors retreated from their pose as priests who guide their parishioners through patient doctrinal repetition—under the ultimate threat of excommunication—and took up that of the American talk show host who keeps the show rolling through an occasional witty quip or timely comment. Youths no longer constituted an obedient flock of believers, but strode to the podium and delivered their own lectures as equals. The strictly vertical relationship of former times had become almost horizontal.

Why did rectification no longer work? It is unlikely that the editors of *China Youth*—or the leadership of China—would be willing to admit that the prerequisites of rectification no longer hold. They would not acknowledge that their legitimacy no longer derives from ideology. To them, the 1980 discussion was an exception, a concession, a safety valve organized to defuse widespread youth disillusionment. *China Youth* debates since 1980 once again have had clear pedagogical intent—encouraging youths to adopt the nationalistic modernization and reform ideals to fill the ideological vacuum.[61]

In 1980, it was youths who no longer held up their end of the rectification bargain. They no longer offered the faith in elite ideology—or in the patriarchal relationship implicit in that ideology—to make the proposition tenable.[62] Alienation was written all over the pages of the 1980 discussion. As a whole, youths were disillusioned with socialism, or at least with socialism as an absolutist philosophy of life automatically passed down from authority to learner. This attitude was revealed particularly in the viewpoints expressed by Pan Xiao, Zhao Lin, the philosophical revisionists, and other more cynical respondents, but was perhaps more fundamentally evident in the overall texture of the discussion itself. The questions raised by youths all predated Marx by centuries. Problems addressed both before and after the Cultural Revolution related in some manner to the relationship between the individual and the collective, but whereas in 1956 youths asked how best to lead their lives within the collective, in 1980 they

[61]See, for example, the discussion beginning in issue 16, July 1981, of "Why Are Progressive Youths Ostracized and Attacked?" This topic is interesting and significant, but it lacks the troubling ambiguity of the "Meaning of Life" debate.

[62]A growing body of survey literature, often concerned with youths still in school, being published in China lends general support to this assertion. See, for example, David S. K. Chu, ed. and trans., "Sociology and Society in Contemporary China, 1979–1983," *Chinese Sociology and Anthropology* 16, 1 (Fall-Winter 1983–84):145–69.

questioned the nature of the collective itself and its right to determine the value of their individual existence. They were not content, moreover, with seeking answers to their questions solely within the body of socialist doctrine. Marx was indeed often cited (Mao was quoted only once), but even those respondents who followed the official line or who claimed to have "rediscovered" genuine Marxism had read Rousseau, Kant, Hegel, and many other Western novelists, philosophers, and social scientists before reaffirming the validity of socialism. More extreme participants drew intellectual sustenance from Sartre, Nietzsche, Social Darwinism, and European surrealism.

Most important, most youths did not base the validity of their conclusions on the authority of any one thinker or school of ideas, but on reason and practice. This attitude of "seeking truth from facts" revealed a skepticism regarding any idea or ideology that they had not thought through or practiced in their own lives. Reason only assumes importance when ideology ceases to be absolute. Many youths seemed devoted to truth as an abstract concept, not necessarily truth as defined in the canons of Marxism-Leninism-Mao Zedong Thought.

But none of these "establishment youths" were the undisciplined hoodlums derided in the Chinese press and executed in the recent "spiritual pollution" campaigns. Participation in a *China Youth* discussion was and is a decidedly political act. Many of these youths were disillusioned with socialism and impatient with political and ideological restrictions that limit their freedom. Many had lost faith in the Party and what it stood for. But as their letters revealed, they had turned their backs not on ideology in general, but on contemporary Chinese dogma in particular. Both their writings and the fact that these writings appeared in the pages of *China Youth* indicated that these young people remain committed to ideology. The question is: can China's leadership formulate an official doctrine that will satisfy youth demands without sacrificing the Party's pretensions to authority?

And here we meet the final irony. The essays in this volume outline certain continuities between contemporary China's establishment intellectuals and their Neo-Confucian predecessors. Both have felt a necessity, bordering on moral obsession, to see their contribution to society and their personal self-fulfillment in terms of service to the state. This moral obsession has been transmuted into acceptance of a Marxist-Leninist doctrine, with all of its own elitist overtones. Deng Xiaoping and his supporters survived the utopian tragedy of the Cultural Revolution and reemerged from the ordeal, in the process endowing their moral obsession with overtones of heroism. They now seek to modernize China through the same set of authoritarian, elitist ideas for which they were condemned in the mid-1960s.

But these policy makers and intellectuals are in danger of ignoring an important discontinuity in modern Chinese history. Part of Mao Zedong's concept of the Chinese revolution required the politicization of the Chinese populace at large. While it is doubtful that peasants and workers ever absorbed the content of Mao's ideas, nonetheless, the structures of the Cultural Revolution—the mass organizations—had the effect of broadening the Chinese political arena and endowing a much larger part of the Chinese people with a political awareness and vocabulary. In the case of Chinese youths, this experience has enabled them to analyze Chinese politics in a manner significantly different from that of their leaders. Cut off from tradition and from the outside, brought up in the new society, they no longer understand the historical logic that animates establishment intellectuals. They argue from a perspective alien both to the Chinese and to the Leninist traditions. The question is whether the revolutionary leaders can communicate with these "revolutionary" successors.[63]

[63]On this generational issue, see William deB. Mills, "Generational Change in China," *Problems of Communism* (November–December 1983):16–35; and Michael Yahuda, "Political Generations in China," *China Quarterly* 80 (December 1979):793–805.

Afterword

Vera Schwarcz

> Our only boldness was a lack of enthusiasm for the endless movements and struggles we participated in. . . . An acute sense of shame can result in selective amnesia. . . . A guilty conscience can make you guarded.
>
> Qian Zhongshu,
>
> Preface, *A Cadre School Life,* 1982

Chinese intellectuals and the Communist Party are still recovering from the nightmare of the "endless movements and struggles" recalled by Qian Zhongshu in 1982.[1] Both of these elements of Chinese society have cause to question their own minimal boldness in the face of events that required a far stronger stance than lack of enthusiasm. The Cultural Revolution, especially, lingers on in the minds of leaders inside and outside the Party. It was a horror that cannot easily be blamed on Mao Zedong alone. Unwilling to admit fully its own responsibility, yet unable to point the finger of blame elsewhere, the Party seems to favor a certain amount of historical amnesia in the current period of recovery. Forgetting past hostilities among the educated and the powerful is thus emerging as a precondition for moving on with the tasks of modernization.

The task of putting the memory of the Cultural Revolution behind—into history, as it were—is, however, not an easy one. The undigested lessons of the 1960s still haunt those intellectuals who are being asked to think of the future rather than the past. These survivors of repeated movements against intellectuals know full well that the forces that had

---

[1]Qian Zhongshu, preface to Yang Jian, *A Cadre School Life: Six Chapters*, tr. Geremie Barme (Hong Kong, 1982).

victimized them in the past can be unleashed readily again. Their guilty conscience is a sign of their continuing inability to counter those forces directly, whether during the Cultural Revolution or now. In this milieu of silent self-accusation, tortured self-questioning, and muted public criticism, the Party thus far is still perceived as the only institution capable of keeping the anti-intellectual forces somewhat at bay.

The Party has entered the post-Mao era with a loud proclamation of its intention to collaborate with intellectuals. As early as 1978, Deng Xiaoping (a survivor of endless struggles himself) used the occasion of a national science conference to declare that highly educated experts were henceforth to be considered a part of the "socialist working class." Mental laborers, he argued, were no different from physical laborers and should therefore be privileged to the same kind of political trust, as well as consideration of their special needs in conducting their work. Deng's argument ran counter both to the Maoist prejudice in favor of the poor and uneducated masses and to the "mental laborers" own sense of superiority in relation to those who labor with their physical strength.

In the wake of Deng Xiaoping's statements, the official media argued for the rehabilitation of highly educated experts on the grounds that the Party has always had a policy of collaboration with intellectuals. Reinterpreting history in this light, the *People's Daily* was able to declare that past struggles—which so haunt the life and imagination of elderly intellectuals such as Qian Zhongshu—were nothing but momentary outbursts of the "outworn prejudices against intellectuals that are the product of the mentality of small producers."[2]

Not surprisingly, this line of reasoning strikes a false note in the minds of those who remember more instances of enmity than collaboration between intellectuals and the Party. The years 1942, 1948–49, 1951, 1954, 1957, 1958, 1962, 1964, 1966–69, 1973–74, 1979, 1981, and 1983 are, according to them, just some in which the Party mounted campaigns against individuals or against an entire stratum of society labeled as "bourgeois intellectuals." Those who have been victimized by these movements, both directly and indirectly, cannot overlook the obvious fact that the Party membership continues to be made up of those with largely rural origins and that "small producers" can all too easily be mobilized once more against highly educated "mental laborers." The task of building up trust between the Party leadership

[2]"Makesi zhuyi he zhishi fenzi de zhengce" [Marxism and the Policy Toward Intellectuals], *Renmin ribao*, April 18, 1980, p. 2.

and the broader intellectual elite in the post-Mao period thus poses a far greater challenge than can be met by policy reversal.

Intellectuals, then, are weary partners in this renewed alliance. They share the official assessment of China's backwardness and are quite prepared to join the effort to make up the shameful loss of training and research suffered by the entire Chinese nation during the 1960s and 1970s. Unlike in earlier periods of modernization, however, many young and middle-aged intellectuals are coming to this round of collaboration more concerned about their own autonomy than the elderly intellectuals described in this book, whose views were shaped in an earlier time. Less prone now to selective amnesia, they recall quite clearly past instances when the Party acclaimed the value of technical knowledge without necessarily safeguarding the right to independent inquiry of all those engaged in the pursuit of knowledge. As evidence, they point to an ongoing Party effort to drive a wedge between establishment and nonestablishment intellectuals, and between technical and scientific experts on the one hand and literary or academic figures on the other. To counter this, intellectuals have tried to portray themselves as spokespersons of the people and thereby to deflect criticism of educated elites as defenders of particularistic interests. And yet this, too, incites the suspicion of a Party that views itself as the vanguard of the proletariat.

The image of intellectuals as *daiyan ren*, literally, word-carriers for the wordless masses—comes through most clearly in the writings of Liu Binyan, the journalist-essayist who continues to be a thorn in the side of Communist authorities. In his 1979 speech entitled "Listen Carefully to the Voice of the People," Liu shows himself to be an unequivocal advocate of the special mission of intellectuals:

> We must answer the people's questions. We have no right to be auditors in the courtroom of history. The people are the judges as well as the plaintiffs. We must supply them with scripts. But before we provide answers, we must first learn. We must understand more about social life than the average person does.[3]

By portraying intellectuals as the conscience of society—as authors of scripts based on superior information about social problems—Liu Binyan is consciously harking back to the Confucian self-definition of

---

[3]Liu Binyan, "Listen Carefully to the Voice of the People," *People or Monsters*, tr. Perry Link and Kyna Rubin (Bloomington: Indiana University Press, 1983), p. 8.

the Chinese intelligentsia. What he is appealing to, more specifically, is an idealized image of the loyal censor who engaged in educating the populace but also in ceaseless remonstrance with a benevolent but erring emperor. The censor, like Liu Binyan's script writer, spoke *for* the people far more frequently than *to* the people. A key precondition for this role was, and remains, some autonomous sphere of investigation and discussion. The hope that such a realm might yet be sanctioned and consolidated leads intellectuals to persevere in their collaboration with the Party today.

Modern heirs of the censor tradition, Chinese intellectuals today still see their mandate in terms of placing superior knowledge in the service of worthy rulers. The questions that linger on from imperial times, however, are: What is to be done when intellectuals cannot gather their knowledge independently from the dictates of political authority? What recourse is there for loyal critics who cannot convince the powerful to follow their counsel? And finally, how can intellectuals maintain their own integrity in the process of seeking to serve within the bureaucratic apparatus?

This concern with integrity is perhaps the most striking feature of the Chinese intellectuals' own self-rehabilitation in the post-Mao era. It stands in marked contrast to the Party's own effort to place past movements into history by condemning the "erroneous" persecution of intellectuals such as Wu Han and Deng Tuo. Once these deceased figures are declared to be role models for today, the assumption goes, other intellectuals can proceed without fear or doubt. Within the intellectual community, however, there is a far more complex inquiry going on. The individual and collective weaknesses of these posthumous models are being scrutinized intensely for hints of what made them so vulnerable to the abuse of those whom they tried to serve so loyally. The absurd self-incrimination of Wu Han toward the end of his life, when he called himself a class enemy of the proletariat, and Deng Tuo's purist last gesture, suicide, are seen as symptoms of these intellectuals' inability to maintain their integrity in times of political crisis.

In the quest to overcome the debilitating weaknesses of their deceased comrades, contemporary intellectuals are turning to the Confucian definition of integrity as *qijie*. This concept is drawn from a long history of the humiliation of the educated by the powerful. It connotes the quality of high-mindedness that traditional literati discovered inside themselves whenever they decided they must take moral initiative out of the hands of corrupt political authority. The practical manifestation of *qijie*, from the Warring States period to the present, is *qinggao*, or inner refusal. In a context in which intellectuals did not have the ear of the politically powerful, *qinggao* suggests a strategy for action when no officially sanctioned action is possible. It enables intellectuals to raise individual voices of public discontent with the status quo, while retaining some distance from the murky realm of factional political intrigue.[4]

Practitioners of *qinggao* are quite useful to political factions out of power. In recent memory, such intellectual gadflies have been particularly helpful to the Communist Party before 1949 and to the modernizing faction during the 1970s. They are considerably more troublesome once power has been consolidated at the center. Contemporary defenders of *qijie* and *qinggao* are aware of this tension and are determined to face its consequences more directly than their predecessors, including the establishment intellectuals of the early 1960s.

The party now needs the educated elite more than ever before. Since its current mandate of power rests on the promise of rapid modernization, it cannot proceed without the active collaboration of highly trained personnel. Intellectuals, thus, have a unique opportunity to press the cause of autonomy. They have, however, embraced this new opportunity with tactics reminscent of those used by the establishment intellectuals. Moralistic appeals to political superiors are still more common than horizontal cooperation among the intellectuals themselves, much less alliances with other social groups. Intellectuals seem quite reluctant to foster public coalitions and, instead, keep hoping that their individual integrity will suffice to insure the trust and the noninterference of enlightened political authorities. This strategy, as shown by the biographies in this book, is a risk-laden one indeed.

While only very timidly making the case for increased autonomy through professional associations, contemporary intellectuals focus instead on calling once more for a thorough enlightenment movement. The intense revival of the May Fourth ideal of *qimeng* in the post-Mao era is the direct result of the intellectuals' inability to work out an acceptable division of labor with political authorities in the modern

[4]The connection between *qijie* and *qinggao* became clearest to me during the course of my research on May Fourth intellectuals carried on in China from 1979 to 1980. The record of that experience, especially the portions relevant to this discussion, may be found in Vera Schwarcz, *Long Road Home: A China Journal* (New Haven: Yale University Press, 1984), pp. 241–48.

era.[5] But the resort to moral rather than institutional remedies is thoroughly traditional. China's educated elites currently are returning to a critique of "feudal mentality," arguing that intellectual freedom does not exist in the People's Republic because the Party as well as the masses have not emancipated themselves from the old ethic of subservience to patriarchal authority. Today, as during the May Fourth movement of 1919, the emphasis of the enlightenment movement is not so much on the institutional structures that limit the autonomy of educated professionals as on the habits of mind that lead the powerful to assume that they can and must "guide" the thought of others. For the most part, however, intellectuals do not recognize their own paternalism in presuming to "speak for the people."

The effort toward emancipation from old habits of mind, moreover, is constantly thwarted by the Party's calls for unity around the goals of state-sponsored modernization. Intellectuals who continue to question the prejudices and superstitions of their bureaucratic superiors are subject to periodic attack as "unpatriotic." Their appeal to the unfinished legacy of the May Fourth Movement is used against them to suggest an overreliance on ideas borrowed from abroad and contempt for the native revolutionary tradition. In the 1980s, as during the late 1910s, advocates of *qimeng* are thus finding themselves on the defensive regarding the nationalistic cause of *jiuguo*—national salvation, currently redefined as "Chinese-style modernization."[6]

Familiar with the tension between *qimeng* and *jiuguo* from the time of the May Fourth movement onward, contemporary intellectuals are able to deal with it more skillfully. They know that beneath the accusations leveled against them stands a long tradition of ambivalence about the West, which the Party shares with the populace at large. Just how far one may go in criticizing the native tradition with the aid of a perspective glimpsed from abroad is a question that modernizing intellectuals have been posing to themselves for more than six decades. Over this period, they have found that the cause of intellectual emancipation is easier to pursue when the political power at the center is weak,

[5]For a fuller discussion of the historical background of the contemporary implications of the May Fourth concept of *qimeng*, see Vera Schwarcz, *The Chinese Enlightenment: Intellectuals and the Legacy of the May Fourth Movement of 1919* (Berkeley: University of California Press, 1985).

[6]Ibid., especially chapters 5 and 6, which deal with the effort to mount a new enlightenment movement in 1935–38 and analyze the process through which mobilization for war against Japan silenced cultural criticism of the native feudal heritage.

corrupt, or both. Thus, the enlightenment movement made more headway during the warlord period than in times when power became concentrated in the hands of a charismatic leader who was able to use the threat of outside aggression to silence criticism of "feudal mentality." Anti-imperialist politics have been used over and over again to blunt the edge of cultural criticism. Mao Zedong, not unlike Chiang K'ai-shek, found it useful to exalt the specialness of the Chinese tradition in times of national crisis. To be loyal to China and to the chairman, then, required nothing less than an uncritical acceptance of the national heritage as reconstructed according to the dictates of chauvinistic nationalism.

Intellectuals have been quite vulnerable to the pressures for conformity that have accompanied the phenomenon of anti-imperialist politics in twentieth-century China. Ardent patriots, they have been in the forefront of national salvation movements from 1919 to the present. But each time highly educated men and women joined the cause of nationalism, they had to defend themselves against those who questioned their "Chineseness" by pointing to their education in the West or to their attachment to such Western values as science and democracy. Nevertheless, intellectuals have continued to develop a notion of critical patriotism quite different from this more chauvinistic nationalism. They continue to draw upon the historical experiences of non-Chinese peoples to highlight China's backwardness in the modern world and to point to the Party's share of responsibility for this predicament. Such critical patriots refuse to see their homeland as unique in the world. Rather, they are convinced that the lessons of modernization from the West and from Japan have considerable bearing on the problems confronting their own society today. Most importantly, they believe that the gains of technological modernization will not be secured unless and until the enlightenment movement is allowed finally to challenge the tenacity of feudal habits of mind.

In the process of comparing China and the West, contemporary intellectuals are learning to be more critical of both. They, as well as some Party leaders, are seeking a middle ground between total fidelity to the native heritage (be that Confucian or revolutionary) and unqualified admiration of the technological accomplishments of the West. Travel abroad, prolonged study of foreign languages and philosophy, and joint research projects between Chinese scientists and colleagues from Japan, the United States, and Europe all provide the context for the elaboration of this middle ground. The short-term chances of success in this project, however, are quite limited. Even in the past eight years, intellectuals' loyalty has been questioned and they have been asked to choose between an allegiance to state-sponsored views of what China needs and their own commitment to a transnational notion of truth.

And yet, in spite of the repeated waves of mistrust since 1976, a struggle is underway to achieve a more relative definition of truth as China is weaned from the overblown certainties of the late Mao era. As a willingness to live with a relativistic definition of truth (political and philosophical) emerges, the Party and intellectuals are now experimenting with new meanings for modernization. The intellectuals' sphere of experimentation is, to be sure, considerably broader than that of the Party. The top leadership has been able to break with so many of the ideas and policies of Mao Zedong only by affirming that there is no real break at all with the "correct" line of the 1940s and 1950s. Many intellectuals, on the other hand, have been less willing and less able to affirm the validity of earlier experience to the tasks ahead. They, more than the Party majority, have argued for a thorough enlightenment precisely because they believe that a repudiation of all outworn ideas is necessary before China can proceed to establish its modernization program on a firm foundation.

A certain amount of refutation of wrong ideas has been sanctioned in the realm of the intellectuals' own expertise. Thus, for example, wrong judgments in historical criticism, in literary policy, and even in scientific practice are being rectified daily. It is more problematic when the intellectuals take their critical point of view into the realm of politics, overspilling the boundaries of specialization. The most instructive example of this was the late 1983 criticism of Zhou Yang and his younger colleague Wang Ruoshui—two highly placed intellectuals in the Party.

Throughout his career as a "literary czar,"[7] from 1936 to 1966, Zhou Yang was the enforcer of the shifting Communist line in art and literature. His power to monitor and to persecute grew greater and greater during the decades after 1942 when writers and artists were forced to subordinate their artistic consciousness to politics. In the wake of his fall from power, however, Zhou Yang has had an opportunity to reflect on the implications of dogmatism in the Mao era. What has

---

[7]Mu Fu has discussed the phenomena of Zhou Yang in terms of the "self-alienation of the literary czar." See "Yihua lun" [On Alienation], *Zhengming* 74 (December 1983):54–55.

made Zhou Yang rather unique on the Chinese political scene in recent years is his willingness to atone publicly for his own ideological mistakes before 1966.

Zhou and Wang emerged as two of the most forceful advocates of enlightenment thought and most visible targets of conservative Party suspicion of intellectual autonomy. They have sought to rehumanize the foundation of Chinese communism. With the aid of the philosophical texts of the early Marx and the backing of the Party's bolder reformers, they launched a broad discussion about the goals of socialist transformation. But this concern with ends as opposed to means brought them into conflict with more doctrinaire members of the Party leadership. Not surprisingly, the conservative rebuttal of their views centered on the charge that they tried to re-Westernize, not only rehumanize, Chinese Marxism. Once again, as so often before, the questions became: How much are intellectuals allowed to learn from abroad? To what uses may they put that knowledge, especially in the political realm?

The campaign against "spiritual pollution," which cost Wang his job as deputy editor-in-chief of *People's Daily* and forced Zhou to make a perfunctory self-criticism, was a backlash against the spirit of enlightenment that may yet prove temporary. For the commitment to intellectual emancipation grows stronger. Ironically, Zhou and Wang have become useful symbols of integrity among intellectuals determined to think for themselves. The willingness of such influential Party intellectuals as Zhou and Wang to pose questions about the ideological foundations of the current line enables others outside of the Party to raise even stronger objections to the view that intellectual modernization is synonymous with the rehabilitation of a few, frequently deceased, critics of Mao Zedong.

Critical-minded intellectuals today differ from their predecessors in the early 1960s in their insistence that critical thought be given a greater and greater role in Chinese political life. Zhou Yang has recently advanced the argument in the following terms:

> Although some intellectuals tried to solve the problem of feudal mentality in the 1940s, they were unsuccessful. Even the Communist Party's land reform campaign in the 1950s did not tackle the deepest aspects of the culture problem. Courage alone—the Communists' slogan "be not afraid to have your head chopped off"—did not suffice in dealing with old habits of mind. Superstitions persist in spite of repeated efforts to wipe out backwardness and ignorance. Enlightenment thought is still needed, you see, because the power of

habits of thought is stronger than any other kind of power. It is
invisible.[8]

The intellectuals' unwillingness to forget that China has a serious
problem of culture makes them rather guarded allies of the Party to this
day. Those like Zhou Yang, who continue to talk about the invisible
power of habits of mind, cannot but bring down upon themselves the
wrath of conservative optimists. They find it difficult to proceed on the
"bright road" of modernization unencumbered by the recollection of
past darkness. Forgetfulness is not an option for intellectuals seasoned
by the history described in this book. They remember too vividly how
frequently they and their martyred colleagues had ignored the voice of
conscience for the sake of Party unity, national salvation, or loyalty to
Chairman Mao. Now, out of fidelity to their own experience, they are
ashamed for what they did not do in the past, that is, question more
insistently the direction of China's development. It is this sense of
shame that makes intellectuals so determined to recapture and hold on
to their own integrity in this new period of collaboration.

[8]Personal interview with Zhou Yang, May 1983. See Wang Ruoshui, "Lun rendao
zhuyi" [On Humanism], in *Renxing rendao zhuyi wenti taolunji* [Essays from the
Debate on Human Nature and Humanism] (Beijing, 1982), p. 387. Much of this interpretation of Wang Ruoshui is indebted to an excellent paper by David Kelly,
"The Socialist Humanism of Wang Ruoshui and the 'Alienation School,'" presented at the conference on Chinese Intellectuals and the State: The Search for A New
Relationship, Harvard University, May 5, 1984.

Index

Absolutists, 232–35
Academy of Science, 59, 82, 102, 138
Academy of Social Sciences, 14, 139, 175, 180
Ai Siqi, 53–86 *passim*
Alienation, 10, 90, 91, 97, 212–46
An Ziwen, 46, 55
Anti-Rightist campaign (1957), xiv, 12, 32, 34, 161, 187, 200
Atlas, Z., 135
Authoritarianism, 113

Bai Hua, xvii, 12, 14, 89, 185–211
Bao Gong, 184
Beidaihe conference (1958), 67
Beijing Daily, 41, 102
Beijing Opera, 38, 108, 165, 189
Beijing University, 14, 38, 102
Black Art Exhibition (1974), 188
Bo Yibo, 55, 56, 82, 90, 139
"Bourgeois liberalism," 185, 192, 196, 199
Brus, Wlodzimierz, 142
Bu Wuji, 101. *See also* Deng Tuo
Bukarin, Nikolai, v, 54, 58, 65, 81, 127
Bureaucratism, ix, 18, 19, 86, 103, 108, 110, 183, 210

Cadre training, 56
Cao Yi'ou (Kang Sheng's wife), 61, 69
Cao Yu, 166
Career patterns, 11–13
Censorship, 201, 250
Central Party School, 5, 13, 23, 45, 52,
56, 57, 69, 70, 76, 80, 83, 84, 85, 91, 204
Chang Guan Lou incident (1961), 34–35, 105, 106
Chen Boda, 53, 57, 58, 62, 63, 64, 83, 86, 106, 147
Chen Hanseng, 128
Chen Kongli, 180
Chen Wutong, 175
Chen Yi (army), 130, 196
Chen Yi (propaganda), 74, 191, 200
Chen Youhua. *See* Bai Hua
Chen Yun, 23, 47, 84, 87, 128–29, 132, 140
Chen Zuohua, 186
Chengdu conference (1958), 63
Chiang K'ai-shek, xiv, 158, 253
China Youth, 103, 214–45
Chinese Communist Party, xiii, xviii, 3–20 *passim*, 128, 130, 131, 247, 248; Beijing, 13, 24, 167, 173; Central Advisory Commission, 52, 89; Central Committee plenums: (7th CC, 2d plenum [1949]), 62; (8th CC, 9th plenum [1961]), 105; (10th plenum [1967]), 75, 145, 167, 183; (11th CC, 3d plenum [1978]), 13, 25, 41, 119, 190; (6th plenum [1981]), 84; (12th CC, 2d plenum [1983]), 89; Central Directive No. 7, 205; constituency, 17, 19; discipline, 15, 39, 49; education, 60–61; intra-Party affairs, 10, 28; leadership, 44–45; Lushan meetings (1959), 69, 139, 164; norms, 8, 16, 152, 153,

About the Contributors

Timothy Cheek is a doctoral candidate in history and East Asian languages at Harvard. He studied in China in 1981 and in 1982-83 on a dissertation grant from the Committee on Scholarly Communication with the People's Republic of China. His research centers on the role of intellectuals and ideology in China. He has published in *The China Quarterly*, *The Australian Journal of Chinese Affairs*, and *Chinese Law and Government*.

Tom Fisher is a senior lecturer in the Department of History at La Trobe University in Melbourne, Australia. He has a B.A. from Antioch, an M.A. from Harvard, and a Ph.D. in history from Princeton. Interested primarily in early Qing history, he is also fascinated by continuities in contemporary China. He has published in *Papers on Far Eastern History*, *Ming Studies*, *Harvard Journal of Asiatic Studies*, and *The Australian Journal of Chinese Affairs*, of which he is a member of the editorial board.

Carol Lee Hamrin is research specialist for China at the Department of State, and professorial lecturer at the School of Advanced International Studies (SAIS), the Johns Hopkins University. Since receiving her Ph.D. from the University of Wisconsin, Madison, her interests have included modern Chinese intellectual history and current Chinese politics and foreign policy. She has published in *Asian Survey* and *Pacific Affairs* and is currently on sabbatical to write a book on the politics of China's open door policy.

John Israel is a professor of Chinese history at the University of Virginia and has written widely on students, politics, and education in twentieth century China. He is author of *Student Nationalism in China, 1927-1937* (1966) and (with Donald W. Klein) *Rebels and Bureaucrats: China's December 9ers* (1976). He is currently writing a history of Southwest Associated University (1938-1946).

Richard Kraus teaches Chinese politics at the University of Oregon. He is author of *Class Conflict in Chinese Socialism* (1981). He is currently writing on the politics of culture and ideology in the People's Republic.

Barry J. Naughton is an assistant professor of economics at the University of Oregon. His current research interests are the industrial planning and management system in China and urban incomes and living standards. Professor Naughton spent a year in China hosted by Wuhan University.

David Ownby is a doctoral candidate in history and East Asian languages at Harvard. He has traveled extensively in China and studied at Nanjing University in 1981-82. He has recently published translations from *China Youth* in *Chinese Sociology and Anthropology*.

Pitman B. Potter is a doctoral candidate in political science and, concurrently, a law student at the University of Washington. His dissertation concerns the Economic Contract Law of the PRC. He has published in *Chinese University of Hong Kong Occasional Papers*, *China Business Review*, and *Chinese Law and Government*.

Vera Schwarcz was born and raised in Romania and educated in the United States. An associate professor of history at Wesleyan University, she is the author of *Long Road Home: A China Journal* (1984) and *The Chinese Enlightenment: Intellectuals and the Legacy of the May Fourth Movement of 1919* (1985).